Reader's Handbook

A Student Guide for Reading and Learning

Great Source Education Group
a Houghton Mifflin Company
Wilmington, Massachusetts

www.greatsource.com

AUTHORS

Laura Robb
Author

Powhatan School, Boyce, Virginia

Laura Robb, author of *Reading Strategies That Work* and *Teaching Reading in Middle School*, has taught language arts at Powhatan School in Boyce, Virginia, for more than 30 years. She is a co-author of the *Reading and Writing Sourcebooks* for grades 3–5 and the *Summer Success: Reading* program. Robb also mentors and coaches teachers in Virginia public schools and speaks at conferences throughout the country on reading and writing.

Ron Klemp
Contributing Author

Los Angeles Unified School District, Los Angeles, California

Ron Klemp is the Coordinator of Reading for the Los Angeles Unified School District. He has taught Reading, English, and Social Studies and was a middle school Dean of Discipline. He is also a coordinator/facilitator at the Secondary Practitioner Center, a professional development program in the Los Angeles Unified School District. He has been teaching at California State University, Cal Lutheran University, and National University.

Wendell Schwartz
Contributing Author

Adlai Stevenson High School, Lincolnshire, Illinois

Wendell Schwartz has been a teacher of English for 36 years. For the last 24 years he also has served as the Director of Communication Arts at Adlai Stevenson High School. He has taught gifted middle school students for the last 12 years, as well as teaching graduate-level courses for National Louis University in Evanston, Illinois.

Design: Ronan Design: Christine Ronan, Sean O'Neill, Maria Mariottini and Candace Haught

Illustrations: Mike McConnell

Printed in the United States of America
International Standard Book Number: 0-669-48858-5 (hardcover)
1 2 3 4 5 6 7 8 9—RRDC—08 07 06 05 04 03 02 01

International Standard Book Number: 0-669-48857-7 (softcover)
1 2 3 4 5 6 7 8 9—RRDC—08 07 06 05 04 03 02 01

READERS AND REVIEWERS

Jay Amberg
Glenbrook High School
Glenview, Illinois

Mary Baker
Beach Middle School
Chelsea, Michigan

Marlene Beirle
Westerville City Schools
Westerville, Ohio

Ann Bender
Guoin Creek Middle School
Speedway, Indiana

Martha Clarke
Roosevelt Center-Dayton
    Public Schools
Dayton, Ohio

Cindy Crandall
Suttons Bay Middle School
Suttons Bay, Michigan

Janet Crews
Wydown Middle School
Clayton, Missouri

Marilyn Crow
Wilmette Public Schools
Wilmette, Illinois

Deanna Day
Tucson, Arizona

Demetra Disotuar
Martin Luther King Lab School
Evanston, Illinois

Pam Embler
Allen Jay Middle School
High Point, North Carolina

Julie Engstrom
Hillside Junior High School
Boise, Idaho

Shelly Fabozzi
Holmes Middle School
Colorado Springs, Colorado

Aimee Freed
Perry Middle School
Worthington, Ohio

Patricia Fry
Templeton Middle School
Sussex, Wisconsin

Barb Furrer
Templeton Middle School
Sussex, Wisconsin

Lorraine Gerhart
Crivitz, Wisconsin

Laurie Goodman
Pioneer Middle School
Hanford, California

Jane Goodson
Brunswick, Georgia

Pam Grabman
Center Middle School
Youngstown, Ohio

Bianca Griffin
Audubon Middle School
Milwaukee, Wisconsin

Dorsey Hammond
Oakland University
Rochester, Michigan

Cheryl Harry
Southfield, Michigan

Jeff Hicks
Whitford Middle School
Beaverton, Oregon

Claire Hiller
Timber Ridge Magnet School
Skokie, Illinois

Terri Huck
John Bullen Accelerated
    Middle School
Kenosha, Wisconsin

Ralph Huhn, Jr.
Key West, Florida

Dana Humphrey
F. Zumwalt North Middle School
O'Fallon, Missouri

Dennis Jackson
Danvers Public Schools
Danvers, Massachusetts

Jean Lifford
Dedham High School
Dedham, Massachusetts

Linda Maloney
Ridgewood Junior High School
Arnold, Missouri

Nancy McEvoy
Anderson Middle School
Berkley, Michigan

Mary McHugh
Franklin School
Belleville, Illinois

Catherine McNary
Proviso West High School
Hillside, Illinois

Marsha Nadasky
Western Reserve Middle School
Berlin Center, Ohio

Cheryl Nuciforo
City School District of Troy
Troy, New York

Lucretia Pannozzo
John Jay Middle School
Katonah, New York

Brenda Peterson
Templeton Middle School
Sussex, Wisconsin

Evelyn Price
Grand Avenue Middle School
Milwaukee, Wisconsin

Richard Santeusanio
Danvers School District
Danvers, Massachusetts

Jennifer Sellenriek
Wydown Middle School
Clayton, Missouri

Jill Vavrek
Proviso West High School
Hillside, Illinois

Dave Wendelin
Educational Service Center
Golden, Colorado

Michel Wendell
Archdiocese of St. Louis
    Cathedral School
St. Louis, Missouri

Roberta Williams
Traverse City East Junior
    High School
Traverse City, Michigan

Sharon Williams
Bay Point Middle School
St. Petersburg, Florida

Contents

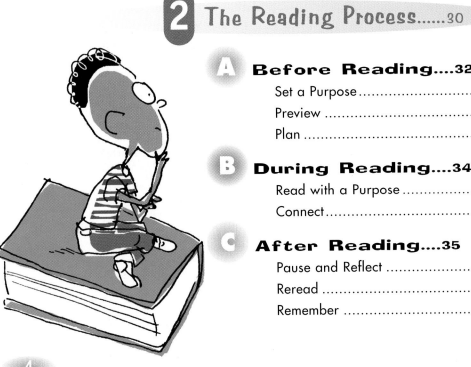

How to Use This Book...13

Goals.................................14
Uses..................................16
Book Organization 17

1 Introduction......22

What Is Reading? 24
Why You Read 25
What Happens When You Read 26
   1. Visualizing Reading 26
   2. The Reading and
     Writing Process 28

2 The Reading Process......30

A **Before Reading....32**
   Set a Purpose...................................32
   Preview 33
   Plan 33

B **During Reading....34**
   Read with a Purpose 34
   Connect..35

C **After Reading....35**
   Pause and Reflect 35
   Reread 36
   Remember 36

3 Reading Know-how.....38

A Essential Reading Skills...40

1. Making Inferences 40
2. Drawing Conclusions 41
3. Comparing and Contrasting........42
4. Evaluating..................................42

B Reading Actively................43

1. Being an Active Reader 43
2. Ways of Reading Actively...........45
3. Finding a Reading Place.............46
4. Finding Time for Reading 46

C Reading Paragraphs......... 47

1. Finding the Subject 48
2. Finding the Main Idea 50

D Kinds of Paragraphs........ 55

E Ways of Organizing Paragraphs 56

1. Time Order 57
2. Location Order 58
3. Cause-Effect Order 59
4. Order of Importance 60
5. Comparison-Contrast Order.........62
6. Classification Order 63

4 Reading Textbooks......64

A Reading Different Subjects

1. Reading History..........................66

2. Reading Geography....................84

3. Reading Science 100

4. Reading Math 117

B Focus on School Reading

1. Focus on Science Concepts 132

2. Focus on Word Problems.............143

C Elements of Textbooks...155

Boldface Terms 156

Charts 157

Glossary 158

Graphs 159

Headings and Titles..............160

Index.................................162

Maps.................................163

Photos and Illustrations 165

Preview 166

Table of Contents 168

5 Reading Nonfiction......170

A Reading Kinds of Nonfiction

1. Reading an Essay 172

2. Reading a Biography 188

3. Reading an Autobiography 204

4. Reading a Newspaper Article 218

5. Reading a Magazine Article 234

B Ways of Reading Nonfiction

1. Focus on Persuasive Writing 247

2. Focus on Speeches 256

3. Focus on Real-world Writing........265

C Elements of Nonfiction...273

Argument or
Persuasive Writing 274

Cause and Effect.................275

Chronological Order 276

Classification and Definition..277

Comparison and Contrast 278

Connotation and Denotation..279

Editorial.............................280

Fact and Opinion 281

Interview 282

Lead 283

Main Idea 284

Problem and Solution 286

Propaganda Techniques........287

Topic Sentence and
Supporting Details 289

Viewpoint 291

6 Reading Fiction......292

A Reading Kinds of Fiction

1. Reading a Short Story.................294

2. Reading a Novel 315

B Ways of Reading Fiction

1. Focus on Characters....................340

2. Focus on Setting 351

3. Focus on Dialogue 360

4. Focus on Plot...........................368

5. Focus on Theme........................376

6. Focus on Comparing
and Contrasting.........................383

C Elements of Fiction 389

Antagonist and Protagonist ..390

Author's Purpose.................391

Character...........................392

Dialogue and Dialect...........394

Genre 396

Mood 397

Point of View 398

Plot 400

Setting 402

Style 403

Symbol 404

Theme 405

7 Reading Poetry......406

A Reading a Poem...408

B Ways of Reading Poetry
1. Focus on Language 422
2. Focus on Meaning 430
3. Focus on Sound and Structure......439

C Elements of Poetry..........446

Alliteration 447
Allusion 448
Exaggeration 449
Figurative Language...........450
Free Verse.......................451
Idiom 452
Imagery 453
Lyric Poem 454
Metaphor 455
Mood 456
Narrative Poem 457

Onomatopoeia 458
Personification...................459
Repetition 460
Rhyme 461
Rhyme Scheme 462
Rhythm 463
Simile..............................464
Stanza 465
Symbol 467
Tone and Voice 468

8 Reading Drama......470

A Reading a Play...472

B Ways of Reading Drama
1. Focus on Theme..........................489
2. Focus on Language 495

C Elements of Drama..........502

Acts and Scenes 503
Cast of Characters 504
Dialogue 505
Monologue.........................506

Plot 507
Setting 509
Stage Directions 510
Theme 511

9 Reading on the Internet......512

A **Reading a Website**................514

B **Elements of the Internet**...527

Bookmark 528	Link 532
Browser 529	Search Engine 533
Email..................530	World Wide Web 534

 10 Reading Graphics......536

A **Reading a Graphic** 538

B **Elements of Graphics** 548

Bar Graph 549	Pie Chart 558
Cartoon 550	Table 559
Diagram 552	Timeline 561
Line Graph.........554	
Map 555	
Photograph 557	

11 Reading for Tests......562

A Reading a Test and Test Questions......564

B Focus on Kinds of Tests
1. Focus on Essay Tests....................580
2. Focus on Vocabulary Tests 584
3. Focus on Social Studies Tests........588
4. Focus on Math Tests 593
5. Focus on Science Tests.................598

12 Improving Vocabulary......606

A Learning New Words 608
1. Building Vocabulary Strength 608
2. Being a Word Collector 609
3. Boosting Your Vocabulary............613

B Building Vocabulary Skills..615
1. Becoming a Context Clue Expert...615
2. Understanding Roots, Prefixes, and Suffixes 621
3. Learning Word Parts 624
4. Dictionary Dipping 626
5. Reading a Thesaurus....................630

C Understanding Specialized Terms and Vocabulary Tests........631
1. School Terms 631
2. Vocabulary Questions 634
3. Analogies 636

Reader's Almanac......640

A Strategy Handbook 641

Close Reading 642
Looking for Cause and Effect 644
Note-taking 646
Outlining 648
Paraphrasing..........650
Questioning the Author 652
Reading Critically 654
Skimming 656
Summarizing 658
Synthesizing 660
Using Graphic Organizers 662
Visualizing and Thinking Aloud....664

B Reading Tools 666

Argument Chart..........667
Cause-Effect Organizer 667
Character Development Chart 668
Character Map 668
Class and Text Notes 669
Classification Notes..........669
Concept Map 670
Critical Reading Chart 670
Double-entry Journal 671
Fiction Organizer 671
5 W's Organizer..........672
Inference Chart 672
Key Word or Topic Notes 673
K-W-L Chart..........673
Magnet Summary 674
Main Idea Organizer 674
Nonfiction Organizer 675
Outline 675
Paraphrase or Retelling Chart..........676
Plot Diagram 676
Process Notes 677
Setting Chart..........677
Storyboard 678
Story Organizer 678
Story String 679
Study Cards 679
Summary Notes..........680
Thinking Tree..........680
Timeline or Sequence Notes 681
Topic and Theme Organizer 681
Two Per Line 682
Two-story Map 682
Venn Diagram 683
Viewpoint and Evidence Organizer 683
Web 684
Website Profiler..........684

C Word Parts: Prefixes, Suffixes, and Roots........685

Prefixes 685
Suffixes 687
Greek and Latin Roots 689

Acknowledgments......693

Author and Title Index....695
Skills and Terms Index....697

How to Use This Book

A "reading handbook" might seem like a strange idea. You are asked to read a book to help you get more out of what you read.

The reading you are asked to do is amazingly complex. You read instructions, tests, novels, newspapers, websites, and books from the library. You need to recognize all sorts of unusual words, make sense of many types of reading, change how fast or slow you read, use strategies, reread, and then remember everything. Who can do all that?

You could probably use a little help to make reading and learning easier. Well, that's what this handbook is—help when you need it.

Goals

What are the goals
of this handbook?
They're simple:

1 Model Good Reading

If you want to shoot a hockey puck or
learn how to skate backward, someone
models it for you. You watch a coach take
shots at the net or the instructor skate
backward. You need the same kind of help for
reading. But you can't just watch people read. You
need to listen to what they are thinking as they read.
That's what this handbook does. It lets you listen in while readers
read. Among other things, the handbook will teach you a clear and
easy reading process. It will tell you what to do step by step.

2 Teach Reading Strategies

The handbook will also show you how much reading know-how you
already have and help you learn reading tools and strategies that will
make you a better reader. Right now you have a lot of know-how
that can help you understand what you read. It can help you make
inferences and help you see the way a text is organized. Using this
know-how is essential to make you a stronger, better reader. But the
difference between being an OK reader and a great one is not brains.
It's having the tools and strategies that help you get the most out of
your reading.

Think about it for a minute. Once you know some strategies for
reading tests, don't you think you'll do a little better on them? Once
you know what to look for when you read a play, won't you be able
to understand it better?

3 Introduce Kinds of Reading

As a reader, you will face a wide number of different kinds of reading—everything from cartoons to the Constitution. You don't read them all the same way. Knowing how to tackle these different kinds of reading does not just come to you in your sleep one night. You need to practice reading different kinds of materials and to read them with someone who can help you.

Graphs, for example, are one kind of reading. You approach reading a graph differently than you do reading the newspaper, a biography, or a novel. You need to understand that different kinds of reading have different patterns of organization. In this handbook, you will see how your purpose changes with different kinds of reading, as do the strategies and tools you use.

Here's a way to think about it. The reading process is like a map. It guides you on any journey. Your reading know-how is stored up there in your brain, just waiting to be let out when you call on it. The tools and strategies of reading are like a backpack full of neat things—compass, pocket knife, water bottle, and so on—that can come in handy on a reading journey.

Let's get started.

So, how do you use this handbook?

1 Guide

Think of this handbook as a friendly guide or answer book. When you don't understand something, look in here. Maybe you are having trouble in math class. Look up "math," and you'll find help on how to read your math book or specific kinds of math problems. If you want tips on how to make sense of a poem, look at the lesson on poetry. It will give you some ways to read poems.

2 Mini-lessons

The handbook is written with lots of tips, tools, and examples. The idea is to make it easier for you to dip in and get on with what you are doing. If you want to learn something about taking notes, look it up, read about it, and apply it. A mini-lesson might be just what is needed. The handbook gives you lots of suggestions and ideas. Try a few of them out, but don't feel like you have to try them all.

3 Desk Reference

Whenever you come across something new you need help with, check for it in the handbook. It contains a Reader's Almanac of reading tools and strategies and Elements sections on key terms. Check in the index or the Almanac to help you find what you want.

4 Different Kinds of Reading

To help you with different kinds of reading, the handbook includes all sorts of materials, from political cartoons and magazines to web pages and tests. The handbook will suggest the kinds of things you need to look for with all different types of reading.

Book Organization

In this handbook, you'll see four different kinds of lessons.

1

Reading Sections

The "reading" lessons model how to read different kinds of materials with the reading process. They include several key parts:

Before Reading

Goals

They tell what the lesson is about.

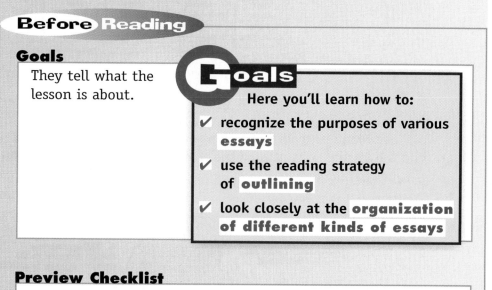

Goals

Here you'll learn how to:

✔ recognize the purposes of various **essays**

✔ use the reading strategy of **outlining**

✔ look closely at the **organization of different kinds of essays**

Preview Checklist

It tells what to look for when you preview a reading.

Preview Checklist

✔ the title and author
✔ the first and last paragraphs
✔ any key words, headings, or words in boldface
✔ any repeated words or phrases

Reading Strategy

In this part of the lesson, you decide on one strategy that will work well for this kind of reading. Each reading lesson focuses on one main reading strategy.

Reading Strategy: **Note-taking**

Reading Tools

Each lesson suggests one or more reading tools to use as you read. Often two, three, or more tools are shown to suggest possible choices, but you don't need to use them all.

5 W'S ORGANIZER

SUBJECT
radio-controlled robots

WHO	WHAT	WHERE	WHEN	WHY
David Colker	duels between BattleBots	on a cable TV program	special exhibition	for fun and entertainment

How Texts Are Organized

Each kind of reading has a way it's organized. This part of the lesson looks at how the writing is organized so you can understand it better.

3. Climax
The situation reaches a critical point. The tension that has been building reaches a peak.

2. Rising Action
Characters try to solve a problem or conflict, but the situation usually grows worse before the problem gets solved.

4. Falling Action
Tension decreases as the conflict begins to be settled.

1. Exposition
Background is given on the setting and situation the main characters find themselves in.

5. Resolution
The solution to the problem occurs at the story's end.

After Reading

Rereading Strategy

Every lesson gives you questions to help you reflect on what you learned. Then, another reading strategy is suggested to help you reread and fulfill your purpose for reading.

Rereading Strategy: **Skimming**

2 Focus Sections

The "focus" lessons are close-ups. They take a closer look at one kind of reading or specific element, such as theme, setting, dialogue, and so on. These briefer lessons zero in on a single subject.

Before Reading

Goals

Each lesson starts out with goals.

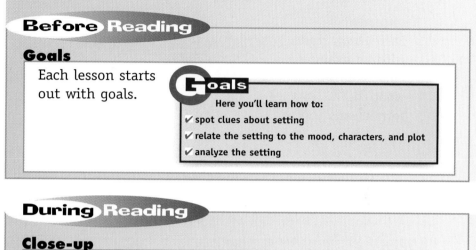

Goals

Here you'll learn how to:

✔ spot clues about setting
✔ relate the setting to the mood, characters, and plot
✔ analyze the setting

During Reading

Close-up

Next, you take a close-up look at one kind of reading through one lens, or point of view.

SETTING CHART

NOVEL NAME: Shiloh

CLUES ABOUT TIME	CLUES ABOUT PLACE
time of day	place names
afternoon	Friendly, Sistersville, Wheeling, and Parkersburg
season	physical environment
summer	high in the hills

After Reading

Summary

Each lesson ends after exploring the one idea (such as setting) and concludes with a brief summary.

Summing Up

■ Writers usually give clues about time and place at the beginning of the story—usually in the first few paragraphs.

■ Setting can help you understand the mood, characters, and plot of a story.

■ A change in the setting often signals a change in action and atmosphere.

Elements Sections

The "elements" mini-lessons explain the key terms related to a genre. They explain the language, or "lingo," so you can talk about what you are reading.

Example

Each lesson starts with an example. First, you see what the term means.

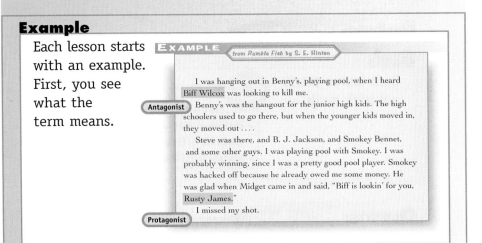

EXAMPLE — from *Rumble Fish* by S. E. Hinton

I was hanging out in Benny's, playing pool, when I heard Biff Wilcox was looking to kill me.

Antagonist — Benny's was the hangout for the junior high kids. The high schoolers used to go there, but when the younger kids moved in, they moved out....

Steve was there, and B. J. Jackson, and Smokey Bennet, and some other guys. I was playing pool with Smokey. I was probably winning, since I was a pretty good pool player. Smokey was hacked off because he already owed me some money. He was glad when Midget came in and said, "Biff is lookin' for you, Rusty James."

Protagonist — I missed my shot.

Description

Next, you read about the term in the example.

DESCRIPTION

The **protagonist** of a story is the main character, or the one most central to the action of the story. The **antagonist** is the person, thing, or force that works against the protagonist. An antagonist can be another character, a family, a society, a force of nature (such as the freezing cold or a tornado), or a force within the main character.

Definition

Each lesson ends with a clear definition of what the term means.

DEFINITION

The **antagonist** is the person or thing working against the protagonist, or hero, of a work. The **protagonist** is the main character of the story.

4 Reader's Almanac

The Reader's Almanac is a collection of reading strategies, tools, and lists of word parts that you might need for easy reference.

Reading Strategies

First, the Almanac describes in detail each of the 12 main reading strategies used in the handbook.

Reading Critically

DESCRIPTION

Reading critically means understanding and evaluating the point a writer is trying to make. To do that, you need to move beyond the facts and details on the page and consider what those facts and details mean. Read the lines and read between the lines. Think about what's missing or has been left out.

Reading Tools

Next, the Almanac describes and gives an example of the 36 main reading tools used in the handbook.

PARAPHRASE OR RETELLING CHART

A Paraphrase or Retelling Chart helps you do two things at once. It helps you understand parts of a text or graphic by putting them in your own words and helps you collect your own thoughts about the work.

Lines	My Paraphrase
Write two or three lines from a text or facts from a graphic here.	*Tell in your own words what these lines mean here.*

My Thoughts

Note your own ideas or reaction to what's said here.

Reading Aids

Finally, the Almanac gives a list of useful reading aids, such as Greek and Latin roots, suffixes, and prefixes.

Root	Origin	Meaning	Examples
aero	Greek	air	aerobics, aerate
agri	Latin	field	agriculture, agrarian
alter	Latin	other	alternate, altercation

Introduction

- **What Is Reading?**
- **Why You Read**
- **What Happens When You Read**

Introduction

To start, you need to have a good idea of what reading really is. What do you think it is? How would you describe it?

What Is Reading?

To understand reading, you need to compare it to something you already know. Reading is a lot like a number of things.

A Tool

For example, you can think of reading as a tool. Like a hammer, reading helps you perform a number of jobs. With a hammer you can pound a nail, close a paint can, and pull out rusty nails. Likewise, by reading you can figure out the instructions to set up a computer, learn which movies are playing over the weekend, or check the weather before an afternoon at the beach with your favorite novel.

A Skill

But reading is also a skill, like swimming or driving. It is something you learn how to do by practicing. Improving your swimming skills makes it possible to do new things. Once you learn how to float in a pool, you can swim in a lake or even go snorkeling in the ocean. The same is true for reading. The more you read, the better you'll get at it. When you learn to read well, you can read anything—with confidence, enthusiasm, and enjoyment.

An Ability

Reading gives you "thinking power." It increases your ability to communicate, to learn, to enjoy, and to imagine. In short, it makes your life fuller, richer, and more fun. Reading helps you make sense of—and be curious about—the world.

Why You Read

Reading is something you can hardly do without. You read so you can learn about a movie before deciding to see it. You read so you can understand a bus schedule, do well on your history test, follow a road map, or get news from a letter by a friend.

Being a good reader will help you not only in school but also in life. As you see in this handbook, reading is vital to almost everything you do.

Here are six good reasons to read.

1 Enjoyment Reading is great entertainment. You read the sports pages, interviews with TV or film stars, mystery novels, and magazine articles because it's fun to read.

2 Information Reading helps you understand the world and your life. You read to learn about current events, computers, guitars, and much more. Reading gives you the information you need.

3 Meaning Reading brings you things that are meaningful— letters, historical documents, great ideas, new facts. Whatever your interests, reading helps you locate and learn about what has meaning for you.

4 Depth Reading expands your mind. It develops your thinking processes and stretches your imagination. It helps you answer questions about what you believe and what the best way to lead your life is.

5 Beauty Reading a well-written story, article, or poem can be highly pleasurable. Just as you appreciate the colors in a painting, you may like the writing style of certain writers. Writers can create art with words.

6 Fun and Ease Reading is almost as easy as talking. You do it almost automatically. You read street signs, headlines in newspapers, names of movies, store display signs, and labels on food. It's a habit.

What Happens When You Read

Part of becoming a better reader is seeing reading for what it really is. You might sometimes hear someone say "the act of reading." Well, reading isn't an act. Reading is very seldom something you just do—zip—and it's over.

Like writing, reading is a process. It occurs over time—a few minutes, a few hours, or even a few weeks in the case of a novel or full-length book.

Visualizing Reading

What happens when you read? What do you see in your mind as "reading"? Jean Lifford and some fellow teachers in Dedham, Massachusetts, began asking this question as a way to understand what their students think happens when they read. It's a brilliant idea.

ONE STUDENT'S SKETCH OF THE READING PROCESS

Take 15–20 minutes to draw what you think happens when you read. Your sketch may be one image or a number of panels, like a comic strip. (See the example on the previous page.) Imagine yourself sitting down and starting to read. What happens?

Your sketch of your reading process may look very different from the sketch of anyone else. People learn in different ways. What works for you may not work for everyone else. And don't worry about how good an artist you are. You're not getting a grade for your sketches. The drawings are just a way to help you discover what happens when you read.

Try it yourself. Follow some simple steps.

1. Close your eyes.
2. Think about what happens when you read a book.
3. Try to see the steps you take as you read a book.
4. Next, sketch what happens when you read.
5. Then, after you've finished, spend a few minutes thinking about what your sketch tells you about the way you read.

The Reading and Writing Process

By now, almost every student has heard about "the writing process."
It is a basic part of teaching writing today. But do you know as
much about the "reading process"? Reviewing the writing process
will make the reading process clearer.

Questions for Writers

The trick of doing anything hard is to make it easy—or at least
easier. The writing process makes a complex activity seem easy by
breaking it down into small steps. Look at some of the questions
you have to answer when writing:

- What are your purpose and subject?
- How long should the writing be?
- Is your subject narrow enough?
- What's your main point?
- What details should you include?
- How should you organize your paper?
- How can you make your paper more clear?
- Is your writing accurate and correct?
- What's the best way to present it?

To simplify all that, the writing process is usually broken down into
five steps:

1. Prewriting
2. Drafting
3. Revising
4. Editing and Proofreading
5. Publishing and Presenting

The process of writing, like that of reading, involves answering many
questions and making all kinds of decisions. The writing process helps
walk writers through the various questions and decisions involved in
creating a written composition.

Questions for Readers

Likewise, a reading process can help you with all of the questions that a reader needs to answer. Look at some of them:

- What are you reading about?
- Why are you reading?
- What do you want to get out of your reading?
- What kind of reading is it?
- Should you read slowly or quickly?
- How do you know if you've understood it?
- How can you remember what you read?
- What can you do if you don't understand something?
- Should you reread?

A reading process makes it easier to deal with these sorts of questions.

This handbook suggests one process for you to follow. It is *not* the only absolutely right way to read. It is just one way to help you read better and understand more.

In time, you will discover other ways that help you read and learn. This handbook will give you a good start for developing your own reading process— *one that works best for you.*

The Reading
Process

Before Reading

During Reading

After Reading

The Reading Process

Here is a brief description of a reading process, one you will use again and again in this handbook.

Before Reading

What you do before you read is the first part of the reading process:

A Set a Purpose

B Preview

C Plan

A Set a Purpose

The first step of reading takes an incredibly short period of time—perhaps as little as a few seconds to a minute or two. All too often we jump right into reading without ever giving ourselves enough time to listen to our own thoughts.

Listen to yourself think. You have decided to read for some reason. What is it? Maybe your teacher made a homework assignment, or you needed to find a name or a date for a paper you're writing. Or maybe you simply wanted to know about how the basketball game turned out. Decide what your reason to read is. Once you know that, you have a purpose. It's like taking a grocery list with you into the store. When you have the list, you know what you need to buy.

In most cases, it's a good idea to put your reading purpose into a question, such as, "What is this novel about, and what makes it interesting?" Looking for an answer to the question gives you a reason to read.

B Preview

When you preview a reading, you look over it. The preview can be long or short, brief or in-depth. How much of a preview you decide to do is up to you. You don't need to give all of your reading the same kind of preview. The newspaper, for example, probably requires only a glance to decide how long an article is. A novel or nonfiction book requires a more detailed preview, such as looking over the cover and checking out the chapter titles.

You preview a reading to get a sense of what to expect and to start thinking about what you might already know about the subject. The point of the preview is learning something about the reading—its length, its difficulty, its vocabulary, its organization, and above all its content. You may only learn one or two things. That's fine. You may learn a whole lot. The idea is to learn enough so that you can decide *how you want to read*.

C Plan

You can probably get home from school four or five different ways— walk, take a bus, ride your bike, wait for a family member to pick you up in a car, or go with a friend. But to get home you need to decide on one of them. If you don't decide, you will still be at school tomorrow when classes begin again.

The same is true of getting what you want from your reading. You need a plan. After you set a purpose, you decide the best way to reach it. You choose a reading strategy and tools. You may decide that, with a textbook, your reading purpose is to learn the causes of the Civil War. A sensible strategy would be note-taking. You take notes every time the text mentions a reason for the war. Or, you could decide to use the strategy of using graphic organizers and create a Cause- Effect Organizer.

Just before reading, pause and decide which reading strategy to use to find what you are looking for.

During Reading

What you do as you read is the
second step in the reading process:

D Read with a Purpose

E Connect

D Read with a Purpose

Have you ever walked into a department
store and asked yourself, "What am I looking
for?" You are overwhelmed by all of the colors, the perfume smells,
the salespeople, and the other customers. You have already walked
through the doors and halfway down the aisle before you stop and
ask, "Wait a minute. What am I here for? What do I want?"

Often you begin reading the same way. You go on for 15 or more
minutes before ever stopping to ask what you are trying to learn.
Instead, think about your purpose as you read. Look for the
information you need to find.

A text makes statements, bombards you with information, hints at
certain meanings, and presents graphs, charts, or photos. It can take
a lot of effort just to see what the writer is telling you. If you read
with a purpose, you'll know how to sort through everything that is
being presented. Don't simply pass your eyes over the words on the
page. Think about what you're reading.

With reading, you create understanding by being clear about *why*
you are reading. By taking the attitude "I will get something out of
reading this," you will learn something. You have to say to yourself,
in effect, "When I'm done reading, I'll know _____." By doing that,
you have created an understanding about what the reading will
mean for you.

E Connect

You also want to connect to what you read. One way to do this is to relate what you are reading to your own life.

Asking questions helps you link the reading to something in your life.

- How does this touch you?
- Where have you seen or heard something like this before?
- What do you find surprising?
- When did something like this happen to you?
- What do you think about it? Is it believable or not?

You will remember more about what you read if you connect it to your life.

After Reading

The last step in the reading process begins once your eyes read the last word:

F Pause and Reflect

G Reread

H Remember

F Pause and Reflect

Take time to pause, look back, and reflect after you read. Ask yourself how well you have met your reading purpose. Instead of immediately moving on to something else, take a moment to look back and ask yourself, "Did I learn what I wanted to learn? Does anything seem confusing? Can I answer the question in my reading purpose?" For example, at the end of a chapter on the background of the Civil War, did you learn the causes for it? Could you state them?

You may or may not have found the information you were looking for. In fact, you might have found something else—for example, information about the two great generals of the war. That's like going into a store to buy shoes and coming out with a sweater. You got something, but it may not be what you wanted to find. You might need to go back to the reading again.

G Reread

For many kinds of reading, it's helpful to reread. Be patient. A comic strip probably doesn't need rereading (if you get the humor of it), but your science or history text probably will. Reading for enjoyment won't require much rereading. But you will need to reread for a lot of other kinds of reading—for example, a science article or the directions for installing new software.

As you go back into a text, reread with a specific purpose. Focus on what you want to learn or what puzzled you the first time.

Then, after rereading, ask yourself again if you have found what you wanted. Insist upon getting what you started out to find.

H Remember

"I forgot" may just be the most common expression heard from students. "I knew it, but I forgot." Where did it go? All of us forget things, but some of us are better than others at remembering. Why?

We remember what we can find. To remember something, you need to know where you put it. Write down what you learned. Create a graphic organizer or drawing. Take some notes. Talk about what you read with a friend. Summarize new ideas. The key to remembering is to "make the information your own."

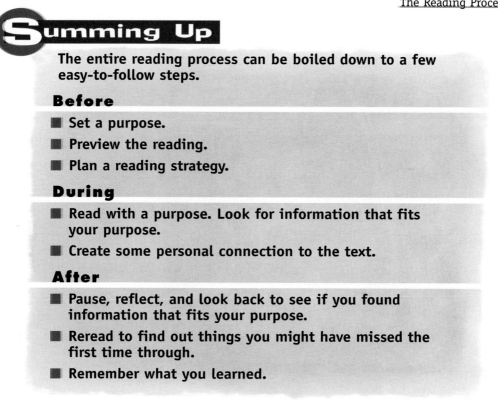

Summing Up

The entire reading process can be boiled down to a few easy-to-follow steps.

Before

- Set a purpose.
- Preview the reading.
- Plan a reading strategy.

During

- Read with a purpose. Look for information that fits your purpose.
- Create some personal connection to the text.

After

- Pause, reflect, and look back to see if you found information that fits your purpose.
- Reread to find out things you might have missed the first time through.
- Remember what you learned.

One Last Word

You are probably thinking, "Do I have to do all that every time? It's hard, and it'll take a lot of time." You're right. Reading well can take a lot of time and is not always easy. But why spend time and not get anything from it?

The fact is you probably do a lot of the steps in the reading process already. But maybe you skip some and rush through others. This handbook will help you be more aware of what happens while you read and help you develop good habits you can practice.

You will see how the reading process works with many different kinds of reading. By going through it step by step, you will see how you can read with more understanding and confidence. Think of the **reading process** as a road map leading you through different kinds of reading, making sure you don't get lost.

Reading
Know-how

- Essential Reading Skills
- Reading Actively
- Reading Paragraphs
- Kinds of Paragraphs
- Ways of Organizing Paragraphs

Reading Know-how

You already have a lot of reading know-how. You just need to unlock it. The best way to become a better reader is not to learn a lot of new things, but to use what you already have.

Essential Reading Skills

Every day you make judgments and comparisons, reach conclusions, and make inferences. You decide whether or not you like some people based on the things they say or do. Those judgments, comparisons, conclusions, and inferences are the same thinking skills you can use when reading. They form the foundation on which all of your reading rests.

Making Inferences

Writers won't tell you everything. Sometimes you need to figure things out on your own. You need to learn how to use everything you read and everything you already know. That's what making an inference means—taking something you read and putting it with something you know already to make an inference.

MAKING INFERENCES

"What I Learned"
+ "What I Already Know"
―――――――――――――
= Inference

For example, a character who is glaring and has clenched fists is probably angry. You do not know that for certain; you infer it. You take the fact that the character was glaring and had clenched fists and put that information with what you already know. You know that's the way people who are angry act, so you infer the character is angry. You read between the lines.

Drawing Conclusions

You draw conclusions all the time. You have probably heard the expression "Why don't you put two and two together?" That means taking bits of information and coming up with something else from what you know. For example, imagine you see a man nearly 6'6" tall in an airport. All you know is that he is tall. But, suppose you saw this man with 10 to 15 other tall men, all of them carrying gym bags and wearing basketball shoes. What conclusion would you probably draw? Taking all that information, you conclude that the men could be part of a basketball team.

Drawing conclusions is fundamental reading know-how. You need to keep track of information you learn and see how it adds up.

DRAWING CONCLUSIONS

FACTS	CONCLUSION
Fact #1 man 6'6" tall	
Fact #2 10-15 other tall men	basketball team
Fact #3 gym bags and basketball shoes	

Comparing and Contrasting

The ability to see how things are alike and different lets you gather important information. You compare the way you dress to what your friends wear. By doing that, you learn more about yourself and your friends. By comparing two books or stories, you can learn more about them.

Comparing and contrasting gives you a particular point of view, which is useful for readers. Often you need to look at a selection from a number of different points of view.

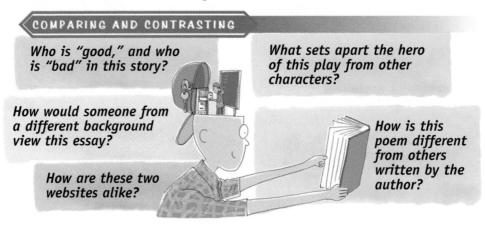

COMPARING AND CONTRASTING

Who is "good," and who is "bad" in this story?

What sets apart the hero of this play from other characters?

How would someone from a different background view this essay?

How is this poem different from others written by the author?

How are these two websites alike?

Often, it is only by comparing or contrasting things from different angles that you can really get to know or understand them.

Evaluating

You also make judgments every day. You decide which friends, movies, and music you like and which you don't. As a reader, you will also be called upon to use what you know to make judgments. For example, suppose a novelist creates a character who speaks rudely and who is sloppily dressed. The writer probably wants you to form a negative opinion of this character. That's probably the reason the writer included actions most readers would disapprove of—to create an impression and send alert readers a signal.

In almost any reading you do, you will need the skills of making inferences, drawing conclusions, comparing and contrasting, and evaluating. These are lifelong skills you build as a reader.

Reading Actively

Be sure that you take the time to think about what you're reading.
That's not as easy as it sounds. The writer is bombarding you with
facts, stories, opinions, and graphics. It's easy to let your mind
wander and simply let the words pass in front of your eyes. But you
need to stay focused and be an active reader.

Being an Active Reader

Being an active reader means thinking
about what you are reading and
making an effort to understand.
It means giving 100 percent of your
attention to reading—not getting
distracted or tuning out when
something is hard. Good readers see
reading as an activity that requires them
to *do* something. They ask themselves
questions, make predictions, and look
for ways to relate to what they read.
They use their reading know-how
by making judgments, drawing
conclusions, and making comparisons
as they read.

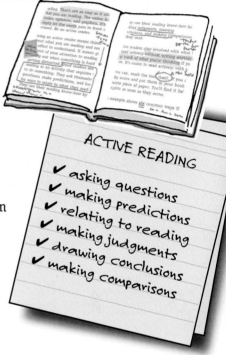

ACTIVE READING

✔ asking questions
✔ making predictions
✔ relating to reading
✔ making judgments
✔ drawing conclusions
✔ making comparisons

Active readers stay involved with what they're reading. It's possible
to read actively without writing anything down. But it's easier to
keep track of what you're thinking if you mark the text or take
notes. It's easier to read actively with a pen or pencil in your hand.

If you can, mark the text itself. If you can't write in your books, use
sticky notes and put them in your books or jot down your ideas on a
separate piece of paper. You'll find it helps to write down your
thoughts as soon as they occur.

The example on the next page shows *six* common ways that an active
reader might mark up a passage or a text.

1. Mark

2. Question

Did the children like that?

When my mother had her children, she wanted all of them to be children, not boys and girls. Everybody could do the same thing. There wasn't no such thing as a boy job or a girl job. The boys had to do just what the girls did. And I liked her for that. She didn't say, "All right now, you boys cut the wood and you girls go and make up the beds." It didn't matter if it was a girl that cut the wood or a boy that cut the wood. Or the boy that made the bed or the girl that made the bed. Every one of my brothers could cook a meal, take care of their wife and their children, just like any woman; like they could put on diapers, comb the baby's hair. They could wash, iron, sew, cook. They could do everything for themselves. Every last one of Momma's children could do that. If they didn't want to get married, they didn't have to get married, because they could do everything for themselves.

3. React

My family is like that.

4. Predict

They probably turned out to be good kids.

My mother told us this: Whatever you have, you make sure it's clean. My mother said some kids have three or four dresses but if you have just one dress, and if your one is standing out nice and clean and your skin is clean, you can beat out the others with three or four dresses because they are no cleaner than you are with one. . . .

5. Visualize

6. Clarify

Having a lot of things isn't important.

Ways of Reading Actively

You may have your own way of reading actively. Readers often develop a style that works best for them, but here are *six* common ways of reading actively.

WAYS OF READING ACTIVELY

① Mark or Highlight *The most common way is to write a sticky note and put it in a text. Or, if you can, mark the text itself by highlighting with a marker or pen. You can also put highlighting tape over passages. This is another way of making some words, phrases, or sentences stand out as IMPORTANT. Highlighting parts of a text in this way helps you come back and find what's important when you reread.*

② Ask Questions *Active readers ask lots of questions. It's one of the best things a reader can do. "Why is the writer talking about this?" "Who says this is true?" "What does that mean?"*

③ React and Connect *When you read, you need to listen to the author and to yourself. You need to think about what you are reading and relate it to your own life. Look for connections between you and the text, comparing and contrasting it to things you know.*

④ Predict *As you read, you constantly wonder how things will turn out. Think ahead when you read. Share your ideas about what's going to happen with a friend. Write down your predictions. They will help you stay interested in what you're reading.*

⑤ Visualize *Because your thoughts are mere flashes in the brain, you need to record them if you want to remember them. Making pictures in your mind can help you "see" what you were thinking and help you remember. A chart, a sketch, a diagram—any of these can help you "see."*

⑥ Clarify *Because so much is happening as you read, you need to be sure of the things you do know. Pull together what you have learned. You can do this by writing notes to clarify things, whether it's a series of points in an argument or an important detail.*

Finding a Reading Place

You need a good reading spot. You can't read actively if you can't concentrate. You can read anywhere—on the bus, in the car, at the park, in the library, or even in your room. But you will find that you get more from your reading if you find one good reading spot. Think of it as the place you go to read.

A GOOD READING PLACE HAS:
✔ good light
✔ peace and quiet
✔ a comfortable chair
✔ a pen, pencil, or highlighter

Finding Time for Reading

You also need to find time to read. Active reading takes practice, and it takes time. As a student, you should be reading an average of at least 30 minutes a day. That does not mean studying or doing homework, but just reading. To find that time, you need to plan for it.

Setting aside a time for reading is a way for you to take control of your life. If you do it, it will pay off.

Reading Paragraphs

There are *two* steps to understanding a paragraph:

1. Finding the subject
2. Finding the main idea

The paragraph, like the sentence, is a basic unit in writing. Each sentence contains a single thought, and each paragraph centers around a single large idea. As a reader, you want to find what each sentence says and what each paragraph is about. Finding what a paragraph is about is called "finding the subject." What the writer wants the reader to understand about the subject is the **main idea**.

To understand a paragraph, you first need to find the subject and then you need to find what the writer is saying about the subject. That's the key to unlocking the meaning of paragraphs.

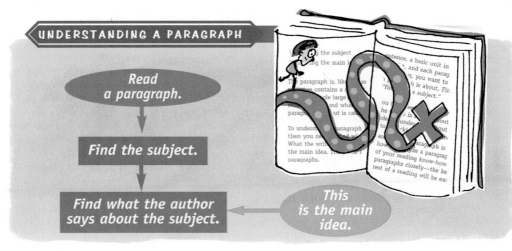

UNDERSTANDING A PARAGRAPH

Read a paragraph.

Find the subject.

Find what the author says about the subject.

This is the main idea.

Because the paragraph is a basic unit of writing, it helps to know how to analyze a paragraph. Reading paragraphs effectively should be part of your reading know-how. Often you will find that by reading a few paragraphs closely—the key paragraphs in a story or essay—you will make the rest of a reading easier to understand.

Finding the Subject

The first thing you need to do as a reader is look for the subject of the paragraph. You can find the subject by looking at several things:

■ the title or heading

■ the first sentence

■ any key or repeated words or names

For example, read this paragraph from an essay.

Title

from "Living Like Weasels" by Annie Dillard

First sentence

Key words

A weasel is wild. Who knows what he thinks? He sleeps in his underground den, his tail draped over his nose. Sometimes he lives in his den for two days without leaving. Outside, he stalks rabbits, mice, muskrats, and birds, killing more bodies than he can eat warm, and often dragging the carcasses home. Obedient to instinct, he bites his prey at the neck, either splitting the jugular vein at the throat or crunching the brain at the base of the skull, and he does not let go. One naturalist refused to kill a weasel who was socketed into his hand deeply as a rattlesnake. The man could in no way pry the tiny weasel off, and he had to walk a half a mile to water, the weasel dangling from his palm, and soak him off like a stubborn label.

Repeated word

1 Look at the title or heading.

Look at all of the clues you can to find the subject of a paragraph. Here, the title "Living Like Weasels" provides the strongest clue. It leads to the question "How do weasels live?" The writer answers that question in the very first sentence.

2 Look at the first sentence.

The first sentence also states the subject plainly: "A weasel is wild." It tells you that this paragraph is about weasels and how weasels live.

Note also that, at first, the writer says *weasel*. Later, Dillard uses a pronoun (*he* sleeps, *he* lives, and so on), but the writer is still talking about the weasel. Watch for that. Writers commonly name a subject and then later use pronouns to refer to it.

3 Look at key or repeated words or names.

Throughout the paragraph some key words have been highlighted, often the subject and verb of the sentence. They help you see what each sentence is about.

KEY WORDS

1st	*that the weasel is wild*
2nd	*what the weasel might think*
3nd	*how the weasel sleeps*
4rd	*how the weasel lives*
5th	*how the weasel hunts*
6th	*how the weasel kills its food*
7th	*about a naturalist who was bitten by a weasel*
last	*how the weasel would not let go of the man's hand*

Examining a paragraph sentence by sentence is not something you will do every day. But the exercise helps show you what you often do automatically as a reader. Your brain takes in what you read in each sentence and comes to the conclusion:

"Hey, this is about how weasels live."

You can follow this plan for finding the subject whenever you have any trouble understanding a passage.

Finding the Main Idea

Once you know the subject of a paragraph, ask yourself, "What's the main idea?" Figure out what the writer is saying about the subject. To find the main idea, you need to know the most important thing the writer wants you to know.

Main Idea in the First Sentence

In the opening paragraph from "Living Like Weasels," you know what the author thinks right away. The main idea comes in the sentence that begins the paragraph: "A weasel is wild." The rest of the paragraph gives some details or examples of the wildness.

You can use an organizer to help you understand Dillard's paragraph and sift the main idea from the details.

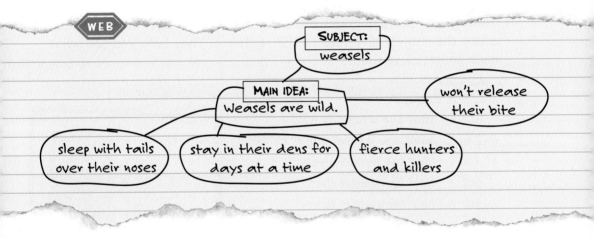

The word *wild* does not tell you right away whether the author likes the weasel's wildness or doesn't like it.

Writers do not—and often cannot—make everything clear in a single paragraph. Why would they want to do that anyway? That would take much of the fun and suspense from their writing.

Nor do writers always put the main idea right in the first sentence of the paragraph. Textbooks often do, and sometimes articles in an encyclopedia do; but writers like variety. As a result, you need to look at a number of places to find the main idea.

Main Idea in the Last Sentence

Writers sometimes prefer to write by showing several examples or details and then giving their main idea. As a reader, you need to recognize what's most important. That will be the main idea. For example, read this paragraph from an autobiography about one man's experience in Poland at the outbreak of World War II.

> **from *Courier from Warsaw* by Jan Nowak**
>
> When I reported for duty in the small town of Dubno, **①** on the Russian border, my **②** Second Squadron of Horse Artillery had already left and was in its battle position on the opposite side of the country, facing the German frontier. The reserve soldiers were collected in the barracks. When I left early in the morning to have breakfast in the officers' mess on Friday, **③** September 1, 1939, I saw **④** another officer running toward me. Waving his hands he shouted excitedly: "The war has started—the fighting started at 5 A.M.!"

Four details

Main idea

Here the main idea comes in a dramatic statement at the very end of the paragraph: the war has begun. This main idea—the beginning of the war—is what connects everything else in the paragraph. The other sentences give details. They tell the author's location (Dubno), his squad (Second Horse Artillery), the day (September 1, 1939), and how he learned about the beginning of the war (from an officer).

These notes show you how the writer built up to the main idea.

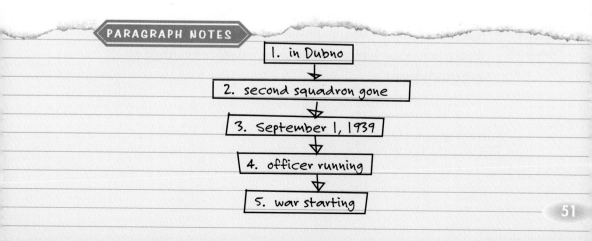

PARAGRAPH NOTES

1. in Dubno
2. second squadron gone
3. September 1, 1939
4. officer running
5. war starting

Implied Main Idea

Things would be easy if writers always put the main idea in the first or last sentence of a paragraph. But they don't. Often, the main idea of a paragraph is implied. That means it is not directly stated in any one sentence, but rather comes from parts of many sentences.

As a reader, you need to *infer* the main idea. That is, you consider what all of the sentences in the paragraph say about the subject and then decide what the author is saying about it.

Look at this example from a history textbook.

Heading

from *Creating America*

The First People in America

First sentence

...Some ancient people may have crossed a land bridge that joined Asia and North America during the last Ice Age. The Ice Age was a time of extreme cold that lasted for thousands of years. Glaciers trapped so much water that ocean levels dropped. A bridge of land, now called Beringia, appeared where the Bering Strait is now. (See map, page 28.) When the earth grew warm again, the glaciers melted and flooded Beringia. Some scientists who hold this theory believe the earliest Americans arrived 12,000 years ago. Other scientists believe humans came to the Americas much earlier. They have found artifacts in South America that tests show to be 30,000 years old. These scientists believe that people came to the Americas by many routes, over thousands of years. Some came by boat, sailing short distances from island to island. This theory may also change as scientists find more evidence of ancient America.

Four details

Heading

The heading gives you as a reader an important clue about the subject—ancient people in America. The first sentence does, too.

First Sentence

Note that the subject of the first sentence is "ancient people." But, to know what the paragraph is saying about ancient people, you need information from many of the sentences.

The first part of the paragraph begins by discussing the idea that the first people came to America during the Ice Age (12,000 years ago) by crossing a land bridge.

Details

In the second part of the paragraph, the writer gives another theory: that people came earlier "by many routes," including boats.

So, what is the writer saying about the first people? Why are two different theories discussed? The main idea seems to be that a number of different theories explain how the first people came to America. You need to piece together information from several of the sentences to come up with that main idea. The writer never directly states that idea about these theories. You have to infer it. That means going through a paragraph, sentence by sentence, piecing together the meaning. At the end, you'll see how everything adds up, and you'll know the main idea. Use an organizer like this one to help you make sense of a paragraph.

MAIN IDEA ORGANIZER

SUBJECT: First People in America

Detail #1	Detail #2	Detail #3	Detail #4
Maybe they came over a land bridge during Ice Age 12,000 years ago.	Scientists found artifacts 30,000 years old.	Maybe they arrived earlier, perhaps by boat.	New evidence might change current thinking.

MAIN IDEA: A number of different theories may explain how the first people came to America.

As a reader, you need to analyze paragraphs when the main idea does not jump out at you. Here's a plan you can follow:

1. First, find the subject.
  • Look at the heading or title.
  • Look at the first sentence.
  • Look at key words.

2. Decide what the author is saying about the subject.
  • Look closely at the first sentence and last sentence.
  • Look to see if the sentences are giving details or explaining a more general idea.
  • Pull together all that the writer is saying about the subject.
  • Then try to state the main idea in your own words.

3. Use a graphic organizer to help you sort out the main idea from the supporting details.
  • Put the subject in a box at the top.
  • List specific things the writer says about the subject in separate boxes.
  • Then sum up all of it to find what the writer wants you to understand about the subject. Write that main idea in a box at the bottom.

Kinds of Paragraphs

Part of the trouble with reading paragraphs comes in understanding the different kinds of paragraphs and the ways paragraphs can be organized.

You are probably already familiar with the *four* types of paragraphs:

KINDS OF PARAGRAPHS

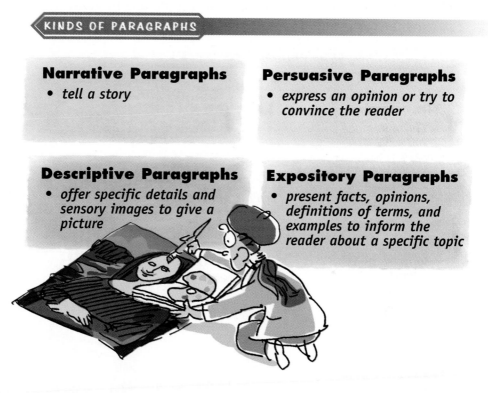

Narrative Paragraphs

- *tell a story*

Persuasive Paragraphs

- *express an opinion or try to convince the reader*

Descriptive Paragraphs

- *offer specific details and sensory images to give a picture*

Expository Paragraphs

- *present facts, opinions, definitions of terms, and examples to inform the reader about a specific topic*

What may be less familiar are the many ways paragraphs can be organized. Each sentence in a paragraph fits together around a single, central idea. But the sentences with details can be organized differently. Knowing some of the ways the details in paragraphs are organized can help you in several ways:

1. See what's important and what's not.

2. Understand the author's purpose.

3. Remember what you read.

Ways of Organizing Paragraphs

One clue to understanding paragraphs is to see how they are organized. Good writers follow a clear order most of the time, but not always. Why should they? No single set of rules exists for the way writers can or cannot write paragraphs. Some paragraphs are long; some may have just one sentence. But the more you read, the more you will notice that the order of the details in many paragraphs can be described in one of these *six* ways:

ORGANIZING PARAGRAPHS

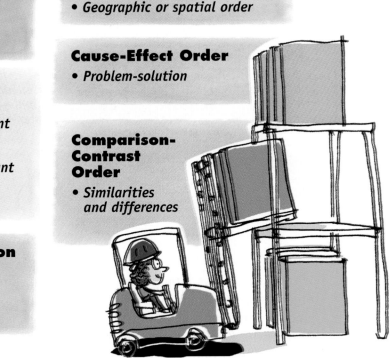

Time Order
- *Chronological order*

Location Order
- *Geographic or spatial order*

Cause-Effect Order
- *Problem-solution*

Order of Importance
- *Most important to least important*
- *Least important to most important*

Comparison-Contrast Order
- *Similarities and differences*

Classification Order
- *Groups or categories*

Let's look closely at each kind of paragraph on the next few pages. Note how each one is put together. Ask yourself:

■ What's the main idea that holds the paragraph together?

■ Where is the idea located—the beginning, middle, end, or all over?

Time Order

In a paragraph organized by time order, the writer tells a series of events in more or less the exact order in which they occurred. Note how Jack London describes the death of a dog-sled dog named Dave in *Call of the Wild*.

> **from *Call of the Wild* by Jack London**
>
> But [Dave] held out till camp was reached, when his driver made a place for him by the fire. Morning found him too weak to travel. At harness-up time he tried to crawl to his driver. By convulsive efforts he got on his feet, staggered, and fell. Then he wormed his way forward slowly toward where the harnesses were being put on his mates. He would advance his forelegs and drag up his body with a sort of hitching movement, when he would advance his forelegs and hitch ahead again a few more inches. His strength left him, and the last his mates saw of him he lay gasping in the snow and yearning toward them. But they could hear him mournfully howling till they passed out of sight behind a belt of river timber.

Series of events

The subject of the paragraph is the last day and moments of the sled dog named Dave. London tells the series of events in time order:

SERIES OF EVENTS

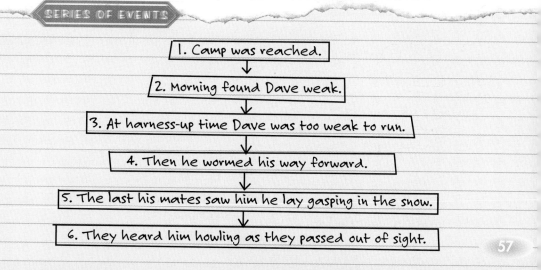

1. Camp was reached.
   ↓
2. Morning found Dave weak.
   ↓
3. At harness-up time Dave was too weak to run.
   ↓
4. Then he wormed his way forward.
   ↓
5. The last his mates saw him he lay gasping in the snow.
   ↓
6. They heard him howling as they passed out of sight.

Location Order

Some paragraphs move in an organized way from one location to another. The idea of this paragraph is to establish what was happening where.

Different locations

I was asleep on the second floor of our narrow, gabled green house in Willemstad, on the island of Curaçao, the largest of the Dutch islands just off the coast of Venezuela. I remember that on that moonless night in February 1942, they attacked the big Lago oil refinery on Aruba, the sister island west of us. Then they blew up six of our small lake tankers, the tubby ones that still bring crude oil from Lake Maracaibo to the refinery, Curaçaosche Petroleum Maatschappij, to be made into gasoline, kerosene, and diesel oil. One German sub was even sighted off Willemstad at dawn.

With paragraphs that follow location order, you can almost draw a map of what the writer is describing. For example, note the order of the locations described in Taylor's paragraph. The details in the paragraph move the reader across the map in a circle.

MAP OF LOCATION

Aruba
② attacked big Lago oil refinery

③ blew up six tankers

Curaçao

① asleep in house on second floor in Willemstad

Willemstad

④ sighted submarine off Willemstad

coast of Venezuela

Cause-Effect Order

In a paragraph organized by cause and effect, the writer begins with the cause and moves to the effects or begins with effects and then explains the cause. Here is a way to picture cause-effect order:

CAUSE-EFFECT ORDER

Cause ⟶ Effects   Effects ⟶ Cause

Read this paragraph for cause and effect.

> **from *Slavery in the United States* by Charles Ball**
>
> "When [the slave traders] put us in irons, to be sent to our place of confinement in the ship, the men who fastened the irons on these mothers, took the children out of their hands, and threw them over the side of the ship, into the water. When this was done, two of the women leaped overboard after the children—the third was already confined by a chain to another woman, and could not get into the water, but in struggling to disengage herself she broke her arm, and died a few days after, of a fever. One of the two women who were in the river, was carried down by the weight of her irons, before she could be rescued; but the other was taken up by some men in a boat, and brought on board. This woman threw herself overboard one night, when we were at sea.

Cause

Three effects

Here Charles Ball organizes the paragraph clearly around why some captured slaves threw themselves overboard. He gives a single cause and then tells the series of chilling effects it creates.

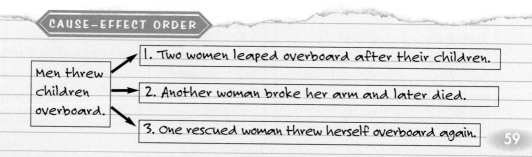

CAUSE–EFFECT ORDER

Men threw children overboard.

1. Two women leaped overboard after their children.
2. Another woman broke her arm and later died.
3. One rescued woman threw herself overboard again.

Order of Importance

When a paragraph is organized by order of importance, the writer may begin with the most important idea and move to the least important idea. Or, the writer can begin with examples and details and build up to the larger idea.

Most Important to Least Important

In this paragraph from a history textbook, the writer starts with the most important idea (given in the first sentence) and moves to details that support this main idea.

from *Creating America*

As the Native Americans of the Plains battled to remain free, the buffalo herds that they depended upon for survival dwindled. At one time, 30 million buffalo roamed the Plains. However, hired hunters killed the animals to feed crews building railroads. Others shot buffalo as a sport or to supply Eastern factories with leather for robes, shoes, and belts. From 1872 to 1882, hunters killed more than one million buffalo each year.

Main idea

Four details

The main idea has four detail sentences supporting it, and the paragraph moves deductively from the most important idea to details about it.

MOST IMPORTANT IDEA FIRST

MAIN IDEA: Buffalo herds dwindled.

Detail #1:	Detail #2:	Detail #3:	Detail #4:
30 million buffalo roaming the plains	killed to feed crews building the railroad west	killed for sport or to be used for shoes, robes, or belts	between 1872 and 1882, more than 1 million killed each year

Least Important to Most Important

Here, in another paragraph from the same textbook, the writing moves from the least important details to the main idea stated in the last sentence.

from *Creating America*

During the height of the fur trade, ① mountain men worked some streams so heavily that they killed off the animals. ② This forced the trappers to search for new streams where beaver lived. The mountain men's ③ explorations provided Americans with some of the earliest firsthand knowledge of the Far West. This knowledge, and the trails the mountain men blazed, made it possible for later pioneers to move west.

Three details

Main idea

This organization is inductive. It begins with one example, then another, and another, taking the reader to the main idea at the end of the paragraph.

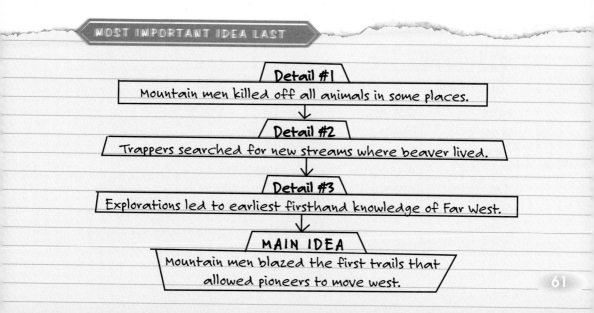

MOST IMPORTANT IDEA LAST

Detail #1
Mountain men killed off all animals in some places.

Detail #2
Trappers searched for new streams where beaver lived.

Detail #3
Explorations led to earliest firsthand knowledge of Far West.

MAIN IDEA
Mountain men blazed the first trails that allowed pioneers to move west.

Comparison-Contrast Order

When a paragraph follows comparison-contrast order, the writer shows how one thing is like or unlike another. In the paragraph below, the writer compares something unfamiliar (wolves) with something that is familiar (dogs).

from *Gray Wolf, Red Wolf* by Dorothy Hinshaw Patent

Subject of comparison

Wolves look similar to German shepherd and husky dogs, but their legs are longer, their chests are narrower, and their feet are bigger. Wolf tails generally hang down, while dog tails often curl up over their backs. Wolves have a scent gland located on the top of their tails that dogs lack.

With a good comparison-contrast paragraph, you can probably make a list showing how the two things being compared are alike and how they are different.

WOLVES vs. DOGS

PART	WOLVES	DOGS
LEGS	longer	shorter
CHESTS	narrower	rounder, fuller
FEET	bigger	smaller
TAIL	hangs down	curls upward
SCENT	special scent gland	no scent gland in tail

Classification Order

When one or more paragraphs follow classification order, the writer tries to group things to show broad similarities. Writers often need to name categories to make it clear how one group is alike or different from another.

Here, in a classification paragraph, the scientist Bill Nye names the main categories of living creatures in the ocean.

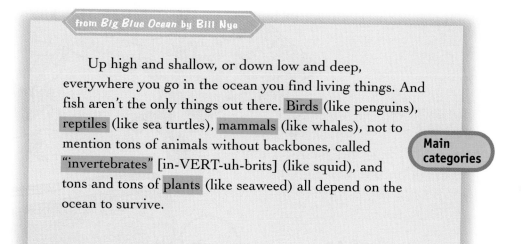

from *Big Blue Ocean* by Bill Nye

Up high and shallow, or down low and deep, everywhere you go in the ocean you find living things. And fish aren't the only things out there. Birds (like penguins), reptiles (like sea turtles), mammals (like whales), not to mention tons of animals without backbones, called "invertebrates" [in-VERT-uh-brits] (like squid), and tons and tons of plants (like seaweed) all depend on the ocean to survive.

Main categories

Classification paragraphs are like a chart put into words.

LIVING THINGS IN THE OCEAN

BIRDS	REPTILES	MAMMALS	INVERTEBRATES	PLANTS
penguins	sea turtles	whales	squid	seaweed

While not all paragraphs will fit in one neat category or another, you will find that knowing the way they are organized can help you understand them.

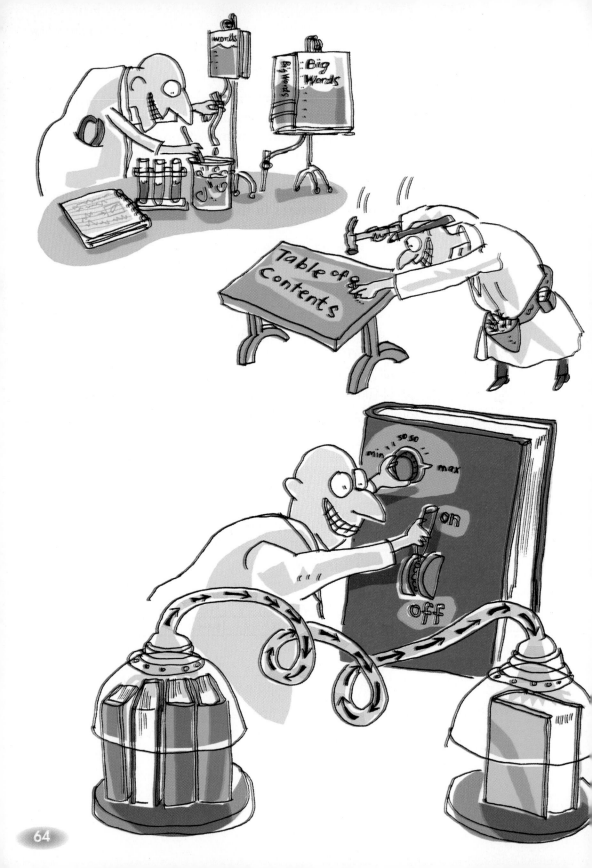

Reading
Textbooks

Reading Different Subjects

Reading History
Reading Geography
Reading Science
Reading Math

Focus on School Reading

Focus on Science Concepts
Focus on Word Problems

Elements of Textbooks

Reading History

History is about more than just names and dates. And reading history textbooks means more than just memorizing the details of a few discoveries or battles. When you read history, you're reading about people's hopes and fears and about conflict, leadership, and decision making. To get the most out of reading history, you need a plan to understand new facts, connect to what's being described, and keep track of what you're learning.

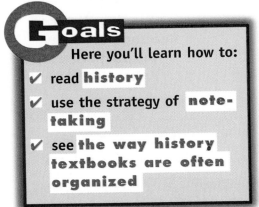

Goals

Here you'll learn how to:

✔ read **history**

✔ use the strategy of **note-taking**

✔ see **the way history textbooks are often organized**

Before Reading

Reading begins when you hear the assignment "Read Chapter 2, 'The Indian Wars.'" You can start thinking about the topic an hour before you sit down to read or a few minutes before you begin running your eyes over the page. The important thing is to start before your eyes begin reading a single word. Move your mind first.

A Set a Purpose

The key to setting a purpose for reading history is to ask questions about what you want to know. "What were the Indian Wars?" "Why did they begin?" These are fine questions. In fact, you can almost always set a purpose by just asking *who, what, where, when,* or *why.*

Answering the 5 W's gives you the most general, basic information about a topic. Use the questions to set your purpose:

Setting a Purpose

- **What** were the Indian Wars?
- **When** did they take place?
- **Who** was involved in these wars?
- **Where** did they take place?
- **Why** did they occur?

B Preview

Next, run your eyes over the next several pages from an American history textbook. Here are a few things to look for as you preview "Indian Wars":

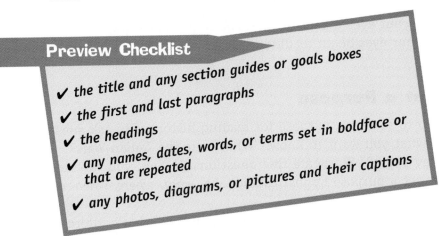

Preview Checklist

✔ the title and any section guides or goals boxes
✔ the first and last paragraphs
✔ the headings
✔ any names, dates, words, or terms set in boldface or that are repeated
✔ any photos, diagrams, or pictures and their captions

The point of previewing is to give you an idea of what to expect before you begin.

As you preview "Indian Wars," think a little about what you may already know about the subject. Do any of the names, terms, or events sound familiar?

2 Indian Wars

SECTION GUIDE

Main Idea
As settlers poured onto their lands, the Plains Indians fought to maintain their way of life.

Goals
As you read, look for answers to these questions:

1. What caused conflicts between Plains Indians and white settlers?

2. What was the outcome of conflicts between white settlers and Indians?

3. What new policy toward Indians did the U.S. government adopt?

Key Terms
reservation
Battle of Little Bighorn
Wounded Knee Massacre
assimilation
Dawes Act

C HIEF CRAZY HORSE spoke for the Indians of the Great Plains when he said the following:

We did not ask you white men to come here. The Great Spirit gave us this country as a home. You had yours. We did not interfere with you. . . . But you have come here; you are taking my land from me.

Government Policy
In the early 1800s the Plains Indians lived and hunted from southwestern Canada to northern Mexico and from the Mississippi to the Rocky Mountains. Beginning in the 1840s, white settlers passed through the Plains to reach the West Coast. The U.S. government asked the Plains Indians to let settlers through safely. It also asked the Indians to limit their hunting to certain areas. Yet the great herds of buffalo, on which the Indians depended, obeyed no such limits. To maintain their way of life, the Indians had to be free to follow the buffalo.

By the mid-1800s the federal government changed its policy. It began to set aside **reservations,** special areas used by a specific group. In return for agreeing to live on these reservations, the Indians were told that the land would be theirs forever. They were also promised food, money, and other help. Over the years, several treaties were signed, placing Indians on reservations.

This photograph of a Blackfoot Indian camp in Montana was taken in 1900. Even after they were forced off most of their lands, the Plains Indians struggled to maintain their way of life.

Clash of Cultures
The Plains Indians and the white settlers who moved onto the Plains looked at the world in different ways. From the settlers' point of view, the resources of the West were there to be used. Getting at those

Textbooks

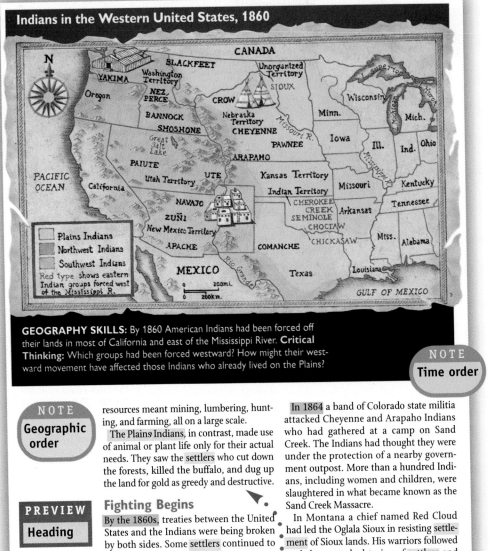

Indians in the Western United States, 1860

Plains Indians
Northwest Indians
Southwest Indians

Red type shows eastern Indian groups forced west of the Mississippi R.

GEOGRAPHY SKILLS: By 1860 American Indians had been forced off their lands in most of California and east of the Mississippi River. **Critical Thinking:** Which groups had been forced westward? How might their westward movement have affected those Indians who already lived on the Plains?

NOTE
Time order

NOTE
Geographic order

resources meant mining, lumbering, hunting, and farming, all on a large scale.

The Plains Indians, in contrast, made use of animal or plant life only for their actual needs. They saw the settlers who cut down the forests, killed the buffalo, and dug up the land for gold as greedy and destructive.

PREVIEW
Heading

Fighting Begins

By the 1860s, treaties between the United States and the Indians were being broken by both sides. Some settlers continued to pass through areas where they were not allowed. Some Indians raided white settlements and wagon trains.

In 1864 a band of Colorado state militia attacked Cheyenne and Arapaho Indians who had gathered at a camp on Sand Creek. The Indians had thought they were under the protection of a nearby government outpost. More than a hundred Indians, including women and children, were slaughtered in what became known as the Sand Creek Massacre.

In Montana a chief named Red Cloud had led the Oglala Sioux in resisting settlement of Sioux lands. His warriors followed and then attacked trains of settlers and construction parties. In 1866 a U.S. Army officer, Captain W. J. Fetterman, pursued a

PREVIEW
Repeated words

NOTE
Time order

party of Sioux who had attacked a supply train. Fetterman led his 80 soldiers into a trap. A much larger band of Sioux fighters was waiting. In the battle, Fetterman's entire group was wiped out.

Little Bighorn

The most famous battle of the Indian Wars took place in June 1876 after tensions had arisen in the Black Hills of the Dakotas. These hills had been set aside by treaty for the Sioux and northern Cheyenne. In 1874, after a U.S. Army exploring party found gold in the Black Hills, miners arrived by the thousands. They cared little that this land was sacred to the Sioux.

Hoping to head off a clash, the government tried to buy the Black Hills from the Indians. The Sioux would not think of selling their land. As war fever mounted through the winter of 1875–1876, Sioux warriors left their reservations. They united under the leadership of two Sioux chiefs—Sitting Bull and Crazy Horse.

On June 25, 1876, George Armstrong Custer and several hundred soldiers came upon a Sioux camp on the bank of the Little Bighorn River. Custer was already famous. He had fought in many Civil War battles. To some he was a daring, brilliant officer. To others he was a dangerous showoff, with his colorful uniform and long blond hair.

Custer's orders were to attack if he found Indians. When he neared the camp on the Little Bighorn, however, he entered a trap set by Sitting Bull and Crazy Horse. A large force of Sioux and Cheyenne overpowered his forces. In what became known as "Custer's Last Stand," all of Custer's men—including Custer himself—were killed.

In the East, people were shocked by news of the **Battle of Little Bighorn.** The government sent thousands more soldiers west to fight the Indians.

Little Bighorn was the last Indian victory in the Indian Wars. Army forces defeated the Sioux in the fall of 1876. Sitting Bull and his followers fled to Canada. Crazy Horse and some 800 of his people surrendered. As Crazy Horse was being arrested, he was fatally stabbed. It was never determined if it was a guard who killed him or another Indian who opposed his aims.

A portrait of Sitting Bull.

PREVIEW
Photo and caption

Textbooks

PREVIEW
Boldface name

PREVIEW
Picture and caption

A Sioux artist painted this scene of the Battle of Little Bighorn. **Critical Thinking:** With what kinds of weapons did the Sioux fight?

PREVIEW

Heading

Chief Joseph

A few months after the death of Crazy Horse, another war began—this one with the Nez Percé people. The Nez Percé were Northwest Indians. They fished for salmon, hunted, and gathered food from eastern Oregon to Idaho. Their leader was Chief Joseph, who refused to sell the lands where his people had lived for centuries.

When the government ordered the Nez Percé to move to a reservation in 1877, Chief Joseph and his followers fled. Army troops followed them. Over the next four months, the Nez Percé traveled some 1,300 miles through Oregon, Idaho, and Montana, looking for safety.

The Nez Percé were about 40 miles from the Canadian border when the army caught up with them. Cold, hungry, weary, and outnumbered, the Nez Percé surrendered. Chief Joseph spoke eloquently for many western Indians when he said:

> 66 Hear me, my chiefs. I am tired; my heart is sick and sad. From where the sun now stands, I will fight no more forever. 99

Southwest Indians

The Indians of the Southwest were also forced onto reservations. In the 1860s the U.S. government ordered Colonel Kit Carson to move the Navajo from their traditional lands in Arizona to a reservation in eastern New Mexico on the Pecos River.

The Navajo refused to surrender. Carson waged total war against them. His soldiers burned their fields, cut down their trees, and slaughtered their animals. In January 1864, freezing and starving, the Navajo finally surrendered. Thus began what the Navajo call the "Long

Walk" east, away from their rugged lands to the edge of the Great Plains. Hundreds died during the trip from lack of food and warm clothing.

Arrival at the reservation did not end their problems. Guarded and watched, the Navajo were forced to dig irrigation ditches and plant crops. Insects killed the crops and the Pecos River overflowed, destroying the irrigation system. Finally, the government admitted that the reservation was a failure. The Navajo returned home.

In the mid-1870s the Chiricahua Apache were moved onto land away from their traditional territory in the Southwest. Geronimo, an Apache leader, led his followers off the reservation. His knowledge of southern Arizona allowed them to escape the U.S. Army time and time again.

Geronimo was finally captured just north of the Mexican border in 1886. He spent the rest of his life forced to live far from his people.

A Way of Life Destroyed

The Indians lost more than battles. Their way of life was destroyed as well. Railroad crews seeking food killed thousands of buffalo. So did professional hunters. Buffalo hunting even became a sport. Settlers would shoot buffalo from passing trains, leaving the carcasses to rot in the sun.

The destruction of the buffalo herds meant another defeat for the Indians. They needed the buffalo for many uses, especially food. As a Lakota Sioux warrior put it:

> 66 Our living was their sport, and if you look at it one way, they might as well have been killing us as the buffalo. 99

Destroying the Indians was what some whites had in mind. "Every buffalo dead is an Indian gone," said one army officer.

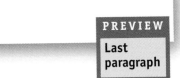

Chief Joseph, leader of the Nez Percé.

NOTE

Geographic order

PREVIEW

Headings

PREVIEW

Last paragraph

C Plan

Now take a minute to think about what you learned in your preview. Even a quick preview will tell you a lot:

■ A number of different kinds of Indians were involved (Southwest, Nez Percé, Blackfoot, Sioux).

■ Several different chiefs were important (Crazy Horse, Red Cloud, Sitting Bull, Chief Joseph, Geronimo).

■ The Indians lost—"A Way of Life Destroyed."

Most of this information comes from the headings. Notice how little you actually have to read and how much the headings alone can tell you.

You have already learned a lot through your preview. But next you need to make a plan to get the details that you need to meet your reading purpose. You want to be sure that the time you spend reading gives you the information to answer the 5 W questions: *who, what, where, when,* and *why.*

Textbooks *(side tab)*

Reading Strategy: Note-taking

So, here's your purpose—to gather general, basic information about the Indian Wars. One excellent strategy to use to collect that information is **note-taking.** Other reading strategies may work too, but note-taking is a very good strategy to use when reading history. Set up your notes to collect the information you want. Try something simple.

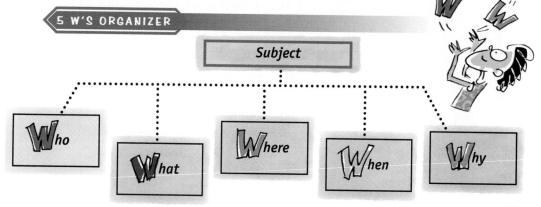

5 W'S ORGANIZER

Subject

Who   What   Where   When   Why

During Reading

Now you are ready to read the chapter. You have a reading purpose and a reading strategy.

D Read with a Purpose

You cannot write in most textbooks. You won't be able to highlight and mark passages right on the pages. As a result, you will need to take some kind of notes in a separate notebook. It is a good idea to have a notebook for each of your subjects—history, science, math, and so on. You can also put sticky notes in your book, but these sometimes don't last very long or get pulled off.

NOTE-TAKING STRATEGIES:

✔ Summary Notes
✔ Webs
✔ Timeline or Sequence Notes
✔ Thinking Tree

You might also want to start keeping a learning log or journal. In it, you can record things you learned and how you learned them. By telling yourself, "I used an organizer like this to understand what happened during the Indian Wars," you can help yourself learn and remember how you learn.

Whether you decide to use notebook paper or sticky notes, try taking notes in different ways. The 5 W's Organizer on page 73 is just one way to organize information. On the next page are some others. Try using one of these different tools for taking notes in a chapter. The point isn't to take all these kinds of notes all the time. The idea is to find one that seems to work best for you.

1. Summary Notes

Learn something from each page or section of your textbook. Take
notes about the most important information. Look for key facts or
names and any terms or ideas in boldface or headings. For instance,
if you read ten pages, you make notes for ten pages. The idea of
Summary Notes is to help you remember what's important.

PAGE-BY-PAGE NOTES

| Page 559 | 1800—Indians lived in peace. 1840—Reservations began. Indians and whites clashed on Plains. |

| Page 560 | 1860s—Treaties were broken. Settlers went through Indian lands and killed buffalo. Indians raided white settlements. |

| Page 561 | 1876—Sitting Bull and Crazy Horse attacked Gen. Custer. Massacre was last major Indian victory. |

Textbooks

2. Webs

You might want to use web diagrams to take your notes. The great
thing about webbing is that the diagrams can take any shape, and
you can add a new part or branch to the subject at any time. Use
Webs to help you keep track of how lots of different topics or facts
fit together. With Webs, you place the subject of the material in the
center and add spokes (or arms) as needed.

WEB NOTES

Plains Indians
Northwest Indians   Indian Wars   Cheyenne—Nebraska
Southwest Indians   Blackfoot—Washington
                                                Apache—New Mexico
                                                Sioux—Montana

• fought settlers who killed buffalo
• fought because of broken treaties
• fought because whites took their land

3. Timeline or Sequence Notes

When you want to follow the order of events, you may want to start with Timeline or Sequence Notes. They give you a way to create an understanding of what happens first, next, and last as you are reading. <u>By jotting down dates and the order of events, you can keep better track of what happens and when things happen.</u> This kind of note-taking gives you a way of seeing how events are tied to one another.

TIMELINE OR SEQUENCE NOTES

early 1800s	Plains Indians lived in peace.
1860	Treaties began to be broken.
1876	Custer lost at Little Bighorn.
1886	Geronimo was captured. Indian Wars ended.

4. Thinking Tree

A Thinking Tree helps you see connections among different parts of a chapter. Suppose you need to know key places, people, and causes of the Indian Wars. The clearer you are about your purpose, the better off you are. Set up your notes to show the main topics and add details related to them. <u>A Thinking Tree works well when you need to show how facts and ideas relate to one another.</u>

THINKING TREE

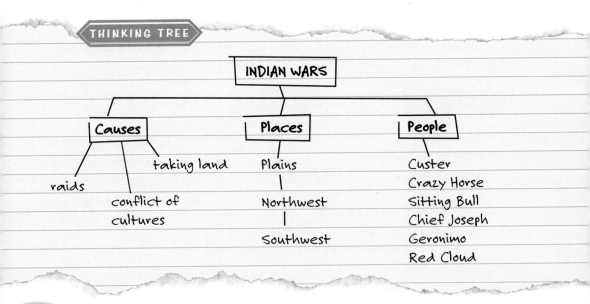

How History Textbooks Are Organized

Active readers can create more understanding than readers who simply turn the pages. Understanding a passage takes time and effort, and it helps to know the kinds of things to look for.

Look back for a moment at the history text on pages 69–72. If you follow the highlighting in the example, you will notice that the reader marked many of the names, dates, and locations. History textbooks like this one often follow **time** (or chronological) **order.** That is, they tell what happened first, then what happened next, then next after that, and so on all the way until the end. As a reader, you ought to look for the organization of the writing because it helps you understand more.

Dates—Time Order

Locations— Geographic Order

Textbooks

This passage also follows **geographic** (or location) **order.** It begins by showing a map of the Indian Territories around 1860. Then the information moves in a clear path, from the Plains, to the Northwest, to the Southwest. Writers organize writing in this way to help readers follow what they are trying to say.

The sticky notes in the margin point out signal words that clue you in on the organization. Throughout the chapter, the dates are given in order, and the writing moves clearly from east to west, then down to the southwest. That's done on purpose to help you understand.

Dates
• 1877
• mid 1870s

Locations
• Oregon
• Idaho
• Montana

Chief Joesph, leader of the Nez Percé.

Chief Joseph

A few months after the death of Crazy Horse, another war began—this one with the Nez Percé people. The Nez Percé were Northwest Indians. They fished for salmon, hunted, and gathered food from eastern Oregon to Idaho. Their leader was Chief Joseph, who refused to sell the lands where his people had lived for centuries.

When the government ordered the Nez Percé to move to a reservation in 1877, Chief Joseph and his followers fled. Army troops followed them. Over the next four months, the Nez Percé traveled some 1,300 miles through Oregon, Idaho, and Montana, looking for safety.

The Nez Percé were about 40 miles from the Canadian border when the army caught up with them. Cold, hungry, weary, and outnumbered, the Nez Percé surrendered. Chief Joseph spoke eloquently for many western Indians when he said:

❝ **Hear me, my chiefs. I am tired; my heart is sick and sad. From where the sun**

Walk" east, away to the edge of the died during the warm clothing.

Arrival at the their problems. G Navajo were force and plant crops. and the Pecos Riv the irrigation sys ment admitted th failure. The Navaj

In the mid-1870 were moved onto ditional territory mo, an Apache le the reservation. H Arizona allowed Army time and tir

Geronimo was fi of the Mexican b the rest of his life people.

A Way of Lif

The Indians lost

E Connect

The idea that you are responsible for your own reading is one of the most important ideas in this handbook. You need to take charge and grab the information you need. Many readers think that information will come to them if they read, but information doesn't just get delivered like the morning paper. You create the understanding you get by taking notes, asking yourself questions, visualizing what's happening, and connecting and reacting to what you read.

Look at the way a reader marked up this example from a history textbook. He or she concentrated on how the United States government treated the Sioux Indians.

> cause   effect
> U.S. Army finds gold
> → tries to take
> over the land
> This seems so
> unfair.

party of Sioux who had attacked a supply train. Fetterman led his 80 soldiers into a trap. A much larger band of Sioux fighters was waiting. In the battle, Fetterman's entire group was wiped out.

Little Bighorn

The most famous battle of the Indian Wars took place in June 1876 after tensions had arisen in the Black Hills of the Dakotas. These hills had been set aside by treaty for the Sioux and northern Cheyenne. In 1874, after a U.S. Army exploring party found gold in the Black Hills, miners arrived by the thousands. They cared little that this land was sacred to the Sioux.

Hoping to head off a clash, the government tried to buy the Black Hills from the Indians. The Sioux would not think of selling their land. As war fever mounted through the winter of 1875–1876, Sioux warriors left their reservations. They united under the leadership of two Sioux chiefs—Sitting Bull and Crazy Horse.

On June 25, 1876, George Armstrong Custer and several hundred soldiers came upon a Sioux camp on the bank of the Little Bighorn River. Custer was already famous. He had fought in many Civil War battles. To some he was a daring, brilliant officer. To others he was a dangerous showoff, with his colorful uniform and long blond hair.

Custer's orders were to attack if he found Indians. When he neared the camp on the Little Bighorn, however, he entered a trap set by Sitting Bull and Crazy Horse. A large force of Sioux and Cheyenne overpowered his forces. In what became known as "Custer's Last Stand," all of Custer's men—including Custer himself—were killed.

In the East, people were shocked by news of the **Battle of Little Bighorn.** The government sent thousands more soldiers west to fight the Indians.

Little Bighorn was the last Indian victory in the Indian Wars. Army forces defeated the Sioux in the fall of 1876. Sitting Bull and his followers fled to Canada. Crazy Horse and some 800 of his people surrendered. As Crazy Horse was being arrested, he was fatally stabbed. It was never determined if it was a guard who killed him or another Indian who opposed his aims.

A portrait of Sitting Bull.

> What happened
> to Sitting Bull?
> Did the
> government
> arrest him?

After Reading

If you are like most readers, you can only understand a limited amount of information the first time you read a selection. After you finish reading, take a moment to decide how much you really understand from the passage.

Good readers are patient. They will read something once just to become familiar with it and then again a second time to understand it better.

OK people, let's take it from the top.

Textbooks

F Pause and Reflect

Right after finishing the last word of a textbook, think about what you have read. Take a few minutes to consider what you learned and pinpoint parts that seemed difficult or confusing. Go back to your reading purpose and ask yourself questions like these:

Looking Back

■ Can I answer the *who, what, where, when,* and *why* questions?

■ Can I summarize 2–3 important ideas in my own words?

■ Do my notes cover the whole chapter, and do I understand them?

Be honest with yourself. Chances are good that you can answer *yes* to some but not all of the questions. It's time to reread to find out what more you can learn.

G Reread

At this point, you probably have a good idea of what the chapter is about. Now is the time to go back through the pages again, looking specifically for the information you need to fill in your notes or help you understand difficult parts. Maybe you forgot to take any notes about dates. Or maybe you're a little unclear about who fought whom at Little Bighorn.

At first, you'll probably greet the idea of rereading with a groan. But soon you'll see how much it helps you understand your assignments. It'll become a habit and something you don't even have to remind yourself to do.

Rereading Strategy: Outlining

When you reread, try a new reading strategy. **Outlining** is a good way to review the key information in a chapter. Remember when you previewed the headings? They can help you create a quick, effective Topic or Sentence Outline. Textbooks are usually carefully organized. The headings are chosen with care. Note how they form a good beginning for an Outline of the Indian Wars.

OUTLINE

INDIAN WARS

I. Government Policy ◀ · · · ·
    A. 1840s—white settlement
    B. mid-1800s—changing policy

Headings from textbook

II. Clash of Cultures ◀ · · · · ·
    A. settlers farming and hunting on the land
    B. Indians using what they needed to live on

III. Fighting Begins
    A. raids on settlements
    B. led by Red Cloud, a Sioux chief

IV. Little Bighorn
    A. miners' invasion of Indian lands in Black Hills
    B. ambush of Gen. Custer

V. Chief Joseph
    A. member of the Nez Percé tribe
    B. ordered to live on a reservation
    C. surrendered with dignity

VI. Southwest Indians
    A. resisted order to live on reservation
    B. Geronimo's revolt

VII. A Way of Life Destroyed

Textbooks

By adding two or three points under each heading, you have outlined the chapter.

A Topic Outline like the one above gives you another way to keep track of what you're learning. The point is that by being an active reader, you have what you need to ace the test—at the end of the week or weeks from now. You have some basic information—*who, what, when, where,* and *why*—and could, for an essay test, write well about the conflicts between the Indians and the white settlers.

H Remember

Often you spend a lot of time reading, but sometimes you may recall very little. As a student, you have to not only read the material but also remember it. At the very end of the reading process, readers need to spend a few moments gathering up what they learned, or they'll forget it.

Here are two suggestions about what you can do to help you remember what you read. Try one of them.

1. Share Your Ideas

Talk about what you learned with a friend or family member. Find out what they know about the Indian Wars. Ask some of your classmates what they found most interesting or surprising. Getting into a conversation about what you read is a great way to remember more about it.

2. Create a Chart or Organizer

The act of creation helps you "make the material your own," and that helps you remember it. By creating some notes, a chart, or a graphic organizer, you give your brain a way to "see" the information you learned.

History texts tell what happened in the past and try to explain *why* it happened. Because of that, you'll find that history teachers will often ask you for the causes of this or that event. So, why not be prepared? Create a Cause-Effect Organizer such as the one below.

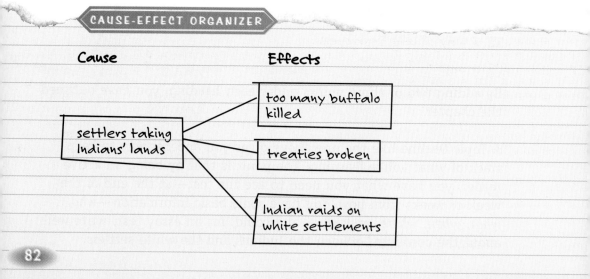

CAUSE-EFFECT ORGANIZER

Cause

Effects

too many buffalo killed

settlers taking Indians' lands

treaties broken

Indian raids on white settlements

Summing Up

When you read a history textbook, use the reading process. Preview the chapter and set a purpose. Then decide on a reading strategy, such as **note-taking.** Keep track of important information by using one of these tools:

- ■ Summary Notes
- ■ Web
- ■ Timeline or Sequence Notes
- ■ Thinking Tree

As you read, look also for **the way the writing is organized—often in time or location order.** Then, after reading, look back. Be sure you learned what you wanted and needed to learn. Use a rereading strategy such as **outlining** to help you go back through the chapter a final time.

Textbooks

83

Reading Geography

If you've had trouble understanding geography or been bored by it, it might be because of how you're reading the textbook. You need to learn how to get *more* out of your reading. Your textbook is the key to unlocking new information. In this lesson, you'll find part of a geography textbook and work through it.

Geography is the study of the earth and its plant and animal life. It includes the study of continents, mountains, bodies of water, and climates of countries around the world. Most geography textbooks are organized by subject. If you look at the table of contents, you'll probably find chapters about such subjects as "Population," "Climate," and "Cities" and the names of continents, such as South America, Europe, and Africa.

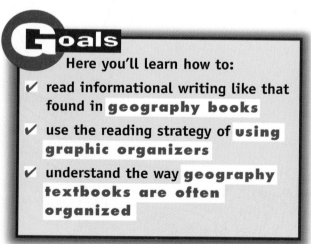

Goals

Here you'll learn how to:

✔ read informational writing like that found in geography books

✔ use the reading strategy of using graphic organizers

✔ understand the way geography textbooks are often organized

Before Reading

Let's say you've been assigned to read the "Population" chapter from your geography textbook. Do you start by turning to the first paragraphs and diving in? No, instead take a few minutes to get ready to read. Think about what you already know about population. Get a sense of what the chapter is about and make a plan for getting the information you want.

A Set a Purpose

Your first step is to set a purpose for reading. What do you need to find out?

One easy way to set your general purpose is to take the title of a chapter or section and rephrase it as a question. The title of the chapter is "Population." You can turn the title into a question by asking, "What is population, and why is it important?"

Also, many textbooks have goals or preview boxes at the beginning of each chapter. They often tell you what's important to watch for as you read. This information can help you adjust your purpose. Now your purpose for reading might include two questions:

Setting a Purpose
■ **What is population, and why is it important?**
■ **How is it changing?**

PREVIEW

Words to Know
- emigrate
- refugee
- population density
- urbanization
- developed country
- developing country
- demographer

Read to Learn . . .
1. where most people in the world live.
2. how scientists measure population.
3. how the earth's population is changing.

Information that helps set purpose for reading

Textbooks

B Preview

Once you know your purpose, your next step is to preview the reading. Remember that a preview can give you an idea of what to expect when you read more carefully.

When you preview a textbook chapter, you run your eyes down each page. Run down the page with your finger. Pay careful attention to these items:

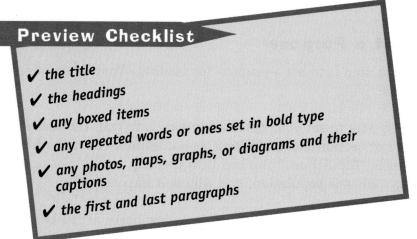

Preview Checklist

✔ the title
✔ the headings
✔ any boxed items
✔ any repeated words or ones set in bold type
✔ any photos, maps, graphs, or diagrams and their captions
✔ the first and last paragraphs

Now that you know what to look for, preview "Population" on pages 87–90.

SECTION 2 Population

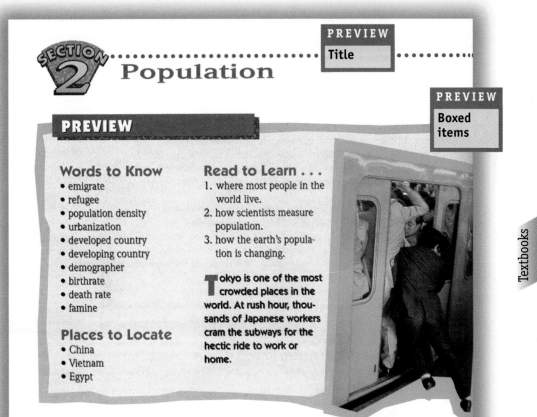

PREVIEW Title

PREVIEW Boxed items

PREVIEW

Words to Know
- emigrate
- refugee
- population density
- urbanization
- developed country
- developing country
- demographer
- birthrate
- death rate
- famine

Places to Locate
- China
- Vietnam
- Egypt

Read to Learn . . .
1. where most people in the world live.
2. how scientists measure population.
3. how the earth's population is changing.

Tokyo is one of the most crowded places in the world. At rush hour, thousands of Japanese workers cram the subways for the hectic ride to work or home.

Although Tokyo is crowded, some parts of the world have few people. What makes one area crowded and another empty? Climate, culture, and jobs are some of the things that help determine where people live.

PREVIEW First paragraph

Movement

Population Patterns

PREVIEW Headings

Some families live in the same town or on the same land for generations. Other people move frequently from place to place. In some cases people choose to leave the country in which they were born. They **emigrate**, or move, to another country. You may know of people who are forced to flee their country because of wars, food shortages, or other problems. They become **refugees**, or people who flee to another country for refuge from persecution or disaster.

Population Distribution People live on only a small part of the earth. As you learned earlier, land covers only about 30 percent of the earth's surface, and half of this land is not useful to humans. People cannot make homes, grow crops, or graze animals on land covered with ice, deserts, or high mountains.

60

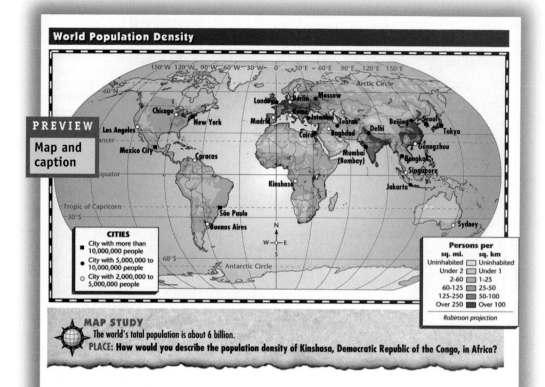

World Population Density

CITIES
- ■ City with more than 10,000,000 people
- • City with 5,000,000 to 10,000,000 people
- ○ City with 2,000,000 to 5,000,000 people

Persons per	
sq. mi.	sq. km
Uninhabited	Uninhabited
Under 2	Under 1
2-60	1-25
60-125	25-50
125-250	50-100
Over 250	Over 100

Robinson projection

MAP STUDY
The world's total population is about 6 billion.
PLACE: How would you describe the population density of Kinshasa, Democratic Republic of the Congo, in Africa?

PREVIEW
Map and caption

Even on the usable land, population is not distributed, or spread, evenly. One reason is that people naturally choose to live in places with plentiful water, good land, and a favorable climate. Other reasons may lie in a people's history and culture.

Look at the map above to see how the world's population is distributed. Notice that people are most concentrated in western Europe and eastern and southern Asia. The United States also has areas of dense population.

Asia is a huge continent in land area. It also has the largest population—nearly 3.6 billion. Africa is the second-largest continent in area and in overall population, with 770 million people. Europe is much smaller in land area, but its 730 million people make it third in population size.

Population Density One way to look at population is by measuring **population density**—the average number of people living in a square mile or square kilometer. Population density gives a general idea of how crowded a country or region is. For example, the countries of Vietnam and Congo have about the same land area. The population density in Vietnam is 625 people per square mile (241 people per sq. km). Congo has an average of only 20 people per square mile (8 people per sq. km).

PREVIEW
Words in bold

PREVIEW
Heading

61

PREVIEW

Heading

World Population Growth

GRAPHIC STUDY

Between A.D. 1 and 1500, the world population grew by only 300 million people.

PLACE: By about how much has the world population grown in just the last 500 years?

Source: *World Almanac,* 1998

PREVIEW

Graph and caption

Notice that density is an *average.* It assumes that people are distributed evenly throughout an area. But this seldom happens. A country may have several large cities where most of its people actually live. In Egypt, for example, overall population density is 171 people per square mile (61 people per sq. km). In reality, about 99 percent of Egypt's people live within 20 miles of the Nile River. The rest of Egypt is desert.

Urbanization Throughout the world, populations are changing as people leave villages and farms and move to the cities. This movement to cities is called **urbanization**. People move to cities for many reasons, but the overwhelming reason is to find jobs. In South America, for example, economic hardships have caused millions of people to move to cities such as São Paulo in Brazil and Buenos Aires, Argentina.

Urban areas are usually centers of industrialization. Countries that are industrialized are called **developed countries**. Those countries that are working toward industrialization are called **developing countries**. The economies of these countries depend mainly on agriculture and developing modern industries.

Human/Environment Interaction

Population Growth

PREVIEW

Headings

How fast has the earth's population grown? In 1800 the number of people in the world totaled about 857 million. During the next hundred years the population doubled to nearly 1.7 billion. By the late 1990s, this figure had risen to about 6 billion people. **Demographers,** or scientists who study population, believe that the earth will have more than 7 billion people by the year 2010. Look at the graph above to see how population has grown since 1800.

Measuring Growth Populations are growing at different rates in different places. To find the growth rate in a specific area, demographers compare the birthrate with the death rate. The **birthrate** is the number of children born each year for every 1,000 people. The **death rate** is the number of deaths for every 1,000 people.

PREVIEW

Words in bold

62

UNIT 1

Textbooks

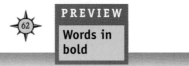

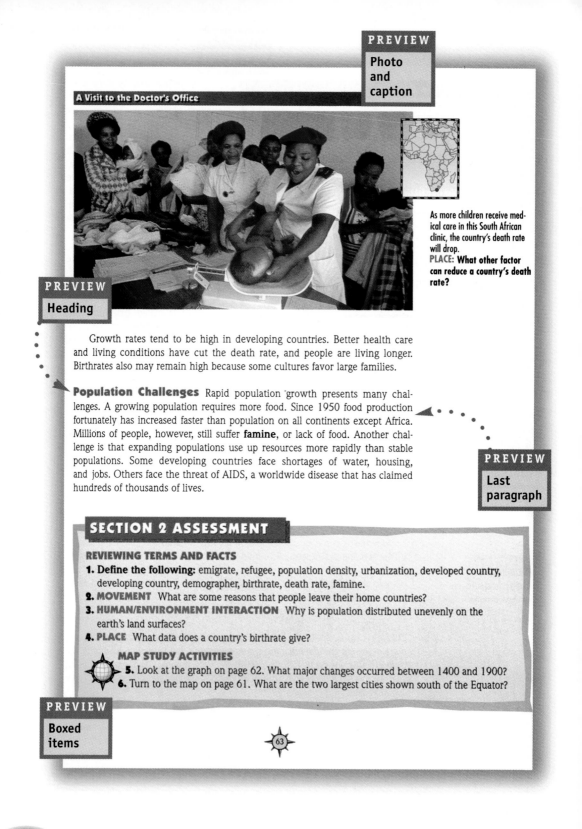

PREVIEW

Photo
and
caption

A Visit to the Doctor's Office

As more children receive medical care in this South African clinic, the country's death rate will drop.
PLACE: What other factor can reduce a country's death rate?

PREVIEW

Heading

Growth rates tend to be high in developing countries. Better health care and living conditions have cut the death rate, and people are living longer. Birthrates also may remain high because some cultures favor large families.

Population Challenges Rapid population growth presents many challenges. A growing population requires more food. Since 1950 food production fortunately has increased faster than population on all continents except Africa. Millions of people, however, still suffer **famine**, or lack of food. Another challenge is that expanding populations use up resources more rapidly than stable populations. Some developing countries face shortages of water, housing, and jobs. Others face the threat of AIDS, a worldwide disease that has claimed hundreds of thousands of lives.

PREVIEW

Last
paragraph

SECTION 2 ASSESSMENT

REVIEWING TERMS AND FACTS

1. **Define the following:** emigrate, refugee, population density, urbanization, developed country, developing country, demographer, birthrate, death rate, famine.
2. **MOVEMENT** What are some reasons that people leave their home countries?
3. **HUMAN/ENVIRONMENT INTERACTION** Why is population distributed unevenly on the earth's land surfaces?
4. **PLACE** What data does a country's birthrate give?

MAP STUDY ACTIVITIES
5. Look at the graph on page 62. What major changes occurred between 1400 and 1900?
6. Turn to the map on page 61. What are the two largest cities shown south of the Equator?

PREVIEW

Boxed
items

63

Plan

What did you learn in your preview? From the headings, graphics, and boldface terms alone, you may have a list that includes these ideas:

■ There are patterns of population.

■ The world's population is 6 billion and growing.

■ Birthrates and death rates affect population.

Now it's time to make your reading plan. You need a good way to find and remember the details you'll be learning as you read the "Population" chapter.

Reading Strategy: Using Graphic Organizers

Using graphic organizers is a good strategy for textbooks. If you're used to taking notes in sentences or in numbered lists, using organizers may seem strange at first. But give it a try. One kind of graphic organizer is a K-W-L Chart. It allows you to keep track of three kinds of things:

■ what you think you already know

■ what you want to know

■ what you've learned

The time to create your K-W-L Chart is now, right before you begin reading. A K-W-L Chart looks like this:

K-W-L CHART

(WHAT I KNOW)	(WHAT I WANT TO KNOW)	(WHAT I LEARNED)

Textbooks

During Reading

Your next step is to read the chapter. Read slowly and carefully, one sentence at a time. Think about the information, ask yourself questions, and jot down notes.

D Read with a Purpose

Always keep in mind your purpose questions for reading: "What is population, and why is it important? How is it changing?" Try not to get distracted. Each time you find a fact or detail that helps answer one of these questions, you should make a note of it.

Choosing the strategy of graphic organizers gives you the option of a number of different tools to use. Experiment. And remember, don't feel like you have to use all of them. Choose one that works for you.

1. K-W-L Chart

Before you begin to read, you write what you know in the K part of the K-W-L Chart. Think about what you learned in your preview. Make notes about that and anything else you happen to know about population—maybe from a TV news program or a conversation with a teacher. Add questions about what you want to find out in the W part. You'll return to the L part later and summarize the most important information. A K-W-L Chart is a good tool for textbooks, especially in history, science, and geography.

K-W-L-CHART FOR POPULATION

(WHAT I KNOW)	(WHAT I WANT TO KNOW)	(WHAT I LEARNED)
Population means number of people.	What is population, and why is it an important idea?	(This part of the chart is filled out after you've finished reading.)
There are patterns of population.	Why is the world's population growing?	
The world's population is 6 billion.	What is the birthrate and death rate?	
Birthrate and death rate are important factors.	Where do most people in the world live?	
Our state has lost population recently.	What is population density?	

2. Concept Map

<u>A Concept Map can help you understand a new term or concept.</u> Use the boxes surrounding the center for important details or ideas about the concept.

CONCEPT MAP

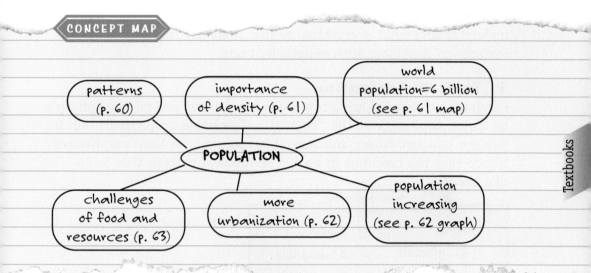

patterns
(p. 60)

importance
of density (p. 61)

world
population=6 billion
(see p. 61 map)

POPULATION

challenges
of food and
resources (p. 63)

more
urbanization (p. 62)

population
increasing
(see p. 62 graph)

3. Main Idea Organizer

Think of the headings in textbooks as clues to the main ideas. Take each major heading and create a topic sentence or main idea. Then, under it, list one key detail for each subheading. <u>By creating a Main Idea Organizer for each major heading in a chapter, you're sure to focus on the most important material.</u>

MAIN IDEA ORGANIZER

MAIN IDEA: There are patterns to the world's population.

DETAIL #1	DETAIL #2	DETAIL #3
Population distribution means that more people live in some areas than in others.	Population density increases and decreases, depending on food and resources.	Urbanization takes people to the cities.

How Geography Textbooks Are Organized

You're probably asking yourself, "How am I supposed to take in all this information?" But, if you figure out the organization of a text (how the information is arranged), you'll have a much easier time understanding what everything means. There are *two* important features to remember with geography texts.

1. Topic Organization

Geography textbooks are often organized around several key concepts or topics. Look back at the "Population" example on pages 87–90. Do you see how two topics and several subpoints have been emphasized? Notice that the headings in bold type follow a pattern that looks like this:

TOPIC ORGANIZATION

I. *Topic*
   A. *subpoint*
   B. *subpoint*
   C. *subpoint*

II. *Topic*
   A. *subpoint*
   B. *subpoint*

If you plug the headings of the "Population" reading into the above outline, you'll end up with this:

TOPIC ORGANIZATION: POPULATION

I. Population Patterns
   A. population distribution
   B. population density
   C. urbanization
II. Population Growth
   A. measuring growth
   B. population challenges

Once you know the pattern, you can look for the main topics and 2–3 subpoints. For instance, the Main Idea Organizer on the previous page illustrates the organization of the "Population Patterns" section into three subpoints, or details.

2. Use of Graphics

Besides paying attention to key topics, you'll also want to be aware of just how much geography books use graphics. Many geography textbooks are filled with maps, graphs, tables, diagrams, and charts. Graphics are included to give you a visual picture of what the words on the page are saying or to highlight an important point. If you don't understand the text, you look at the map. If you don't understand the map, look again at the text. The textbook is organized so words, maps, graphs, tables, and charts work together.

Each time you come to a graphic, take a moment to study it carefully. Notice the visual itself and read all the text on it. Then ask yourself what point the visual is trying to make. Almost always, the point of the visual can be summed up in one or two sentences. For example, study the graph below. What point is it making?

Textbooks

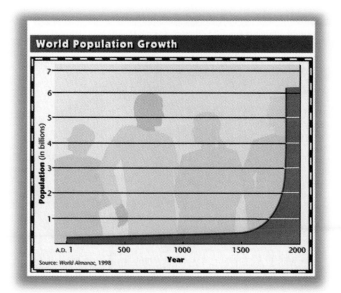

ONE-SENTENCE SUMMARY

Our world's population is exploding!

E Connect

When you read, you may make personal connections to a text without even realizing it. You read about places and say to yourself, "Wow, I've been there." Or you read about a topic such as climate and think, "I wonder how they measure the average rainfall." Think about how what you read about population connects to experiences, interests, or issues in your own life.

These connections to a text help you understand and stay interested in what you are reading. Often readers make notes about their connections as they go and then return to them later as a way of reviewing what they learned.

I dislike getting shots. I hate it, but it prevents disease.

A Visit to the Doctor's Office

I know people are living longer in the U.S. than ever before.

As more children receive medical care in this South African clinic, the country's death rate will drop.
PLACE: What other factor can reduce a country's death rate?

Growth rates tend to be high in developing countries. Better health care and living conditions have cut the death rate, and people are living longer. Birthrates also may remain high because some cultures favor large families.

Population Challenges Rapid population growth presents many challenges. A growing population requires more food. Since 1950 food production fortunately has increased faster than population on all continents except Africa. Millions of people, however, still suffer **famine**, or lack of food. Another challenge is that expanding populations use up resources more rapidly than stable populations. Some developing countries face shortages of water, housing, and jobs. Others face the threat of AIDS, a worldwide disease that has claimed hundreds of thousands of lives.

This summer's benefit concert is for famine relief.

After Reading

Once you finish reading a chapter, it's time to figure out what you've learned. Don't be in a hurry to close up the book and put it away. Take a few minutes to reflect on what you've read.

F Pause and Reflect

As soon as you finish a reading from your geography book, ask yourself, "Have I met my reading purpose?" Filling in the L column of your K-W-L Chart (page 92) will help you see what you learned. Ask yourself questions such as these:

Looking Back

■ **Can I answer my reading purpose questions?**

■ **Can I identify several key topics and main ideas?**

■ **Do the graphs and maps make sense?**

■ **If there are study questions, can I answer them?**

G Reread

If you're like most readers, you'll decide you should probably do a little rereading. Hardly anyone gets everything right the first time through a chapter. Textbooks are loaded with information. You can usually absorb only so much on a first reading. So, it's a good idea to double back and reread.

Sometimes, you'll want to do a quick general rereading of the whole chapter or a particularly hard-to-understand section. Other times, you'll decide to search for a particular graphic, heading, or term. You may want to look up something a teacher mentioned in class that you'd forgotten or review the definitions you think will be on a test.

Textbooks

rereading Strategy: **Note-taking**

Rereading Strategy: Note-taking

Note-taking is an excellent rereading strategy. Keep a pen or pencil handy when you reread. If you find something important, you'll want to be able to jot it down. Add it to an organizer you've already made or write it on a sticky note or in your notebook. Making Study Cards is an excellent and simple kind of note-taking tool that you may want to try.

Study Cards can help you keep track of small chunks of material, key words or terms, and important concepts. You can write the notes in your class notebook or on individual 3 x 5 file cards. Study Cards will come in handy when it's time to study for a quiz or test.

STUDY CARDS

Question:
What is population density?

Question:
Where do most people in the world live?

Answer:
the average number of people living in a square mile or square kilometer (page 61)

Answer:
western Europe, eastern and southern Asia, and areas of the United States (page 61)

H Remember

The notes and organizers you made should help you store the most important facts and details from the chapter in your memory—without your even realizing it. After reading, take five minutes and "make the material your own."

Try one of these ideas.

1. Write a Letter or Email

Put the material in your own words by writing about it to a friend. Imagine you were telling your friend the three most important facts you learned from this chapter.

2. Make a Practice Test

Make a practice test on the material. Use it to review with or to quiz your friends. You can create your own way to ace the test.

PRACTICE TEST FOR POPULATION

1. What is not a reason the world's population is always changing?
   a. People move from country to country.
   b. People often move to cities.
   c. People like to go shopping.
   d. People move where there are resources.

2. What is the world's total population?
   a. about 6 million
   b. about 6 billion
   c. about 60 billion
   d. about 600 billion

Summing Up

Use the reading process when you have an assignment in a geography textbook. Remember to pay attention to **how information is organized around several main topics and presented in graphics.** The strategy of **using graphic organizers** can help, especially when you use one of these tools:

- ■ K-W-L Chart
- ■ Concept Map
- ■ Main Idea Organizer

Use the rereading strategy of **note-taking** to help you find details you might have missed on your first reading.

Reading Science

Have you ever picked up a science textbook and thought for a moment that you were reading a foreign language? What on earth do all those big words mean? If you're having trouble reading or understanding science, it might be because of *how* you're reading the textbook.

Science is the study of the natural world. This includes animal and plant life, the earth, water, space, weather, technology, and a whole host of other things. One course may focus on the *natural sciences*. The natural sciences are concerned with living organisms—how they grow, develop, function, and reproduce.

Other times your class may focus on the *physical sciences*. The physical sciences are concerned with the properties, functions, and structure of nonliving matter—for example, electricity and energy.

Here you'll read part of a science textbook chapter entitled "Exploring the Ocean." Take what you learn here and apply it to your own science textbook.

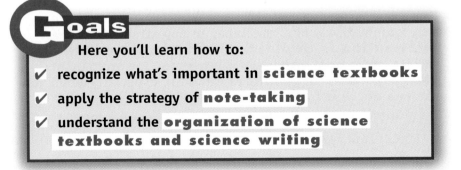

Goals

Here you'll learn how to:

✔ recognize what's important in science textbooks

✔ apply the strategy of note-taking

✔ understand the organization of science textbooks and science writing

Before Reading

The purpose of a science textbook is to teach you to think like a scientist. The articles, explanations, and definitions in a science text tell you *what* a scientist thinks about. The diagrams, graphs, charts, and webs tell you *how* a scientist thinks. Both kinds of information are important.

A Set a Purpose

Your first step is to set a purpose. Whether you're reading a science article, a part of a science chapter, or a science book, your general reading purpose will be more or less the same:

Setting a Purpose

■ **What is the subject?**
■ **What is the author saying about it?**

B Preview

In most cases, you can find out the subject of a science chapter simply by reading its title. You'll want to do a quick preview to get a sense of what the pages are all about.

Look for the following features as you glance through each page:

Preview Checklist

✔ *the title and headings*
✔ *any boxed items or highlighted questions*
✔ *any repeated words or terms set in boldface*
✔ *any photos, maps, graphs, or diagrams*
✔ *the first and last paragraphs*

For practice, preview these opening pages from a science chapter called "Exploring the Ocean."

Textbooks

SECTION 1 Exploring the Ocean

DISCOVER .... ACTIVITY

What Can You Learn Without Seeing?

1. Your teacher will provide your group with ten plastic drinking straws and a covered box containing a mystery object. The top of the box has several holes punched in it. Using the straws as probes, try to determine the size, shape, and location of the object inside the box.

2. Based on the information you gathered, describe your object. What can you say about its length, shape, and position? Write down your hypothesis about the identity of the object.

3. Remove the box top to reveal the object.

Think It Over

Inferring Explain how you used the method of indirect observation in this activity to learn about the object.

PREVIEW

First paragraph

PREVIEW

Highlighted questions

PREVIEW

Repeated name

PREVIEW

Graphic and caption

GUIDE FOR READING

◆ What factors make ocean-floor research difficult?

◆ What are some features of the ocean floor?

Reading Tip As you read, make a list of features found on the ocean floor. Write one sentence about each feature.

Imagine going on a voyage around the world lasting three and a half years. Your assignment: to investigate "everything about the sea." Your vessel: a former warship, powered by sails and a steam engine. Its guns have been removed to make room for scientific gear. On board there are thermometers for measuring the temperature of ocean water and hundreds of kilometers of cable for lowering dredges to the bottom of the ocean. With the dredges, you scrape sand, muck, and rock from the ocean floor. You drag trawl nets behind the ship to collect ocean organisms.

The crew of a British ship, HMS *Challenger*, began such a voyage in 1872. By the end of the journey, the scientists had gathered enough data to fill 50 volumes and had collected more than 4,000 new organisms! It took 23 years to publish all the information they learned about oceanwater chemistry, currents, ocean life, and the shape of the ocean floor. The voyage of the *Challenger* was so successful that it became the model for many later ocean expeditions.

Figure 1 This engraving shows HMS *Challenger* in the Indian Ocean in 1874, two years into its journey around the world.

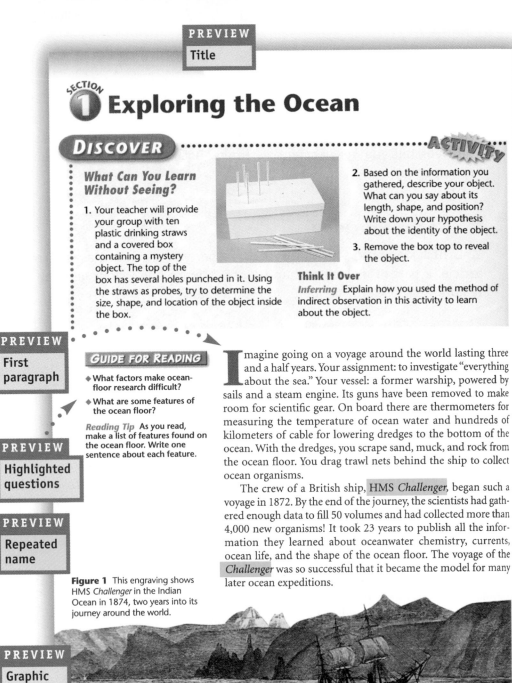

Voyages of Discovery

For thousands of years before the *Challenger* expedition, people explored the ocean. Knowledge of the ocean has always been important to the people living along its coasts. The ocean has provided food and served as a route for trade and travel to new settlements.

The Phoenicians, who lived along the Mediterranean Sea, were one of the earliest cultures to explore the oceans. By 1200 B.C., they had established sea routes for trade with the other nations around the Mediterranean. After the Phoenicians, people of many European, African, and Asian cultures sailed along the coasts to trade with distant lands.

In the Pacific Ocean around 2,000 years ago, the Polynesians left the safety of the coastline and boldly sailed into the open ocean. Their knowledge of winds and currents enabled the Polynesians to settle the scattered islands of Hawaii, Tahiti, and New Zealand.

As modern science developed and trade increased, ocean exploration changed. Nations needed accurate maps of the oceans and lands bordering them. Governments also wanted their countries to be known for new scientific discoveries. For example, in the late 1700s, the British government hired Captain James Cook to lead three voyages of exploration. Cook's crew included scientists who studied the stars and collected new species of plants and animals.

Within a century of Cook's voyages, almost all of Earth's coastlines had been mapped. Scientists then turned to the study of the ocean's waters and invented methods to explore its unknown depths. The *Challenger* expedition marked the beginning of the modern science of oceanography.

☑ *Checkpoint* *What are two reasons why people have explored the oceans?*

Figure 2 Polynesian sailors used stick charts to navigate the Pacific Ocean. The curved sticks represent currents and winds. The pieces of coral might represent rocks or small islands. *Interpreting Maps* Use the map to explain why navigation tools were important to the Polynesians.

Exploring the Ocean Floor

INTEGRATING TECHNOLOGY Following the *Challenger*'s example, governments and universities sponsored many other major ocean research expeditions. Until recently, however, the ocean floor was unexplored, and much of the life in the oceans was unknown. Why did it take so long to reach this part of the ocean? Studying the ocean floor is difficult because the ocean is so deep—3.8 kilometers deep on average, more than twice as deep as the Grand Canyon. As you learned in Chapter 4, conditions are very harsh at such depths. First, because sunlight does not penetrate far below the surface, the deep ocean is in total darkness. Second, the water is very cold—only a few degrees above freezing. Finally, there is tremendous pressure due to the mass of water pushing down from above.

Because of the darkness, cold, and extreme pressure, scientists have had to develop new technology to enable them to study the deep ocean floor. Since humans cannot survive these conditions, many of the inventions have involved indirect methods of gathering information. One of the simplest methods, used by the *Challenger*'s crew, was to lower a weight on a long line into the water until the weight touched the bottom. The length of line

NOTE

Problem-solution order

Technology and Ocean Exploration

The time line includes several inventions that have helped scientists overcome the challenges of studying the ocean world.

PREVIEW

Photo and caption

1943 SCUBA

Jacques Cousteau and Emile Gagnan invented SCUBA, which stands for "**s**elf-**c**ontained **u**nderwater **b**reathing **a**pparatus." A tank containing compressed air is strapped to the diver's back and connected by a tube to a mouthpiece. SCUBA enables divers to explore to a depth of 40 meters.

| 1915 | 1930 | 1945 | 1960 |

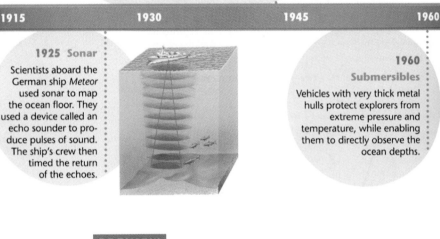

1925 Sonar

Scientists aboard the German ship *Meteor* used sonar to map the ocean floor. They used a device called an echo sounder to produce pulses of sound. The ship's crew then timed the return of the echoes.

1960

Submersibles

Vehicles with very thick metal hulls protect explorers from extreme pressure and temperature, while enabling them to directly observe the ocean depths.

PREVIEW

Diagram

that got wet was approximately equal to the water's depth at that location. This method was slow and often inaccurate, as the line would descend at an angle. Nevertheless, these depth readings produced the first rough maps of the floor of the North Atlantic.

A major advance in ocean-floor mapping was sonar, a technology invented during World War I to detect submarines. **Sonar**, which stands for **so**und **na**vigation and **r**anging, is a system that uses sound waves to calculate the distance to an object. The sonar equipment on a ship sends out pulses of sound that bounce off the ocean floor. The equipment then measures how quickly the sound waves return to the ship. Sound waves return quickly if the ocean floor is close. Sound waves take longer to return if the ocean floor is farther away.

✓ *Checkpoint* **How is sonar an indirect way of gathering data?**

PREVIEW

Last paragraph

In Your Journal

Each of the inventions shown on these two pages helped solve a problem of ocean exploration. Find out more about one of these inventions. Write a short newspaper article telling the story of its development. Include details about the people who invented it and how it added to people's knowledge of the oceans.

Textbooks

1986

Remote Underwater Manipulator

The Remote Underwater Manipulator, or RUM III, is about the size of a small car. It is controlled by a computer aboard a ship at the surface. Without a crew, the RUM III can collect samples, take photographs, and map the ocean floor.

| 1975 | 1990 | 2005 | 2020 |

1978 Satellites

Seasat A was the first satellite in Earth's orbit to study the oceans. Since satellites make millions of observations a day, they provide data on rapidly changing and widespread ocean conditions. Such data include temperatures, algae growth patterns, and even the movement of large schools of fish.

1995

Gravity Mapping

The United States Navy used advanced satellite data to create a new map of the ocean floor. The satellite detected slight changes in gravity related to the shape of the ocean floor, providing accurate measurements within a few centimeters.

PREVIEW

Timeline and captions

Plan

What did you notice on your preview? From the headings, graphics, and repeated terms alone, you now know a lot:

- A part of the chapter will focus on exploration of the ocean floor.
- Ocean floor research is difficult.
- There is a long history of ocean research.
- The *Challenger* investigated the ocean.

Maybe you already know a little about what the ocean floor is like. Or maybe you've already heard about the *Challenger*. Add your prior knowledge to what you learned from the preview. Now you're ready to make a reading plan. Choose a reading strategy that can best help you remember all the new terms and concepts and can help you find out what the author is saying.

 **Reading Strategy: Note-taking**

One excellent strategy to use with a science textbook is **note-taking.** Of course, it's not the only strategy you can use, nor is it useful only for science. You've probably taken lots of notes before—in classes or in the library. But how many different ways of taking notes do you know? By looking at how note-taking works with science texts, you will see some of the many forms it can take.

For example, try using a Thinking Tree to organize your notes. Begin with the chapter title on top. Next, add the first major heading below it. Add details below that, and so on.

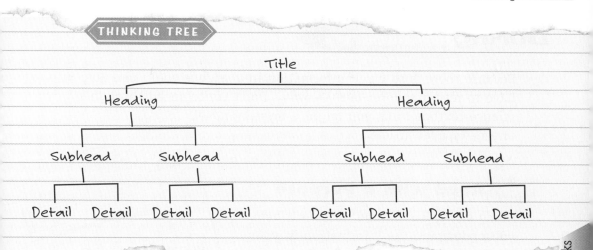

THINKING TREE

Title

Heading   Heading

Subhead   Subhead   Subhead   Subhead

Detail   Detail   Detail   Detail   Detail   Detail   Detail   Detail

Textbooks

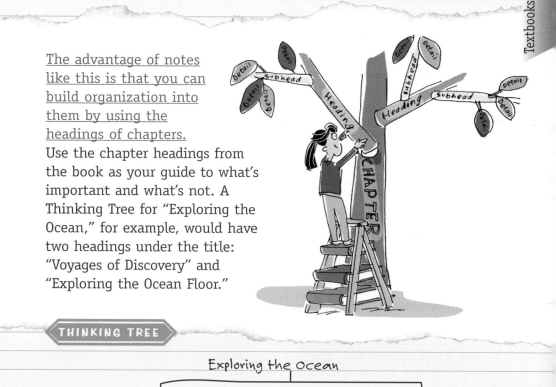

<u>The advantage of notes like this is that you can build organization into them by using the headings of chapters.</u> Use the chapter headings from the book as your guide to what's important and what's not. A Thinking Tree for "Exploring the Ocean," for example, would have two headings under the title: "Voyages of Discovery" and "Exploring the Ocean Floor."

THINKING TREE

Exploring the Ocean

Voyages of Discovery   Exploring the Ocean Floor

Now that you have a reading purpose and a reading strategy, you're ready to begin.

During Reading

Because there is so much information in a science book, you may have to read a chapter fairly slowly. Don't try to speed through a science textbook like you might a mystery novel or a newspaper article.

D Read with a Purpose

Going slowly and taking notes will help you understand the information in your science textbook more easily. Try different kinds of note-taking for different kinds of material. In addition to the Thinking Tree, here are five other styles of note-taking and their purposes. Each is a tool that can help you with a specific task—classifying, learning terms, sequencing, and so forth. Choose one that might work with your specific assignment.

NOTE-TAKING TOOLS

✔ Class and Text Notes
✔ Key Word Notes
✔ Study Cards
✔ Process Notes
✔ Classification Notes

1. Class and Text Notes

A traditional form of note-taking is 2-column notes. Use the left-hand column to write information from class and the right-hand column to record details from your reading. Class and Text Notes pull together the information your teacher gives in class with what you read in the textbook.

CLASS AND TEXT NOTES

EXPLORING THE OCEAN

Class	Notes from the Text
importance of Sonar	stands for sound navigation and ranging
	uses sound waves to figure distances
	invented during World War I
Jacques Cousteau	invented SCUBA in 1943

2. Key Word Notes

Here is another way of taking 2-column notes. Notes from the textbook go on the right-hand side and summary words or key words go on the left. Key Word Notes help you study and organize information around important concepts. Using them helps you sort out what's important from everything else.

▶ KEY WORD NOTES ▶

EXPLORING THE OCEAN

Key Words	Text Notes
exploration methods	Challenger and weighted lines
	Polynesians and stick charts
important explorers	U.S. Challenger
	James Cook's 3 voyages

Textbooks

3. Study Cards

Sometimes it's a good idea to take notes on index cards. Study Cards help you learn key concepts and terms. They also work well with study groups and when studying for quizzes or tests.

▶ STUDY CARDS ▶

CONTINENTAL SHELF

a gently sloping, shallow area of the ocean floor that extends outward from the edge of the continent

4. Process Notes

Science texts often describe the stages of growth, the steps in an experiment, or the process of discovery or invention. <u>Process Notes help you keep track of key steps or stages in a sequence.</u>

EARLY MAPPING OF OCEAN FLOOR

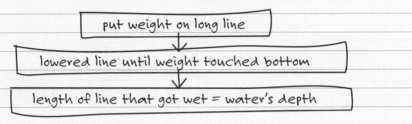

put weight on long line

↓

lowered line until weight touched bottom

↓

length of line that got wet = water's depth

5. Classification Notes

Science texts often describe different kinds or types and explain the characteristics of each group. <u>Classification Notes help you organize separate types or kinds and note characteristics about them.</u>

EXPLORING	METHOD	FINDING
Phoenicians	wooden boats?	sea routes
Polynesians	?	islands
James Cook	3 voyages	new species
Challenger	sailing ship	50 volumes of Information 4,000 organisms

When you read, you can use any one of these types of note-taking to help you organize what you are learning. Think of each kind of note-taking as a tool that can help you with a specific task—classifying, sequencing, studying, remembering terms, and so forth.

How Science Texts Are Organized

To think like a scientist, you need to understand *three* important thought patterns: 1) cause-effect order, 2) classification order, and 3) problem-solution order. Much of science focuses on these three patterns.

> **1. Cause-Effect Order**
> **2. Classification Order**
> **3. Problem-Solution Order**

Scientists ask questions and attempt to explain the world.

- What causes waves in an ocean? (cause-effect order)
- What kinds of fish live in the ocean? (classification order)
- How were the difficulties of exploring the ocean floor overcome? (problem-solution order)

1. Cause-Effect Order

Science is concerned with how and why things happen: how a chrysalis turns into a butterfly, why the earth rotates, what makes the stars shine, and so on. Cause-effect order is used to explain how and why these things happen. At its most basic, cause and effect looks like this:

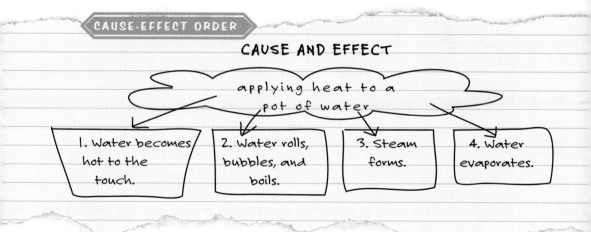

CAUSE-EFFECT ORDER

CAUSE AND EFFECT

applying heat to a pot of water

1. Water becomes hot to the touch.
2. Water rolls, bubbles, and boils.
3. Steam forms.
4. Water evaporates.

Textbooks

2. Classification Order

In science, classification means dividing things into groups or types that have shared characteristics. In natural science, for example, fish are classified as vertebrates because of their backbones. Scientists have grouped fish according to what sort of backbone they have. The classification of fish looks like this:

CLASSIFICATION ORDER

GROUP 1	GROUP 2	GROUP 3
jawless fishes	cartilaginous fishes	bony fishes
lampreys	sharks	perch

3. Problem-Solution Order

Scientists like to say that nature corrects its own problems. This may be true, because many of the problems and solutions you read about in science occur naturally. Go back to page 104 and notice the problem-solution order in the section about new technology being invented.

PROBLEM-SOLUTION ORDER

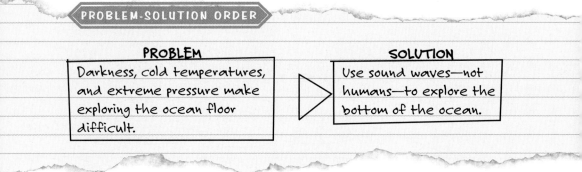

PROBLEM	SOLUTION
Darkness, cold temperatures, and extreme pressure make exploring the ocean floor difficult.	Use sound waves—not humans—to explore the bottom of the ocean.

When you read science texts, you will see these three kinds of patterns again and again. Use organizing tools like the ones above to help you better understand what you read and how you can think like a scientist.

E Connect

One reason you may have trouble studying science is that you don't see how it relates to you. After all, why do you need to know about the exploration of the ocean? Who cares how deep the ocean is?

One good way to overcome this problem is to look for connections you can make to the material.

As you read, make notes about things that are familiar or that interest you. You may be surprised to find how many connections you can make between a scientific subject and your own experience. Look at how one reader connected to a graphic from the "Exploring the Ocean" section.

Textbooks

1986
Remote Underwater Manipulator

The Remote Underwater Manipulator, or RUM III, is about the size of a small car. It is controlled by a computer aboard a ship at the surface. Without a crew, the RUM III can collect samples, take photographs, and map the ocean floor.

> This sounds like something in a movie I saw about the search for the Titanic on the ocean floor.

> How much does this thing cost?

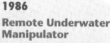

1990   2005   2020

Satellites

Seasat A was the first satellite in Earth's orbit to study the oceans. Since satellites make millions of observations a day, they provide data on rapidly changing and widespread ocean conditions. Such data include temperatures, algae growth patterns, and even the movement of large schools of fish.

1995
Gravity Mapping

The United States Navy used advanced satellite data to create a new map of the ocean floor. The satellite detected slight changes in gravity related to the shape of the ocean floor, providing accurate measurements within a few centimeters.

After Reading

Each time you finish reading a science chapter, take a minute or two to be sure you've gotten what you needed from the text.

F Pause and Reflect

First, return to your reading purpose. Do you know what the author is saying about ocean exploration? Ask yourself how much you've really learned about the subject. Sometimes there might be questions printed in a review or summary box that you can try to answer to get a sense of how well you've understood the material. Otherwise, ask yourself questions like these:

Looking Back

■ **Do I understand what are the main topics?**
■ **Can I explain the key terms?**
■ **Do the graphics, pictures, and captions make sense?**

G Reread

If you're honest with yourself, you'll probably find that you can't answer *yes* to all these questions. Maybe reviewing your notes or asking the teacher a question is all you'll need to do. But maybe you'll feel like you need to reread at least part of the chapter.

Rereading Strategy: Skimming

The strategy of **skimming** makes sense if you are looking for specific information and when you know what you don't know. That may sound crazy, but it happens a lot.

For instance, maybe you realize you don't know what *sonar* means. Perhaps you draw a blank when the teacher mentions it in class or you notice you forgot to fill in part of the Thinking Tree you made. Glance through the chapter (or use the index) to find where *sonar* was discussed and reread just that passage. Jot down what it means.

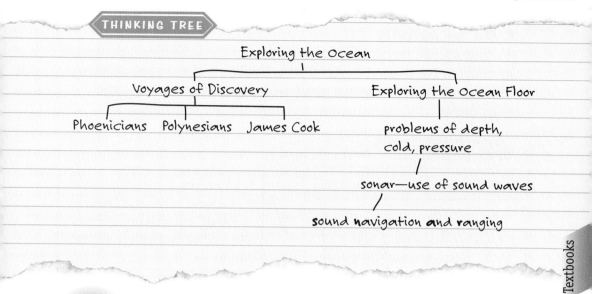

THINKING TREE

Exploring the Ocean

Voyages of Discovery   Exploring the Ocean Floor

Phoenicians   Polynesians   James Cook   problems of depth,
cold, pressure

sonar—use of sound waves

sound navigation and ranging

Textbooks

H Remember

Unlike some subjects, science is a hands-on discipline. This means that very often you can take what you've learned and create something interesting. Try one of these suggestions to help remember the information in a science textbook.

1. Make a Sketch

In a learning journal or notebook, make a diagram of something you learned about. Draw a plant or animal, an invention, or a place that was important in the chapter.

2. Do an Activity

To make science feel "real," try doing one of the activities described in the chapter. For example, later in the "Exploring the Ocean" chapter, students are invited to map a room. Below are Sequence Notes one reader created to make it easier to follow the steps involved.

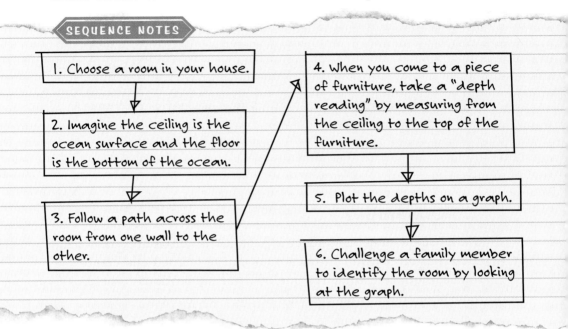

SEQUENCE NOTES

1. Choose a room in your house.

2. Imagine the ceiling is the ocean surface and the floor is the bottom of the ocean.

3. Follow a path across the room from one wall to the other.

4. When you come to a piece of furniture, take a "depth reading" by measuring from the ceiling to the top of the furniture.

5. Plot the depths on a graph.

6. Challenge a family member to identify the room by looking at the graph.

Summing Up

When you read a science textbook, follow the reading process and use the strategy of **note-taking**. Choose one of many different note-taking tools:

- ■ Thinking Tree
- ■ Class and Text Notes
- ■ Key Word Notes
- ■ Study Cards
- ■ Process Notes
- ■ Classification Notes

Remember, too, that the **structure of writing** in science texts explains why things happen (cause-effect), how things are divided into types (classification), and how problems are or might be solved (problem-solution). Use the rereading strategy of **skimming** to help you be sure you have noted and understood all of the important information in a chapter.

Reading Math

One of the great things about math textbooks is that the writing is brief and to the point. There are no extra words.

On the other hand, one of the *worst* things about math textbooks is that the writing is brief and to the point. This means that each word—no matter how small or simple—counts for a whole lot. Each explanation, tip, diagram, and caption is important. If you miss something, you may have trouble later on.

You probably think that to be a good math student, you need to be good with numbers. That's true. But you also need to be a good reader. You need to be the kind of reader who knows how to get the most out of a math book.

Goals

Here you'll learn how to:

✔ read about **math and math concepts**

✔ use the strategy of **visualizing and thinking aloud**

✔ understand the **organization of math textbooks**

Before Reading

When you read math, what you already know is very important. Many new math concepts you learn hinge on a previous concept. (For example, you can't *divide* if you don't know how to *multiply*.) Math is like a staircase that stretches on and on. If you miss a step, you may stumble. This is why you must read slowly and carefully.

Any time you read or study math, you need to work at peak concentration. This means that you shouldn't sit down to read a math chapter when you're feeling tired, hungry, or distracted. Schedule your math study time for when you're feeling fresh— first thing in the morning, for example, or right after dinner.

A Set a Purpose

When your assignment is to read some or all of a math chapter, begin by setting your purpose. In most math textbooks, the main subject is identified in the chapter or section title. A question about that subject will make a good purpose question.

For example, for a section in your math textbook called "Variables and Equations," your reading purpose might be simple:

Setting a Purpose
■ **What's important about variables and equations?**

B Preview

Often new math facts or concepts you learn build upon a previous math fact or concept. For this reason, it's a good idea to *review* before you *preview*. This means that you should return to the notes, diagrams, and practice exercises you completed in a previous or related chapter and think about what you learned.

After your review, begin your preview. Watch for key terms and concepts. The reason you preview is to get an idea of what to expect during your reading. Look for these items:

Preview Checklist

✔ *any titles, headings, and highlighted terms*

✔ *any boxed items*

✔ *any words in boldface*

✔ *any models, diagrams, or examples*

✔ *the introductory paragraph*

For practice, preview these two pages from a math chapter about variables and equations.

Textbooks

1.6

Connections to Algebra: Variables and Equations

PREVIEW
Title

What you should learn:

Goal 1 How to use mental math to solve an equation

Goal 2 How to write an equation to represent a real-life problem

PREVIEW
Words in bold

Why you should learn it:

Knowing how to write and solve equations can help with your finances. An example is finding the total income at a garage sale.

Goal 1 **Solving Equations**

PREVIEW
Introductory paragraph

An **equation** is a mathematical statement with an equal sign "=" in it. Here is an example.

$$3 \times n = 12 \qquad \textit{Equation}$$

This equation also has a **variable** in it. The variable, n, can be replaced by any number. When you **solve** an equation, you find the value of the variable that makes the equation true.

For example, the solution of the equation $3 \times n = 12$ is 4 because $3 \times 4 = 12$. The variable may also have the value 2, but 2 is not a solution because 3×2 does not equal 12.

Example 1 *Solving Equations*

PREVIEW
Example

Use mental math to solve each equation. Check your result.

a. $12 + p = 23$ b. $36 \div m = 4$ c. $x - 13 = 27$

Solution

a. You need to find a number that can be added to 12 to get 23. The solution is $p = 11$.

Check	$12 + p = 23$	*Original equation*
	$12 + 11 \stackrel{?}{=} 23$	*Substitute 11 for p.*
	$23 = 23$	*Solution checks.* ✔

b. You need to find a number that 36 can be divided by to get 4. The solution is $m = 9$.

Check	$36 \div m = 4$	*Original equation*
	$36 \div 9 \stackrel{?}{=} 4$	*Substitute 9 for m.*
	$4 = 4$	*Solution checks.* ✔

c. You need to find a number that you can subtract 13 from to get 27. The solution is $x = 40$. You should check this solution. ■

PREVIEW
Boxed item

Study Tip

Later in this book and in future math classes, you will study other strategies for solving equations. Whatever strategy you use, be sure that you always check your solution by substituting it into the original equation.

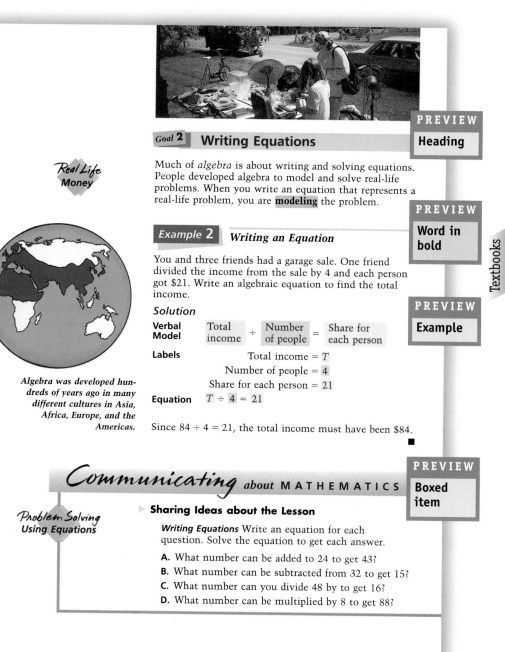

Real Life
Money

Goal 2   **Writing Equations**

Much of *algebra* is about writing and solving equations.
People developed algebra to model and solve real-life
problems. When you write an equation that represents a
real-life problem, you are **modeling** the problem.

Example 2   *Writing an Equation*

You and three friends had a garage sale. One friend
divided the income from the sale by 4 and each person
got $21. Write an algebraic equation to find the total
income.

Solution

Verbal Model					
	Total income	÷	Number of people	=	Share for each person

Labels

$$\text{Total income} = T$$
$$\text{Number of people} = 4$$
$$\text{Share for each person} = 21$$

Equation $T \div 4 = 21$

Since $84 \div 4 = 21$, the total income must have been $84. ■

Algebra was developed hundreds of years ago in many different cultures in Asia, Africa, Europe, and the Americas.

Communicating about MATHEMATICS

Problem Solving
Using Equations

▶ **Sharing Ideas about the Lesson**

Writing Equations Write an equation for each
question. Solve the equation to get each answer.

A. What number can be added to 24 to get 43?

B. What number can be subtracted from 32 to get 15?

C. What number can you divide 48 by to get 16?

D. What number can be multiplied by 8 to get 88?

Textbooks

121

Plan

What did you notice on your preview? From the headings, boxed items, and boldface terms, you may have learned a lot:

■ *Equation, variable,* and *modeling* are key terms in this chapter.

■ You'll need to use mental math to solve the problems.

■ Checking your work will be important.

You might have noticed other items as well. Keep them in mind when you make your reading plan.

It's often a good idea to talk over math material with a classmate. In math, two minds can be better than one. You may be very good with long division but have trouble with fractions. Your partner may be exactly the opposite—great with fractions, but weak with long division. If you work together, you and your partner can help each other over trouble spots—and have some fun.

TIPS FOR WORKING WITH A PARTNER

1. Stay on Track *Keep your focus. Avoid distractions. If you're solving equations, don't start talking about your new CD or last night's basketball game. Do your work first.*

2. Be Prepared *Make sure you have everything you need. Bring your book, your notebook and homework papers, scratch paper, and a pencil.*

3. Be Patient *Sometimes you may find yourself asking your partner the same questions several times. Other times, you'll be the one who needs to explain something more than once. Take turns listening and talking. Don't get frustrated and don't give up.*

Reading Strategy: Visualizing and Thinking Aloud

One of the best learning strategies for math is the combination of **visualizing and thinking aloud**. You can do it by yourself or with a friend or two. Math is about ideas. They are abstract. You need to "see" those ideas and help put them in terms you understand. You can do that by making a mental image of math ideas.

Probably the easiest way to visualize is to create a sketch or draw. For example, consider this sample problem from the chapter you previewed:

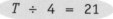

$$T \div 4 = 21$$

You need to translate that equation into something that makes sense to you. For example, suppose you and three friends (4) did a weekend garage sale. Each of you made $21. The total amount you made *(T)* divided by the 4 of you equals 21. How much did you make all together on the garage sale? Try to sketch it out.

VISUALIZING

The strategy of thinking aloud can help you talk through the steps of a problem. Besides being abstract, math often involves a number of steps. For example, with the equation above, the reading part is simple. You're done in an instant ($T \div 4 = 21$). But what does it mean? Talk your way through it.

THINK ALOUD

T is the variable. I need to figure out what that is.
The next part is the sign for division (÷).
So, I divide T by 4 to get the answer 21.
If something (T) divided by 4 equals 21, then 4 times 21 equals T.
Imagine T has 4 parts. Each is 21.
When you add them up, you get 84. That means T = 84.

Textbooks

During Reading

During your careful reading, you'll need to identify the most important information in the chapter and then use that information to help you solve math problems.

D Read with a Purpose

As you read the chapter and do the problems, use the four-step problem-solving plan below to help you. Take the first example given in the chapter "Variables and Equations":

$$a.\ 12 + p = 23$$

PROBLEM-SOLVING PLAN

Step 1. Read
Read the problem several times until you understand it.

This is an equation that has a variable, p.

Step 2. Plan *Think about what you need to do to solve the problem. Collect and organize the data or information.*

To solve this problem, you need to find a number that can be added to 12 to get 23.

Step 3. Solve
Use your strategy to solve the problem. Don't give up if you can't get the answer right away.

The solution is $23 - 12 = p$, or p added to 12 to get 23.

Step 4. Check
End by checking your work. Be sure your answer seems reasonable.

Use 11 for p in the equation. If it equals 23, then it's right.

Sometimes a problem will be easy. You can breeze through the four steps. Other times, you may get stuck on steps 2 and 3. If you have trouble organizing the information and finding the right answer, then try either visualizing, thinking aloud, or both.

Make a Sketch

It's always a good idea to visualize (make mental pictures of) the math problems you read. Draw a quick picture to stand for numbers in a problem. Making a sketch may lead you to the solution, as in the example below.

VISUALIZING

$12 \div 3 = x$

$x = 4$

Visualizing also means drawing a picture of concepts and terms that are described. For example, a picture of an equilateral triangle is easier to remember than the definition of the term.

VISUALIZING

An equilateral triangle is a triangle whose sides are all the same length.

2" 2"

equilateral triangle

2"

Textbooks

Talk Through a Problem

Another excellent technique to use with math diagrams or equations is to talk through what you've read. This means you use words to explain what the diagram or equation means. Consider this example:

$36 \div m = 4$

This means that 36 divided by some number equals 4. I know that I need to put the variable, m, alone on one side of the equation. What if I divided 36 by 4? That would be 9.

Now, will 9 work as the answer for m?

Yes, $36 \div 9$ does equal 4.

Thinking aloud lets you do two things:

- Listen to yourself and put the ideas in words you understand.
- Work toward a solution one step at a time.

How Math Texts Are Organized

All math books are divided into chapters. Each chapter covers a major topic in mathematics. In many books, chapters are further divided into sections. Often these are numbered with decimals: 1.3, 1.4, 1.5, 1.6, and so on. Each decimal is a new section of the chapter.

Most math chapters have *four* main elements:

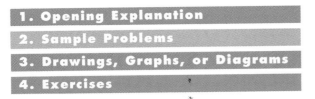

1. Opening Explanation
2. Sample Problems
3. Drawings, Graphs, or Diagrams
4. Exercises

Notice that all of these parts appear on the second page of the example.

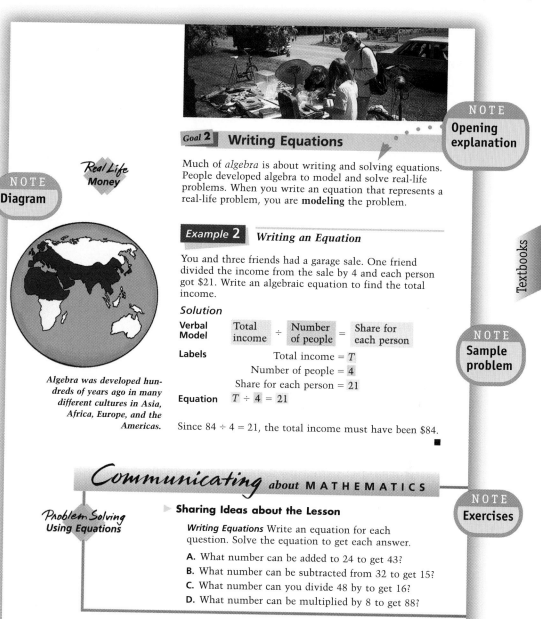

NOTE
Opening explanation

NOTE
Diagram

Real Life
Money

Goal 2 **Writing Equations**

Much of *algebra* is about writing and solving equations.
People developed algebra to model and solve real-life
problems. When you write an equation that represents a
real-life problem, you are **modeling** the problem.

Example 2 **Writing an Equation**

You and three friends had a garage sale. One friend
divided the income from the sale by 4 and each person
got $21. Write an algebraic equation to find the total
income.

Solution

| **Verbal Model** | Total income | ÷ | Number of people | = | Share for each person |

Labels   Total income = T
         Number of people = 4
         Share for each person = 21

Equation $T \div 4 = 21$

Since $84 \div 4 = 21$, the total income must have been $84. ■

*Algebra was developed hundreds of years ago in many
different cultures in Asia,
Africa, Europe, and the
Americas.*

NOTE
Sample problem

Communicating about **MATHEMATICS**

Problem Solving
Using Equations

▶ **Sharing Ideas about the Lesson**

Writing Equations Write an equation for each
question. Solve the equation to get each answer.

A. What number can be added to 24 to get 43?

B. What number can be subtracted from 32 to get 15?

C. What number can you divide 48 by to get 16?

D. What number can be multiplied by 8 to get 88?

NOTE
Exercises

When you read, begin with the explanation and then study the
sample problems, graphs, and diagrams. Next, complete the exercises.
Cover the answer section with a piece of paper to see if you've got
the right idea. If you're having trouble working the sample exercises,
return to the opening explanation and reread.

E Connect

You can have trouble with math if you don't see how it applies to real life. You should know that you use math in almost everything you do on a day-to-day basis. You estimate the time it will take you to reach school. You calculate the number of hours you spent on a project. You use measurement when you try on a new pair of jeans. You use addition to add up the amount you're owed for your allowance and subtraction to figure out the amount of change you should get back after buying your lunch. These are all examples of how you use math in your daily life.

Carrots 35¢ lb

EVERYDAY USES OF MATH
✔ estimate distance
✔ calculate time
✔ measure length and width
✔ add and subtract money

You can make math feel more real if you make connections to your own life. Say, for example, you are reading a word problem involving subtraction. You can make the problem more interesting and easier to remember if you turn it into a situation you can relate to or an experience you've had. Here's one way to make a connection.

THINK ALOUD

PROBLEM	CONNECTION
What number can be subtracted from 32 to get 15?	The score in the basketball game was something like that—about 32 to 15. How much did the other team win by?

Finish by solving the problem. (The answer is 17.)

After Reading

Each time you finish reading a math chapter, take the time to reflect on what you've read.

F Pause and Reflect

First, return to your reading purpose. Think about what you've learned. Ask yourself questions like these:

Looking Back

- ■ **Do I understand the key vocabulary?**
- ■ **Can I explain what each term means?**
- ■ **Do I understand the sample problems?**
- ■ **Can I take what I learned and use it to solve problems that appear on sample exercises or tests?**

If you can't answer *yes* to each of the questions, you'll need to do some rereading or ask your study group for help.

G Reread

Unless you're a math whiz, chances are that some of the terms or examples are not completely clear. Go back to the pages with the problems or terms that are still giving you difficulty.

Rereading Strategy: Note-taking

Note-taking is an excellent rereading strategy to use on hard material. You may find it useful to take careful notes about the sample problems your teacher solves in class. Use your notes to rework the sample problems and help you figure out what questions to ask.

For math concepts, taking notes on key words also works well. Divide a sheet of notebook paper in half. Label the left-hand column "Key Terms." Label the right-hand column "Examples." Try to write your own examples instead of using the ones in the book. This will help you work through the material.

Textbooks

VARIABLES AND EQUATIONS

KEY TERMS	EXAMPLES
Equation—mathematical statement that has an equal sign in it	$8 \times 3 = 24$
Variable—symbol or letter that can stand for a quantity that changes	$3 \times N = 12$ (N is the variable)
Modeling—writing an equation that shows a real-life problem	(number of lunches) $\times$ ($2.00 per lunch) = total amount due to cafeteria Equation: $18 \times \$2.00 = \$36.00$

H Remember

You can expect regular homework assignments in most math classes. Be sure to complete each one, even if you're not required to turn it in. You can also try one of these ways of helping you remember what you learned.

1. Keep a Math Journal

Keep a math notebook or journal. Use it to keep track of definitions, sketches, drawings, and sample tests. If your teacher doesn't require it, you might start one on your own. Bring it with you to each class. Keep a list of key terms and their definitions. Make notes about sample problems you work through as a class.

2. Create Sample Tests

One great trick is to make up your own sample tests. Look over a chapter and ask yourself what's important. Imagine the sorts of questions that might be on a test. Try to take the test yourself or work through it with a partner.

Your self-test will help you remember what you learned. Plus, you will be prepared for the real thing.

VARIABLES AND EQUATIONS

1. What is a variable?

2. An equation is a mathematical statement with an _____ .

3. Solve these equations.

   a. $80 \div d = 4$ b. $x - 12 = 636$ c. $12 \times m = 48$

4. Write an equation for this problem and solve:
   Mom has 3 pizzas. Each pizza has 8 slices. Mom needs to feed 4 children. How many slices can each child have?

(ANSWERS: 3a. $d = 20$ 3b. $x = 648$ 3c. $m = 4$ 4. 6 slices)

Textbooks

Summing Up

When you read math chapters, keep in mind the reading strategy of **visualizing and thinking aloud.** Choose one of these helpful tools:

- ■ Diagrams or Sketches
- ■ Think Alouds
- ■ Key Word Notes

Remember also to look for the way the **material is often organized into four parts:** an opening explanation; sample problems; drawings, graphs, and diagrams; and exercises. Then, if you still don't understand, try rereading and **taking notes** on the hardest material.

Focus on Science Concepts

Your science textbook is filled with *concepts*. Some of these concepts are simple to understand. Others take a lot more effort.

In science and other subjects, *concept* is another word for "big idea." For example, "The earth revolves around the sun" is an important concept in science. As a reader of science writing, you need to understand what these concepts mean. And, many times, you need to learn the process or steps involved and the terms used to describe them.

Goals

Here you'll learn how to:

✔ **use tools that can help you read about and understand science concepts**

✔ **remember and keep track of science terms**

Before Reading

Many of the concepts you'll find as you read science involve two things:

- a process or series of steps
- a number of terms you need to remember

Previewing the reading will help you get a basic idea of the process and the terms you'll be learning about. Here you'll read about how cells grow. As you preview the sample pages, look for the following items:

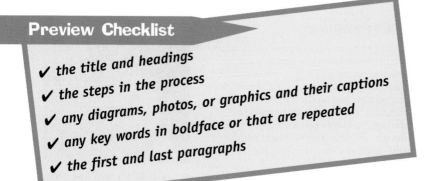

Preview Checklist

✔ the title and headings
✔ the steps in the process
✔ any diagrams, photos, or graphics and their captions
✔ any key words in boldface or that are repeated
✔ the first and last paragraphs

Textbooks

As you preview, you may want to jot down some terms or processes. Think of these as "starter" notes. You will take better, more complete notes when you read the chapter. But, as a way to start, taking some notes on your preview may be helpful.

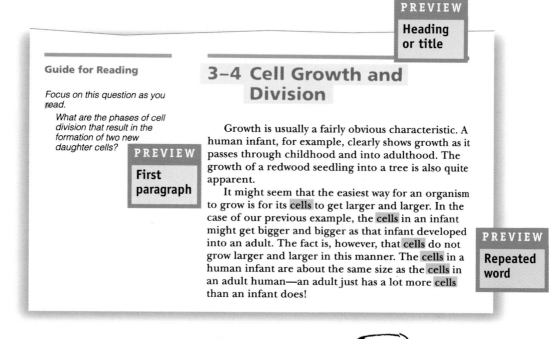

PREVIEW

Heading or title

Guide for Reading

Focus on this question as you read.

What are the phases of cell division that result in the formation of two new daughter cells?

3–4 Cell Growth and Division

PREVIEW

First paragraph

Growth is usually a fairly obvious characteristic. A human infant, for example, clearly shows growth as it passes through childhood and into adulthood. The growth of a redwood seedling into a tree is also quite apparent.

It might seem that the easiest way for an organism to grow is for its cells to get larger and larger. In the case of our previous example, the cells in an infant might get bigger and bigger as that infant developed into an adult. The fact is, however, that cells do not grow larger and larger in this manner. The cells in a human infant are about the same size as the cells in an adult human—an adult just has a lot more cells than an infant does!

PREVIEW

Repeated word

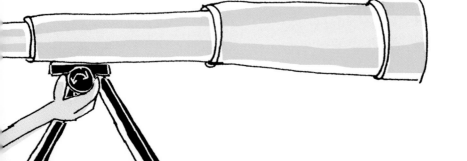

Limits on Cell Growth

Why don't cells get bigger and bigger as an organism grows? The answer involves the transportation of materials into and out of a cell. If a cell continued to grow larger and larger, at some point the cell membrane would not be able to handle the flow of materials passing through it. That is, the amount of raw materials needed by the larger cell would not enter the cell fast enough. The amount of wastes produced by the larger cell could not leave the cell fast enough. The larger cell would then die.

Cell Division

In order for the total number of cells to increase and for an organism to grow, the cells must undergo **cell division.** During cell division, one cell divides into two cells. Each new cell, called a daughter cell, is identical to the other and to the parent cell.

If a parent cell—a skin cell, leaf cell, or bone cell, for example—is to produce two identical daughter cells, then the exact contents of its nucleus must go into the nucleus of each new daughter cell. Recall that the chromosomes, which contain the blueprints of life, are located in the nucleus. If a parent cell simply splits in half, each daughter cell will get only half the contents of the nucleus—only half the chromosomes of the parent cell.

Fortunately, this does not happen. To understand why not, you must know about the process of cell division in more detail. **Cell division occurs in a series of stages, or phases.** Each has a scientific name. It is not important that you memorize the scientific name for each phase. But it is important that you understand the nature of cell division and how a parent cell divides into two daughter cells.

PHASE 1: CHROMOSOMES ARE COPIED During the first phase of cell division, which is called interphase, the cell is performing its life functions, but it is not actually dividing. If you were to observe the nucleus during this phase, you would not be able to see the rodlike chromosomes. Instead, the chromosomes would appear as threadlike coils called **chromatin.** In animal cells, two structures called centrioles (SEHN-tree-ohlz) can be seen outside the nucleus. The centrioles play a part in cell division. Plant cells do not have centrioles.

Figure 3–23 *The adult tiger does not have larger cells than its cub, just more of them. Why can't cells grow larger and larger and larger?*

ACTIVITY

CALCULATING

How Many Cells?

Suppose a cell divides once a day. How many cells will there be in a week? A month? A year?

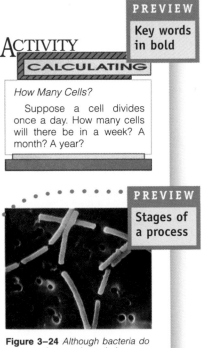

Figure 3–24 *Although bacteria do not contain a nucleus, their chromosomes still must double before the bacterial cells can divide into two identical daughter cells.*

PREVIEW

Key word
in bold

Figure 3–25 *During cell division, one cell divides into two cells. In multicellular organisms, this ensures growth and development and the replacement of dead or injured cells. What is the first stage of cell division called?*

Near the end of phase 1, the process of cell division begins. At this time, all the chromosomes (which still appear as threadlike coils of chromatin) are duplicated. That is, a copy of each chromosome is produced. As a result, the normal chromosome number in the cell doubles. Each chromosome and its sister chromosome (its copy) are attached at an area called the centromere. The sister chromosomes are now called chromatids.

PREVIEW

Stages of
a process

PHASE 2: MITOSIS BEGINS It is during the second phase, which is called prophase, that cell division really gets going. At this point, the process of cell division is called **mitosis** (migh-TOH-sihs). Mitosis is the process by which the nucleus of a cell divides into two nuclei and the formation of two new daughter cells begins.

During phase 2, the threadlike chromatin in the nucleus begins to shorten and form the familiar rodlike chromosomes. Each chromosome is made up of two identical chromatids attached at the centromere. Around this time the two centrioles (in animals cells) begin to move to opposite ends of the cell. In addition, a meshlike spindle begins to develop between the two centrioles, forming a "bridge" between the opposite ends of the cell. (Although plant cells do not contain centrioles, a spindle still forms in the cell at this time.) Near the end of phase 2 of cell division, the nuclear membrane surrounding the nucleus begins to break down, and the nucleolus in the nucleus disappears.

Textbooks

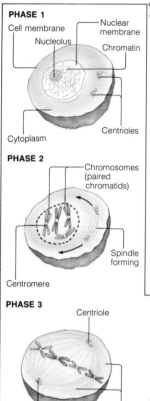

PHASE 1
Cell membrane
Nucleolus
Nuclear membrane
Chromatin
Cytoplasm
Centrioles

PHASE 2
Chromosomes (paired chromatids)
Spindle forming
Centromere

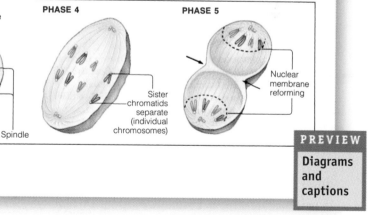

PHASE 3
Centriole
Centriole
Spindle

PHASE 4
Sister chromatids separate (individual chromosomes)

PHASE 5
Nuclear membrane reforming

PREVIEW

Diagrams
and
captions

PHASE 3: CHROMOSOMES ATTACH TO THE SPINDLE During phase 3 of cell division, which is called metaphase, the chromosomes begin to attach to the middle of the meshlike spindle that runs from end to end in the cell. The chromosomes are attached to the spindle by the centromere, which still connects each chromatid to its identical sister chromatid.

PHASE 4: CHROMOSOMES BEGIN TO SEPARATE During phase 4 of cell division, which is called anaphase, the sister chromatids separate from each other. One chromatid from each pair of sister chromatids begins to move toward one end of the cell along the spindle. The other chromatid of the pair begins to move toward the other end. The chromatids are again called chromosomes.

PHASE 5: TWO NEW NUCLEI FORM During phase 5 of cell division, which is called telophase, the chromosomes begin to uncoil and lose their rodlike appearance. The chromosomes again appear as chromatin and a nuclear membrane forms around the chromatin at each end of the cell. In each nucleus, a nucleolus reappears. At this point, the process of mitosis is complete. But cell division still has one more phase to go.

PHASE 6: TWO DAUGHTER CELLS FORM The sixth and final phase of cell division, which is called cytokinesis (sigh-toh-kuh-NEE-suhs), involves the division of the cytoplasm in the cell. The membrane surrounding the cell begins to move inward until the cytoplasm is pinched into two nearly equal parts. Each part contains a nucleus with identical chromosomes. The cell membrane forms and two new daughter cells are produced. In plant cells, a cell wall also forms around each daughter cell.

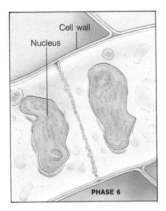

Figure 3–26 *At the same time that telophase is taking place in the nucleus, cytokinesis is taking place in the cytoplasm. Cytokinesis is the division of the cytoplasm and its contents into two individual daughter cells. In plant cells, as shown here, the cytoplasm is divided by a cell plate, which will become the new cell membrane.*

You probably learned a lot from your quick preview:

- The process of cell division has six steps or stages.

- There are limits on cell growth.

- Key terms include *cells, cell division, chromatin,* and *mitosis.*

What else did you learn? How can you best keep track of what you're learning? Making a Concept Map is a great way of exploring a complex idea or process. Start out with some blank boxes that you can fill in as you read.

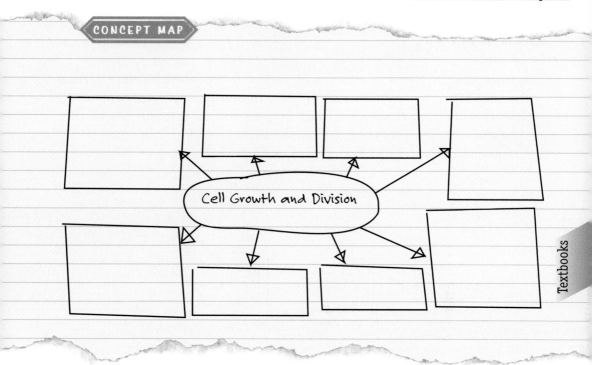

CONCEPT MAP

Cell Growth and Division

Textbooks

A Concept Map helps when you know you will be reading about one idea or concept. The beauty of a Concept Map is that you don't have to know much about the concept—only that it's about one thing. Around the concept, you can cluster terms, stages, or characteristics about the process. That's how a Concept Map can help you. It pulls together, or clusters, the important information so that it is easier to remember. Don't worry about the exact number of boxes you make at this point. You can add more or leave some blank.

Sometimes Concept Maps include examples, characteristics of the concept, and definitions of terms. You can add these too, if you want. The important thing is to collect and organize the information around a concept.

you are here

During Reading

Once you have your reading plan and your organizer in place, you are ready to go. When you can, jot down notes about the concept in your organizer. Remember, the first time you go through the article or chapter, your notes don't have to be perfect. You can come back and add other details later.

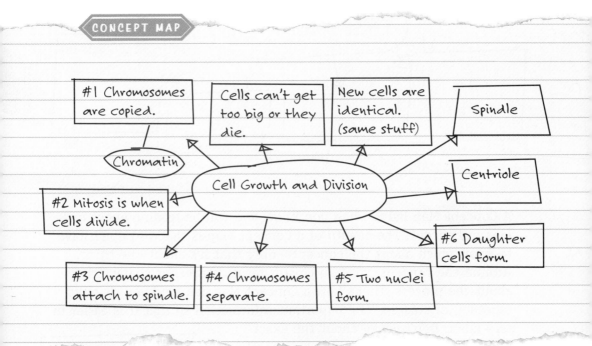

CONCEPT MAP

#1 Chromosomes are copied.

Cells can't get too big or they die.

New cells are identical. (same stuff)

Spindle

Chromatin

Cell Growth and Division

Centriole

#2 Mitosis is when cells divide.

#6 Daughter cells form.

#3 Chromosomes attach to spindle.

#4 Chromosomes separate.

#5 Two nuclei form.

The key to remembering is to organize new information. That's where the Concept Map comes in: it pulls together new terms and ideas.

Sometimes, however, a Concept Map won't be enough. So, you should also know about a few other kinds of tools that can help you collect information.

Reading Strategy: Using Graphic Organizers

It makes a lot of sense to **use graphic organizers** to help clarify and organize what you learn as you read about scientific concepts. Different organizers work well with different kinds of material. You might choose one to help you study for a test and another to prepare you to do a short oral summary. The point is to choose an organizer that will work for you.

1. Thinking Tree

<u>A Thinking Tree works best when you can't predict what a concept will be about or where it will lead.</u> With a Thinking Tree, you can make as many branches as you want and add them anywhere you want. The idea behind a Thinking Tree is to let your notes branch out from the concept.

Textbooks

THINKING TREE

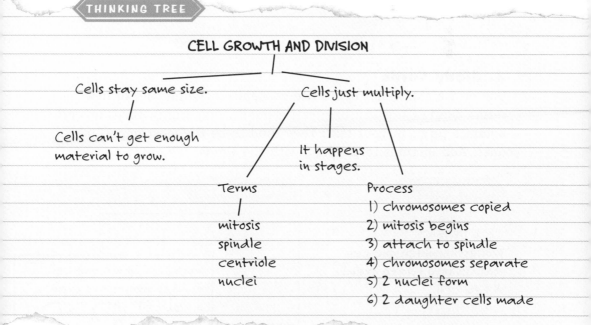

CELL GROWTH AND DIVISION

Cells stay same size.

Cells can't get enough material to grow.

Cells just multiply.

It happens in stages.

Terms

mitosis
spindle
centriole
nuclei

Process

1) chromosomes copied
2) mitosis begins
3) attach to spindle
4) chromosomes separate
5) 2 nuclei form
6) 2 daughter cells made

2. Process Notes

On your preview, you might have noticed the diagram showing a series of stages in cell division. Process Notes can help you keep track of the steps in the process, especially a long or complex one.

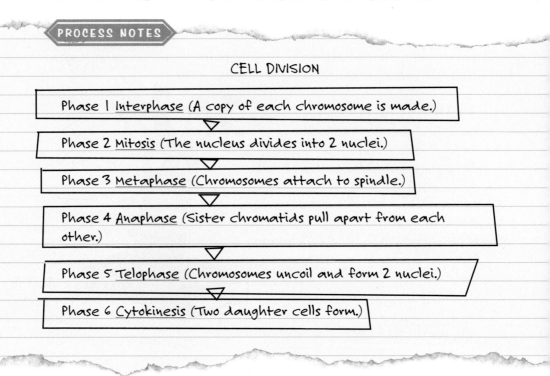

PROCESS NOTES

CELL DIVISION

Phase 1 Interphase (A copy of each chromosome is made.)

Phase 2 Mitosis (The nucleus divides into 2 nuclei.)

Phase 3 Metaphase (Chromosomes attach to spindle.)

Phase 4 Anaphase (Sister chromatids pull apart from each other.)

Phase 5 Telophase (Chromosomes uncoil and form 2 nuclei.)

Phase 6 Cytokinesis (Two daughter cells form.)

3. Study Cards

One of the challenges of science concepts is the number of new terms. Study Cards can help you memorize key words. Focus on the boldface terms in your text. They tend to be the most important ones. Add pictures to go along with the words.

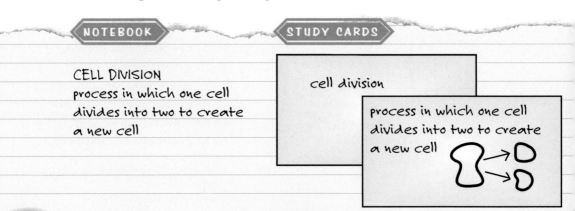

NOTEBOOK

CELL DIVISION
process in which one cell
divides into two to create
a new cell

STUDY CARDS

cell division

process in which one cell
divides into two to create
a new cell

After Reading

Once you finish reading the chapter or article about science concepts, it's time to sort out what you've read.

Science writing often takes careful reading and rereading. Having to reread an article doesn't mean you're not smart. It just means that you weren't able to take everything in the first time around.

In rereading, you'll most likely want to concentrate on only some parts. But how can you know what you don't know? That's a good question. Here are three suggestions to help you work through science readings. Try one and stick with it if it works. The point is not to have a lot of things to do. The point is to do something that works.

1. Look at Your Notes

Be sure that your notes make sense to you and are clear. If not, find the information that will make them clear. Add terms or steps that you might have skipped over.

2. Create a Study Guide

You don't need to be a genius to make a study guide. Just ask yourself what might be on the test. You might want to work with a partner at this point. Make up questions based on the headings and key terms. Each of you can answer the other's questions.

STUDY GUIDE

1. How would you describe the concept of cell division?

2. What are the key stages?

3. What does the term mitosis mean?

4. What does the term daughter cell mean?

Textbooks

3. Redraw or Retell Information

One good way of finding out just how well you understand a concept or process is to put it into your own words. Think about the explanations you've read and the diagrams you've studied. Can you explain them in a paragraph or drawing of your own?

For example, look again at the diagram on page 135 that shows cell division. You might find it easier to remember this diagram (and the steps in the process) if you redraw it into something that is meaningful to you. For example, change the cells to food:

DRAWING

1. coconut

2. apple with seeds

3. pumpkin

4. watermelon

5. one pear

6. two pears

Once you redraw the diagram as a food chain, you will find the steps in the process easier to memorize. The different foods are familiar to you, and they can help you remember what's new and less familiar.

Summing Up

- Science concepts usually involve a process and a number of key terms.
- Using graphic organizers helps you keep track of important information.

Focus on Word Problems

For many students, *word problems* are the most challenging part of studying math. Is this true for you? Do you think word problem questions are harder than ones with numbers or diagrams? If so, pay attention to this lesson.

Goals

Here you'll learn how to:

✔ **follow a four-step plan when solving word problems**

✔ **visualize what the problem is asking**

✔ **recognize the basic organization of word problems**

Before Reading

Word problems can be misleading because they're so short. In truth, sometimes the shortest word problems are the trickiest. You'll need to read them carefully and slowly. You'll also need a plan for solving them.

The good news about word problems is that they can all be solved in essentially the same way. Use the problem-solving plan described in the "Reading Math" lesson (page 124) to help you with even the toughest problems.

FOUR-STEP PLAN FOR WORD PROBLEMS

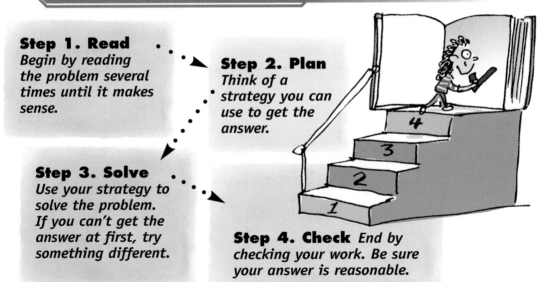

Step 1. Read
Begin by reading the problem several times until it makes sense.

Step 2. Plan
Think of a strategy you can use to get the answer.

Step 3. Solve
Use your strategy to solve the problem. If you can't get the answer at first, try something different.

Step 4. Check *End by checking your work. Be sure your answer is reasonable.*

Read through the problem once without making any notes. Ask yourself these questions:

- Who or what is the topic?
- What is given? What information do I know?
- What "unknown" am I supposed to find?

On your second reading, make notes. Use a highlighter if you can, or jot notes on a separate sheet of paper.

EXAMPLE

■ Ticket sales for this year's annual concert at Riverside Stadium were $1,050,000. The sponsor predicts next year's ticket sales will be 40% more than they were this year. How much does the sponsor think ticket sales will be next year?

NOTES

TOPIC: ticket sales
GIVEN: last year's total:
$1,050,000
Prediction: 40% more
TO FIND: next year's
ticket sales

Textbooks

Next, choose a strategy that will help you solve the problem. The best all-purpose strategy to use with word problems is to **visualize and think aloud.**

Reading Strategy: **Visualizing and Thinking Aloud**

When you visualize, you make a mental picture. For the problem you just read, you might make a mental picture of a ticket or ticket booth with the ticket sales amount written on the front. Sketch in your notebook or on scratch paper.

VISUALIZING

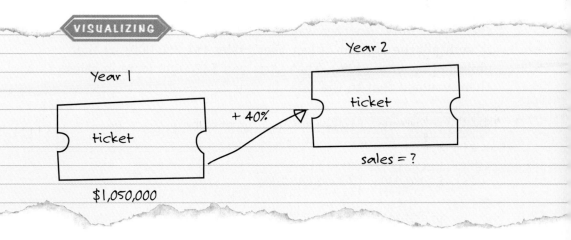

A drawing or chart can help you see the relationships between pieces of information. A drawing could be all you need to figure out how the equation should be written when it's time to solve the problem.

During Reading

After you've decided on a plan, it's time to solve the problem. You'll probably want to read through parts of it again as you work. With your notes and the sketch, write an equation that reflects the information in the problem.

Thinking aloud can help here. It lets you know what you understand and what you don't.

THINK ALOUD

The sponsor thinks sales will be 40% higher. So, take the sales and put 40% more with it. That would be 100% of sales in Year 1 plus 40%, or 100% + 40% = 140%. That's the same as 1.4, if you write 140% as a decimal.

So,

$1,050,000 × 1.40 = Z
Z = next year's sales

Multiply the numbers in the equation, and the solution is $1,470,000. Solving the problem in another way is a good way to check your work. Another way to find out next year's ticket sales is to multiply the amount of last year's sales ($1,050,000) by the projected increase (40%). That gives you $420,000 more in sales. Then, you add that to the sales in Year 1.

CHECKING YOUR WORK

$1,050,000 × 1.40 = $1,470,000

or

$1,050,000 + 420,000 = $1,470,000
Year 1 sales + 40% more = Year 2 sales

How Word Problems Are Organized

All word problems have *two* characteristics in common:

1. They use words along with numbers, symbols, or diagrams to present a problem.

2. You solve them by changing the words into numbers and writing your own equations.

Order of Numbers

Keep in mind that the numbers in a word problem may be jumbled. You can't write an equation or formula simply by jotting down the numbers in the exact way that they are presented. You need to ignore the order the numbers are presented in and think carefully about how the equation should be written.

ORDER OF NUMBERS

Problem
Lila has four ducks. At the end of the day, she has six. How many new ducks came later?

Incorrect
(the way the numbers are presented in the problem)
4 + 6 =
4 − 6 =

Correct
(rearrangement of numbers in the problem)
6 − 4 =

Use of Words

Many word problems also use the word *of* or the word *is* in a special way. Remembering these guidelines can help you come up with the right equations:

■ The word *is* means "equal" or "equal to."

100 ÷ 4 is 25 ➜ 100 ÷ 4 = 25

■ The word *of* means multiplication.

⅓ of 20 ➜ ⅓ × 20 = 6⅔

50% of 20 = 10 ➜ 50% × 20 = 10

Making Sense of Sentences

Some word problems, like the one below, are long. They use many words in several sentences. As a reader, you'll need to be clear about what is given and what you need to find.

EXAMPLE

A car rental company charges $50.00 per day plus $0.40 per mile for a full-size car. Ms. Moss rents a full-size car for two weeks (14 days). She drives a total of 500 miles. How much will she pay the rental company when she returns the car?

NOTES

TOPIC: rental car

GIVEN: car's daily rate ($50)

car's mileage rate ($.40 per mile)

number of days (14) and miles (500)

TO FIND: how much Ms. Moss has to pay

(**ANSWER:** 50(14) + .40(500) = 900. The cost is $900.00.)

Making Sense of Diagrams

Other word problems include one or more graphics or diagrams. In the diagram below, you are given more information than you might at first think. Once you sort out what you know, the challenge is to come up with the right equation.

EXAMPLE

How much fence do you need to enclose this field?

400 yds.

400 yds.

200 yds.

400 yds.

Textbooks

NOTES

TOPIC: fence

GIVEN: the field is 800 yards long (400 + 400) and 600 yards wide (200 + 400)

TO FIND: how much fence is needed to go around the field. I need to use an equation to find the perimeter.

(ANSWER: (800 × 2) + (600 × 2) = 2,800. The total is 2,800 yards.)

After Reading

Sometimes even when you read a math problem carefully and make notes, you just don't get it. Maybe you can't decide where to start or maybe, when you checked, your answer was wrong or just doesn't seem reasonable.

When you're having trouble with a word problem, try one of the following helpful tips:

PROBLEM-SOLVING TIPS

1. Guess, Check, and Revise *Figure out what you know, make a guess, and then check your guess. Revise if needed.*

2. Work Backward *Use this method if you're given the answer ahead of time. Working backward can help you figure out the steps that lead up to the answer.*

3. Use Simpler Numbers *Substitute simpler numbers for difficult ones. After you solve with the simple numbers, go back and solve again with the real numbers.*

4. Work with a Partner *Talk through the problem with a partner. Sometimes it helps to explain what you know to someone else. Your partner may ask just the right question you forgot to ask.*

Let's look at each tip more closely.

Tip #1: Guess, Check, and Revise

When you do a puzzle, you make a first guess about which pieces fit together. Then you check and revise until you find pieces that match. You can use this same process when solving word problems. To see how the process works, think about this word problem:

> **EXAMPLE**
>
> Mr. Quinn bought two types of paper. The graph paper cost $3.00 a package, and the lined paper cost $2.25 a package. He bought a total of 10 boxes and spent a total of $28.50. How many packages of each type did Mr. Quinn buy?

Begin by reviewing what you know:

- the total number of packages (10)
- the cost of a package of each type ($3.00 and $2.25)
- the total cost ($28.50)

GUESS, CHECK, AND REVISE

GUESS (sum must be 10)	CHECK (total must be $28.50)	REVISE
graph — 5 lined — 5	5(3.00) + 5(2.25) = 15.00 + 11.25 = 26.25	Guess is too low. Make a guess that raises the total.
graph — 7 lined — 3	7(3.00) + 3(2.25) = 21.00 + 6.75 = 27.75	Guess is still too low. Buy more of the more expensive paper.
graph — 8 lined — 2	8(3.00) + 2(2.25) 24.00 + 4.50 = 28.50	This is right!

- Is the total cost $28.50? Yes, 8($3.00) + 2($2.25) = $28.50.
- Is the total number of boxes 10? Yes, 8 + 2 = 10.
- Does the answer make sense? Yes, the numbers are reasonable.

ANSWER: Mr. Quinn bought 8 packages of graph paper and 2 packages of lined paper.

Textbooks

Tip #2: Work Backward

Some problems will present the answer and ask you to figure out the steps that led to the answer. If this is the case, use the problem-solving technique of "work backward." Think about this problem:

EXAMPLE

Lena and five of her friends are at a pizza parlor. Each person bought one slice. Their bill was $8.70, which included $0.36 sales tax. How much does one slice of pizza cost before tax?

Begin by reviewing what you know and what's given:
- the final cost of the pizza ($8.70)
- the amount of tax ($0.36)
- the number of people (6)

You can use this information to work backward. First, find the total cost of the six slices. Then keep working backward to find the cost of one slice.

WORK BACKWARD

Final cost:	8.70	Since the tax is added to the total
Tax:	-0.36	cost of the six slices, subtract the
		tax from the total for the cost
Cost before tax:	8.34	before tax.
	8.34 ÷ 6	Note there are six people total.
	= 1.39	To find the cost of one slice, divide
		the total cost before tax by 6.

Then, check your answer.

Cost of one slice: $1.39
Multiply by total number of slices:

$1.39
x   6
$8.34

Add the tax:
Total cost:

+$.36
$8.70

ANSWER:
A slice of pizza costs $1.39 before tax. That seems reasonable.

Tip #3: Use Simpler Numbers

Any time you are asked to solve a difficult problem, try to solve it using simpler numbers.

EXAMPLE

The clothing shop buys shirts wholesale and then marks them up 62%. At the end of the year, the shirts go on sale for 33% off. If the wholesale price for each shirt was $48, what is the sale price?

First, read the problem and think of a "solve strategy." This problem will be easier to answer if you make the numbers easier. Try rounding them. Use 60%, 30%, and $50.00.

USE SIMPLER NUMBERS

1. Rephrase the question using round numbers.	A store marks up shirts about 60%. The shirts are on sale for about 30% off. The wholesale price is $50.00. What is the sale price?	
2. Find the original price of the shirts.	60% of 50 = 0.60 × 50 = 30 50 + 30 = 80	Add the markup to the wholesale amount to find the original price.
3. Find the discount and sale price at 30 % off.	30 % of 80 = 0.30 × 80 = 24 80 − 24 = 56	The sale price is the difference between the original price and the discount.

After you've used easy numbers to plan your solution, you can follow the same steps with the real numbers and a calculator. Since you already know the equations, the problem will be a snap to solve.

Original price:
62% of $48 =
0.62 × $48 = $29.76
$48 + $29.76 = $77.76
Sale price:
33% of $77.76 =
0.33 × $77.76 = $25.66
$77.76 − $25.66 = $52.10

ANSWER:
The sale price for each shirt is $52.10. That seems reasonable. The answer is close to the answer that used simpler numbers.

Textbooks

Tip #4: Work with a Partner

If you think it will help, work with a partner and check your answers together. (See page 122 in "Reading Math.") Talk through the problem together. Look at any notes or sketches you made. Explain to your partner the aspects of the problem:

- what the topic is
- what information you already know
- what "unknown" you need to find
- the equation or formula you wrote to express the problem

Putting your problem-solving steps into words can help you remember them. Working with a partner can also help you spot errors that you missed when you were rereading on your own.

Summing Up

- **Use a four-step plan for solving word problems: read, plan, solve, and check.**
- **Visualizing and thinking aloud can help you keep track of the information.**
- **Don't give up if you don't get the answer right away. Try one of the problem-solving tips.**

Elements of Textbooks

Just as the human body has a heart, lungs, bones, blood vessels, and other key parts, so textbooks also have consistent elements. You are probably familiar with them, having seen textbook headings, captions, glossaries, and indexes over the years. Still, you might want to take a moment to review the elements of a textbook. Not only do you need to know where these elements are and how to find them, but you need to be clear about what their purpose is.

Elements of Textbooks

Boldface Terms	156
Charts	157
Glossary	158
Graphs	159
Headings and Titles	160
Index	162
Maps	163
Photos and Illustrations	165
Preview	166
Table of Contents	168

Boldface Terms

Boldface type is a signal: **pay attention.** It signals that you ought to slow down and look closely at words in bold.

EXAMPLE

Key names, events, and terms

British Troops and Taxes

<u>King George III</u>, the British monarch, wanted to enforce the proclamation and also keep peace with Britain's Native American allies. To do this, he decided to keep 10,000 soldiers in the colonies. In 1765, Parliament passed the <u>Quartering Act</u>. This was a cost-saving measure that required the colonies to quarter, or house, British soldiers and provide them with supplies. General Thomas Gage, commander of these forces, put most of the troops in New York.

Britain owed a large debt from the French and Indian War. Keeping troops in the colonies would raise that debt even higher. Britain needed more <u>revenue,</u> or income, to meet its expenses. So it attempted to have the colonies pay part of the war debt. It also wanted them to contribute toward the costs of frontier defense and colonial government.

In the past, the king had asked the colonial assemblies to pass taxes to support military actions that took place in the colonies. This time, however, Parliament voted to tax the Americans directly.

In 1764, Parliament passed the <u>Sugar Act.</u> This law placed a tax on sugar, molasses, and other products shipped to the colonies. It also called for strict enforcement of the act and harsh punishment of smugglers.

DESCRIPTION

Textbooks have certain words or phrases in **boldface**. This change in type signals that the information is more important than the text around it.

Publishers use the size and boldness of type to highlight what's most important. Be sure you pay special attention to the terms, names, and events shown in boldface.

DEFINITION

Boldface terms are those that appear in heavy, darker type. Boldface is used to help signal that a word, term, or event is important and to make it stand out.

Charts

Like maps, charts present information, often with pictures and symbols rather than only words.

EXAMPLE

Chart listing data

		1601–1810
Slaves Imported to the Americas (in thousands)		
REGION/COUNTRY	1601–1700	1701–1810
British N. America	*	348
British Caribbean	263.7	1,401.3
French Caribbean	155.8	1,348.4
Spanish America	292.5	578.6
Dutch Caribbean	40	460
Danish Caribbean	4	24
Brazil (Portugal)	560	1,891.4

*=less than 1,000

Source: Philip D. Curtin, The Atlantic Slave Trade

Chart showing comparison

Changes in Ideas About Democracy

JEFFERSONIAN DEMOCRACY	JACKSONIAN DEMOCRACY
government for the people by capable, well-educated leaders	government by the people
democracy in political life	democracy in social, economic, and political life
championed the cause of the farmer in a mainly agricultural society	championed the cause of the farmer and the laborer in an agricultural and industrial society
limited government	limited government, but with a strong president

SKILLBUILDER **Interpreting Charts**

1. *What do you think was the most important change in democracy?*
2. *Did Jefferson or Jackson exercise more power?*

DESCRIPTION

Most **charts** pack lots of information in a small space. No one expects you to remember every morsel of information in a chart. The chart is there so that you can understand the general point and then refer to the chart again as needed. Use charts as a resource.

Think aloud to yourself, "What is the point of this chart?" You might even write down the point. Just be sure you remember the main idea when you read a chart.

DEFINITION

Charts give information, show processes, or make comparisons.

Glossary

All school subjects have their own specialized terms, and most textbooks list them in a glossary. It usually appears in the back of the textbook.

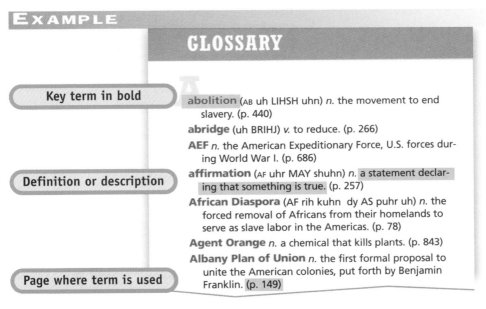

GLOSSARY

Key term in bold

abolition (AB uh LIHSH uhn) *n.* the movement to end slavery. (p. 440)

abridge (uh BRIHJ) *v.* to reduce. (p. 266)

AEF *n.* the American Expeditionary Force, U.S. forces during World War I. (p. 686)

Definition or description

affirmation (AF uhr MAY shuhn) *n.* a statement declaring that something is true. (p. 257)

African Diaspora (AF rih kuhn dy AS puhr uh) *n.* the forced removal of Africans from their homelands to serve as slave labor in the Americas. (p. 78)

Agent Orange *n.* a chemical that kills plants. (p. 843)

Albany Plan of Union *n.* the first formal proposal to unite the American colonies, put forth by Benjamin Franklin. (p. 149)

Page where term is used

DESCRIPTION

The purpose of the **glossary** (like these Elements pages in this handbook) is to give you the specialized language of the subject. This vocabulary is usually vital for your understanding of the subject.

Frequently the key terms or specialized vocabulary words for a chapter are listed at the beginning in a chapter preview. Take time to look at these terms. Knowing the words of a subject—or lingo—helps you know the subject itself.

DEFINITION

The **glossary** is an alphabetical list of key people, places, events, and terms. It is a tool to help you understand the language of the subject.

Graphs

Graphs present information with lines, pictures, and symbols rather than words. Graphs pack lots of information in a small space.

EXAMPLE

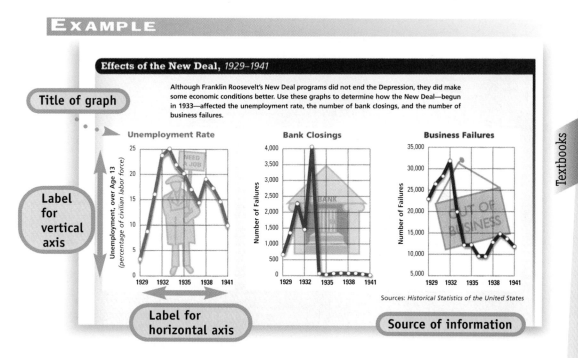

Effects of the New Deal, *1929–1941*

Although Franklin Roosevelt's New Deal programs did not end the Depression, they did make some economic conditions better. Use these graphs to determine how the New Deal—begun in 1933—affected the unemployment rate, the number of bank closings, and the number of business failures.

Title of graph

Label for vertical axis

Label for horizontal axis

Source of information

Sources: *Historical Statistics of the United States*

Textbooks

DESCRIPTION

As with a chart, a **graph** is shown to make a point. Read the title, the labels on the vertical and horizontal axes, and any other text. Then try to summarize the idea of the chart in your own words. For example, the graphs above show this idea:

The number of bad things (like business failures, bank closings, and unemployment) went down because the New Deal worked and helped people.

DEFINITION

Graphs use pictures and symbols to show information.

Headings and Titles

The headings in a textbook announce the topics that will be covered. The first big heading is usually called the title.

EXAMPLE

Unit heading

UNIT 1 — BEGINNINGS TO 1763

Three Worlds Meet

Chapter heading

CHAPTER 1 — The World in 1500 — Beginnings–1500

Chapter subheadings

Section 1 Crossing to the Americas
Section 2 Societies of North America
Section 3 Societies of West Africa
Section 4 Societies of Europe
Section 5 Early European Explorers

Subheading

① Crossing to the Americas

TERMS & NAMES
archaeologist
artifact
migrate
culture
domestication
civilization
irrigation
Mound Builders

MAIN IDEA
Ancient peoples came from Asia to the Americas and over time developed complex civilizations.

WHY IT MATTERS NOW
Archaeologists and other scientists continue to make new discoveries about these ancient people.

ONE AMERICAN'S STORY
To do her work, Solveig Turpin must climb rugged cliffs, step over rattlesnakes, and dodge sharp cactus spines. For more than 20 years, she has searched the caves and cliffs of Texas for paintings that ancient people left on rock walls. Turpin is an **archaeologist**. That is a scientist who studies the human past by examining the things people left behind. One painting that Turpin found shows a red, 9-foot-long panther. She believes it shows a religious leader who turned himself into an animal.

A VOICE FROM THE PAST
This is the Shaman [religious leader] who transforms into the largest and most powerful animal here. . . . I like to call [the shamans] supreme because they were over everything.
Solveig Turpin, quoted in *In Search of Ancient North America*

Archaeologist Solveig Turpin wears a shirt displaying the rock art of ancient peoples as she discusses her work.

Archaeologists make theories about the past based on what they learn from bones and artifacts. **Artifacts** are tools and other objects that humans made. They give clues about who ancient people were and how they lived. This section discusses some theories about early Americans.

The First People in America

Part heading

As many societies do, many Native Americans have stories explaining the origin of their people. Some believe the gods created their ancestors. Others believe their ancestors were born of Mother Earth. In contrast, scientists think that the first Americans **migrated**, or moved, here from Asia. But scientists disagree about how and when this move took place.

Some ancient people may have crossed a land bridge that joined Asia and North America during the last Ice Age. The Ice Age was a time of extreme cold that lasted for thousands of years. Glaciers trapped so much water that ocean levels dropped. A bridge of land, now called Beringia, appeared where the Bering Strait is now. (See map, page 28.) When the earth grew warm again, the glaciers melted and flooded Beringia. Some scientists who hold this theory believe the earliest Americans arrived

The World in 1500 **27**

The ruins of the Anasazi Cliff Palace, in modern-day Colorado, stand as a reminder of the Native American societies that existed before the arrival of Europeans.

22

24

Headings and Titles, continued

DESCRIPTION

The **headings and titles** in a textbook go from broadest to narrowest. The order looks something like this:

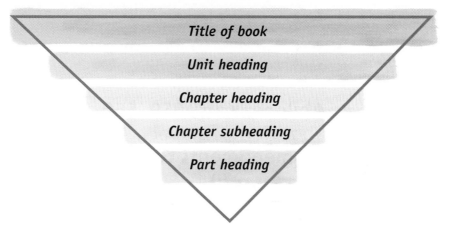

Title of book

Unit heading

Chapter heading

Chapter subheading

Part heading

The purpose of headings and titles is to create an order, from the broadest topic to the narrowest topic.

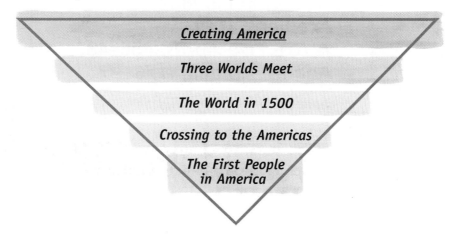

Creating America

Three Worlds Meet

The World in 1500

Crossing to the Americas

The First People in America

DEFINITION

Headings and titles list the big ideas in the textbook and go from biggest (the title of the book) to smaller (unit headings, chapter headings, and chapter subheadings) to the smallest (part headings).

Index

The index at the very back of the textbook gives the location of every important idea, term, definition, person, and place.

EXAMPLE

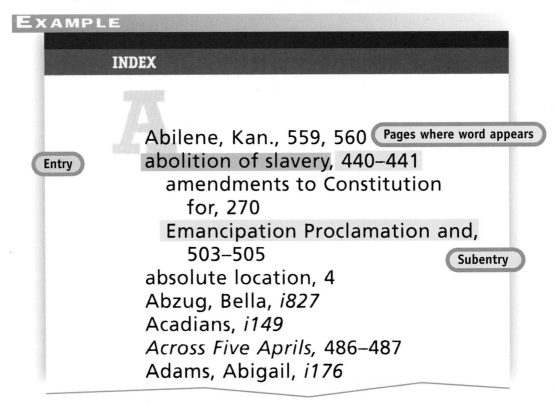

INDEX

Abilene, Kan., 559, 560 — (Pages where word appears)

Entry — abolition of slavery, 440–441
   amendments to Constitution
     for, 270
   Emancipation Proclamation and,
     503–505 — (Subentry)
absolute location, 4
Abzug, Bella, *i827*
Acadians, *i149*
Across Five Aprils, 486–487
Adams, Abigail, *i176*

DESCRIPTION

An **index** is a search tool—sort of like a search engine, but in a book. Use an index when you need to find things, such as specific terms or names.

DEFINITION

An **index** lists topics, terms, people, and places in the textbook and gives the page number where they were used. Think of the index as a search tool you can use to help you find what you need.

Maps

The map here shows information about the War of 1812. By reading the map, you can get a quick summary of this war.

EXAMPLE

Reading a Map

A **Lines** Lines indicate political boundaries, roads and highways, human movement, and rivers and other waterways.

B **Symbols** Symbols represent such items as capital cities, battle sites, or economic activities.

C **Labels** Labels are words or phrases that explain various items or activities on a map.

D **Compass Rose** A compass rose shows which way the directions north (N), south (S), east (E), and west (W) point on the map.

E **Scale** A scale shows the ratio between a unit of length on the map and a unit of distance on the earth. A typical one-inch scale indicates the number of miles and kilometers that length represents on the map.

F **Colors** Colors show a variety of information on a map, such as population density or the physical growth of a country.

G **Legend or Key** A legend or key lists and explains the symbols, lines, and colors on a map.

H **Lines of Longitude** These are imaginary, north-south lines that run around the globe.
Lines of Latitude These are imaginary, east-west lines that run around the globe. Together, latitude and longitude lines form a grid on a map or globe to indicate an area's absolute location.

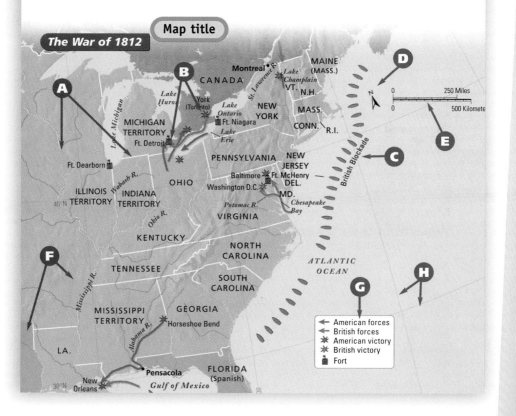

Map title

The War of 1812

American forces
British forces
American victory
British victory
Fort

Maps, continued

DESCRIPTION

The location of something is a vital part of its information.
Maps are information presented in visual form and tell you *where* something is.

Remember to read the title of the map because it tells the main idea. Look for the scale, which tells you how to read distance. Note also the map legend or key, which tells you what the symbols on the map mean.

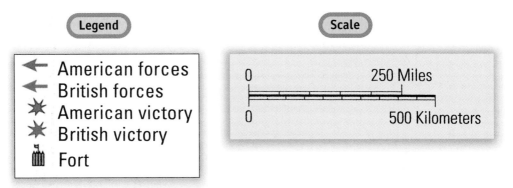

Then, try to put in your own words what the map is showing you. Together, the title, legend, and scale of a map will give you the "big picture."

DEFINITION

Maps present information in visual form and show where something is or where it happened.

Photos and Illustrations

One of the quickest ways to get a feel for a textbook chapter is to look at its photos and illustrations. What is shown?

Caption

These Native American students in Oklahoma Territory in 1901 posed for a class picture at the school where they were sent to learn the culture of white people.

were preparing for war. The army was sent to track down the Ghost Dancers. They rounded them up, and a temporary camp was made along Wounded Knee Creek in South Dakota, on December 28, 1890. The next day, as the Sioux were giving up their weapons, someone fired a shot. The troopers responded to the gunfire, killing about 300 men, women, and children. The **Wounded Knee Massacre,** as it was called, ended armed resistance in the West.

Textbooks

By seeing the subjects of the **photos and illustrations,** you will get an idea of what's in the chapter. That's because the photos and illustrations are used to emphasize or make important points.

The words below or beside photos, graphs, and charts are called *captions*. Most of the time, they tell you the reason for putting the picture or illustration in the text. Take the time to read captions. They can often say in a few lines what the author takes paragraphs to explain.

The **photos and illustrations** in the textbook emphasize the key points and add interest. Use them to help you find out what's in the chapter.

Preview

Most textbooks include a preview at the beginning of the chapter. It acts like a summary, packing into one small space all of the important things to know about the chapter.

EXAMPLE

CHAPTER 6

The Road to Revolution 1763-1776

Section 1 **Tighter British Control**
Section 2 **Colonial Resistance Grows**
Section 3 **The Road to Lexington and Concord**
Section 4 **Declaring Independence**

Mini-table of contents

Angry colonists watch the arrival of British troops in Boston.

156

Interact with History

A colonist reads a copy of a new British tax law.

Tax stamps are burned.

Protesters include men, women, and children.

The year is 1765. Your neighbors are enraged by Britain's attempt to tax them without their consent. Britain has never done this before. Everyone will be affected by the tax. There are protests in many cities. You have to decide what you would do.

Would you join the protest?

What Do You Think?
• What is the best way to show opposition to policies you consider unjust?
• Is there anything to be gained by protesting? Anything to be lost?
• Does government have the right to tax without consent of the people? Why or why not?

Timeline giving overview

1763 Proclamation of 1763 becomes law.
1765 Stamp Act is passed.
1767 Townshend Acts are passed.
1769 Spanish begin to establish military posts and missions in California.
1770 Boston Massacre
1773 Boston Tea Party
1774 Intolerable Acts are passed; First Continental Congress meets.
1775 Battles of Lexington and Concord
1776 Declaration of Independence is signed.

USA World 1763

1763 Treaty of Paris ends Seven Years' War in Europe.
1765 Chinese forces invade Burma.
1772 Captain Cook explores the South Pacific.
1774 Reign of Louis XVI begins in France.

1776

Preview, continued

Big idea of the chapter

Key idea about this period

Key terms

Tighter British Control

TERMS & NAMES
King George III
Quartering Act
revenue
Sugar Act
Stamp Act
Patrick Henry
boycott
Sons of Liberty

MAIN IDEA	WHY IT MATTERS NOW
Americans saw British efforts to tax them and to increase control over the colonies as violations of their rights.	Colonial protests were the first steps on the road to American independence.

ONE AMERICAN'S STORY

James Otis, Jr., a young Massachusetts lawyer, stormed through the streets of Boston one day in 1760. He was furious. His father had just been denied the post of chief justice of the Massachusetts colony by the royal governor. To Otis, this was one more example of Britain's lack of respect for colonial rights. Another example was its use of search warrants that allowed customs officers to enter any home or business to look for smuggled goods. Otis believed these searches were illegal.

Otis took up a case against the government that involved these search warrants. In court in February 1761, Otis spoke with great emotion for five hours about the search warrant and its use.

A VOICE FROM THE PAST

It appears to me the worst instrument of arbitrary power, the most destructive of English liberty and the fundamental principles of law, that was ever found in an English law-book.

James Otis, Jr., quoted in *James Otis: The Pre-Revolutionist* by J. C. Ridpath

Spectators listened in amazement. One of them, a young lawyer named John Adams, later wrote of Otis's performance: "Then and there, in the old Council Chamber, the child Independence was born."

In making the first public speech demanding English liberties for the colonists, James Otis planted a seed of freedom. In this section, you will read more about the early protests against Britain's policies in America.

James Otis, Jr., argues in court against illegal search warrants in 1761.

The Colonies and Britain Grow Apart

During the French and Indian War, Britain and the colonies fought side by side. Americans took great pride in being partners in the victory over the French. However, when the war ended, problems arose. Britain wanted to govern its 13 original colonies and the territories gained in the war in a uniform way. So the British Parliament in London imposed new laws and restrictions. Previously, the colonies had been allowed to develop largely on their own. Now they felt that their freedom was being limited.

Textbooks

DESCRIPTION

Spend time going through the **preview.** Read its questions or goals (if it has them) and look at the headings and key terms. The key terms are the special vocabulary for the chapter and are usually listed at the beginning and underlined or boldface in the chapter itself. Going through the preview is like warming up before you exercise. You need to do it to get ready.

DEFINITION

The **preview** can be several pages or part of a page. Its purpose is to help you look ahead to what will be in the chapter.

Table of Contents

In the very first pages, textbooks have a table of contents. Think of it like a big outline—an overview—of everything in the book. It shows you the topics you'll be reading about and how they're organized. Look at the information a single page contains:

EXAMPLE

1. UNIT TITLE gives the "big idea" and dates.

2. CHAPTER TITLES give mini-themes.

3. FEATURES list items of special interest.

4. PART TITLES break down the main ideas.

5. PAGE NUMBERS give location of each part.

UNIT 2 — Creating a New Nation 1763–1791

CHAPTER 6 1763–1776

The Road to Revolution — 156
INTERACT WITH HISTORY Would you join the protest? — 157
1 Tighter British Control — 159
2 Colonial Resistance Grows — 163
  INTERDISCIPLINARY CHALLENGE
  Fight for Representative Government! — 168
3 The Road to Lexington and Concord — 170
  LITERATURE CONNECTIONS Johnny Tremain — 174
4 Declaring Independence — 176
  INTERACTIVE PRIMARY SOURCE The Declaration of Independence — 182
  HISTORY WORKSHOP Raise the Liberty Pole — 188

CHAPTER 7 1776–1783

The American Revolution — 190
INTERACT WITH HISTORY What would you sacrifice to win freedom? — 191
1 The Early Years of the War — 193
  CITIZENSHIP TODAY Exercising Free Speech — 198
2 The War Expands — 200
3 The Path to Victory — 206
  TECHNOLOGY OF THE TIME Artillery of the Revolution — 208
4 The Legacy of the War — 211
  ECONOMICS IN HISTORY Free Enterprise — 214

CHAPTER 8 1776–1791

Confederation to Constitution
INTERACT WITH HISTORY How do you form a government?
1 The Confederation Era
  GEOGRAPHY IN HISTORY The Northwest Territory
2 Creating the Constitution
3 Ratifying the Constitution
  INTERACTIVE PRIMARY SOURCES The Federalist, Number 51/
  Objections to the Constitution

CONSTITUTION HANDBOOK The Living Constitution — 242
Seven Principles of the Constitution — 244
  INTERACTIVE PRIMARY SOURCE
  The Constitution of the United States — 248

CITIZENSHIP HANDBOOK — 280
The Role of the Citizen — 280
Building Citizenship Skills — 284
Practicing Citizenship Skills — 287

George Washington

x

Table of Contents, continued

DESCRIPTION

What you really have here is a ready-made study outline:

Unit 2. Creating a New Nation (1763–1791)

I. The Road to Revolution (1763–1776)
   A. Tighter British Control
   B. Colonial Resistance Grows
   C. The Road to Lexington and Concord
   D. Declaring Independence

II. The American Revolution (1776–1783)
   A. The Early Years of the War
   B. The War Expands
   C. The Path to Victory
   D. The Legacy of the War

This **table of contents** includes dates, so even the timeline of events can be seen. From this outline, you can create great notes for your history class. Add two or three details under each part, and you will have a strong summary of the contents of this chapter.

SUMMARY NOTES

> I. The Road to Revolution (1763–1776)
>   A. Tighter British control begins.
>   1. British troops and taxes create problems.
>   2. Stamp Act leads to boycott.
>   B. Colonial resistance grows.
>   1. Townshend Acts try to raise revenue from colonies.
>   2. Sam Adams and Sons of Liberty protest.
>   3. Boston Massacre was first major act of violence.
>   4. Boston Tea Party protests the Tea Act.

DEFINITION

The **table of contents** lists the major chapters and parts of a book along with their page numbers. The purpose of a table of contents is to help you find specific parts of the book quickly and easily.

Textbooks

Reading
Nonfiction

Reading Kinds of Nonfiction

Reading an Essay
Reading a Biography
Reading an Autobiography
Reading a Newspaper Article
Reading a Magazine Article

Ways of Reading Nonfiction

Focus on Persuasive Writing
Focus on Speeches
Focus on Real-world Writing

Elements of Nonfiction

Nonfiction

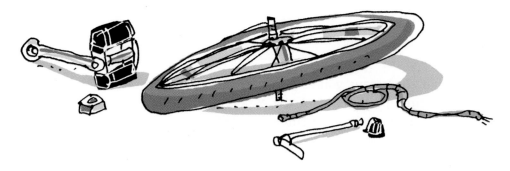

Reading an Essay

An **essay** is a short work of nonfiction that deals with a single subject. Essays can be lighthearted or serious, formal or informal. Sometimes they are meant to entertain, and sometimes they persuade, teach, or reveal an interesting idea. Essays often appear in magazines and newspapers.

You'll probably read two common kinds of essays at school: *narrative essays* and *expository essays.*

In a narrative essay, the writer tells a story, often in order to make a point or express a personal opinion. The writer of an expository essay explains something. He or she makes a point and then supports that point in the body of the essay. In this lesson, you'll read an expository essay, "America the Not-so-Beautiful."

Goals

Here you'll learn how to:

✔ recognize the purposes of various **essays**

✔ use the reading strategy of **outlining**

✔ look closely at the **organization of different kinds of essays**

Before Reading

One way to begin is to think of an essay in *three* parts:

- the introduction
- the body
- the conclusion

Most of the essays you've been writing since you were little have had these three parts. Most of the essays you're likely to read will have them, too. Knowing the three parts of an essay can help you track the writer's ideas.

A Set a Purpose

Most of the time your purpose for reading an essay is figuring out the author's message and what you think about it. Use general purpose questions like these:

Setting a Purpose

- ▪ **What is the subject of the writing?**
- ▪ **What is the author saying about the subject?**
- ▪ **How do I feel about the author's message?**

B Preview

Previewing an essay can give you important information about the subject and at least some clues about the author's message. When you preview an essay, look for these key elements:

Preview Checklist

✔ *the title and author*
✔ *the first and last paragraphs*
✔ *any key words, headings, or words in boldface*
✔ *any repeated words or phrases*

Now preview the first part of "America the Not-so-Beautiful" by Andy Rooney. Watch for items on your checklist. Make notes about anything you think is interesting or important.

Nonfiction

America the Not-so-Beautiful

by
Andy Rooney

PREVIEW

Title and author

PREVIEW

First paragraph

PREVIEW

Repeated phrases

Next to saving stuff I don't need, the thing I like to do best is throw it away. My idea of a good time is to load up the back of the car with junk on a Saturday morning and take it to the dump. There's something satisfying about discarding almost anything.

Throwing things out is the American way. We don't know how to fix anything, and anyone who does know how is too busy to come, so we throw it away and buy a new one. Our economy depends on us doing that. The trouble with throwing things away is, there is no "away" left.

Sometime around the year 500 B.C., the Greeks in Athens passed a law prohibiting people from throwing their garbage in the street. This Greek law was the first recognition by civilized people that throwing things away was a problem. Now, as the population explodes and people take up more room on earth, there's less room for everything else.

NOTE

End of introduction, beginning of body

The more civilized a country is, the worse the trash problem is. Poor countries don't have the same problem because they don't have much to discard. Prosperity in the United States is based on using things up as fast as we can, throwing away what's left, and buying new ones.

We've been doing that for so many years that (1) we've run out of places to throw things because houses have been built where the dump was and (2) some of the things we're throwing away are poisoning the earth and will eventually poison all of us and all living things.

Ten years ago most people thought nothing of dumping an old bottle of weed or insect killer in a pile of dirt in the back yard or down the drain in the street, just to get rid of it. The big companies in America had the same feeling, on a bigger scale. For years the chemical companies dumped their poisonous wastes in the rivers behind the mills, or they put it in fifty-gallon drums in the vacant lots, with all the old, rusting machinery in it, up behind the plants. The drums rusted out in ten years and dumped their poison into the ground. It rained, the poisons seeped into the underground streams and poisoned everything for miles around. Some of the manufacturers who did this weren't even evil. They were dumb and irresponsible. Others were evil because they knew how dangerous it was but didn't want to spend the money to do it right.

The problem is staggering. I often think of it when I go in a hardware store or a Sears, Roebuck and see shelves full of poison. You know that, one way or another, it's all going to end up in the earth or in our rivers and lakes.

I have two pint bottles of insecticide with 5 percent DDT in them in my own garage that I don't know what to do with. I bought them years ago when I didn't realize how bad they were. Now I'm stuck with them.

The people of the city of New York throw away nine times their weight in garbage and junk every year. Assuming other cities come close to that, how long will it be before we trash the whole earth?

Nonfiction

PREVIEW

Repeated words

Of all household waste, 30 percent of the weight and 50 percent of the volume is the packaging that stuff comes in.

Not only that, but Americans spend more for the packaging of food than all our farmers together make in income growing it. That's some statistic.

Trash collectors are a lot more independent than they used to be because we've got more trash than they've got places to put it. They have their own schedules and their own holidays. Some cities try to get in good with their trash collectors or garbage men by calling them "sanitation engineers." Anything just so long as they pick it up and take it away.

We often call the dump "the landfill" now, too. I never understood why land has to be filled, but that's what it's called. If you're a little valley just outside town, you have to be careful or first thing you know you'll be getting "filled."

PREVIEW

Key words from title

If 5 billion people had been living on earth for the past thousand years as they have been in the past year, the planet would be nothing but one giant landfill, and we'd have turned America the beautiful into one huge landfill.

NOTE

End of body, beginning of conclusion

The best solution may be for all of us to pack up, board a spaceship, and move out. If Mars is habitable, everyone on Earth can abandon this planet we've trashed, move to Mars, and start trashing that. It'll buy us some time.

PREVIEW

Last paragraph

C Plan

What clues did you find about the subject of the essay? You may have decided that the essay seems to be about several topics:

▮ throwing things out

▮ the dump

▮ trash

▮ poison

▮ garbage

What do you already know about recycling, landfills, and the environment? Your previous knowledge, together with what you picked up during a preview, gives you a good idea of the subject before you begin your careful reading.

Now you can make a plan to get the information you need. Ask yourself, "How can I figure out what the author's message is? What do I think about it?"

Reading Strategy: Outlining

Outlining is a strategy that works well for expository essays. It can help you identify the three main parts of the essay: the introduction, the body, and the conclusion. It can also help you see how an author develops and supports (or doesn't support) an argument.

Set up a simple Topic or Sentence Outline on a separate piece of paper before you start reading. Use a Roman numeral for each of the three parts. And give yourself plenty of room. At this point you don't really know how many details the writer will include. The following is a sample of the sort of Outline you might want to use. You may decide to add or subtract as you go, so use a pencil.

Nonfiction

I. Introduction
   A. introductory detail
   B. introductory detail
   C. thesis statement (if it appears here)
II. Body
   A. support for thesis
      1. example
      2. example
   B. support for thesis
      1. example
      2. example
   C. support for thesis
      1. example
      2. example
III. Conclusion
   A. concluding detail
   B. concluding detail
   C. thesis statement (if it appears here)

During Reading

As you're reading an essay, stay focused. Ask yourself what an author is saying about the subject and how you feel about what's being said.

D Read with a Purpose

With an expository essay like "America the Not-so-Beautiful," first look for the subject. From your preview, you know the subject of the essay is trash or throwing things out. Now watch carefully for the author's message about that subject.

1. Finding the Main Idea

What is Rooney saying about trash and throwing things out? Get the answer to that question, and you'll have the **main idea**, or the thesis statement.

Look again at the first two paragraphs of Rooney's essay.

Nonfiction

from "America the Not-so-Beautiful"

Next to saving stuff I don't need, the thing I like to do best is throw it away. My idea of a good time is to load up the back of the car with junk on a Saturday morning and take it to the dump. There's something satisfying about discarding almost anything.

Throwing things out is the American way. We don't know how to fix anything, and anyone who does know how is too busy to come, so we throw it away and buy a new one. Our economy depends on us doing that. The trouble with throwing things away is, there is no "away" left.

NOTE
Main idea

By the end of the second paragraph, you should have a good idea of Rooney's main point: that the American habit of throwing things out is a problem.

2. Finding Supporting Details

Once you've found the author's main point, you can begin picking out the **supporting details**. They are the facts, examples, statistics, and quotations used to support or prove the author's message. Support can come from many places:

- published facts, statistics, examples, and explanations
- comments from experts or other people who know about the topic
- the writer's own experiences

Making an Outline as you read is an excellent way to sort out the kinds of details that appear in an essay. Here is an Outline one reader made of "America the Not-so-Beautiful."

I. Introduction
   A. Rooney describes his trash "habits."
   B. Main point: Throwing things out is the American way.
     This is a problem.
II. Body
   A. Our economy depends on using things up as fast as we can.
     This is wasteful.
     1. People don't fix things.
     2. Our economy depends on us buying new things.
   B. What we're throwing away can poison us. Big companies
     carelessly dump poisonous waste.
     1. People don't know how to dispose of dangerous products.
     2. Poison seeps into the ground.
   C. There's nowhere to put all the stuff we're throwing away.
     1. People of New York City throw out nine times their
       weight in trash.
     2. Wasteful packaging is used.
     3. Landfills are filled.
III. Conclusion
   A. If people don't change their habits, the planet will be filled
     with trash.
   B. The best solution may be for all of us to move to Mars
     and trash it.

This is a very detailed Sentence Outline. Yours can be a lot simpler.
The point is to follow what the author is saying.

How Essays Are Organized

Knowing the ways essays are organized can make your job as a reader easier. Many essays follow one of several basic structures.

1. **Narrative Essay Organization**
2. **Expository Essay Organization**
3. **Essay Openings**

1. Narrative Essay Organization

If the essay is a narrative essay, it tells a story and usually follows a chronological order: first this happened, then this, and then this. If the author's main point is stated directly, it's told near the end, if not in the last paragraph or sentence. The story is used to make the author's point.

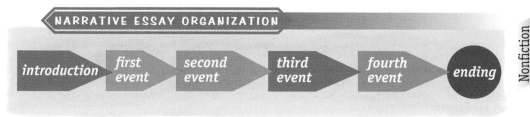

NARRATIVE ESSAY ORGANIZATION

introduction → first event → second event → third event → fourth event → ending

2. Expository Essay Organization

Expository essays are usually built around details that support a main idea or thesis statement. The support for the main idea almost always appears in the body of the essay. But *where* the main idea is may vary. The most common places for the main idea are either the first one or two paragraphs or the last one or two. The overall organization follows one of these models.

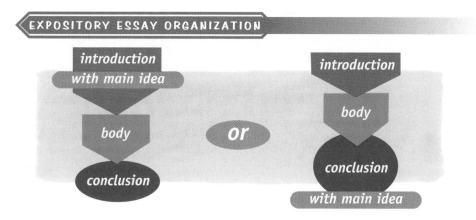

EXPOSITORY ESSAY ORGANIZATION

introduction with main idea → body → conclusion

or

introduction → body → conclusion with main idea

Nonfiction

3. Essay Openings

Even when the main idea comes near the beginning, it's usually not the very first sentence. Writers like to lead up to the point they want to make. They often will begin with one, two, or three sentences or paragraphs that "hook" the reader. A bit later, the writer offers the main idea. This is a common pattern of organization. Rooney uses it. One popular kind of essay opening is called a *funnel pattern* because it starts with a broad idea and narrows to a specific point at the bottom. It looks like this:

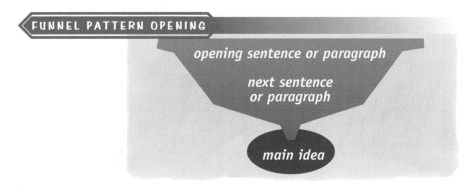

FUNNEL PATTERN OPENING

opening sentence or paragraph

next sentence
or paragraph

main idea

The funnel pattern works the same way an appetizer does when you're eating a meal. You begin with something that gets you interested and ready for what's coming next.

Knowing how essays are commonly organized makes it easier for you to pick out the main point and the important details. You'll have a better idea of where to look. A Main Idea Organizer is another way of making sense of what the author's saying.

MAIN IDEA ORGANIZER

TITLE:	"America the Not-so-Beautiful"	
MAIN IDEA: Throwing things out is the American way. This is a problem.		
DETAIL	DETAIL	DETAIL
Our economy depends on using things up as fast as we can. This is wasteful.	What we're throwing away can poison us.	There's nowhere to put all the stuff we're throwing away.
CONCLUSION: The way Americans get rid of trash creates big problems.		

E   Connect

Your purpose when reading an essay is not just to find the writer's message, but also to evaluate it and react to it.

Stay involved as you're reading. Relate the subject to your own life. Your during-reading reactions to the essay can help you decide how you feel. With which of Rooney's comments do you agree? Do you have any personal experiences with what he's talking about? By making a personal connection with an essay, you will remember it more and get in the habit of drawing upon what you already know.

Look how one reader reacted to part of Rooney's essay.

from "America the Not-so-Beautiful"

I have two pint bottles of insecticide with 5 percent DDT in them in my own garage that I don't know what to do with. I bought them years ago when I didn't realize how bad they were. Now I'm stuck with them.

We have stuff like this in our garage, too. There's a special pick-up once a year.

Nonfiction

After Reading

When you finish reading an essay, take a minute or two to reflect on what you understand—and what you don't.

F Pause and Reflect

After you've finished reading an essay, see if you can answer these questions:

Looking Back

- **What is the subject?**
- **What is the author saying about the subject?**
- **How do I feel about the author's message?**

In other words, did you meet your reading purpose?

G Reread

Your goal should be to restate the author's main point in your own words, to identify several points the author uses as support, and to have an opinion about what the author has said. If you're confused about how to outline or find that you don't follow what the author is saying, it's probably a good idea to return to the essay and do some rereading.

Rereading Strategy: Questioning the Author

Questioning the author is a terrific strategy to use when you're not 100 percent sure why you're having a hard time understanding something. If you're like most people, you're frustrated or embarrassed that part of a text is difficult to understand. You just want to skip over or forget about the hard parts.

Instead, take a deep breath. Zero in on what doesn't make sense. Think about the decisions the author made. Ask questions like these:

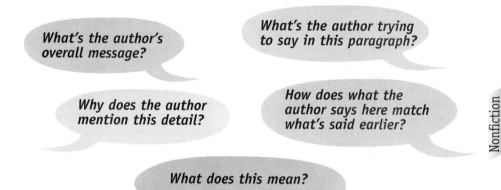

What's the author's overall message?

What's the author trying to say in this paragraph?

Why does the author mention this detail?

How does what the author says here match what's said earlier?

What does this mean?

Nonfiction

You can work on answering the questions however you want—writing in a journal, talking with friends, or making an organizer like the one below. Double-entry Journals help you focus your ideas about short passages you read. Notice how one reader used a Double-entry Journal to make sense of part of Rooney's second paragraph.

DOUBLE-ENTRY JOURNAL

WHAT WRITER SAYS	WHAT I THINK WHEN I READ
"Throwing things out is the American way. We don't know how to fix anything, and anyone who does know how is too busy to come, so we throw it away and buy a new one."	Why does he say people don't fix anything? Some people obviously do fix things—service people, mechanics, etc. That's just a fact. He must be exaggerating, probably trying to be funny. At the end when he mentions Mars, he's also trying to exaggerate.

H Remember

Questioning the author can be a useful rereading strategy, and it may be a way of helping you remember what you read. Here are a couple of things to try.

1. Write Questions and Answers

Write questions to the author and create answers to them. You might even set up your notes like an interview.

QUESTIONS AND ANSWERS

QUESTION: What's the point of your essay anyway?
ANSWER: I wanted to make people more aware of how much they throw away and how harmful all this trash can be.

2. Write a Summary

Another surefire way to remember "America the Not-so-Beautiful" is to summarize it. Put into your own words what the author has said and then explain how the writing made you feel.

Here's one way to summarize "America the Not-so-Beautiful."

SUMMARY

Andy Rooney's essay "America the Not-so-Beautiful" is really interesting. He talks all about trash and says that Americans make too much of it. He says this is a big problem for a number of reasons. First, he explains that our economy depends on people throwing things away. I think that means that a lot of businesses would fail if people started reusing things instead of buying new ones. He also says that we've run out of space to put all this trash. Plus, all this trash is poisoning the earth.

I think Andy Rooney made a lot of good points in his essay. He has some statistics and draws on his own personal experience. But I'm mad that he didn't give a real solution for the problem. I think if you complain about something, you should also come up with a way to make it better. Andy Rooney should have done this.

Summing Up

When you read an essay, remember to use the reading process and the reading strategy of **outlining**. It can help you see how the author supports the main idea. Being aware of **how an essay is organized** can also make it easier to figure out the author's message. Try using one of these tools:

- Outline
- Main Idea Organizer
- Double-entry Journal

Then, as you reread, the strategy of **questioning the author** can help you make sense of parts you didn't get the first time.

Reading a Biography

A **biography** is the story of a person's life, written by another person. The writer of a biography is called the *biographer*. The person the biographer is writing about is the *biographical subject*.

Biographies can be written about anyone, but most published biographies are about famous people. Good biographies make the readers feel that they know the subject inside and out. Here you'll read parts of a biography of Harriet Tubman.

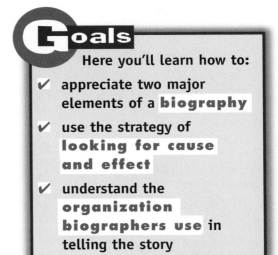

Goals

Here you'll learn how to:

✔ appreciate two major elements of a **biography**

✔ use the strategy of **looking for cause and effect**

✔ understand the **organization biographers use** in telling the story

Before Reading

Most biographers have *two* goals in mind when writing:

1. They want to tell an interesting story about the events of a person's life.

2. They want to create a portrait, or impression, of that person so that you can understand what he or she was really like.

Harriet Tubman

A Set a Purpose

Most of the time when you pick up a biography—for fun or for a school assignment—you're not reading to find one particular fact about the subject. Your curiosity is more general. When you read a biography, ask yourself two key questions:

Setting a Purpose

■ **What kind of life did this person have?**

■ **What was he or she really like?**

Make two questions like these your purpose for reading.

B Preview

Have you heard of the subject before? What do you already know about him or her? Even if the subject isn't completely new to you, spend a few minutes previewing. When you preview, pay attention to these items:

Nonfiction

Preview Checklist

✔ the title and author
✔ the front, back, and inside covers
✔ the table of contents or chapter titles
✔ any photographs or illustrations
✔ any dedication, preface, introduction, or note to the reader
✔ the first paragraph or two of the text
✔ any repeated words

Now preview the covers and table of contents of Ann Petry's biography, *Harriet Tubman: Conductor on the Underground Railroad*.

Harriet Tubman

CONDUCTOR ON THE UNDERGROUND RAILROAD

HARRIET TUBMAN

*Conductor on the
Underground Railroad*

by ANN PETRY

In the squalid slave quarters of a Tidewater plantation in Maryland, Harriet Tubman was born. She was a quiet girl, but a bright one, and her parents hoped that she might learn a trade so that she would not have to work in the fields. It was the most she could hope for, they said.

But Harriet had a dream for a better life for her people. She heard the whisperings of slave revolts, escapes from other plantations, the underground railroad. She acquired amazing physical strength and moral courage; she learned to recognize the signs in nature that would enable her to escape. And escape she did.

But freedom was not enough. After she escaped she went back for others. She walked, ran, hid, coaxed, cajoled, and prayed, until three hundred of her people had been delivered into freedom. She became the legendary "Moses" whom every plantation owner feared, and none had ever seen. But all her life she remained the tender, understanding Tidewater girl she was born.

Ann Petry brings all her controlled narrative skill to bear on the heroic story of a great woman. In vivid flowing style, she makes Harriet Tubman into a living figure and re-creates in vivid scenes an era of struggle, hardship, and unshakable faith.

"It is an amazing story, and Ann Petry has told it convincingly. Her technique of ending each chapter with one or two italicized paragraphs, highlighting some contemporary event in the conflict over slavery, serves to keep Harriet's story in focus with those unhappy times."—*New York Herald Tribune.*

Jacket by Ernest Crichlow

BY ANN PETRY

Contents

NOTE

Moves
from birth
to death

PREVIEW

Chapter
titles

1.   THE QUARTER I
2.   THE FIRST YEARS 12
3.   SIX YEARS OLD 21
4.   HIRED OUT 30
5.   FLIGHT 39
6.   THE UNDERGROUND ROAD 49
7.   "SHUCK THIS CORN" 59
8.   MINTA BECOMES HARRIET 70
9.   THE PATCHWORK QUILT 79
10. "A GLORY OVER EVERYTHING" 89
11. STRANGER IN A STRANGE LAND 102
12. FREEDOM'S CLOTHES 116
13. THE LEGEND OF MOSES 123
14. THE RAILROAD RUNS TO CANADA 131
15. "GO ON OR DIE" 139
16. "BE READY TO STEP ON BOARD" 149
17. "MOSES ARRIVES WITH SIX PASSENGERS" ... 157
18. A WAGON LOAD OF BRICKS 170
19. THE OLD FOLKS GO NORTH 184
20. THE LECTURE PLATFORM 201
21. WITH THE UNION ARMY 213
22. THE LAST YEARS 229
     INDEX 243

Nonfiction

Plan

What have you learned from your preview?

- ◼ Harriet Tubman was an African American.
- ◼ She was born a slave but escaped to freedom.
- ◼ She helped other slaves to freedom.

Maybe you picked up some other clues about Tubman's life and how the book is organized. The point is that now you have some useful background. With a purpose and a sense of what to expect, it's time to make a reading plan.

Since your purpose involves deciding what your subject was really like, you'll want to pay attention to what seem to be the most important events. Think about how those events shaped the biographical subject.

Reading Strategy: Looking for Cause and Effect

You probably know that the events of your life can shape who you are. That's true for everyone—you as well as the people you read about in biographies. Keep track of these "life-shaping" events on a Cause-Effect Organizer. Make notes on the Causes or Events side as you are reading. Fill in the Effect part when you've finished. Remember, you can use a Cause-Effect Organizer for a whole book, just one or two chapters, or important scenes.

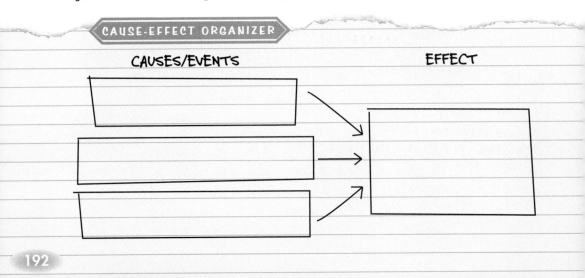

CAUSE-EFFECT ORGANIZER

CAUSES/EVENTS   EFFECT

During Reading

What should you be doing as you read a biography? Here are some questions that can keep you focused and on track:

- What are the important events in this person's life?
- How did these events shape his or her life?
- How would I describe this person?
- How do I feel about the person described?

D Read with a Purpose

Now read a part of Ann Petry's biography of Harriet Tubman. Take notes as you read. Track major events on the Cause-Effect Organizer you made before reading.

As you read, you'll be continuously creating, sharpening, and changing your impression of Harriet Tubman. What does each new event tell you about her?

Nonfiction

from *Harriet Tubman*

Harriet was back on the Brodas plantation, back in the slave quarter. Miss Susan brought her back and told the master that Minta wasn't "worth a sixpence."

Old Rit sniffed her contempt for Miss Susan when she saw Minta. The child was little better than skin and bones. She was as filthy as though she'd been living in a hog wallow, and her neck and back were covered with scars, old scars crisscrossed with fresh ones from the beating Miss Susan and her husband had given her because she ran away.

It was slow work, but Old Rit got the fresh scars healed up, and then when Harriet began to get a little flesh on her bones, Brodas hired her out again.

NOTE
Harriet is sent back.

NOTE
Harriet is in bad shape.

NOTE
She starts to work again.

NOTE

New event—
she goes to
work in the
fields.

In a way, Harriet had won a victory—though Rit did
not think so. Harriet worked in the fields from then on.
Brodas hired her out to a man who kept her out of doors.
She loaded wood on wagons, split rails, and knew more
about mules and hoes and plows than she did about the
interior of a house. Despite her strong sturdy body, she was
still a child. Yet she was often ordered to perform jobs that
would have taxed the strength of a full-grown, able-bodied
man. If she failed in any of these backbreaking jobs, she
was beaten.

Her appearance began to change. The solemn-eyed, shy
little girl, hesitant of speech, had disappeared. She was
replaced by a sullen-eyed creature, the lids hanging heavily
over the eyes. She had the calloused work-hardened hands
of a field slave.

NOTE

Hard work
causes
Harriet to
get stronger.

She no longer wore the tow-lined shirt, the one garment
worn by the children. She wore a long one-piece dress, tied
around the middle with a piece of rope. She looped the
skirts up when she was in the field. She was still
barefooted.

NOTE

She works
hard all
day.

She worked from dawn to dusk, working in the rain, in
the heat of the sun. Her muscles hardened. She sang when
she was in the fields or working in the nearby woods. Her
voice was unusual because of the faint huskiness. Once
having heard it, people remembered it. The low notes were
rich and deep. The high notes were sweet and true. Like the
other slaves, she made up the words and the melody of most
of the songs that she sang, never singing them exactly the
same way.

In 1831, Harriet started wearing a bandanna. It was
made from a piece of brilliantly colored cotton cloth. She
wound it around her head, deftly, smoothly, and then tied it
in place, pulling the knots tight and hard. This new
headgear was an indication that she was no longer regarded
as a child. These colorful bandannas were worn by young
women; they were a symbol of maturity.

NOTE

She's
becoming
a grown
woman.

from *Harriet Tubman*, continued

Though the life she led was cruelly hard, she was more nearly content than she had ever been before. She was working outdoors. She felt free in the fields. No matter how hard the job assigned to her, she could always pause for a moment in her work and watch the slow drift of clouds overhead, study the swift flight of the birds. Even in summer, when heat waves rose from the land, there was a fresh smell from the woods close by.

Sometimes this short, straight-backed young girl hummed under her breath, or sang, while she hoed the corn or tugged on the reins when a refractory mule refused to budge. True, work in the fields had calloused her hands, but it had given her a strong, erect body. She carried her head proudly as she sang.

That year, 1831, when Harriet regarded herself as sufficiently grown up to wear a bandanna, she kept hearing a strange, fascinating story, told and retold, in the quarter, in the fields. This same story about a slave named Tice Davids was being told in the Big House, too. But with a difference. The slaves told it with relish, the masters with distaste.

Tice Davids ran away from his master in Kentucky.

NOTE
Effect is she feels freer and content.

Nonfiction

NOTE
She's interested in story of Tice Davids.

What did you learn about Harriet Tubman from these pages? What is your impression of her? Look closely at the highlighting and the notes on the pages. If you get the sense that this was an important period in Tubman's life, you're right. Harriet's hard work in the fields caused a change in how she felt about herself.

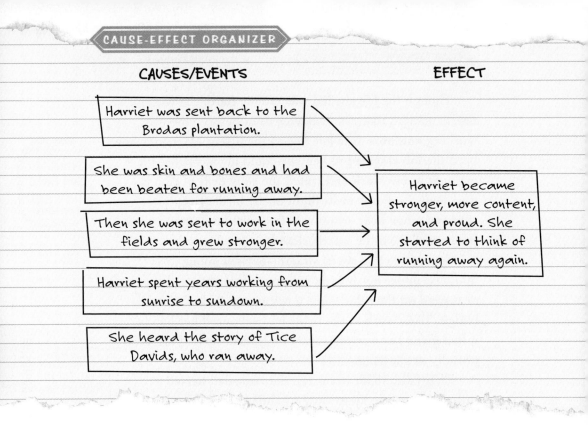

CAUSES/EVENTS

Harriet was sent back to the Brodas plantation.

She was skin and bones and had been beaten for running away.

Then she was sent to work in the fields and grew stronger.

Harriet spent years working from sunrise to sundown.

She heard the story of Tice Davids, who ran away.

EFFECT

Harriet became stronger, more content, and proud. She started to think of running away again.

How Biographies Are Organized

Most biographies begin with the birth and family history of the subject. That's what Ann Petry does with the story of Harriet Tubman. A biographer then follows the subject through his or her childhood, young adulthood, and adult years. The events tell the story of a person's life.

The chapters often make the **chronological** (or time) **order** of the subject's life clear. By describing the key periods of a person's life, the biographer hopes to create an interesting portrait and explain how the subject developed into the person he or she was.

1. Details about Time
2. Details about Place
3. Details about Key Events
4. Details about the Subject

adulthood

young
adulthood

school-age years

early years

completed portrait

Reader forms
impression of subject.

Nonfiction

As you read a biography, look for details about changes in the person's life. Sometimes the changes are in the place he or she lives or what job he or she has. Other times the changes are in the subject's feelings or values.

1. Details about Time

Look back at the excerpt. Notice the highlighting of these words and phrases:

- *from then on*
- *In 1831*
- *than she had ever been before*
- *That year, 1831*

Highlighting these words and phrases allows you to track the sequence of events in Tubman's life. These phrases tell what happened first, second, third, and so on.

2. Details about Place

In a biography, where the person lives usually has a strong effect on his or her life. (For example, think about how different Harriet Tubman's life would have been had she been born in a free state like New Hampshire, rather than in Maryland, a slave state.) Notice how these "place" words and phrases were highlighted:

- *on the Brodas plantation, back in the slave quarter*
- *in the fields*
- *in the Big House*

3. Details about Key Events

Making a list or even a simple Timeline can help you keep track of important events. Look again at the excerpt for some of the events the reader marked. Notice how the reader kept track of them with these notes:

TIMELINE

around 1826   1831

- Harriet is beaten for running away and returned home.
- She is hired out to work in the fields.
- She begins wearing a bandanna.
- She hears story of Tice Davids.

4. Details about the Subject

Besides paying attention to facts about important events, you should also look for details about what the person was like. That's part of the portrait. Here's the way one reader kept track of details about Harriet Tubman in a Character Map.

CHARACTER MAP

HOW SHE ACTS AND FEELS
- shy
- sings
- feels content outdoors and appreciates nature
- interested in story of Tice Davids

HOW OTHERS FEEL ABOUT HER
- Miss Susan thinks she's worthless.
- Old Rit cares about her and watches over her.
- Brodas and new master know she's strong and beat her if she doesn't work hard enough.
- She's no longer seen as a child.

HARRIET TUBMAN

HOW I FEEL ABOUT HER
I admire her. I could never do that kind of hard work every day without getting angry or giving up.

HOW SHE LOOKS AND TALKS
- is skinny and covered with scars
- gets stronger, more muscles
- has calloused hands
- wears long dress and bandanna
- has husky voice and sullen eyes

Nonfiction

E Connect

Whenever you read a biography, think about your impression of the person described. Ask yourself:

> **Do I like this person? Why or why not?**

> **Do I admire him or her? Why or why not?**

> **Would I want to be like this person?**

Almost all biographers will have a bias in their writing. They try to form a certain impression in their readers. They try to portray the person as likable or unlikable and hope that you agree. Your job as a reader is to figure out how you feel about the person being described and then decide whether or not you agree with the biographer.

One way to connect with a biography this way is to record your own thoughts as you read. Make predictions, comment on your reactions to what's happening, and connect events to your own experiences and ideas. Note the comments that one reader jotted on sticky notes about the following paragraph. It describes a time when Harriet is lying ill after having refused to follow her master's orders. As a reader, the parts you highlight or notes you take should relate to your reading purpose. They will help you get a good idea of what the subject was like and what kind of life he or she led.

from *Harriet Tubman*

That night, in the slave cabins in the quarter, they talked about Harriet. If she lived, she would be sold South; the overseer and the master would not keep an intractable, defiant slave, a slave who refused to help the overseer tie up a runaway, blocking the door like Harriet did. She would be sold. It was a dangerous thing that she had done. Dangerous, yes, but a brave thing, too. Why wasn't she afraid? What had made her so bold?

I admire her for taking such a big risk.

I predict she won't be sold. Maybe she'll escape.

After Reading

When you finish reading a biography, your job is not over. Take a moment or two to stop and think about what you've learned.

F Pause and Reflect

Go back to your reading purpose. Have you gotten the information you need? Ask yourself questions like these about what you learned:

Looking Back

- **What are several important events in the subject's life?**
- **How did these events affect the subject?**
- **What was the person really like?**
- **How do I feel about the subject?**
- **Can I support how I feel with evidence from the reading?**

Nonfiction

G Reread

If you find you can't answer all of your questions, then you probably need to do some rereading. Rereading can be quick and easy. Think of rereading as your chance to pick up on important details that you missed the first time around.

EVENTS
PERSONS
FEELINGS

Rereading Strategy: Outlining

Suppose you can recall the details of several events late in the subject's life, but you've forgotten the earlier periods. **Outlining** is a great strategy to use when you want to remind yourself of the "big picture" of the subject's life. Return to the text. Page through the book and outline the important events in the subject's life. Use the index to locate details. The outline form below on the left will work for almost any biography you read. (Of course, the number of details will vary.) On the right is the first part of a completed Topic Outline for *Harriet Tubman: Conductor on the Underground Railroad*.

TOPIC OUTLINE

Title or Subject
   I. Early Years
      A. *important event*
      B. *important event*
   II. School-age Years
      A. *important event*
      B. *important event*
   III. Young Adulthood
      A. *important event*
      B. *important event*
   IV. Adulthood
      A. *important event*
      B. *important event*

HARRIET TUBMAN
I. Early Years
   A. born a slave in Maryland in 1820
   B. sent to work as a maid at age six
   C. hated the work and was beaten severely
   D. sent back to the Brodas plantation
II. School-age Years
   A. worked from sunrise to sundown in the fields
   B. listened to other slaves talk and began to understand the injustice of slavery

H Remember

Many times, it's not important to remember a lot of the details in a biography. If you were reading for fun, you got caught up in the subject's life and enjoyed the reading experience. But other times—perhaps because of an assigned book report or a speech you need to do—you'll want to remember what you've read. Here are a couple of suggestions to try.

1. Write a Summary

In your reading journal or notebook, create a brief summary of the key events shaping the subject's life. For example, you would note that Harriet was born around 1820, but you might also want to note that she first heard about Tice Davids running away in 1831. That event seems to be one shaping force in her lifetime.

2. Make Study Cards

A more formal way of recording what you learned is through Study Cards. Use them to help you prepare for a reading quiz or to do some writing about the subject. If your teacher leaves it up to you to create a final product, think about putting together a 60-second talk about the biographical subject. Put notes on index cards and then refer to them as you give your talk.

> **STUDY CARD**
>
> Harriet Tubman: Early Years
> • born a slave in 1820: Dorchester County, Maryland
> • born on Brodas plantation
> • originally named Araminta Greene

Nonfiction

Summing Up

Now think of all you have learned about reading biographies. Remember that many biographies are **organized in chronological order** and trace key events in the person's life from birth throughout adult life. The reading strategy of **looking for cause and effect** can help you understand the subject's life. Use one of these tools to keep track of what you're learning:

- ■ Cause-Effect Organizer
- ■ Timeline
- ■ Character Map
- ■ Outline
- ■ Study Cards

The rereading strategy of **outlining** can help you to pick out and remember events that shaped the person in important ways.

Reading an Autobiography

An **autobiography** is a form of nonfiction in which a person tells the story of his or her life. The main difference between an autobiography and a biography is that an autobiography is written by the subject, not by someone else.

The person who writes the autobiography is called the *autobiographer*. Most autobiographers write with the purpose of reflecting on their own lives. They want to explain to readers what made them the way they are.

Autobiographies are as different as the people who write them. Here you'll read part of *Up from Slavery,* the autobiography of Booker T. Washington.

Goals

Here you'll learn how to:

✔ recognize the major elements of an **autobiography**

✔ use the reading strategy of **synthesizing,** or pulling together key topics

✔ understand the **organization of autobiographies**

Before Reading

Most autobiographers have these *two* goals in mind when writing:

1. They want to tell the story of their lives in an interesting or dramatic way.

2. They want to create a self-portrait that readers can relate to and perhaps admire.

To meet these goals, the autobiographer chooses which stories and details to include. Your job as reader is to view this self-portrait the writer has created and then decide how you feel about the autobiographer. To begin, follow the steps in the reading process. That's a good first step to becoming an active reader of autobiographies.

A Set a Purpose

As always, begin by setting your purpose. What do you want to find out? Most of the time, you'll be looking for answers to these two questions as you read:

Setting a Purpose

- **What kind of life did this person have?**
- **How do I feel about him or her?**

The questions sound simple, but answering them will require careful reading on your part. Make these two questions your purpose for reading.

B Preview

After you set your purpose, preview the autobiography. It shouldn't be hard to get a general idea of what an autobiography will be like. Look for the following items:

Preview Checklist

✔ the title and author
✔ the front, back, and inside covers
✔ any dedication, preface, introduction, or note to the reader
✔ any summaries or reviews
✔ the table of contents or any chapter titles
✔ any photographs or illustrations
✔ the first paragraph or two

Now preview the front and back covers of Booker T. Washington's autobiography, *Up from Slavery.*

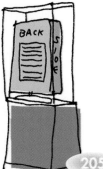

Nonfiction

PENGUIN CLASSICS

BOOKER T. WASHINGTON

UP FROM SLAVERY

PREVIEW

Author and title

PREVIEW

Photo of author

PENGUIN CLASSICS

BOOKER T. WASHINGTON

UP FROM SLAVERY

INTRODUCTION BY LOUIS R. HARLAN

PREVIEW

Brief summary

During his unchallenged reign as black America's foremost spokesman, former slave Booker T. Washington treaded a dangerous middle ground in a time of racial backlash and disfranchisement: as he publicly acquiesced to whites on issues of social equality, he fiercely exhorted blacks, through his national political machine, to unite and improve their lot.

Though Washington worked ceaselessly, through many channels, to gain moral and financial support for his people and for his beloved Tuskegee Institute, *Up from Slavery,* his autobiography, helped him at these endeavors more than all other efforts combined. Vividly recounting Washington's life—his childhood as a slave, his struggle for education, his founding and presidency of the Tuskegee Institute, his meetings with the country's leaders, *Up from Slavery* reveals the conviction he held that the black man's salvation lay in education, industriousness, and self-reliance. Louis R. Harlan's introduction fully assesses the impact of this simply written, anecdotal life story that bears the mark of a man of real courage, talent, and dedication.

PREVIEW

Key events in his life

The cover shows a photograph of Booker T. Washington taken in 1906. Frances Benjamin Johnston Collection, Library of Congress.

Autobiography

ISBN 0-14-039051-0

90000

U.K.   £7.99
CAN. $12.99
U.S.A. $9.95

9 780140 390513

Nonfiction

C Plan

What did you notice on your preview?

- Booker T. Washington was an African American.
- He was well educated and successful.
- He was born a slave but became famous because of his work at the Tuskegee Institute.

Did you learn anything else? Perhaps you have already heard of Booker T. Washington. You may even know a little about when he lived and what made him famous. A good preview will give you a head start on your reading.

When you've finished previewing, make a reading plan to help you meet your reading purpose.

Reading Strategy: Synthesizing

One excellent strategy for reading an autobiography is to synthesize, or pull together, a number of key topics. **Synthesizing** is like gathering up the pieces of a puzzle and figuring out how they fit together. This strategy gives you a full picture of the writer because these topics are likely to appear in almost every autobiography:

- childhood
- family
- school
- work
- major achievements
- major problems
- character traits

As you read, look for what the author says about them. Key Word or Topic Notes, like the ones on the next page, are an easy way to focus on these areas of a person's life. List the topics on the left-hand side of the page and leave yourself plenty of room to fill in details as you read.

KEY TOPICS	NOTES FROM READING
childhood	(Facts and details about the author's childhood go here.)
family	(Facts and details about the author's family go here.)
school	(Facts and details about the author's education go here.)
work	(Facts and details about the author's jobs go here.)
major achievements	(Facts and details about achievements go here.)
major problems	(Facts and details about big problems go here.)
character traits	(Facts and details about the author's personality go here.)

Nonfiction

If the autobiography is long or you need to remember a lot of the details, you might need to add other topics. (By the time you finish a longer reading, you may have a total of eight or nine key topics and several pages of notes!) Your notes will come from all different parts of the text, so leave lots of space to add more details as you go along. You'll have more notes for some of the key topics than you will have for others.

During Reading

Now it's time to begin reading the autobiography and put your plan to work.

D Read with a Purpose

Remember your reading purpose: to find out about the kind of life Washington had and to decide how you feel about him.

As you read, make notes in the margins of the book if you can. Or use separate paper or sticky notes. Focus on key topics and group together notes on important details from throughout the book.

Now read this excerpt from a chapter of *Up from Slavery*. Notice details about Washington's jobs and his feelings about school.

---

from *Up from Slavery*

ONE day, while at work in the coal-mine, I happened to overhear two miners talking about a great school for colored people somewhere in Virginia. This was the first time that I had ever heard anything about any kind of school or college that was more pretentious than the little colored school in our town.

NOTE
Works in mine

NOTE
Comparing two schools

In the darkness of the mine I noiselessly crept as close as I could to the two men who were talking. I heard one tell the other that not only was the school established for the members of my race, but that opportunities were provided by which poor but worthy students could work out all or a part of the cost of board, and at the same time be taught some trade or industry.

NOTE
Thinks Hampton sounds great

As they went on describing the school, it seemed to me that it must be the greatest place on earth, and not even Heaven presented more attractions for me at that time than did the Hampton Normal and Agricultural Institute in

from *Up from Slavery,* continued

Virginia, about which these men were talking. I resolved at once to go to that school, although I had no idea where it was, or how many miles away, or how I was going to reach it; I remembered only that I was on fire constantly with one ambition, and that was to go to Hampton. This thought was with me day and night.

NOTE
Determined to get an education

After hearing of the Hampton Institute, I continued to work for a few months longer in the coal-mine: While at work there, I heard of a vacant position in the household of General Lewis Ruffner, the owner of the salt furnace and coal-mine. Mrs. Viola Ruffner, the wife of General Ruffner, was a "Yankee" woman from Vermont. Mrs. Ruffner had a reputation all through the vicinity for being very strict with her servants, and especially with the boys who tried to serve her. Few of them had remained with her more than two or three weeks. They all left with the same excuse: she was too strict. I decided, however, that I would rather try Mrs. Ruffner's house than remain in the coal-mine, and so my mother applied to her for the vacant position. I was hired at a salary of $5 per month.

NOTE
Knows job will be hard

Nonfiction

I had heard so much about Mrs. Ruffner's severity that I was almost afraid to see her, and trembled when I went into her presence. I had not lived with her many weeks, however, before I began to understand her. I soon began to learn that, first of all, she wanted everything kept clean about her, that she wanted things done promptly and systematically, and that at the bottom of everything she wanted absolute honesty and frankness. Nothing must be slovenly or slipshod; every door, every fence, must be kept in repair.

NOTE
What he learns from Mrs. Ruffner

What did you learn about Booker T. Washington? You can arrange the information in Key Topic Notes.

KEY TOPICS	NOTES FROM READING
school	• school in his town not very good • hears about Hampton Institute in Virginia • thinks it sounds like heaven
work	• works in a coal mine • takes job with Mrs. Ruffner
character traits	• wants to get a good education • not afraid of a challenge

Sometimes you may want to concentrate on one or two of the common topics in an autobiography. Use a reading tool called a Character Trait Web to help you explore the writer's personality. Paying attention to character traits can sharpen your understanding of the author and help you get ready to write about the book.

CHARACTER TRAIT WEB

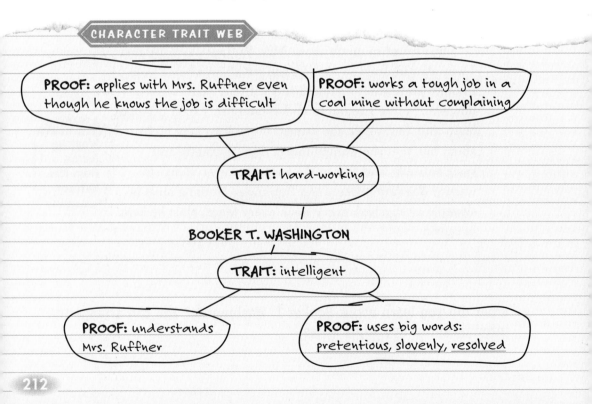

PROOF: applies with Mrs. Ruffner even though he knows the job is difficult

PROOF: works a tough job in a coal mine without complaining

TRAIT: hard-working

BOOKER T. WASHINGTON

TRAIT: intelligent

PROOF: understands Mrs. Ruffner

PROOF: uses big words: pretentious, slovenly, resolved

How Autobiographies Are Organized

Autobiographies are as individual as the people who write them. But most autobiographies share several common features.

▪ Autobiographies are usually written in the first person. Watch for pronouns such as *I, we,* and *our*.

▪ Autobiographies are somewhat biased or "slanted"; you hear only one person's point of view.

▪ As a reader, you need to decide how you feel about the writer and his or her self-portrait.

▪ Autobiographies are usually told in chronological, or time, order.

To keep track of what happens in an autobiography, create a Timeline in your reading notebook. Begin with the author's birth and note important milestones, or events, in his or her life.

Here is a Timeline one reader created for the events in the first part of *Up from Slavery.*

Nonfiction

TIMELINE

1858?	1865	1872	1876	1881
born a slave in Virginia	freed after Civil War, goes to West Virginia	started school at Hampton Institute	got first teaching job	went to Tuskegee

E Connect

Once you have a good sense of what the author is really like, decide how you feel about him or her. Remember that when you read an autobiography, you need to think about your *impression* of the person described. Do you like this person? Would you want to be *like* this person? Why or why not? As you read, jot down your reactions on sticky notes. Here is one reader's impression of Booker T. Washington.

> from *Up from Slavery*
>
> Mrs. Ruffner always encouraged and sympathized with me in all my efforts to get an education. It was while living with her that I began to get together my first library. I secured a dry-goods box, knocked out one side of it, put some shelves in it, and began putting into it every kind of book that I could get my hands upon, and called it my "library."

He's very creative.

This was a great way to keep his dream alive.

You might also collect your feelings about the author in an Inference Chart.

INFERENCE CHART

WHAT CHARACTER SAID OR DID	MY IMPRESSION OF HIM . . .
He worked hard jobs (like mining).	I really admire that he was willing to do anything possible to realize his dream.
He used long, formal words like resolved, secured, sympathized, and pretentious.	He sounds very educated.
He made a "library" out of a box.	He seems very creative and hopeful.

After Reading

After you've finished reading an autobiography, take a few moments to think about the kind of self-portrait the author created.

F Pause and Reflect

A few hours or the next day after you finish reading an autobiography, always stop and figure out what you've learned about the person. Ask yourself questions like these:

Looking Back

- **What are several important events in this person's life?**
- **What kind of life did this person have?**
- **How do I feel about him or her?**

Two things are important. First, you want to be able to talk or write about those questions. Second, you should be able to draw on specific events in the writer's life to support your views.

G Reread

If you find it hard to answer these questions, or you have a hard time finding evidence from the text to support your feelings, it's a good idea to return to the text for a little rereading. Concentrate on parts that you can't remember much about or that confused you the first time around.

Nonfiction

For example, suppose after reading *Up from Slavery* you're still not sure about what gave Washington the drive to accomplish all that he did. Look over the notes you took about the key topics, such as *family*, *school*, or *jobs*. Use what you wrote to jog your memory about important events and concentrate on **looking for cause and effect**. Think about how Washington reacted to events. How did particular ones shape his personality?

Often, rereading begins with a question. Let's say your question after reading the whole book is: What caused Washington to create the Tuskegee Institute in Alabama?

Find the pages that have to do with that part of Washington's life. Look for pages that mention Tuskegee and reread them. After just a little rereading, you'd discover that Booker T. Washington created Tuskegee Normal and Agricultural Institute with the desire that it would give African Americans the education and skills they would need to compete in the world after the Civil War.

Here's how one reader used a Cause-Effect Organizer to keep track of what motivated Booker T. Washington.

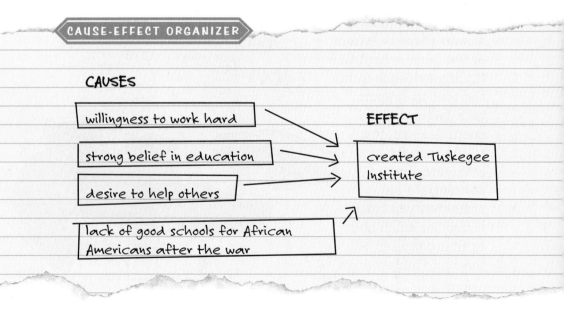

CAUSE-EFFECT ORGANIZER

CAUSES

willingness to work hard

strong belief in education

desire to help others

lack of good schools for African Americans after the war

EFFECT

created Tuskegee Institute

H Remember

When you're reading an autobiography for fun, you don't need to worry about remembering specific details. But, if you need to remember what you read, here are two easy activities to help you.

1. Write a Summary

Use the book's chapter titles and your notes to write a summary of the writer's life. Put important details in your notebook or reading log. Go through the key topics of the writer's life in chronological order and end with a sentence about how the events shaped him or her.

2. Write a Book Review

You can also try writing a review of the autobiography. Look at book reviews in magazines or newspapers to get an idea of how they're organized. In this type of writing, your opinion of the author and his or her work will be very important. Here's the beginning of one review of *Up from Slavery*:

Nonfiction

BOOK REVIEW

Booker T. Washington's autobiography, Up from Slavery, tells the amazing story of how he went from being a slave to starting a college. The book is not easy reading. Washington uses a lot of big words that can make following what's going on difficult.

Summing Up

When you read an autobiography, follow the reading process and use the reading strategy of **synthesizing**, or pulling together, key topics. Choose from a number of tools that can help you get a sense of the author's life:

■ Key Topic Notes   ■ Inference Chart
■ Character Trait Web ■ Cause-Effect Organizer
■ Timeline

Remember, too, that focusing on **chronological order** and **looking for cause and effect** when you reread can be very useful.

Reading a Newspaper Article

If you're like most people, you want to know what's happening in the world—whether it's news about an earthquake in another country or the outcome of a local baseball game. One way you can find out what's happening around the world and in your community is by reading a newspaper.

Here you'll read a newspaper article about robots. Take what you learn here and use it when you read other newspaper articles.

Goals

Here you'll learn how to:

✔ appreciate what's in **newspaper articles**

✔ use the strategy of **reading critically**

✔ understand the **organization of many news stories**

Before Reading

The reading process is helpful even for light reading like reading the newspaper. It helps you evaluate information and form your own opinions about what you read.

A Set a Purpose

No one reads every single article in a newspaper. Instead, you scan the headlines and choose the articles you want to read, based mainly on your interests and curiosity. The headlines will usually tip you off to the subject of the article. Sometimes you read a newspaper article for fun. Other times, you read because you need particular information for a school project or assignment.

Once you decide to read a particular article, your general purpose is to find out what the article has to say about its subject. One way to set your purpose is to take several words from the headline and use them to form a question.

For example, take the headline "Robots get ready to rumble." One possible question could be the following:

Setting a Purpose

■ **What do robots do when they rumble, and what's the point of it?**

What do you think of that question? Would you have come up with something else? That's OK. Lots of different purpose questions would work. Plus, once you know what a newspaper article is about, your purpose in reading may change. Challenge yourself to go beyond the obvious. Ask yourself a good, meaningful question, and you will find yourself getting more from your reading.

Nonfiction

B Preview

Newspaper articles are easy to preview because they're written for readers who are in a hurry. As you glance through an article, look for these items:

Preview Checklist

✔ the headline and author
✔ any words that are repeated or in bold or larger type
✔ the opening paragraphs (the lead)
✔ any photographs and captions
✔ any maps, diagrams, charts, or other graphics

A news article usually has something called the **lead**. Its purpose is to grab the reader's attention. It also answers the most important questions, called the 5 W's. Create a 5 W's Organizer to keep track of information in the lead.

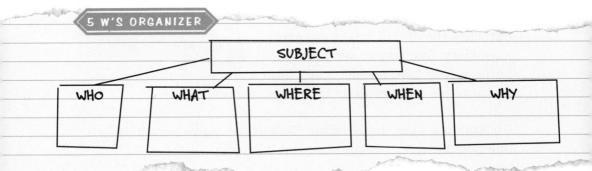

5 W'S ORGANIZER

SUBJECT

WHO | WHAT | WHERE | WHEN | WHY

Now preview the beginning of the article "Robots get ready to rumble." See how many of the 5 W's you can answer.

PREVIEW
Photo

PREVIEW
Opening paragraphs

PREVIEW
Headline and author

Nonfiction

Robots get ready to rumble

David Colker
Los Angeles Times

In my hands are the controls to a 210-pound killer robot named Biohazard.

The crowd yells—some for me, but mostly for my robotic minion. A huge video screen follows every move of my robot's grudge match against opponent Ginsu. Rotary saws pop up from the arena floor. Huge hammers smash down with so much force that they shake the room.

And the crowd gets louder.

I am not worthy.

I am a guest controller in an exhibition round of "BattleBots," the highly successful cable television show that pits radio-controlled robots against each other in three-minute duels. Object: Inflict as much damage as possible by slamming opponents against metal spikes, hacking them with buzz saws, or flipping them over like motorized turtles. It's R2-D2 as gladiator.

Normally, this is not my scene. But there is something about "BattleBots"—with its garage tinkerer ethic and bumper car sensibility—that is irresistibly American and even a bit nostalgic. The garage inventor is an icon epitomized by Henry Ford creating an automobile or Orville and Wilbur Wright building an airplane. "BattleBots" provides a brutally Darwinistic arena in which inventors can prove the worth of their creations.

On hand at this special exhibition are eight robots that have appeared on the Comedy Central show, all looking more menacing than they do on TV. They are not walking robots like in 1950s science fiction films, but low-to-the-ground, compact machines capable of astonishing speed, agility and malice.

PREVIEW
Repeated words

221

C Plan

What did you learn from your preview? From just this brief sample of the article, look at how much you have learned.

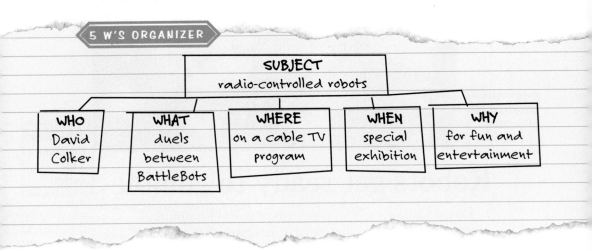

5 W'S ORGANIZER

SUBJECT
radio-controlled robots

WHO	**WHAT**	**WHERE**	**WHEN**	**WHY**
David Colker	duels between BattleBots	on a cable TV program	special exhibition	for fun and entertainment

If you can find out this much in just a few minutes, why do you need a plan for reading a newspaper article? Why should you do anything else? Actually, good readers *do* have a plan, or strategy, in mind when they read a newspaper article. Most of them are just not aware of it.

Reading Strategy: Reading Critically

Often without even thinking about it, active readers adopt the strategy of **reading critically** when they read newspaper articles. What exactly does critical reading mean? It means going beyond the facts to see what point the writer is making. It means evaluating evidence and deciding if it is convincing. Finally, critical reading means recognizing that important information may be left out.

For short articles, you can probably keep your ideas in your head. But for longer articles, set up a chart like the one that follows. It can help you sort out and evaluate the evidence.

CRITICAL READING CHART

QUESTIONS	MY THOUGHTS
1. Is the main idea or viewpoint clear?	(Look for the author's central point or opinion on a topic.)
2. What evidence is presented?	(Evidence can include facts and statistics, quotations from experts, statements by eyewitnesses, and personal experiences.)
3. Are the sources authoritative and reliable?	(An authoritative source is one with a great deal of experience or expertise. A reliable source is one that is not biased.)
4. Is the evidence convincing?	(Evaluate how much evidence is presented.)
5. Is there another side of the story?	(Often a newspaper article only gives one side of a story. You may need to identify a possible opposing viewpoint.)

Nonfiction

A chart like this helps you sort out facts and opinions and reminds you to question what you read. Critical readers look at all angles of a story and evaluate what to believe.

During Reading

The first few steps in the reading process for newspaper articles took you only several minutes. Now it's time to read the entire article.

ROBOTS UNFAIRLY PRESENTED IN MEDIA

Read with a Purpose

As you begin reading the rest of the feature article on the BattleBots, think about your purpose in reading:

> **What do robots do when they rumble, and what's the point of it?**

Pay attention to the sorts of facts and opinions the author gives you. You may want to jot down your thoughts about the evidence on a Critical Reading Chart.

"Robots get ready to rumble," continued

Overkill sports a mean-looking saw blade. Tazbot looks like a giant metallic insect with a pick ax. Diesector has two axes. Ginsu uses rotary blades for wheels. Toe Crusher does damage with a hammerlike spike. Minion carries a firefighter's emergency saw. The flying saucerlike Ziggo has spinning steel blades. The impervious-looking BioHazard inflicts robot pain with its sheer power and lifting arm.

> **NOTE**
> Author's opinions

Unlike the robots, the creators of the machines on hand for the event are soft-spoken, thoughtful and even shy. "I get all my aggression out during the matches," says Christian Carlberg, father of Minion, Overkill and Toe Crusher.

> **NOTE**
> Quotation from expert

Not surprisingly, Carlberg, 30, of Santa Monica, Calif., works in a field that requires hands-on electronic and engineering capability. He's a Walt Disney Co. "imagineer" who designs attractions for a new theme park in Tokyo.

> **NOTE**
> Fact

All the BattleBot-makers design and build their creations piece by piece in garages, rented spaces or, when a sympathetic supervisor looks the other way, at work. None are in it for the money. The machines cost $1,000 to $70,000 to build, according to "BattleBots" production coordinator Erica Smentowski. The top prize in last November's competition in Las Vegas: $6,000.

> **NOTE**
> Expert source

Most robotmakers showed an aptitude for building machines at an early age. On the BattleBots Web site (www.battlebots.com), Donald Hutson—creator of Diesector and Tazbot—lists his influences as: "My mom and Legos." His day job in San Diego is customizing and repairing home medical equipment.

Each killer bot is a unique creation. Carlberg's Web site (www.coolrobots.com) goes into detail on how each of his machines was developed, giving beginners a template from which to work. His highly shielded Minion has lost only one regulation match. "It climbed up a wall and got stuck there," he says during the competition, shaking his head. "Embarrassing but true."

And all part of the game. For the children who grew up on Lego and building things in shop, destruction is the soulmate of creation. And the crowds love it.

As tuxedoed ring announcer Mark Beiro makes preliminary comments in championship prize fight-style, drawing out names like "Diiiiiiiiiiiiiiiesector!" some of the bot creators gather around to offer hints. "It's not like being in a car when you are driving," says Carlberg. "It's out there, and you are here. You can't feel what it's doing."

Carlo Bertocchini, the creator of BioHazard, goes over the remote control unit I'll be using. It's fairly straightforward—a small joystick on the right side controlled by the thumb sets the direction and speed of the bot.

"When the robot is speeding away from you, you move the stick as you see it. But when it is coming toward you, you have to think in reverse—pushing the stick to the right is going to turn it left," he says. "I try to imagine myself actually on the bot."

He also advises keeping the lifting of BioHazard up at all times unless it's maneuvered under an opponent. Otherwise it could snag on something.

NOTE
Facts

NOTE
Opinions

Nonfiction

NOTE
Quotation from expert

NOTE
Personal experience

Isn't he afraid that someone who is not an expert in driving a bot will inadvertently do it damage?

"No offense," he says with a friendly smile, "but an amateur driver is not going to get up the speed to really get in trouble."

In the first match of the evening, Carlberg's Toe Crusher is pitted against Jonathan Ridder's Ziggo. Although this is an exhibition, the two go at each other fiercely, with Ziggo almost flying across the floor and using its whirling blades to inflict early harm. Carlberg, who remains so calm he could almost be described as serene, strikes back with Toe Crusher's metal scoop and hammering spike.

NOTE
Opinion

When it's all over, no winner is declared but both vehicles have suffered, especially Toe Crusher. The scoop has been entirely sawed off, the tires are slashed and there are dents all over.

Carlberg is unfazed, saying he allowed some of the damage to happen to make a better show of the match. Carlberg says fixing Toe Crusher with the parts they would normally have on hand would take only about half an hour. "That's not Toe Crusher," he says, pointing to the damaged machine.

Then he points to his head.

"Toe Crusher is up here."

A few matches later, the air thick with smoke caused by metal scraping against metal, it's my turn. I'll be facing Ginsu, driven by Howard Shiffman, president of Chicago's Tiger Electronics, which organized the special match to promote its coming line of BattleBot toys.

NOTE
Expert source

Bertocchini stands at my side, giving last-minute hints. I tentatively press the right stick and BioHazard—made of titanium, magnesium, aluminum and steel—instantly responds, spinning left then right as lithely as a ballet dancer.

NOTE
Personal experience

I speed BioHazard forward, hungry for a bot clash. But controlling the bot, especially under the influence of a huge

"Robots get ready to rumble," continued

adrenaline rush, is not so easy, and I miss Ginsu by a couple of feet. Ginsu rides up over me and digs in its blades, inflicting some dents.

I'm in trouble if I don't get control—and fast, since this is only a one-minute bout. But then Ginsu gets overanxious, hanging up on the spikes as it rears back for an attack. After a couple of tries, I finally hit it head on, BioHazard's sharpened edges under Ginsu.

No mercy. Under Bertocchini's tutelage, I use the lift arm to hoist Ginsu into the air to the cheers of the audience. He drops down and again rides over me, but suddenly the match—which seems to have taken 10 minutes instead of one—is over.

Bertocchini congratulates me, and his wife, Carol, runs over to declare, "You got him, you got him!" Other bot creators kindly agree that I would have won the match if a judge had rendered a decision. No matter, my adrenaline is pumping as the crowd clears.

BioHazard is still in the arena. Bertocchini lets some kids from the audience try driving it a bit. Noah Posnick, 15, is among them with his proud dad looking on.

Noah is concentrating with almost painful intensity as he puts BioHazard through its moves. "That was an amazing experience," he says with reverence, turning back to join his father.

My 15-year-old within knows exactly what he means. Had there been an awards ceremony, I would have wished my father could have been there to see me.

Nonfiction

NOTE
Eyewitness

NOTE
Opinion

If you're just reading the article for fun, you probably don't need to write anything down. But what if you're reading the article as part of a class assignment? Or maybe you're planning on using it in a research project on high-tech toys. Sometimes it's a good idea to fill out a Critical Reading Chart.

QUESTIONS	MY THOUGHTS
1. Is the main idea or viewpoint clear?	Yes—Colker thinks the fights are fun.
2. What evidence is presented?	Colker uses facts, expert sources, eyewitness accounts, and personal experience.
3. Are the sources authoritative and reliable?	Yes, he talks with Christian Carlberg and other makers of BattleBots.
4. Is the evidence convincing?	By taking part in a duel, Colker got a firsthand look at BattleBots and what it's like to run them. He also draws on many other people's experiences.
5. Is there another side of the story?	The match was held to help promote a line of toys. The article doesn't really look critically at the violence issue. The question is, "Is watching these violent battles really a good idea, especially for kids?"

What do you think of the article? Would you have answered the questions any differently? Even if you don't take the time to set up a chart like this, you need to consider whether the evidence a writer provides is reliable and persuasive.

JURY

How Newspaper Articles Are Organized

Finding the facts and opinions in a newspaper article is easier if you understand how information is often organized. Many news stories follow a standard organization called the *inverted pyramid*. In this method of organization, the lead is followed by details presented in order of importance, from most to least important. The lead and the details focus on answering the basic journalistic questions—the 5 W's (*who, what, where, when,* and *why*).

INVERTED PYRAMID

Lead

Most important details

Less important details

Least important details

Nonfiction

"Robots get ready to rumble" follows this inverted pyramid structure, but only in a general way. Look back at the beginning of the article on page 221. The article starts by trying to grab the reader's attention. The first several short paragraphs set up an exciting scene. The lead begins with this paragraph:

from "Robots get ready to rumble"

Lead

    I am a guest controller in an exhibition round of "BattleBots," the highly successful cable television show that pits radio-controlled robots against each other in three-minute duels. Object: Inflict as much damage as possible by slamming opponents against metal spikes, hacking them with buzz saws, or flipping them over like motorized turtles. It's R2-D2 as gladiator.

**Who?
What?
Where?
When?
Why?**

This *buried lead* gives a lot of information about *who, what, where, when,* and *why*. The writer goes on to describe some of the BattleBots, their creators, and their duels.

E Connect

Connecting with the news you read will make the information more meaningful and memorable for you. Let the writing spark your own thoughts, questions, and reactions.

Notice how one reader marked up the news article on the battling robots. The "other side" of this article is never really told.

> **from "Robots get ready to rumble"**
>
> In the first match of the evening, Carlberg's Toe Crusher is pitted against Jonathan Ridder's Ziggo. Although this is an exhibition, the two go at each other fiercely, with Ziggo almost flying across the floor and using its whirling blades to inflict early harm. Carlberg, who remains so calm he could almost be described as serene, strikes back with Toe Crusher's metal scoop and hammering spike.

This sounds very violent.

Is violent entertainment a good idea?

By making connections like these, you can ask yourself other questions that the newspaper article may not have answered. Good writers try to present different sides of a story. But, all too often, the need to entertain readers outweighs everything else. When you read the newspaper, take the time to ask questions about what you read, especially whether what you're reading is the *whole* story.

I think this is going to be too violent for you.

After Reading

Readers usually go through a newspaper quickly. Often they're eating breakfast, riding in a car or bus, or watching TV. If they have to find particular facts in an article, they do it fast. They don't take much time to reflect on what they've read. But, if you want to remember what you've read and use the information later, you'll need to take some time.

F Pause and Reflect

After you've read a newspaper article, take a few moments to look back. Have you met your reading purpose? Ask yourself a couple of questions:

Looking Back

- Can I state the author's main idea or viewpoint in my own words?
- Do I understand how the article is organized?
- Can I answer the *who, what, where, when,* and *why* questions?
- Have I examined the author's evidence and judged how reliable it is?

G Reread

Sometimes one quick trip through a news article is all you'll need. But other times you may need to reread parts of an article to understand what's being said or to examine the evidence more closely. Check definitions of words you don't know, scan photographs and graphics, and identify key facts and opinions. One good way to check that you've understood an article's viewpoint is to restate key ideas in your own words.

Nonfiction

Summarizing

As you reread, try **summarizing** the parts of the article that give important opinions. First, list the subject of the article and what the writer says about it. Then create a list of four or five of the important details. Your summary shouldn't be long. Find the information that answers the 5 W's and think about the overall message the author is trying to express.

SUMMARY NOTES

SUBJECT: robots that fight
AUTHOR'S VIEWPOINT: It's fun to watch robots battle.
1. "BattleBots," cable television show
2. unique names like Overkill or Diesector
3. cost from $1,000 to $70,000
4. robots with saws, hammers, and axes on them trying to
   destroy the other robots
5. popular—matches, toys, websites

A few quick notes are all you need to make. They will give you the details you need to write a summary.

H Remember

Here are two simple things you can do to help you remember the newspaper articles you read.

1. Talk about the Article

One way people often remember news stories is by mentioning them in conversations. If you listen to the conversations people have, you'll hear them talk about what they are reading. Newspaper articles are the stuff of conversations.

2. Write a Summary

After making notes like the ones on page 232, jot down a summary of an article in your journal. Create a 30-second summary that you can read to someone else. Below is a summary of "Robots get ready to rumble."

SUMMARY

"Robots get ready to rumble" is written by David Colker. It's about Colker's experiences watching and participating in an exhibition of battling radio-controlled robots. Colker describes the robots and the matches in a lot of detail. He thinks they're a lot of fun, but they seem kind of violent to me.

Nonfiction

Summing Up

When you read a newspaper article, use the strategy of **reading critically**. It can help you look at all sides of an article. Looking for the **lead** and an **inverted pyramid organization** will help you pick out important details. Keep track of the information and your ideas by using one of these tools:

- 5 W's Organizer
- Critical Reading Chart
- Summary Notes

Use the strategy of **summarizing** when you reread.

Reading a Magazine Article

What interests do you have? Do you like to read about computers, sports, or music? Whatever subject interests you, you're likely to find a magazine article on it.

Here you'll apply the reading process to an article about sharks that's called "A Killer Gets Some Respect."

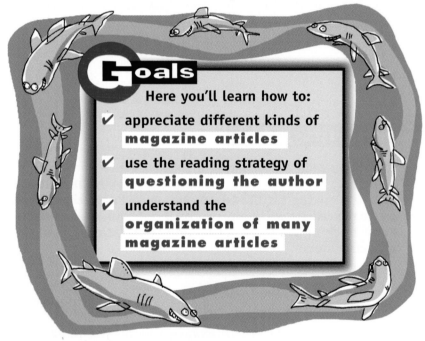

Goals

Here you'll learn how to:

✔ appreciate different kinds of **magazine articles**

✔ use the reading strategy of **questioning the author**

✔ understand the **organization of many magazine articles**

Before Reading

Much of the time you read magazine articles simply for fun and enjoyment. You quickly glance at the title and photographs to see if the subject interests you. If it does, then you just read at your own pace for as long as the article holds your attention. For "fun" reading, the reading process is short and sweet.

At other times, you read magazine articles not just to enjoy them but also to learn from them. Then you'll need to read more slowly and carefully.

A Set a Purpose

It's easy to establish a general purpose for reading. Just ask yourself, "What do I hope to learn from this article?" With magazine articles, most of the time you read to find out about a topic. Use key words in the title to form reading purpose questions:

Setting a Purpose

- **What do I need to know about sharks?**
- **Are sharks really killers?**

B Preview

Previewing is a way of preparing your mind for the information you're about to read. Through previewing, you get an idea of the subject, and you start remembering what you already know about it. Look for these items when you preview a magazine article:

Preview Checklist

✔ the title and author
✔ any photographs, illustrations, and captions
✔ any headings or any large type
✔ the first paragraph
✔ the general length or number of pages

Now preview "A Killer Gets Some Respect" on pages 236–239.

Nonfiction

CLOSE ENCOUNTERS

LOUISE SOURISSEAU was snorkeling with her friend Martha Morrell on the Hawaiian island of Maui when Sourisseau felt the rough skin of a tiger shark dragging across her calf. Sourisseau watched in horror as the 10-foot-long shark swam past her and repeatedly attacked her friend, biting off both her legs and an arm. Morrell, the 42-year-old wife of a plantation owner, died instantly on that November day in 1991.

Less than a year later, 18-year-old Aaron Romento was body surfing on Oahu when a tiger shark appeared and bit him in three places on the right leg. Surfers nearby pulled him ashore but the bites had severed Romento's femoral artery, and he bled to death before they could get him to a hospital.

These two fatalities, coupled with six other confirmed shark attacks in Hawaii from 1991 to 1992, triggered a media frenzy. Shark sightings were front-page news in Hawaiian newspapers, along with photos of shark hunters hoisting catches as vengeance for the human deaths. A bill was introduced in the Hawaiian legislature to initiate a $200,000 program to send more hunters after the animals.

The initial response to the Hawaiian shark attacks was much the same as in the late 1950s, when tiger sharks killed a surfer. Back then the state launched a $300,000 program to get even, and nearly 4,700 sharks of several species died as a result. But many things had changed in the intervening three decades, causing legislators to pause this time. One change was a new awareness of and respect for Native Hawaiian beliefs, which viewed certain tiger sharks as sacred *aumakua*, or guardian spirits. There was also a new ecological consciousness that included respect for the ocean and its wild denizens. And there was a dawning awareness of the plight of sharks, millions of which die in commercial fisheries each year for each human that is reported killed by a shark.

Another key to the bill's eventual defeat was the role of wildlife biologists, in particular 51-year-old Kim Holland, an associate

A KILLER GETS SOME RESPECT

STEPHEN M. KAJIURA

In Hawaii, scientists are helping to dispel some long-standing myths about tiger sharks

By Michael Tennesen

SHARK STATS: Although tiger sharks appear menacing (right), public fears about the fish are unwarranted. The odds of being attacked by a shark in Hawaiian waters are about one in five million. When a rare attack does occur, killing sharks nearby will have little impact, says biologist Kim Holland (above, examining a captured shark.)

researcher at the Hawaii Institute of Marine Biology. Holland pointed out that the basic biology of tiger sharks was not well understood a decade ago. "We didn't know if shark control would do any good," says Holland, a native of England who moved to Hawaii. "The scientific community could not give sound answers as to whether or not a limited, focused fishing effort could in fact have any chance of catching the shark or sharks that did the dirty deed."

Holland and a group of graduate students, including Brad Wetherbee and Chris Lowe from the University of Hawaii, decided to look into this question shortly after the attacks in the early 1990s. The answers they found have helped to dispel some long-standing myths about tiger sharks and are leading to a less hostile attitude toward the fish in Hawaii and elsewhere.

Tiger sharks (so-called because they are striped, a feature most prevalent in juveniles) are found all over the world in tropical and temperate waters. On the Atlantic coast, the species ranges from Massachusetts in the north to Uruguay in the south. On the Pacific coast, it is found from Southern California to Peru. The creature is one of about 400 species of sharks worldwide, ranging from the deepwater 10-inch-long dwarf shark to the 40-foot-long whale shark. Several of these species are capable of biting a human, but great white sharks, bull sharks and tiger sharks are responsible for 99 percent of attacks, according to the International Shark Attack File.

Holland feels the public fear of sharks is unwarranted, however. There were 26 shark attacks from 1990 to 1997 in Hawaii with 3 fatalities, compared to 40 fatal drownings each year in Hawaiian waters. With 20 million people entering Hawaiian waters each year, the odds of being attacked by a shark are about one in five million. What's more, only about one-fifth of those attacked by sharks worldwide are killed. Apparently sharks do not like the taste of human flesh. "Tiger sharks are efficient hunters," says Holland. "If sharks liked human flesh, we'd see a lot more fatalities."

To get more information about tiger sharks, especially their movements and

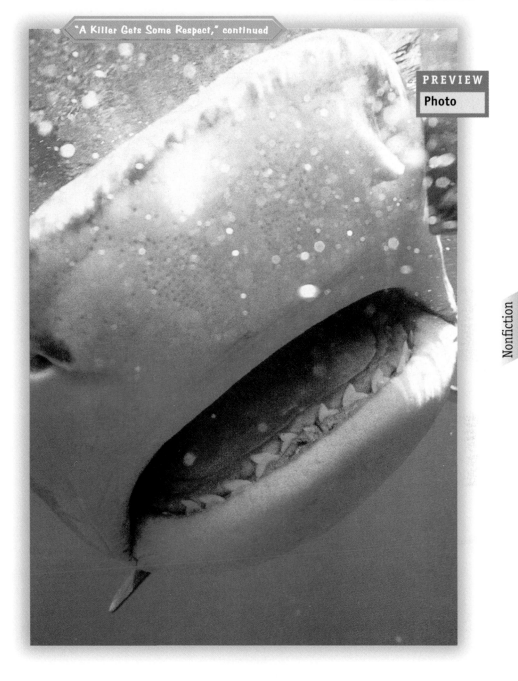

"A Killer Gets Some Respect," continued

Nonfiction

home ranges, Holland and his fellow researchers needed to get transmitters on some of the fish. So they started setting fishing lines for sharks offshore near Honolulu International Airport. Thirty-yard leaders baited with fish heads were attached to a main line about 400 yards long. Tiger sharks hooked on these leaders could keep swimming—vital to the creatures since they must move to breathe. The baited lines brought in an average of one tiger shark a night.

To tag the animals, the biologists used an 18-foot Boston whaler that was not much bigger than some of the sharks they captured (which ranged from 7 to 14 feet in length). Hooked sharks were brought alongside the whaler, restrained with ropes and then flipped over. Once turned over, the tiger shark would go into a trancelike condition called tonic immobility. This allowed the biologists to surgically implant a transmitter without using an anesthetic. When completed, the hook was removed and the shark released.

The biologists noted that female tiger sharks had many scars on their backs. These wounds are usually a side-effect of mating, when males restrain females by biting them on the back and fins. Both male and female sharks have thick hides, however; one researcher describes the skin of a tiger shark as being 6 to 10 times the tensile strength of ox hide.

Sharks are equipped with several rows of teeth that when lost are replaced rapidly. (Some species of sharks may lose as many as 30,000 teeth during their lives.) Behind those teeth are powerful jaws armed with elastic muscles, which enable the fish to distend its mouth and swallow huge pieces of food. In Australia, one 11-foot tiger shark was found with an entire horse's head, intact, inside its stomach.

Although horses' heads are not a staple of the tiger shark's diet, the creatures do have wide-ranging tastes. Smaller sharks eat mostly fish, along with birds, but as tiger sharks grow larger their diet switches to dolphins, other sharks and rays. Tiger sharks also go after seemingly inedible prey such as puffer fish, stingrays, triggerfish and sea snakes. Researchers aren't sure

"Tiger sharks are efficient hunters. If sharks liked human flesh, we'd see a lot more fatalities."

how the sharks survive the barbs, bites and stings of these prickly prey.

Tiger sharks have a variety of sensors for locating prey. Like other sharks, they have a line of vibration detectors located along their sides that enable them to pick up the pressure waves of a moving animal. The sharks also use special organs below the skin of their snouts that allow them to detect faint electrical fields generated by living creatures. Sometimes the sharks pick up the electrical fields generated by motors and mistake them for prey, however. Bill Gilmartin, a federal government biologist who studied Hawaiian monk seals, reported a 12-foot tiger shark that burst out of the water behind his boat and engulfed the propeller with its jaws, lifting the entire craft.

Holland's crew got used to tiger sharks banging up against its boat. The researchers tagged some 200 sharks and fitted 40 with transmitters that could be tracked by boats or listening devices set on the ocean floor. What the transmitters revealed was that tiger

Moana Park?" asked Jim Cook, chairman of the Western Pacific Fishery Management Council.

Surprisingly, another reason for the defeat of the legislation was a call for moderation from shark bite survivors. Honolulu author Greg Ambrose interviewed 10 victims of tiger shark attacks for his book *Shark Bites* and was amazed at the epiphany each had. "In every case the tiger shark actually had their teeth upon them and was biting into their flesh, but let them go," wrote Ambrose. "The lesson they learned was that the shark didn't want the people, that their mighty fear of sharks had been totally unfounded. In most cases they've become eloquent spokespersons for sharks."

One of those victims was Jonathan Mozo, a photographer who lives on Oahu. On the morning of June 10, 1993, he was surfing at Goats, a spot on the north shore. Suddenly he felt a piercing pain and crushing pressure on his lower legs. He looked back and saw his feet and his board in the mouth of a tiger shark. As he watched, the animal opened its mouth and swam forward for a bigger bite. Mozo screamed, yanked his feet out of the creature's mouth and paddled shore as fast as he could. His friends put tourniquets around his ankles to keep him from bleeding to death, as surfer Aaron Romento had done a few months earlier. It took more than 100 stitches to sew Mozo back up, but he was surfing again only two months later.

Mozo expresses the feelings of many Hawaiians who have now come to accept the tiger shark as part of the marine environment. "I have no feelings of hatred against the shark," he says. "I don't want revenge. I don't think they should be eliminated. We are not the masters of sea. If it were our territory we'd have been born with gills and fins. I was out there a guest in his world. I just feel lucky he let me live."

Michael Tennesen, a frequent contributor to National Wildlife, *swims in the ocean near his home in Southern California but worries more about automobile traffic on land than the sharks in the water.*

sharks travel long distances for their food.

All of the tiger sharks tracked swam more than 10 miles offshore in the first 24 hours after release and did not return to the area during the following 48 hours. It was not unusual for one of these fish to cover 30 to 40 miles a day. And though they eventually revisited monitoring sites, they did so on an irregular basis, with intervals ranging anywhere from two weeks to 10 months.

The implication of this discovery was that if tiger sharks don't stay close to one area, "It makes no sense to kill sharks in the vicinity of an attack and expect to solve the problem," Holland says.

The local news media gave extensive coverage to Holland's findings, and that helped quell the call for revenge in the Hawaiian legislature. Not everyone was happy with the idea of letting the sharks off, however. "If we had 30 people attacked in the last 10 years by wild dogs in Ala Moana Park [a seaside park near Honolulu], how many wild dogs would be in Ala

N THE MOVE: Tiger sharks roam temperate and tropical waters around the world. Their taste in prey is also wide-ranging, from small fish and birds to dolphins, rays and even other sharks. Razor-sharp teeth, powerful jaws and elastic muscles allow the fish to bite off and swallow huge pieces of food. Holland's research has shown that tiger sharks may swim 30 or 40 miles a day in their search for food, and it may take them weeks or months to return to a given area.

PREVIEW

Photo and caption

Nonfiction

NOTE

Eyewitness account

NOTE

About the author

August/September 2000

C Plan

Are you surprised at how much you find out by previewing the article? From the title and photographs you can learn what the article is about (sharks). The title, photo caption, and sentence in large type on the first page also give you the author's viewpoint: Tiger sharks need more respect, and fears about them are unwarranted.

Now that you have a general sense of what the article is about and have set your purpose questions, you need a plan to get the answers.

Reading Strategy: Questioning the Author

For magazine articles, the best strategy many times is **questioning the author**. That involves thinking about the decisions the author made. You want to identify the writer's viewpoint and see how it is supported. To do this, you'll ask questions as you read:

- How does the author think or feel about the subject?
- How does the author support or develop his or her main idea?
- What do I think about it?

One tool to help you sort out your ideas about questions like these is a Main Idea Organizer. Filling in a Main Idea Organizer helps you see how separate ideas, examples, or paragraphs fit together.

MAIN IDEA ORGANIZER

SUBJECT			
MAIN IDEA			
DETAIL 1	DETAIL 2	DETAIL 3	DETAIL 4
CONCLUSION			

During Reading

If you're asking questions of the author, you're reading actively. Questioning the author will help you focus on the author's ideas and sort out your own feelings on the subject. That also helps you figure out how the author's point relates to what you already know.

D Read with a Purpose

Start your questioning by thinking about your purpose: finding out about sharks and whether they're really killers.

Think about what you already know about sharks. Are you afraid of them? What do they look like? Use your own previous knowledge to help you write questions. Start out simple—maybe one or two questions about each page you read. Below are one reader's questions and possible answers to them.

Nonfiction

QUESTIONS AND ANSWERS

PAGE 1
Why does the writer begin with two stories about shark attacks?
(He probably wants to grab the reader's interest.)

PAGE 2
Why include such a scary picture of a shark?
(He wants to scare us and get our attention.)

PAGE 3
Why does he include all of the information about tiger sharks?
(He wants to help readers understand what their lives are like.)

PAGE 4
Why does he end with the story of a shark attack?
(The victim makes it sound like the shark was defending itself.)

Answering questions like the ones above helps you understand the author's purpose in writing the article. You can begin to piece together what the author is saying and why.

Understanding how magazine articles are often organized makes it easier to pick out what's important.

Time Order

Some magazine articles tell a story, detailing the main events in the order they occurred. For a narrative article of this kind, the events follow chronological, or time, order. This Story String shows how narrative articles are organized.

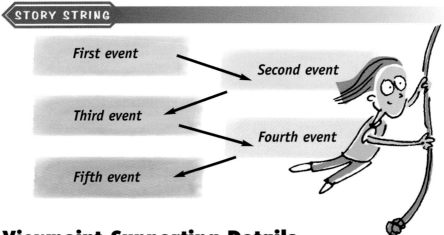

STORY STRING

First event

Second event

Third event

Fourth event

Fifth event

Viewpoint–Supporting Details

But not all magazine articles are organized in time order, especially those expressing a viewpoint or a main idea. Look back at the beginning of "A Killer Gets Some Respect." Two quick stories about shark attacks serve to grab the reader's attention. Then the article begins developing the author's main idea—that sharks should be respected, not destroyed out of fear.

The author explains how people have reacted to shark attacks in the past. He then explains why attitudes toward sharks are now changing. The rest of the article supports the author's point that we should try to understand and respect sharks. Go back to the article again and find different kinds of evidence the author used: facts and statistics, experts' views, and eyewitness accounts. The Viewpoint and Evidence Organizer that follows illustrates the article's structure.

VIEWPOINT AND EVIDENCE ORGANIZER

SUBJECT
Attitudes about sharks

AUTHOR'S VIEWPOINT
Sharks should be understood and respected, not destroyed out of fear.

FACTS AND STATISTICS	PERSONAL EXPERIENCES	WHAT EXPERTS SAY	EYEWITNESS ACCOUNTS
There were only eight shark attacks in Hawaii from 1991 to 1992. The odds of a shark attack are about one in five million.	None	Sharks eat lots of different food and cover 30 to 40 miles a day.	Jonathan Mozo says we're not masters of the sea. We're guests in the shark's world.

Nonfiction

E Connect

Even though you're reading a magazine article to get information, it's still important to react to what you're learning. Active readers make connections between their experiences and ideas and what they're reading about. As you read "A Killer Gets Some Respect," what were your reactions? Note how one reader responded to the conclusion of the article.

from "A Killer Gets Some Respect"

Mozo expresses the feelings of many Hawaiians who have now come to accept the tiger shark as part of the marine environment. "I have no feelings of hatred against the shark," he says. "I don't want revenge. I don't think they should be eliminated. We are not the masters of sea. If it were our territory we'd have been born with gills and fins. I was out there a guest in his world. I just feel lucky he let me live."

Michael Tennesen, a frequ̶...
...life, swi̶...
Souther̶...
...ut auto̶...

He makes a strong point. It's the shark's world, not ours.

Did the shark really make that decision? I doubt it.

After Reading

"A Killer Gets Some Respect" ends with the personal story of a surfer who was attacked but still forgives sharks. How much should that emotional story affect your feelings about the article? Has the author persuaded you to support his viewpoint?

F Pause and Reflect

Any time you finish reading, you need to look back on what you read. Recall your reading purpose. Did you meet it? Ask yourself questions like these:

Looking Back

- **What have I learned about the topic?**
- **What is the author's main idea?**
- **Are there parts that I don't understand?**
- **Do I agree with the author's viewpoint?**

From your reading, you probably learned a number of facts about sharks. But whether the evidence has persuaded you to agree with the author's viewpoint may be tougher to answer. The question "Are sharks really killers?" requires that you take a stand. To decide whether you agree or disagree with the author, you may need to go back to the article and reread parts of it.

G Reread

Writers do not always present both sides of every issue. Most of the time they present their viewpoint in the hopes of convincing you— the reader—of adopting the same position. As a reader, you need to evaluate what is presented as supporting evidence and what is not. Only then can you make up your mind and evaluate the writer's viewpoint.

Rereading Strategy: **Reading Critically**

In "A Killer Gets Some Respect," the writer's point is that the public shouldn't be so afraid of the sharks. Do you agree? As a reader, you need to weigh the evidence for and against his viewpoint.

To do that, you need to **read critically**. Look at all the evidence that's presented. Then think about what's *not* shown. Making a Critical Reading Chart can help you evaluate what you read.

CRITICAL READING CHART

1. VIEWPOINT	• Sharks should be understood and respected. • They shouldn't be killed out of fear.
2. KINDS OF EVIDENCE	• facts about sharks and attacks • expert source, Kim Holland • eyewitness account of victim
3. RELIABILITY OF SOURCES	• knowledgeable scientists • Hawaii Institute of Marine Biology
4. QUALITY OF EVIDENCE	• good quotations and lots of data • Where do attack statistics come from?
5. ANOTHER SIDE OF THE STORY	• What about quotes from people who favored the bill to kill sharks?

Nonfiction

Did the author get a wide enough range of experts? Only one person on the other side is mentioned. A magazine called *National Wildlife* would most likely support respect for wildlife. For the opposite viewpoint, you would need to do more research.

H Remember

Using the information you read helps you remember it. Try one of these ways to improve your chances of remembering.

1. Tell a Friend

Sometimes the easiest thing you can do after you read something is to share it with a friend. Mention what you learned in a phone conversation or during lunch. Ask a classmate who's read the same article what he or she thought of it. When you share what you read, you are more likely to remember it.

2. Write a Journal Entry

You may not always want to share your thoughts. Another option is to write them in a journal. The act of retelling them—even in just a few sentences—will help the article stick in your mind.

JOURNAL ENTRY

> Shark attacks may not happen a lot, but they can be deadly. One guy got more than 100 stitches after he was bitten by a shark. I can't believe that he wasn't even that mad about it. He thought he was wrong to be in the shark's world. The chances of a shark attack are about one in five million. Just hope you're not the one!

Summing Up

When you read magazine articles, remember to use the reading process and the reading strategy of **questioning the author.** Use tools like these to help clarify the writer's viewpoint and see the way **articles are organized** with supporting evidence:

- Main Idea Organizer
- Viewpoint and Evidence Organizer
- Critical Reading Chart

Use the strategy of **reading critically** to see what evidence has been presented and what hasn't.

Focus on Persuasive Writing

Persuasive writing is all around you. An ad for a new sports drink is persuasive writing. So is an email from a friend asking for a copy of your science notes.

Persuasive writing makes an argument. It is meant to convince you to do, say, or think what the writer wants you to do, say, or think. Among other things, persuasive writing can ask you to:

■ take action

■ consider an idea

■ support a cause

■ spend money

■ accept an opinion

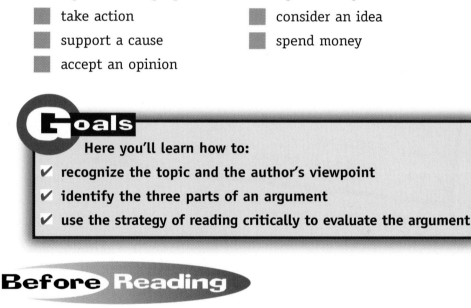

Goals

Here you'll learn how to:

✔ **recognize the topic and the author's viewpoint**

✔ **identify the three parts of an argument**

✔ **use the strategy of reading critically to evaluate the argument**

Before Reading

With persuasive writing, begin by looking for the topic and the author's main point or opinion about it. The writer's opinion is called the viewpoint. A **viewpoint** is a statement of belief that the author wants to explain and then support.

Usually the viewpoint is just one sentence long. It may include such phrases as "I think we should . . ."; "The point is . . ."; or "What it means in the end is . . . ."

The viewpoint can appear almost anywhere in the text. The most common places for the viewpoint are either the first one or two paragraphs or the last one or two. The overall organization often follows one of these models.

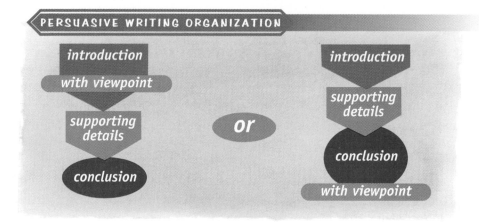

PERSUASIVE WRITING ORGANIZATION

introduction
with viewpoint

supporting details

conclusion

or

introduction

supporting details

conclusion
with viewpoint

Look for the topic and viewpoint in the first part of the editorial below. In your preview, pay particular attention to these items:

Preview Checklist

✔ the title or headline
✔ the first paragraph
✔ any repeated words, phrases, or sentences

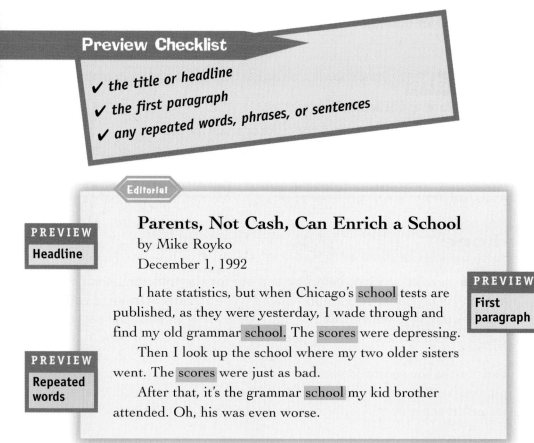

Editorial

PREVIEW
Headline

Parents, Not Cash, Can Enrich a School
by Mike Royko
December 1, 1992

PREVIEW
First paragraph

I hate statistics, but when Chicago's school tests are published, as they were yesterday, I wade through and find my old grammar school. The scores were depressing.

PREVIEW
Repeated words

Then I look up the school where my two older sisters went. The scores were just as bad.

After that, it's the grammar school my kid brother attended. Oh, his was even worse.

What clues did you find about Royko's topic and viewpoint? Once you have an idea about the topic and viewpoint, get ready to begin reading critically.

Reading Strategy: **Reading Critically**

You need to evaluate any arguments you read, and the best way to do that is by **reading critically**. Start by recognizing the author's viewpoint. As you read the rest of Mike Royko's editorial, watch how he supports his opinion.

During Reading

Whenever you read persuasive writing, it's tempting to decide quickly whether you agree or disagree. But be patient. Don't rush to a conclusion about how you feel about an argument before you're sure what the argument is.

Every good argument is made up of three parts. Note the three basic parts in the Argument Chart below and look for them as you read.

ARGUMENT CHART

Viewpoint	**Support**	**Opposing Viewpoint**
This is a statement of belief that the author wants to explain and support. It is also called the "opinion statement" or "assertion."	*This is the facts, figures, statistics, and examples used to support the assertion.*	*Since every argument has two sides, the writer must anticipate how readers might object to his or her views and then answer those objections.*

The three parts of an argument can appear in any order. They can also be mixed together. As a critical reader, you need to check that all three parts are present. If one part is missing, the argument is flawed.

Now, read the beginning of Royko's editorial on page 248 again. Then, go on and read the rest. As you do, look for the three parts: *viewpoint, support,* and *opposing viewpoint.*

Nonfiction

There was a time when all three schools would have done well, if they had conducted tests in those days. If not excellent, at least adequate.

I'm confident, because the kids in my class could all read and write, some quite well; my sisters were voracious readers by the time they graduated, and my brother's fundamentals were good enough to get him to college and a successful business career.

So what's changed? Why were we able to get the basics out of these inner-city schools, as they are now called, but today's kids are barely learning to read a street sign?

Money? That's the first thing that will come to many minds. The children going to those schools today are from poor families. And that's true.

But it was true when we were in the same schools. My sisters graduated at the height of the Great Depression, when relatives and neighbors borrowed coal from those lucky enough to work, when the only welfare was called "relief" and it meant standing in line for a box of groceries.

My brother and I had it a little better, but by today's standards, we were close to or below the poverty level. So were the families of many of our classmates.

But there was a difference, although it can't be found in any of the statistics, including how much each community spends on students.

It's called family. The families weren't perfect. For perfection, there were the "Andy Hardy" movies, which wasn't the way life was in the cold-water flats around Humboldt Park.

But in most of the flats, there was some semblance of a family life, even if the parents spoke broken English or none at all.

And if you look hard enough, that's what those long tables of statistics tell us.

You have to skip beyond the obvious. Sure, in the

wealthy suburbs, where they spend $9,000 or $10,000 a year per pupil, compared with Chicago's $6,000, the results are excellent. But should that be a surprise?

So forget the wealthy suburbs. Look at the middle-class, working-class suburbs, where there are as many blue collars as white collars, where they aren't spending any more on each student than Chicago does. In many, they spend even less.

Yet they get results. Most are at the state and national averages or above.

Eldon Gleichman is superintendent of an elementary school district in Des Plaines, which is seldom compared with, say, the affluent Lake Forest.

He has 3,360 pupils. "This year, one-third of our kindergartners don't speak English... In fact, 58 percent of our kids don't speak English at home."

But despite being more fluent in Spanish, Polish, and Russian, the kids scored above average.

It isn't easy, Gleichman says, "Parents are busier and busier in their lives. It's getting harder and harder, but we get the parents involved. Parental involvement—that's really where it's all at. The key is whatever goes on in the classroom and whatever goes on in the living room. It's a team effort."

Or the superintendent of a district in a southwest suburb, who said: "The parents are here. They listen to kids read, they get involved in our reading contests—book weeks—where children read to parents who must verify their children are reading.

"The parents are an extension of the school, just as we here at school are an extension of the parent. We have similar expectations, and the children know it.

"But one thing to keep in mind about spending. Yes, we don't spend any more [than Chicago], but we have the luxury of spending directly on the kids. We don't have

NOTE
Support from expert

NOTE
Support from expert

Nonfiction

251

security guards. We don't need building security or money to clean up vandalism or fix broken windows."

Just about every suburban school superintendent or principal says the same thing. From the principal of a middle-class district in the western suburbs:

NOTE
Support from expert

"When we have an open house, it's packed. Parents give visible support for what their kids are involved in. Parents give their time to be at the school, to call the teacher, to be with their kids.

"You can't focus on how much we spend on students. Just looking at the simple numbers doesn't tell the whole story."

NOTE
Opposing viewpoint

Exactly. And crying out for more money for Chicago's schools isn't the answer, unless the money is spent in a way that will get results.

But how do you use money to replace a family structure that isn't there? If you know the answer to that question, then pass it along to the eighth-grade teacher at a West Side school who wearily told me:

"I try to teach, but it isn't easy when my smartest student is a girl who is already pregnant with her second child."

So when you hear the educational experts talk about the problems of Chicago's schools, tossing programs and plans in every direction, unless they use words like "family" and "parents" tune them out.

And get ready for next year's bleak statistics.

Were you able to find all three parts—the viewpoint, support, and opposing viewpoint? Here is how one reader used an Argument Chart to keep track of Royko's ideas.

ARGUMENT CHART

VIEWPOINT	SUPPORT	OPPOSING VIEWPOINT
• Parents, not cash, make a school succeed. • Families need to be involved.	#1 The Roykos were poor, but kids did well in school because of family. #2 Des Plaines school has involved parents and high scores. #3 School in southwest suburbs has parents involved in reading contests. #4 School in western suburbs has no money, but it has packed open houses, and the parents spend time at the school.	• Royko admits that some will say more money means better test scores. • Royko argues against those who say money is the reason: ". . . crying out for more money for Chicago's schools isn't the answer, unless the money is spent in a way that will get results."

Nonfiction

Making a chart like this can help you see how persuasive writing is organized. Royko states his viewpoint in the title. He next looks at his own experience and that of his family and asks a question: "So what's changed?" He gives one possible answer, money, but then rejects it. Family, not money, makes schools and students successful.

Royko goes on to give examples of some successful schools in the suburbs. Those schools—and their test scores—help Royko support his viewpoint. In his conclusion, Royko repeats his opinion that the opposing viewpoint of experts who just want to spend more money on education is wrong.

After Reading

When you've finished reading, think back again about the argument. What's your opinion of it? How does it relate to your life? Has it affected your own view of the subject? Rereading parts of it can help you focus on key points. Try these suggestions to make your rereading pay off.

1. Connect with the Writing

After you've finished reading, think about your own response to the writing. What are your own feelings about the topic? Do you have any experiences with what the writer is talking about? Note how one reader reacted to a particular part of Royko's argument.

from "Parents, Not Cash, Can Enrich a School"

"You can't focus on how much we spend on students. Just looking at the simple numbers doesn't tell the whole story."

Exactly. And crying out for more money for Chicago's schools isn't the answer, unless the money is spent in a way that will get results.

How can more money hurt? We need more money for books at my school.

2. Evaluate the Argument

For an argument to be effective, the viewpoint must be clear, convincing, and supported well. What's your opinion of how persuasive Royko's argument was? Were you impressed by his support? What other evidence might have strengthened his point? Jot some notes to questions like these on your Argument Chart or in a reading notebook. What do you think of this reader's evaluation of Royko's writing? What rating would you give it?

READING LOG

His assertion was really clear and easy to find. It was right in the headline! That helped me get a handle on the argument right away. He mentioned several different schools, but the principals could have been biased. There have to be poor schools with involved parents that still have bad test scores. He might have explained why people think more money will help. What would they do with the money if they had it? All in all, I'd rate the argument an 8 out of 10.

3. Decide How You Feel

After you decide whether an argument is convincing, you'll want to consider how *you* feel about the author's viewpoint. After all, you can think an author has made a poor argument but agree with his or her conclusion. Take some time to listen to your own thoughts.

One way of deciding how you feel about a topic is to form your own argument about it. Organize your thoughts into the three parts of an argument in case you're asked to state your own opinion.

Nonfiction

MY ARGUMENT

VIEWPOINT	SUPPORT	OPPOSING VIEWPOINT
I agree with Royko's claim that getting more parents involved, not spending more money, is what makes schools better.	#1 In our district, parents must help at school a certain number of hours. #2 If you don't have help at home with homework, you might have trouble with a subject. Having new books or a fancy school wouldn't help. #3 Kids in our district don't have much money, but they have good standardized test scores!	• Family support isn't the only thing. • You could have parents who really cared and still not have the kids succeed.

Summing Up

- Good persuasive writing has three parts: viewpoint, support, opposing viewpoint.
- Use the strategy of reading critically to analyze an argument and evaluate its effectiveness.

Focus on Speeches

Usually you listen to speeches rather than read them. But sometimes you may have to read historic or political speeches for class assignments. Speeches fall into two general types—informative and persuasive. Using the reading process when you read speeches will help you understand and evaluate them.

Goals

Here you'll learn how to:

✔ **sharpen your critical reading skills**

✔ **understand how speeches are organized**

✔ **recognize common propaganda techniques**

Before Reading

You may not have read any—or very many—speeches. Relax. Reading a speech is like reading other kinds of nonfiction. What you want to find out first is what the speaker's trying to say. Your purpose, as a reader, is to figure out the speaker's purpose. If you're reading a persuasive speech, you want to know what the speaker's position, or viewpoint, is. If you're reading an informative speech, you want to know what the main idea is.

Nonfiction

Previewing can tell you a lot. It won't take long, and what you learn about the subject, the speaker, and the occasion at which the speech was delivered will make it easier for you to follow the speaker's idea. It's like looking over a map of an amusement park before walking through the entry gate. It'll be easier to get where you want to go. In most cases, this background information appears before the speech. The most important part of previewing the speech is to read and understand this information. The following items can give you clues about the speaker's purpose:

Preview Checklist

✔ the title
✔ any background information
✔ the opening and closing paragraphs
✔ any repeated words or phrases
✔ overall length of the speech

Now preview this famous speech by former president Ronald Reagan.

"The future doesn't belong to the fainthearted" by Ronald Reagan

OVAL OFFICE OF THE WHITE HOUSE, 28 JANUARY 1986

Only a few hours after the Challenger space shuttle exploded during take-off, then president Ronald Reagan delivered this address to the country. Reagan's speechwriter, Peggy Noonan, made the speech memorable for its inspirational tone and its closing lines, quoted from the poem "High Flight" by John Gillespie Magee, a Canadian pilot killed in World War II.

Nineteen years ago, almost to the day, we lost three astronauts in a terrible accident on the ground. But we've never lost an astronaut in flight; we've never had a tragedy like this. And perhaps we've forgotten the courage it took for the crew of the shuttle; but they, the *Challenger* Seven, were aware of the dangers, but overcame them and did their jobs brilliantly. We mourn seven heroes: Michael Smith, Dick Scobee, Judith Resnik, Ronald McNair, Ellison Onizuka, Gregory Jarvis, and Christa McAuliffe. We mourn their loss as a nation together.

For the families of the seven, we cannot bear, as you do, the full impact of this tragedy. But we feel the loss, and we're thinking about you so very much. Your loved ones were daring and brave, and they had that special grace, that special spirit that says, "Give me a challenge and I'll meet it with joy." They had a hunger to explore the universe and discover its truths. They wished to serve, and they did. They served all of us.

We've grown used to wonders in this century. It's hard to dazzle us. But for twenty-five years the United States space program has been doing just that. We've grown used to the idea of space, and perhaps we forget that we've only just begun. We're still pioneers. They, the members of the *Challenger* crew, were pioneers.

And I want to say something to the schoolchildren of America, who were watching the live coverage of the shuttle's takeoff. I know it is hard to understand, but sometimes painful things like this happen. It's all part of the process of exploration and discovery. It's all part of taking a chance and expanding man's horizons. The future doesn't belong to the fainthearted; it belongs to the brave. The *Challenger* crew was pulling us into the future, and we'll continue to follow them . . .

PREVIEW
Repeated words

There's a coincidence today. On this day 390 years ago, the great explorer Sir Francis Drake died aboard ship off the coast of Panama. In his lifetime the great frontiers were the oceans, and a historian later said, "He lived by the sea, died on it, and was buried in it." Well, today we can say of the *Challenger* crew: Their dedication was, like Drake's, complete.

The crew of the space shuttle *Challenger* honored us by the manner in which they lived their lives. We will never forget them, nor the last time we saw them, this morning, as they prepared for the journey and waved goodbye and "slipped the surly bonds of earth" to "touch the face of God."

PREVIEW
Closing paragraph

Nonfiction

What did you learn from previewing Reagan's speech? The answer is that you learned a lot. President Reagan was speaking to the nation about the death of the *Challenger* astronauts. His speech is a eulogy, meant to honor and remember the dead.

Once you know something about the speaker, the occasion, and the topic, you need a reading strategy. A good strategy for understanding a speech is **reading critically**. To read critically, you first need to identify the speaker's viewpoint. Then, you identify how the speaker supports his or her position. A speaker may use any of the following as support:

- facts and statistics
- comparisons and contrasts
- firsthand experience or examples
- opinions of experts
- research results
- logical reasoning
- appeals to emotion

Of course, there are all kinds of speeches. While some persuade, others inform, entertain, or do a combination of all three. Not all of them depend on the same sort of evidence. Some speeches will rely more on logic, others more on emotion. What's important is that you think about *what* the speaker is saying and *how* he or she is saying it. In other words, be a critical reader.

During Reading

Now you're ready to read President Reagan's speech (pages 258–259) slowly and carefully. Follow these two tips as you go.

1. Find the Three Main Parts of a Speech

A standard way to organize a speech is to include an introduction, a body, and a conclusion. The speaker usually states his or her viewpoint or main idea in the introduction. Next, he or she gives evidence supporting it in the body and then restates the viewpoint in the conclusion. Sometimes a speaker may also answer objections to the viewpoint in the body.

But many speeches do not follow this common pattern of organization. For instance, some may not have all three parts, and some speakers don't state their main ideas or viewpoints in the introduction. But get in the habit of looking for the three parts. It can help you follow the sequence of ideas. One way of identifying the three parts is by making a list with three headings. Another is to use a simple organizer like the one below. It shows the three basic parts of President Reagan's speech.

Nonfiction

NONFICTION ORGANIZER

TITLE: "The future doesn't belong to the fainthearted."

SUBJECT: <u>Challenger</u> explosion

INTRODUCTION: Paragraph 1
    says we mourn courageous people

BODY: Paragraphs 2–5
    says how brave the astronauts were to explore space

CONCLUSION: Paragraph 6
    says they lived with honor and won't be forgotten

2. Identify the Main Idea and the Support

Having an overall sense of the organization of a speech makes it easier to focus on the speaker's point and how he or she supports it. Reagan is trying to communicate the opinion expressed in the title: Those who explore are courageous. In his introductory paragraph, he admits that Americans may have forgotten how much courage the crew members had. In the body of the speech, he emphasizes their bravery.

What kind of support does he present? It's not the usual mixture of facts, statistics, eyewitness accounts, or quotes from experts that you might think of as "evidence." Take a closer look at the body of the speech. Use a Main Idea Organizer like the one below to examine how Reagan supports his point.

MAIN IDEA ORGANIZER

TITLE: "The future doesn't belong to the fainthearted."			
MAIN IDEA: Explorers like the astronauts are brave.			
DETAIL 1	**DETAIL 2**	**DETAIL 3**	**DETAIL 4**
Three earlier astronauts died.	Astronauts are pioneers.	Expanding the frontiers is risky. The risks are part of the discovery process.	Challenger astronauts are like Sir Francis Drake, who also died while exploring.
CONCLUSION: The Challenger astronauts lived with honor and won't be forgotten.			

The speech compares the *Challenger* astronauts to earlier astronauts who died during a mission and to the explorer Sir Francis Drake. It describes the *Challenger* mission of exploration in heroic terms—a task only for the brave, for those who know the great risks but take them anyway.

After Reading

After you read a persuasive speech, take a little time to think about the speaker's position. Don't just settle for understanding what the speaker is saying. Take the next step. Judge whether or not the argument is effective. Are you convinced by it?

If you took notes, you can identify the viewpoint and how it is supported. But is that all that makes a speech convincing?

You may need to reread a speech carefully before you can truly evaluate its effectiveness. As you reread, look for some of the common techniques speechwriters use to persuade you.

COMMON PROPAGANDA TECHNIQUES

1. Bandwagon
Everybody agrees or is doing it.

2. Stacking the Deck
Only the good side is mentioned. Unfavorable facts are withheld.

3. Plain Folks Appeal
Common, everyday people support it.

4. Broad Generalization
Broad statements that have little substance are made.

5. Snob Appeal
The "best" people support it.

6. Circular Thinking
The conclusion just restates the beginning.

7. Loaded Words
Words that have strong emotional associations— such as mother, family, and patriotism—are used.

President Reagan doesn't use facts, statistics, or expert opinion to prove his point. So what gives President Reagan's speech its great emotional power? Which techniques did he use? If you answered loaded words, you're right. Look again at some of the words he used to describe the *Challenger* astronauts:

Nonfiction

"Your loved ones were **daring** and **brave**, and they had that special **grace**, that special **spirit** that says, 'Give me a **challenge** and I'll meet it with **joy**.'"

"...they, the *Challenger* Seven, were aware of the **dangers**, but overcame them and did their jobs **brilliantly**. We mourn seven **heroes**...."

"...this morning, as they prepared for the journey and waved goodbye and 'slipped the surly bonds of earth' to 'touch the **face of God**.'"

Often the power of a speech comes through its appeals not to our heads, but to our hearts (our emotions). Reagan's speech uses powerful descriptive language with strong positive connotations.

The speech paints an inspirational portrait of seven brave heroes who were ready to sacrifice their lives. If you're reading critically, you'll understand what a speaker's saying and be able to judge whether or not it's effective.

Summing Up

- Find out when and why the speech was given and who the audience was.
- Many speeches have three parts: introduction, body, and conclusion.
- Use the strategy of reading critically to help you identify the speaker's point and evaluate how well it's supported.
- Be on the alert for common propaganda techniques, such as loaded words or the bandwagon appeal.

Focus on Real-world Writing

The reading you do *outside* of school (often called "real-world" or "informational" reading) can be as important as the reading you do *inside* of school. Informational reading helps you stay informed, up-to-date, and knowledgeable about the world around you. For this reason alone, it's a good idea to learn how to be a better reader of real-world writing.

Goals

Here you'll learn how to:

✔ **identify a purpose when reading real-world writing**
✔ **understand the organization of the writing**
✔ **skim to find the information you need**

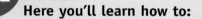

Before Reading

Two types of real-world reading that you do all the time are free-reading and informational reading.

1. Free-reading

Some of the real-world reading you do will be purely for pleasure. Your purpose for reading comic books, emails or chat room messages from friends, and late-night novels is enjoyment. No one will ask you questions about this type of reading or quiz you on your comprehension. Still, this type of reading is important because it can improve the speed at which you read and widen your vocabulary.

2. Informational Reading

The other type of real-world reading you do is informational reading: contest rules, manuals for software, how-to instructions, and so forth. You won't be tested on it. However, you still need to read with a plan.

Nonfiction

Real-world Reading Plan

Try using a plan the next time you pick up a set of instructions or a brochure. You might be surprised to find that this plan can help you spend *less* time and get you *more* information.

REAL-WORLD READING PLAN

Step 1
Identify your purpose for reading.

Step 2
Understand the organization of the writing.

Step 3
Find what you need to know.

Step 4
Remember the information and apply it to your own life.

Think about the first two steps before you start reading. What do you need to find out? Knowing your purpose tells you which parts of the writing will be most important.

Identifying a Reading Purpose

Real-world writing can contain lots of different information. As a result, you will probably have a very specific purpose in reading each of the real-world documents that follow.

READING PURPOSE

REAL-WORLD EXAMPLE	READING PURPOSE
1. Student Handbook	to find if religious holidays are excused absences or not
2. Computer Game Instructions	to learn how to load software and begin playing
3. Train Schedule	to find out which train will arrive in Hubbard Woods closest to 6:00 p.m. on a Friday

As you preview the three examples, look for the information you need. Your job as a reader is to sift out all the stuff that's not important and get to what is.

1. Student Handbook

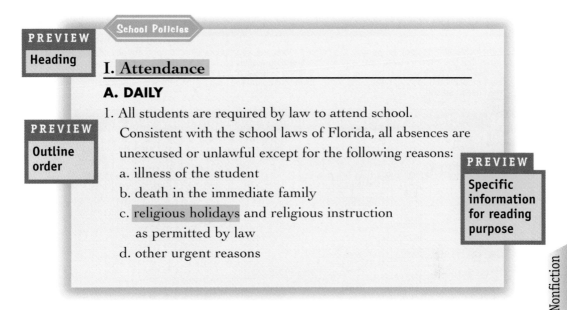

School Policies

I. Attendance

A. DAILY

1. All students are required by law to attend school. Consistent with the school laws of Florida, all absences are unexcused or unlawful except for the following reasons:
   a. illness of the student
   b. death in the immediate family
   c. religious holidays and religious instruction as permitted by law
   d. other urgent reasons

2. Computer Game Instructions

Getting Started

The Play, File Manager, Music, and Screen Settings can be accessed from the main menu. It is not necessary to use the main menu for most games or the use of most CDs. Simply place a disc in the top of the machine. Then the power starts automatically and the sound or image will be displayed automatically on the screen, if "auto start" is in the "ON" position (see page 31 for details).

1. Use the Directional Pad (or Thumb Pad, located on the left) to highlight the desired icon.
2. Press the A Button to choose the icon.
3. Then click, and the game or music will start.

Nonfiction

3. Train Schedule

PREVIEW
Words in large type

Chicago to Kenosha HOW TO READ THIS TIMETABLE

First locate at the top of the page in the colored block, the appropriate direction and the day of the week that you plan to travel. Next, identify the boarding station on the farthest left column. Follow across to the right to determine the departure times of trains at that station. Select the train that best meets your personal needs and move down that column to identify the arrival time at your destination station.

PREVIEW
Headings

Chicago to Kenosha – Monday through Friday cont'd

STATIONS	333	335	337	339	341	343	345	RAV 1	347	349	351	353	355	357	359	361	301
	PM	PM	PM	PM	PM	PM	PM	PM	PM	PM	PM	PM	PM	PM	PM	PM	AM
OGILVIE TRANSPORTATION CENTER LV:	4:35	5:07	5:10	5:15	5:21	5:35	5:45	5:50	6:00	6:31	6:35	7:35	8:35	9:35	10:35	11:35	12:3
Clybourn	4:43		5:18	5:23	5:29	5:43		5:58	6:08		6:43	7:43	8:43	9:43	10:43	11:43	12:4
Ravenswood	4:48		—	5:34	5:49			6:04	6:13		6:48	7:48	8:48	9:48	10:48	11:48	12:4
Rogers Park	4:53		5:26		5:38			6:08	6:18		6:52	7:52	8:52	9:52	10:52	11:52	12:5
Main St., Evanston	4:57		—	5:33	5:41			6:12	6:22		6:55	7:55	8:55	9:55	10:55	11:55	12:5
Davis St., Evanston	4:59		5:31	5:36	5:44	5:56		6:15	6:25	6:50	6:58	7:58	8:58	9:58	10:58	11:58	12:5
Central St., Evanston	—		5:34	5:38	5:47		6:05	6:18	6:28	—	7:01	8:01	9:01	10:01	11:01	12:01	1:01
Wilmette	5:03	5:28	—	5:41	—		6:08		6:31	6:54	7:04	8:04	9:04	10:04	11:04	12:04	1:04
Kenilworth	—		5:38	—	5:51		6:11		6:34		7:06	8:06	9:06	10:06	11:06	12:06	1:06
Indian Hill	5:07		—	5:44	—		6:14		6:36		7:08	8:08	9:08	10:08	11:08	12:08	1:08
Winnetka	—		5:41	—	5:54	6:02	6:17		6:38	6:58	7:10	8:10	9:10	10:10	11:10	12:10	1:10
Hubbard Woods	5:11		—	5:48	—	6:06	6:20		6:42		7:13	8:13	9:13	10:13	11:13	12:13	1:13
Glencoe	—		5:46	—		6:10	6:24		6:45	7:02	7:16	8:16	9:16	10:16	11:16	12:16	1:16
Braeside	5:15	5:36	—	5:52	—	6:14	6:28		6:48		7:19	8:19	9:19	10:19	11:19	12:19	1:19
Ravinia Park	—							6:30	6:50		7:20	8:20	9:20	10:20	11:20	12:20	—
Ravinia	—		5:50	5:56	—	6:17	6:31	—	6:51		7:21	8:21	9:21	10:21	11:21	12:21	1:21
Highland Park	5:19	5:42	5:53	5:59	—	6:21	6:35	—	6:54	7:08	7:24	8:24	9:24	10:24	11:24	12:24	1:24
Highwood	5:22	—	—	6:02	—	6:24	—		6:57		7:27	8:27	9:27	10:27	11:27	12:27	1:27
Sheridan	5:25	5:47	5:58	—	—	6:27	6:40	—	7:00		7:29	8:29	9:29	10:29	11:29	12:29	1:29
Forest	5:29	5:52	—	6:08	—	6:32	6:45	—	7:04	7:16	7:33	8:33	9:33	10:33	11:33	12:33	1:33
ll	5:33	5:56	6:04	—	—	6:36	6:50		7:08	7:19	7:36	8:36	9:36	10:36	11:36	12:36	1:36
kes	5:37	—	6:08	6:14	—	—			7:12		7:40	8:40	9:40	10:40	11:40	12:40	1:40
icago	5:40		6:11	6:17	—	6:41			7:15		7:45	8:45	9:45	10:45	11:45	12:45	1:45
n	5:45	6:06	6:16	6:22	—	6:47	7:00		7:22	7:28	7:52	8:50	9:50	10:50	11:50	12:50	1:50
	—	6:15	6:25	—	—	6:55	—		—	7:37	—	—	—	10:59	—	—	1:59
Harbor (ILL.)	—	6:20	6:30	—	—	6:59	—		—	7:41	—	—	—	11:03	—	—	2:03
(WIS.) AR:	—	6:30	6:40	—	—	7:10	—		—	7:51	—	—	—	11:15	—	—	2:15

PREVIEW
Specific information for reading purpose

PREVIEW
Headings

Chicago to Kenosha – Saturday

STATIONS	305	315	801	321	325	807	809	RAV 1	353	357	359	301
	AM	AM	AM	PM	PM	PM	PM	PM	PM	PM	PM	AM
OGILVIE TRANSPORTATION CENTER LV:	6:35	8:35	10:35	12:35	2:35	4:35	5:35	5:50	7:35	9:35	10:35	12:35
Clybourn	6:43	8:43	10:43	12:43	2:43	4:43	5:43	5:58	7:43	9:43	10:43	12:43
Ravenswood	6:48	8:48	10:48	12:48	2:48	4:48	5:48	6:04	7:48	9:48	10:48	12:48
Rogers Park	6:53	8:52	10:52	12:52	2:53	4:52	5:52	6:08	7:52	9:52	10:52	12:52
Main St., Evanston	6:56	8:55	10:55	12:55	2:56	4:55	5:55	6:12	7:55	9:55	10:55	12:55
Davis St., Evanston	6:59	8:58	10:58	12:58	2:59	4:58	5:58	6:15	7:58	9:58	10:58	12:58
Central St., Evanston	7:02	9:01	11:01	1:01	3:02	5:01	6:01	6:18	8:01	10:01	11:01	1:01
Wilmette	7:05	9:04	11:04	1:04	3:05	5:04	6:04		8:04	10:04	11:04	1:04
Kenilworth	7:07	9:06	11:06	1:06	3:07	5:06	6:06		8:06	10:06	11:06	1:06
Indian Hill	7:09	9:08	11:08	1:08	3:09	5:08	6:08		8:08	10:08	11:08	1:08
Winnetka	7:11	9:10	11:10	1:10	3:11	5:10	6:10		8:10	10:10	11:10	1:10
Hubbard Woods	7:14	9:13	11:13	1:13	3:14	5:13	6:13		8:13	10:13	11:13	1:13
Glencoe	7:17	9:16	11:16	1:16	3:17	5:16	6:16		8:16	10:16	11:16	1:16
Braeside	7:20	9:19	11:19	1:19	3:20	5:19	6:19		8:19	10:19	11:19	1:19
Ravinia Park						5:20	6:20	6:30	8:20	10:20	11:20	—
Ravinia	7:22	9:21	11:21	1:21	3:22	5:21	6:21	—	8:21	10:21	11:21	1:21
Highland Park	7:26	9:24	11:24	1:24	3:25	5:24	6:24	—	8:24	10:24	11:24	1:24
Highwood	7:29	9:27	11:27	1:27	3:28	5:27	6:27	—	8:27	10:27	11:27	1:27
Fort Sheridan	7:31	9:29	11:29	1:29	3:30	5:29	6:29	—	8:29	10:29	11:29	1:29
Lake Forest	7:35	9:33	11:33	1:33	3:34	5:33	6:33	—	8:33	10:33	11:33	1:33
Lake Bluff	7:38	9:36	11:36	1:36	3:37	5:36	6:36	—	8:36	10:36	11:36	1:36
Great Lakes	7:42	9:40	11:40	1:40	3:41	5:40	6:40	—	8:40	10:40	11:40	1:40
North Chicago	7:47	9:45	11:45	1:45	3:46	5:45	6:45	—	8:45	10:45	11:45	1:45
Waukegan	7:51	9:50	11:50	1:50	3:52	5:50	6:50	—	8:50	10:50	11:50	1:50
Zion	7:59	—	11:59	1:59	—	5:59	6:59	—	—	10:59	—	1:59
Winthrop Harbor (ILL.)	8:03	—	12:03	2:03	—	6:03	7:03	—	—	11:03	—	2:03
KENOSHA (WIS.) AR:	8:15	—	12:15	2:15	—	6:15	7:15	—	—	11:15	—	2:15

Understanding the Organization

All writing has some kind of organization. For example, many long documents have a table of contents or index, and directions often have numbered steps. Did you notice how differently the three examples were organized? One used an outline order, one used a numbered list, and one had headings in rows and columns. As a reader, you need to find how the writing is organized—and fast. That's the secret to finding the information to suit your purpose. Get in the habit of looking for these features:

■ words in large or boldface type

■ headings

■ numbered lists or outlines

■ diagrams or graphics

Reading Strategy: **Skimming**

The reading strategy to use when you need to find very specific information is **skimming**. Let your eyes move quickly over each page. Look for headings or key words that relate to your reading purpose. When you skim, you act like a miner looking for gold. You sift lots of sand in your pan looking for a few small nuggets of gold—that is, for the information you need.

Nonfiction

269

During Reading

Most real-world writing is intended for a very wide audience. The writer of a bus schedule or game manual has no way of knowing what individual readers will need, so often the writer offers as much information as possible. As a reader, you have to distinguish between what's needed and what's not.

For example, look back at the train schedule on page 268. The specific time of the train stopping at the Hubbard Woods station is highlighted. That's all a reader may need. The trouble is finding it in all that fine print and all those numbers.

So, here are a few useful tips to find what you need.

Tip #1: Use a Highlighter

As you read, use a highlighter to mark information that meets or is close to your purpose. Ignore information that has nothing to do with your purpose. A highlighter can help you "pull out" the important information.

Tip #2: Pay Attention to Headings

As you skim a page, use headings to direct your eyes. Keep your purpose in mind. Just skip over lists, columns, or paragraphs that aren't what you need. All of the train schedules may list your town (Hubbard Woods), but some schedules are for weekends, and some are for trains departing from Hubbard Woods.

Tip #3: Avoid the Jargon

Many times, finding out what you need to know involves wading through technical language or jargon. *Jargon* is language used in a certain profession or by a particular group of people. Jargon must be "translated" before you can understand what it means. But don't dig out your dictionary. In a lot of real-world writing—even the most technical types—you'll find context clues that can help.

After Reading

With most real-world writing, you finish reading with a feeling of either "mission accomplished" or "failure." You probably either found the information you needed or you didn't. You got on the right train or installed the software successfully—or you didn't.

Try Again

If you didn't find what you need, you can take a few obvious steps.

1. Reread

Go back through the directions, schedule, or manual one more time. Go a little more slowly. Look again for headings. Maybe you weren't looking in the right place the first time. Check again. For example, the morning or Saturday train schedule won't help you if you're traveling on Friday evening. If you're looking for your school's policy on religious holidays, it won't be covered in the section on dress code.

2. Ask a Friend for Help

Sometimes what you want to find is right under your nose, but you just can't see it. (In fact, that probably happens a lot.) Perhaps a friend or brother or sister has looked for the same thing or might know where you should look. Show someone else what you looked at and ask for help.

Nonfiction

Remember and Use the Information

Suppose you do find what you want. What's next? The last step of reading real-world information is to remember it—at least long enough to use it. Accomplishing what you wanted to is the proof of your reading success.

A lot of real-world writing is meant to be read once, used, and then forgotten. But some information in real-world writing may be important to you now *and* in the future. That's why for this writing you might want to jot down a few notes or highlight key parts. For example, you'll need to remember the instructions for programming the VCR so you can tape the shows you like.

To figure out whether you need to retain what you've read, ask yourself:

- Will I need this information again soon?
- Can I see myself wanting to reread or review this information in the future?
- Will the information change how I act or behave?

You live in an information world. Tons of information bombard you each day. As a reader, you need to sift through it and find what's important and what's not.

Summing Up

- **Be sure you know your purpose for reading.**
- **Pay attention to how the writing is organized.**
- **Use the strategy of skimming to find what you want.**

Elements of Nonfiction

You'll often want to talk or write about the nonfiction you're reading. Being familiar with the terms people use to describe essays, biographies, or magazine and news articles will make that easier to do. This part of the handbook contains important terms for nonfiction. Turn to this glossary of terms as needed—perhaps the next time you're asked to discuss the propaganda techniques in an argument or the connotation and denotation of a word. Look up the term, read the example, study the definition, and then apply what you've learned.

Elements of Nonfiction

Argument or Persuasive Writing	274
Cause and Effect	275
Chronological Order	276
Classification and Definition	277
Comparison and Contrast	278
Connotation and Denotation	279
Editorial	280
Fact and Opinion	281
Interview	282
Lead	283
Main Idea	284
Problem and Solution	286
Propaganda Techniques	287
Topic Sentence and Supporting Details	289
Viewpoint	291

Nonfiction

Argument or Persuasive Writing

At the heart of any argument or persuasive writing is a clear, strong opinion.

EXAMPLE

from "A Uniformly Good Idea" by Steve Forbes

Schools across the country should follow the example of Long Beach, Calif., which is requiring public-school students to wear uniforms.

Viewpoint

DESCRIPTION

Argument or persuasive writing attempts to prove something is true or convince you, the reader, to adopt the same viewpoint as the writer.

When reading persuasive writing, watch for the writer's viewpoint, or opinion statement. Look carefully at what support he or she offers for the opinion statement. An organizer of Steve Forbes's whole argument looks like this:

ARGUMENT SUPPORT

VIEWPOINT: Schools should require public-school students to wear uniforms.		
DETAIL #1	DETAIL #2	DETAIL #3
Nobody stands out because of his or her clothes.	Kids can focus on schoolwork, not worry about what they should wear.	Uniforms will help kids feel a sense of school spirit and togetherness.

DEFINITION

Argument or persuasive writing attempts to prove something is true or convince you to adopt the same viewpoint as the writer. Good persuasive writing contains a clear opinion statement and at least three supporting details.

Cause and Effect

The purpose of most cause-effect writing is to answer this question: "Why did this happen?" Essays, biographies, autobiographies, newspaper stories, and textbook articles frequently use cause-effect patterns.

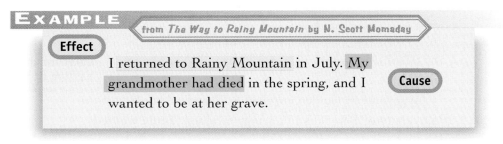

EXAMPLE

from *The Way to Rainy Mountain* by N. Scott Momaday

Effect

I returned to Rainy Mountain in July. My grandmother had died in the spring, and I wanted to be at her grave.

Cause

DESCRIPTION

In **cause-effect order**, the event or situation that happens first and brings about—or causes—another is the cause. The event or events that happen as a result are the effects. Remember that there can be one cause or many causes for a single effect.

Also, an effect can itself become a cause. In the example above, for instance, the author's return to Rainy Mountain causes other events to happen later.

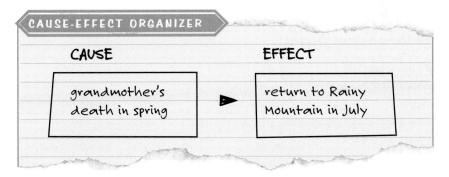

CAUSE-EFFECT ORGANIZER

CAUSE	EFFECT
grandmother's death in spring	return to Rainy Mountain in July

DEFINITION

Cause and effect is a relationship between two or more events in which one event brings about another. The event that happens first is the cause; the one that follows is the effect.

Chronological Order

Nonfiction writers often arrange details in the order in which they happen in time. This passage from a biography entitled *Galileo* covers events in a nine-year period. Note the cues about time.

EXAMPLE

from *Galileo* by Leonard Everett Fisher

In 1575 eleven-year-old Galileo was sent to the school of the Jesuit Monastery of Santa Maria di Vallombrosa to study. . . .

Clues for the passing of time

At seventeen Galileo enrolled as a medical student at the University of Pisa. His financially strained family wanted him to become a rich doctor.

Three years later . . . Galileo's attention was caught by a lamp swinging overhead. He timed its movements with the beat of his pulse.

DESCRIPTION

In **chronological order**, events are described in the order they happened in time. You can tell if a piece is written chronologically by watching for times, dates, and transition words such as *first, next, later,* and so on. Listing items or making a Timeline can help you track the order of details.

TIMELINE

1564	1575	1581	1584
Galileo born	goes to school	enrolls as medical student	notices lamp swinging and makes discovery

DEFINITION

Chronological order is the arrangement of details in time order. This means that the writer explains an event, experience, or series of steps in the order in which they actually occurred.

Classification and Definition

Textbooks and other nonfiction writing sometimes need to explain what terms mean. Usually they group things and tell what is special about them.

EXAMPLE

from "Meteoroids, Meteors, and Meteorites"

Earth is often "invaded" by objects from space. Most of these invaders are **meteoroids** (mee-tee-uh-roids), chunks of metal or stone that orbit the sun. Scientists think that most meteoroids come from the asteroid belt or from comets that have broken up. Each day millions of meteoroids plunge through Earth's atmosphere. When the meteoroid rubs against gases in the atmosphere, friction causes it to burn. The streak of light produced by a burning meteoroid is called a **meteor**. Meteors are also known as shooting stars.

Definitions

Nonfiction

DESCRIPTION

With **classification and definition**, the writers begin by naming the term and placing it in the appropriate class or explaining it. Usually the author provides other details that show how the term is different from others in its class. In the passage above, the writer pinpoints the difference between a *meteoroid* and a *meteor*.

DEFINITIONS

METEOROID	METEOR
chunk of metal or stone that orbits the sun	streak of light from meteoroid burning as it enters Earth's atmosphere

DEFINITION

Classification and definition writing is used to explain and describe a thing or concept and how it looks, acts, and fits in among other members of a group.

Comparison and Contrast

Writers will often use comparison and contrast when explaining something that is not familiar. Comparing or contrasting it to something that you do know helps you understand it.

EXAMPLE

from "The Raven" by Barry Lopez

I am going to have to start at the other end by telling you this: there are no crows in the desert. What appear to be crows are ravens. You must examine the crow, however, before you can understand the raven. To forget the crow completely, as some have tried to do, would be like trying to understand the one who stayed without talking to the one who left.

Understanding one thing by comparing it to another

DESCRIPTION

Comparison involves pointing out what two (or more) things have in common. **Contrast** involves pointing out differences. In the essay "The Raven," Barry Lopez compares and contrasts crows to ravens. Good writers know that two things can be compared only if they are two types of the same thing (for example, two types of birds). Both differences and similarities can help you see the subject (in this case, the raven) in a new light.

DEFINITION

A **comparison** points out similarities between two things.
A **contrast** points out differences between two things.

Connotation and Denotation

The words a writer chooses can say a little or a lot. Look at the words Bailey White uses to describe turkeys in the following paragraph.

EXAMPLE

from "Turkeys" by Bailey White

... the big concern of ornithologists in our area was the wild turkey. They were rare, and the pure-strain wild turkeys had begun to interbreed with farmers' domestic stock. The species was being degraded. It was extinction by dilution, and to the ornithologists it was just as tragic as the more dramatic demise of the passenger pigeon or the Carolina parakeet.

Serious-sounding words

DESCRIPTION

Words with almost the same dictionary meaning, or **denotation**, can have very different **connotations**, or expanded meanings. For example, *cheap* and *thrifty* have close to the same dictionary meaning, but do you see a difference between the two? Saying someone is cheap seems more of a criticism; thrifty seems like a more natural description of how someone acts and even implies a wise use of what's available.

Writers often use certain words because of their emotional meanings. "Extinction by dilution" sounds serious; so does "demise." Bailey White uses these fancy, formal words for humor. She chooses big, serious words for a fairly small thing (the number of pure wild turkeys) that doesn't have much, if any, effect on the lives of most people. But she makes it sound very serious, and her exaggeration adds a touch of humor.

DEFINITION

Connotation is the emotional feelings that surround a word.
Denotation is the strict, literal meaning of a word.

Nonfiction

Editorial

In the newspaper article below, a writer expresses concern about overcrowding at a school.

EXAMPLE

from a newspaper article

VOTE "YES" FOR A NEW SCHOOL

When Rosa Parks Middle School opened its doors this past September, some students learned that they would be sitting on the floor rather than at their desks. Others were asked to pile their books and jackets on tables instead of in assigned lockers. Worse yet, most after-school clubs were asked to hold their meetings in the hallways or off school grounds.

Supporting details

You might be wondering what's wrong with RPMS. The answer is simple: there's nothing wrong with the *students*. But this school, like several others in the district, is terribly overcrowded. . . .

Statement of opinion

DESCRIPTION

An **editorial** is a brief persuasive essay that expresses an opinion, or viewpoint, about a timely and important topic. In an editorial, the writer 1) offers an opinion; 2) supports the opinion with a variety of facts, quotes, or statements; and 3) concludes by restating the opinion. Editorials frequently appear in newspapers and magazines.

DEFINITION

An **editorial** is an essay or article that gives an opinion about a timely or important topic.

Fact and Opinion

Most nonfiction writing, such as this account of the Civil War, is filled with both facts and opinions.

from *The Boys' War* by Jim Murphy

An estimated 2,898,304 would serve in the Union army during the war, while the Confederate side would see almost 1,500,000 join.   **Facts**

    Creating good soldiers began with the officers. Many men had become officers through political favoritism or because they had been able to sign up enough recruits to make a regiment. Others were elected by the soldiers themselves, usually because they were popular, easygoing fellows.   **Opinion**

Nonfiction

DESCRIPTION

A **fact** is a statement that is known to be true. An **opinion** is someone's personal belief about a topic. As a reader, you need to know when you read a fact and when you read an opinion. You also need to evaluate the facts and opinions you read.

When you read the facts, make it a habit to look at the source of the information. When you read opinions, be sure they are well supported with facts, experiences, accounts of experts, and other reliable sources.

DEFINITION

A **fact** is a statement that can be proved. An **opinion** is a statement that reflects a writer's belief. An opinion cannot be proved, but it should be supported with strong, compelling facts and details.

Interview

Have you ever interviewed anybody for a school project or survey? Reading an interview lets you learn about a person and see what his or her opinions are on a variety of subjects. What can you tell about writer Dave Barry from this conversation?

EXAMPLE

from an online interview with author Dave Barry

Interviewer: Where do you suggest up-and-coming novelists look for help in their first years?

Dave Barry: It's tough. The best thing, I think, is to find an agent who believes in you. . . .

Interviewer: Do you feel that grammar and spelling have declined since the advent of the Internet or are we just exposed to more ignorant people?

Dave Barry: Geez, that's a good question. I think it's mostly the latter—in fact, I think the Internet might actually *improve* literacy eventually, since it forces people to write. . . .

Questions and answers

DESCRIPTION

An **interview** is a planned conversation. Interviews can be short or long, formal or informal. The interviewer prepares in advance a set of questions, and the "interviewee" then answers them. The questions can cover both personal and professional topics. Interviews may be done in person, over the phone, or online.

DEFINITION

An interview is a series of questions and answers between two or more people. The purpose is an exchange of information about a given topic.

Lead

The opening paragraph or paragraphs of a newspaper, magazine, or Internet article establish what the article is all about.

EXAMPLE

from the *Chicago Tribune*

1. What

2. Who

3. When

4. Where

In the most dramatic shift in the region's demographic landscape since the great migration of Southern blacks more than a half-century ago, a surge of new Hispanic residents in the 1990s propelled a population boom throughout the Chicago region and fueled the first rebound in Chicago's population since just after World War II.

DESCRIPTION

Lead is the journalism term for the opening paragraph or paragraphs of an article. A lead answers the most important basic journalistic questions: *who, what, where, when,* and *why*. These are called the 5 W's. When you preview a news or feature article, begin by looking for and skimming the lead. It will tell you what you can expect to learn in the rest of the article.

Leads like this one don't always answer all of the 5 W's in a single sentence. This lead tells you a lot:

● *who*—Hispanic residents

● *what*—shift in population

● *where*—Chicago region

● *when*—in the 1990s

Be on the lookout, too, for **buried leads**. They show up in the second, third, or fourth paragraph of an article.

DEFINITION

A lead is the opening paragraph or paragraphs of a newspaper, magazine, or Internet article. The lead establishes what the article is about and often answers the important questions: *who, what, where, when,* and *why*.

Main Idea

In this paragraph, a writer describes what happened on Mount St. Helens. Can you tell what the main idea is?

EXAMPLE

> from *Volcano: The Eruption and Healing of Mount St. Helens* by Patricia Lauber

For well over a hundred years the volcano slept. Each spring, as winter snows melted, its slopes seemed to come alive. Wildflowers bloomed in meadows. Bees gathered pollen and nectar. Birds fed, found mates, and built nests. Bears lumbered out of their dens. Herds of elk and deer feasted on fresh green shoots. Thousands of people came to hike, picnic, camp, fish, paint, bird-watch, or just enjoy the scenery. Logging crews felled tall trees and planted seedlings.

Subject

DESCRIPTION

The **main idea** is the "big idea" of a whole work or a single paragraph. It is the point the author is trying to get across. Identifying the main idea, or thesis, helps you to understand what the writing is all about.

Sometimes the author will state the main idea directly. More often, the writer will imply the main idea and expect you, as a reader, to make inferences, or reasonable guesses, about it.

The main idea is different from the subject or topic. The subject is what the writing is about: *the volcano*. The main idea is the point the writer wants to make about the subject: *For many years before the volcano erupted, it was a beautiful, peaceful place.* The main idea of a piece of writing is a full sentence, not just a word or a phrase.

To find the main idea in a piece of writing, use this formula:

Main Idea, continued

FINDING THE MAIN IDEA

Subject	Volcano
+ **What the author says about the subject**	+ **It was a beautiful, peaceful place.**
= **The main idea**	= **The volcano was for many years a beautiful, peaceful place.**

In the paragraph about the volcano, the writer never states the main idea. You need to infer the main idea, using information from the sentences in the paragraph.

INFERENCE CHART

TEXT	WHAT I CAN CONCLUDE
"For well over a hundred years the volcano slept."	The writer wants to contrast the peaceful scene with what happened when the volcano erupted.

As a reader, remember that the main idea of a piece of writing can be in *three* places:

1. in the beginning, perhaps the first sentence
2. in the end, perhaps the last sentence
3. not stated but implied through all the sentences

DEFINITION

The **main idea** is the central idea in a piece of writing. It is the point that the author wants you to remember most. Some writers will state the main idea directly. Others will expect you to make inferences about the main idea.

Problem and Solution

Writers often try to explain a problem and how it was solved, as shown here.

EXAMPLE

> from *Lincoln* by Russell Freedman

The war had become an endless nightmare of bloodshed and bungling generals. Lincoln doubted if the Union could survive without bold and drastic measures. By the summer of 1862, he had worked out a plan that would hold the loyal slave states in the Union, while striking at the enemies of the Union. **Problem**

On July 22, 1862, he revealed his plan to his cabinet. He had decided, he told them, that emancipation was "a military necessity, absolutely essential to the preservation of the Union." For that reason, he intended to issue a proclamation freeing all the slaves in rebel states that had not returned to the Union by January 1, 1863. **Solution**

DESCRIPTION

Nonfiction writers often use a **problem-solution** pattern to organize information. Frequently, paragraphs will be arranged in a problem-solution order. Sometimes whole books will be devoted to "solving" one problem—for example, explaining why dinosaurs died out. When you read, take notes and use organizers to help you keep track of problem-solution organization.

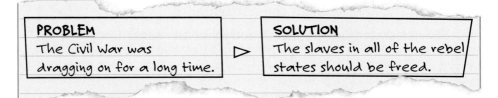

PROBLEM	SOLUTION
The Civil War was dragging on for a long time.	The slaves in all of the rebel states should be freed.

DEFINITION

In **problem and solution** writing, the author identifies and describes a problem and then offers one or more possible solutions.

Propaganda Techniques

Writers use all kinds of techniques to make their arguments persuasive. Look at how one writer explores the issue of whether or not it's wrong to cheat.

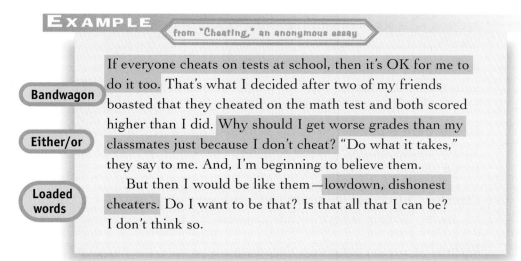

E X A M P L E

from "Cheating," an anonymous essay

Bandwagon

Either/or

Loaded words

If everyone cheats on tests at school, then it's OK for me to do it too. That's what I decided after two of my friends boasted that they cheated on the math test and both scored higher than I did. Why should I get worse grades than my classmates just because I don't cheat? "Do what it takes," they say to me. And, I'm beginning to believe them.

But then I would be like them—lowdown, dishonest cheaters. Do I want to be that? Is that all that I can be? I don't think so.

D E S C R I P T I O N

Propaganda techniques are methods people use to make what they say or write convincing. Sometimes they're used on purpose, to appeal to emotion, not logic. Other times, fallacies, or flaws in logic, are the result of fuzzy or sloppy thinking. Look through the following list of common propaganda techniques. Think about the number of times you've seen them in ads, speeches, editorials, or essays.

Listen for the use of propaganda techniques in the conversations of your friends and in the advertisements on TV. Have you ever heard statements like these?

He's an idiot.

You're either for us, or you're against us.

Come on, everyone will be there.

Nonfiction

Propaganda Techniques, continued

KINDS OF PROPAGANDA TECHNIQUES

Appeal to Ignorance Suggesting that if no one has ever proved a claim false, then it must be true: "Scientists can't prove that there's no life on Mars, can they?"

Bandwagon Suggesting that since everyone else does it or believes it, it must be right or good: "If everyone is skipping school that day, it's OK for me to do it too."

Broad Generalization Making a broad statement that something is true about all members of a group: "Everyone says that Latin is for losers."

Circular Thinking Beginning with the very point you're trying to prove: "This is a boring class because it's not interesting."

Either/Or Analyzing a complex situation as if it has only two sides: "Either we upgrade the computer network in this school, or we doom our students to failure in the world of work."

Loaded Words Using emotionally charged words that will produce strong positive or negative feelings: "Many radicals support that bill, which will hurt the hardworking moms and dads who make America strong."

Oversimplification Making complicated issues or problems seem overly simple or easy to solve: "Whether capital punishment is right boils down to one simple issue: fairness."

Straw Man Exaggerating or oversimplifying the other side so it can be rejected as ridiculous: "Those who support strict dress codes don't care about students' happiness."

DEFINITION

Propaganda techniques are methods—not based in fact—that are used to make arguments more persuasive. Critical readers need to watch out for them, whether they were used on purpose or by accident.

Topic Sentence and Supporting Details

A tightly organized paragraph is about one topic. It often begins with a topic sentence that is followed by three or more supporting details. Most of the time, the paragraph ends with a concluding sentence that sums up what the paragraph is about.

EXAMPLE

from Houghton Mifflin Social Studies

Topic sentence

On the British side, Britain's soldiers were full-time and well trained. This was their profession. 1 They were well supplied with uniforms and weapons. 2 Britain also hired German soldiers to fight in America. 3 Some Americans who were still loyal to the king also fought for Britain. These Loyalists were called Tories, after a group of politicians in England who supported the king. 4 The British army also recruited thousands of American slaves by promising them freedom.

Supporting details

DESCRIPTION

Writers do not always follow the pattern of a **topic sentence** followed by **supporting details** in all of their paragraphs, but it is an excellent model and used a lot in textbooks. The topic sentence states (or strongly suggests) the focus of the paragraph. It usually appears somewhere near the beginning of the paragraph, although it can appear in the middle or at the end.

In a tightly organized paragraph, all sentences relate to the topic. They support the topic sentence in the same way that a table's legs support the top of the table.

The graphic organizer below shows the structure of the example paragraph.

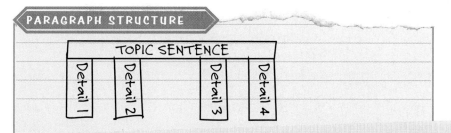

PARAGRAPH STRUCTURE

TOPIC SENTENCE

Detail 1   Detail 2   Detail 3   Detail 4

Nonfiction

Topic Sentence and
Supporting Details, continued

ORGANIZATION OF A PARAGRAPH

TOPIC SENTENCE: "On the British side, Britain's soldiers were full-time and well trained."

DETAILS:

"They were well supplied with uniforms and weapons."	"Britain also hired German soldiers to fight in America."	"Some Americans who were still loyal to the king also fought for Britain."	"The British army also recruited thousands of American slaves by promising them freedom."

All of the sentences in the example describe the topic, Britain's soldiers. The details, or evidence, writers use to support a topic sentence can be examples, facts, personal experiences, opinions from experts, comparisons or contrasts, and definitions. Understanding the organization of paragraphs will help you spot what's most important.

DEFINITION

A **topic sentence** states or strongly suggests the focus of a paragraph. In tightly organized paragraphs, the surrounding sentences all relate to or support the topic sentence. These sentences are called the **supporting details.**

Viewpoint

Writers usually make their opinions clear. As you read this paragraph, see if you can discover the author's viewpoint about the subject.

EXAMPLE

from *Ida B. Wells* by Dennis and Judith Fradin

Clues about viewpoint

The story of these twelve condemned men is a sad commentary on American society in the early 1900s. They and their families had been sharecroppers—farmers who . . . . were paid low prices for their crops and generally lived in extreme poverty. In Phillips County, Arkansas, along the Mississippi River, sharecroppers had tried to join together into a union to demand better prices for their cotton. Outraged by the idea of poor black farmers demanding anything, armed gangs of white ruffians from Arkansas, Tennessee, and Mississippi poured into Phillips County and murdered dozens of black sharecroppers.

DESCRIPTION

In persuasive writing, the writer often will state his or her **viewpoint** directly. Other times, the author gives hints about his or her viewpoint and expects readers to make inferences (reasonable guesses) about the argument. In the example above, the authors' description of the sharecroppers shows their sympathy for the poor black farmers. They were paid "low prices" and lived in "extreme poverty." They were attacked by "armed gangs of white ruffians." This choice of words tells you what the authors' viewpoint is.

DEFINITION

Viewpoint is the author's perspective, or opinion, on an issue or topic. Sometimes the author's viewpoint is presented directly. Other times, readers need to infer how the writer feels about the issue or topic.

Nonfiction

Reading
Fiction

Reading Kinds of Fiction

Reading a Short Story
Reading a Novel

Ways of Reading Fiction

Focus on Characters
Focus on Setting
Focus on Dialogue
Focus on Plot
Focus on Theme
Focus on Comparing and Contrasting

Elements of Fiction

Fiction

Reading a Short Story

"What is the meaning of that story?" "What was the author trying to say in that story?" Maybe you ask yourself questions like that sometimes. Short stories can be funny, spooky, amazing, or just plain impossible to figure out. The key to reading and enjoying them is asking yourself the right kinds of questions and being able to answer them.

Goals

Here you'll learn how to:

✔ appreciate the genre of the **short story**

✔ use the strategy of **using graphic organizers**

✔ understand **the way short stories are often organized**

Before Reading

Let's say you sit down to read the short story "Charles" by Shirley Jackson. What should you do first? What should you do before actually starting to read the first paragraph?

You may be in a rush to get going, but be patient. Take a few minutes to get an idea of what the story is about. And remember that there's no *one* way to read a story. The way you read a story should be *your* way. Not everyone will do it that way, and that's fine. Chart your own course. Here you will see one way to begin.

A Set a Purpose

The ultimate reason to read a short story is pleasure. You read because it's fun. Period. You like a good story in the same way you like a good movie or a good song. But what happens if reading "Charles" is an assignment? If you are like most students, you may be wondering what you are supposed to get out of the story.

Your purpose for reading needs to be more than "The teacher told me to read it" or "I want to do well on the test." Ask yourself what you might find in the story. Start with the title and make it part of a question. Your purpose for reading might be this question:

Setting a Purpose

◼ **Who is Charles, and what is he like?**

This question comes from looking at the title. That's always a good—and obvious—place to start when you're searching for a purpose.

B Preview

Short stories can be hard to preview. They often don't have a lot of pictures or art, and most stories don't have subheadings. So, what do you do? Look for these items:

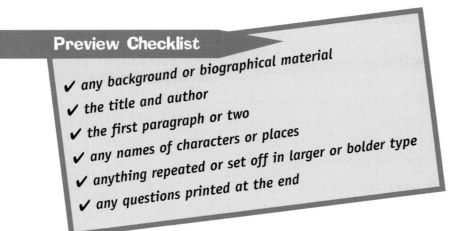

Preview Checklist

✔ any background or biographical material

✔ the title and author

✔ the first paragraph or two

✔ any names of characters or places

✔ anything repeated or set off in larger or bolder type

✔ any questions printed at the end

Now preview "Charles" on pages 296–303.

Fiction

Charles

by

Shirley Jackson

PREVIEW

Title and author

PREVIEW

Background and biographical information

> ## What you need to know about . . .
>
> **THE SELECTION**—"Charles" is a short story that was first published in 1949. In this story (and in many others), Jackson makes an important point—what *you see* is not necessarily what *you get*.
>
> **THE AUTHOR**—Shirley Jackson (1916–1985) was an American writer who was best known for her short story "The Lottery," a chilling tale about a town that stones to death one member of the community every year. Jackson wrote six novels in her career, including *The Haunting of Hill House* (1959) and *We Have Always Lived in the Castle* (1962). She was considered a master of **gothic horror** and psychological suspense.
>
> **THE THEME**—Growing up
>
> **FURTHER READING**—"The Lottery" by Shirley Jackson

"Charles," continued

PREVIEW

Character name

PREVIEW

Mother telling the story

The day my Laurie started kindergarten, he renounced[1] corduroy[2] overalls with bibs and began wearing blue jeans with a belt; I watched him go off the first morning with the older girl next door, seeing clearly that an era of my life was ended, my sweet-voiced nursery-school tot replaced by a long-trousered, swaggering[3] character who forgot to stop at the corner and wave good-bye to me.

PREVIEW

First two paragraphs

He came home the same way, the front door slamming open, his cap on the floor, and the voice suddenly becoming raucous[4] shouting, "Isn't anybody *here*?"

At lunch he spoke insolently[5] to his father, spilled Jannie's milk, and remarked that his teacher said that we were not to take the name of the Lord in vain.

PREVIEW

Character of father

"How *was* school today?" I asked, elaborately casual.

"All right," he said.

"Did you learn anything?" his father asked.

Laurie regarded his father coldly. "I didn't learn nothing," he said.

"Anything," I said. "Didn't learn anything."

"The teacher spanked a boy, though," Laurie said, addressing his bread and butter. "For being fresh,"[6] he added, with his mouth full.

"What did he do?" I asked. "Who was it?"

---

1 **renounced** (rĭ nounst´) *v.* declared that you have given up.

2 **corduroy** (kôr´də roi´) *n.* thick cotton cloth with close velvet-like ridges.

3 **swaggering** (swăg´a ring) *adj.* way of walking, acting, or speaking in a bold, superior manner.

4 **raucous** (rô´ kəs) *adj.* hoarse and harsh-sounding.

5 **insolently** (ĭn´sa lənt lē) *adv.* boldly rude and insulting.

6 **fresh** (frĕsh) *adj.* too bold and rude.

Fiction

PREVIEW

Character name

PREVIEW

Repeated words

Laurie thought. "It was Charles," he said. "He was fresh. The teacher spanked him and made him stand in a corner. He was awfully fresh."

"What did he do?" I asked again, but Laurie slid off his chair, took a cookie, and left, while his father was still saying, "See here, young man."

The next day Laurie remarked at lunch, as soon as he sat down, "Well, Charles was bad again today." He grinned enormously and said, "Today Charles hit the teacher."

"Good heavens," I said, mindful of the Lord's name, "I suppose he got spanked again?"

"He sure did," Laurie said. "Look up," he said to his father.

"What?" his father said, looking up.

"Look down," Laurie said. "Look at my thumb. Gee you're dumb." He began to laugh insanely.[7]

"Why did Charles hit the teacher?" I asked quickly.

"Because she tried to make him color with red crayons," Laurie said. "Charles wanted to color with green crayons so he hit the teacher and she spanked him and said nobody play with Charles but everybody did."

The third day—it was Wednesday of the first week—Charles bounced a see-saw on to the head of a little girl and made her bleed, and the teacher made him stay inside all during recess. Thursday Charles had to stand in a corner during story-time because he kept pounding his feet on the floor. Friday Charles was deprived of blackboard privileges because he threw chalk.

On Saturday I remarked to my husband, "Do you think kindergarten is too unsettling[8] for Laurie? All this

NOTE

Conflict at school

---

7 **insanely** (ĭn sān' lē) *adv.* in a way of someone who is not sane or who is mentally ill.

8 **unsettling** (un set´ling) *adj.* not ordered; disturbing.

toughness, and bad grammar, and this Charles boy sounds like such a bad influence."

"It'll be all right," my husband said reassuringly.[9] "Bound to be people like Charles in the world. Might as well meet them now as later."

On Monday, Laurie came home late, full of news. "Charles," he shouted as he came up the hill; I was waiting anxiously on the front steps. "Charles," Laurie yelled all the way up the hill, "Charles was bad again."

"Come right in," I said, as soon as he came close enough. "Lunch is waiting."

"You know what Charles did?" he demanded, following me through the door. "Charles yelled so in school they sent a boy in from first grade to tell the teacher she had to make Charles keep quiet, and so Charles had to stay after school. And so all the children stayed to watch him."

"What did he do?" I asked.

"He just sat there," Laurie said, climbing into his chair at the table. "Hi, Pop, y'old dust mop."

"Charles had to stay after school today," I told my husband. "Everyone stayed with him."

"What does this Charles look like?" my husband asked Laurie. "What's his other name?"

"He's bigger than me," Laurie said, "and he doesn't have any rubbers and he doesn't ever wear a jacket."

Monday night was the first Parent-Teachers meeting, and only the fact that the baby had a cold kept me from going; I wanted passionately to meet Charles's mother. On Tuesday Laurie remarked suddenly, "Our teacher had a friend come to see her in school today."

"Charles's mother?" my husband and I asked simultaneously.

PREVIEW

Repeated words

Fiction

PREVIEW

Repeated words

---

9 **reassuringly** (rē′ ə shŭr′ ing lē) *adv.* restoring calm or confidence.

"Naaah," Laurie said scornfully. "It was a man who came and made us do exercises; we had to touch our toes. Look." He climbed down from his chair and squatted down and touched his toes. "Like this," he said. He got solemnly back into his chair and said, picking up his fork, "Charles didn't even *do* exercises."

"That's fine," I said heartily. "Didn't Charles want to do exercises?"

"Naaah," Laurie said. "Charles was so fresh to the teacher's friend he wasn't *let* to do exercises."

"Fresh again?" I said.

"He kicked the teacher's friend," Laurie said. "The teacher's friend told Charles to touch his toes like I just did, and Charles kicked him."

"What are they going to do about Charles, do you suppose?" Laurie's father asked him.

Laurie shrugged elaborately. "Throw him out of school, I guess," he said.

NOTE
Situation at school getting worse

Wednesday and Thursday were routine. Charles yelled during story hour and hit a boy in the stomach and made him cry. On Friday Charles stayed after school again and so did all the other children.

With the third week of kindergarten, Charles was an institution in our family; the baby was being a Charles when she cried all afternoon; Laurie did a Charles when he filled his wagon full of mud and pulled it through the kitchen; even my husband, when he caught his elbow in the telephone cord and pulled telephone, ash tray, and a bowl of flowers off the table, said, after the first minute, "Looks like Charles."

NOTE
Situation getting better

During the third and fourth weeks it looked like a reformation in Charles. Laurie reported grimly at lunch on Thursday of the third week, "Charles was so good today the teacher gave him an apple."

"What?" I said, and my husband added warily, "You mean Charles?"

"Charles," Laurie said. "He gave the crayons around and he picked up the books afterward, and the teacher said he was her helper."

"What happened?" I asked incredulously.

"He was her helper, that's all," Laurie said, and shrugged.

"Can this be true, about Charles?" I asked my husband that night. "Can something like this happen?"

"Wait and see," my husband said cynically. "When you've got a Charles to deal with, this may mean he's only plotting."

He seemed to be wrong. For over a week Charles was the teacher's helper; each day he handed things out and he picked things up; no one had to stay after school.

"The P.T.A. meeting's next week again," I told my husband one evening. "I'm going to find Charles's mother there."

"Ask her what happened to Charles," my husband said. "I'd like to know."

"I'd like to know myself," I said.

On Friday of that week things were back to normal. "You know what Charles did today?" Laurie demanded at the lunch table in a voice slightly awed. "He told a little girl to say a word and she said it and the teacher washed her mouth out with soap and Charles laughed."

"What word?" his father asked unwisely, and Laurie said, "I'll have to whisper it to you, it's so bad." He got down off his chair and went around to his father. His father bent his head down and Laurie whispered joyfully. His father's eyes widened.

"Did Charles tell the little girl to say *that*?" he asked respectfully.

PREVIEW

Repeated words

Fiction

NOTE

Conflict continuing

"She said it *twice*," Laurie said. "Charles told her to say it *twice*."

"What happened to Charles?" my husband asked.

"Nothing," Laurie said. "He was passing out the crayons."

Monday morning Charles abandoned the little girl and said the evil word himself three or four times, getting his mouth washed out with soap each time. He also threw chalk. My husband came to the door with me that evening as I set out for the P.T.A. meeting. "Invite her over for a cup of tea after the meeting," he said. "I want to get a look at her."

NOTE
Tension building

"If only she's there," I said prayerfully.

"She'll be there," my husband said. "I don't see how they could hold a P.T.A. meeting without Charles's mother."

At the meeting I sat restlessly, scanning each comfortable matronly[10] face, trying to determine which one hid the secret of Charles. None of them looked to me haggard[11] enough. No one stood up in the meeting and apologized for the way her son had been acting. No one mentioned Charles.

PREVIEW
Character of teacher

After the meeting I identified and sought out Laurie's kindergarten teacher. She had a plate with a cup of tea and a piece of chocolate cake; I had a plate with a cup of tea and a piece of marshmallow cake. We maneuvered up to one another cautiously, and smiled.

"I've been so anxious to meet you," I said. "I'm Laurie's mother."

"We're all so interested in Laurie," she said.

---

10 **matronly** (mā′ trən lē) *adv.* like a wife or widow, especially an older married woman.

11 **haggard** (hăg′ərd) *adj.* looking worn from pain, worry, or hunger.

"Well, he certainly likes kindergarten," I said. "He talks about it all the time."

"We had a little trouble adjusting, the first week or so," she said primly, "but now he's a fine little helper. With occasional lapses, of course."

"Laurie usually adjusts very quickly," I said. "I suppose this time it's Charles's influence."

"Charles?"

"Yes," I said laughing, "you must have your hands full in that kindergarten, with Charles."

"Charles?" she said. "We don't have any Charles in the kindergarten."

NOTE
Climax

Fiction

Questions to Consider

1. Who is Charles?
2. Who are the other characters?
3. What does Laurie's mother mean when she says, "With the third week of kindergarten Charles was an institution in our family. . . ."?
4. Why is Laurie's mother so eager to meet Charles's mother?

PREVIEW
Questions

C Plan

What did you learn in the preview?

■ The introduction said "what *you see* is not necessarily what *you get.*"

■ The story is about a kindergarten boy named Laurie and another boy named Charles.

■ Laurie's mother is telling the story.

■ Charles is a bad kid who is always making trouble.

You can find out all of this in about two minutes, tops. You probably learned much more in your previewing. But, at the very least, you could get a start on understanding the story just by looking in a few of the right places. In fact, with short stories the crucial thing is not to skip the previewing.

What you learned from your preview will help you make a plan to get the information that you want about Charles. Finding out about him is your purpose, so think of a way to get information. Here are several possible ways to do that.

1. Ask Yourself Questions

One method would be asking yourself questions about him that you are curious about. For example:

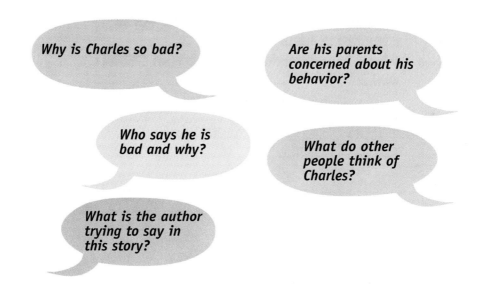

Why is Charles so bad?

Are his parents concerned about his behavior?

Who says he is bad and why?

What do other people think of Charles?

What is the author trying to say in this story?

2. Focus on One Part

Another method would be to focus your reading on learning as much as you can about Charles. Mark or highlight everything having to do with him. Mark when he first appears in the story. Mark what he says, what is said about him, and what details are given about him.

3. Watch What Changes

You can also try to pay attention to what changes. Is anything different about Charles at the end of the story from the beginning? By looking at the changes that occur in a story, you will get an idea of what the author was trying to say.

Reading Strategy: Using Graphic Organizers

The best strategy to do all that is probably to **use graphic organizers.** You can use different organizers depending on what your purpose question is and what you want to focus on. Some work really well for gathering details about setting or theme. Others are more useful for characters or plot. For example, with a Story Organizer like the one below, you can chart what happens at the beginning, middle, and end of the story and note what changes. It's helpful to set it up before you start to read, so it'll be ready when you need it.

Fiction

STORY ORGANIZER

BEGINNING	MIDDLE	END

During Reading

Now that you have a purpose and a reading strategy, it's time to read "Charles."

D Read with a Purpose

Go through the story at your own pace. "Speed reading" is way overrated. Fast is not necessarily better. Read as slowly as you need to read in order to understand what's happening. Think about Charles and what he's like as you go. Take your time.

Record some of your ideas as you read by using one or more graphic organizers. They can help you zero in on a particular part of the story—for example, the character of Charles. For that, you might use a Character Map. It focuses on your purpose—to find out about the character Charles.

Here are a few helpful organizers you can use for reading short stories. Try one or two. Decide for yourself which ones work best for you. Remember, more isn't always better.

1. Character Map

Occasionally with stories you may want to use a kind of graphic called a Character Map. This reading tool works best when you are focusing on one or more characters.

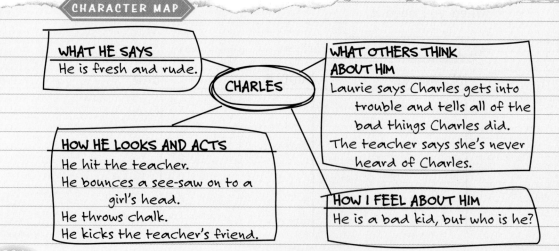

CHARACTER MAP

WHAT HE SAYS
He is fresh and rude.

CHARLES

WHAT OTHERS THINK ABOUT HIM
Laurie says Charles gets into trouble and tells all of the bad things Charles did.
The teacher says she's never heard of Charles.

HOW HE LOOKS AND ACTS
He hit the teacher.
He bounces a see-saw on to a girl's head.
He throws chalk.
He kicks the teacher's friend.

HOW I FEEL ABOUT HIM
He is a bad kid, but who is he?

2. Storyboard

To find what happens in a story, use a simple Storyboard with a few words and sketches. The simplest kind looks like the one below. This kind of organizer works best with stories and simple plots.

STORYBOARD

BEGINNING	MIDDLE	END
Laurie tells about a boy named Charles in his kindergarten class.	Charles does lots of bad things.	Laurie's mother learns that the teacher has never heard of Charles.

Fiction

3. Story String

Another kind of graphic organizer includes more details and lists a number of things that happen in the story. It is often called a Story String because it links together each event in a story as if by a string. This kind of graphic works best for a long story with a plot that has a lot of twists and turns.

STORY STRING

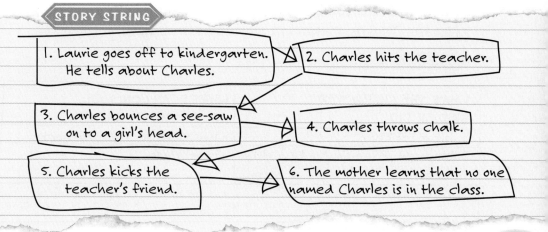

1. Laurie goes off to kindergarten. He tells about Charles.
2. Charles hits the teacher.
3. Charles bounces a see-saw on to a girl's head.
4. Charles throws chalk.
5. Charles kicks the teacher's friend.
6. The mother learns that no one named Charles is in the class.

4. Fiction Organizer

Still another kind of organizer that works well with stories is a Fiction Organizer. There will be times your teachers will ask you to do a book report. <u>One good way to gather all of the information you need about characters, setting, and plot is with a Fiction Organizer.</u>

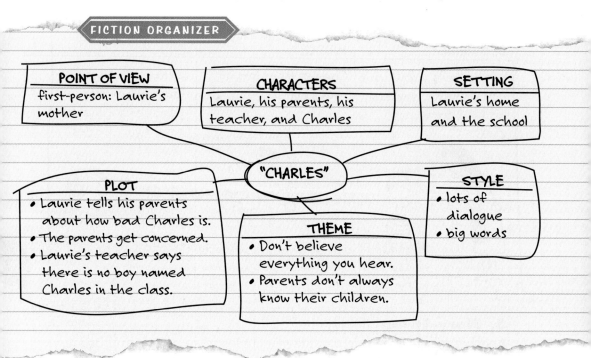

FICTION ORGANIZER

POINT OF VIEW
first-person: Laurie's mother

CHARACTERS
Laurie, his parents, his teacher, and Charles

SETTING
Laurie's home and the school

"CHARLES"

PLOT
• Laurie tells his parents about how bad Charles is.
• The parents get concerned.
• Laurie's teacher says there is no boy named Charles in the class.

THEME
• Don't believe everything you hear.
• Parents don't always know their children.

STYLE
• lots of dialogue
• big words

5. Inference Chart

Use an Inference Chart to gather together your ideas about what a character is like. Look at what the character says or does and see what conclusions you can draw. <u>This kind of organizer works best when you have to interpret or make inferences about a character.</u>

INFERENCE CHART

WHAT THE CHARACTER SAID OR DID	WHAT I CAN CONCLUDE ABOUT THE CHARACTER
1. hit a teacher	• has no respect for authority
2. bounced a see-saw on to a girl's head	• is reckless
3. threw chalk	• does not listen and has little control

How Stories Are Organized

The plots of many short stories can be divided into five basic parts. As you read, look for these parts. Go back to "Charles" on pages 297–303 and notice what the reader marked. The reader kept track of the conflict, tension, and climax—three key elements. You can keep track of plot events by making a Plot Diagram.

PLOT DIAGRAM

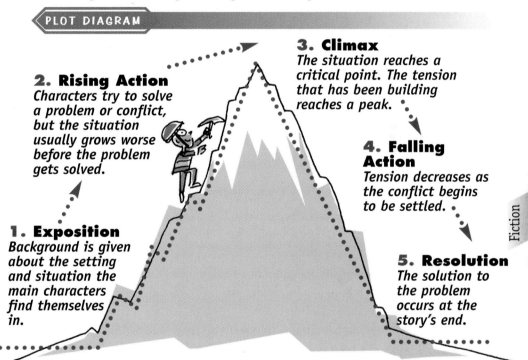

2. Rising Action
Characters try to solve a problem or conflict, but the situation usually grows worse before the problem gets solved.

3. Climax
The situation reaches a critical point. The tension that has been building reaches a peak.

1. Exposition
Background is given about the setting and situation the main characters find themselves in.

4. Falling Action
Tension decreases as the conflict begins to be settled.

5. Resolution
The solution to the problem occurs at the story's end.

Fiction

Of course, this five-part story organization isn't a "one-size-fits-all" formula. Not all stories have all five of these parts. In fact, "Charles" doesn't. The story drops off quickly right after Laurie's teacher says there is no boy named Charles in the class. We don't even get one sentence about how Laurie's mother reacts to the news. The plot structure of this story might look like this:

PLOT DIAGRAM OF "CHARLES"

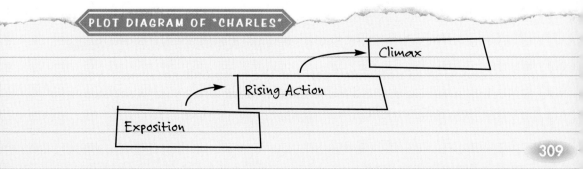

Climax

Rising Action

Exposition

E Connect

Part of the fun of reading stories is relating what you're reading about to your own life. Yes, you may need to figure out what the characters are like, summarize the plot, or discuss the theme. Those may be specific reading purposes that your teacher assigns. But don't forget to make connections between your own life and the story.

When you read a story, explore your own reactions to it. What does it make you think about? What experiences of your own does the story remind you of? What other stories is it like?

Look at how one reader responded to a conversation between Laurie and his parents.

from "Charles"

Laurie's a brat like my neighbor.

"How *was* school today?" I asked, elaborately casual.
"All right," he said.
"Did you learn anything?" his father asked.
Laurie regarded his father coldly. "I didn't learn nothing," he said.
"Anything," I said. "Didn't learn anything."
"The teacher spanked a boy, though," Laurie said, addressing his bread and butter. "For being fresh," he added, with his mouth full.
"What did he do?" I asked. "Who was it?"
Laurie thought. "It was Charles," he said. "He was fresh. The teacher spanked him and made him stand in a corner. He was awfully fresh."

My parents wouldn't let me act that way.

"What did he do?" I asked again, but Laurie slid off his chair, took a cookie, and left, while his father was still saying, "See here, young man."

By choosing to note some parts of the story and not others, you are being an active reader. You're making decisions about what meaning the story has for you.

After Reading

"Charles" ends with a surprise. Guess what? The teacher has never heard of this boy who is such a troublemaker. You were probably reading along thinking of Charles as a bad guy. You had one idea of what the story was about. Then, suddenly, everything changes in the last line.

F Pause and Reflect

When a story has a surprise ending, you'll probably want to go back and look at the story again. Go over the story in your head. How well do you understand it?

You thought you had a pretty good idea of what kind of boy Charles is. But now you learn that Charles does not exist. What do you really know about him? Is he a made-up character? Ask yourself questions like these to check on your understanding of a story:

Looking Back

■ **Do I follow what happened?**
■ **Can I describe what the main characters are like?**
■ **Did the ending come as a surprise? Why or why not?**
■ **Does anything in the story confuse me?**
■ **What is the story's theme?**

All of these questions give you a good reason to do some rereading.

G Reread

Good writing creates questions, suggestions, hints, possibilities, and ideas. The way to follow up on them is by going back through the story again, looking for more information.

Fiction

Close Reading

One powerful strategy for looking back is called **close reading**. It works especially well for brief works such as short stories or poems. Close reading refers to looking very carefully, word by word, at part or all of a work. Zoom in on particular words, sentences, and paragraphs that catch your eye. Maybe they seem important; maybe they puzzle you. Ask yourself why the author used a certain word or why a detail was included.

If you can read this you're too close

For example, let's go over the story opening sentence by sentence. What clues does it give you? Use a Double-entry Journal to record your reactions.

DOUBLE-ENTRY JOURNAL

TEXT OF "CHARLES"	WHAT I THINK ABOUT IT
"The day my Laurie started kindergarten, he renounced corduroy overalls with bibs and began wearing blue jeans with a belt. . . ."	He "gave up" overalls, because he wanted to seem grown-up.
"I watched him go off the first morning with the older girl next door, seeing clearly that an era of my life was ended, my sweet-voiced nursery-school tot replaced by a long-trousered, swaggering character who forgot to stop at the corner and wave good-bye to me."	"I watched" suggests the mother is telling the story because he's her "tot." Era was ended—the one of her "sweet-voiced nursery-school tot." What's starting? Now Laurie is trying to act "cool."

Looking at Point of View

In rereading, you may also want to look at the information you get in the story and where it comes from. From the sentence "I watched him go off . . . ," you can guess that Laurie's mom is telling the story. But how does she learn about Charles? As you reread, pay attention to who says what about Charles.

Once you see that Laurie gives his mom most of the information about Charles, you have to wonder. How true is what he tells her? Is Laurie the kind of kid who might make things up?

Comparing Characters

Comparing and contrasting two characters can help you see them in a clearer light. Note in this Venn Diagram how Laurie and Charles are alike and different. The center part shows their likenesses and the outside shows how they are different.

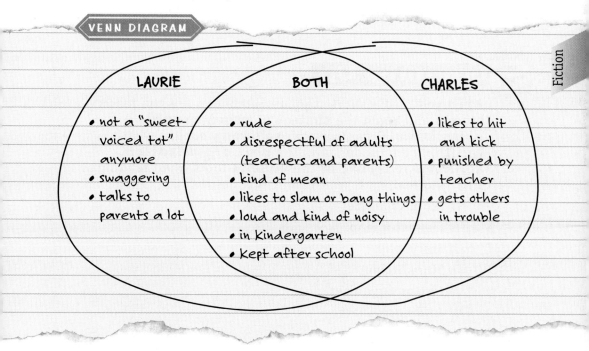

VENN DIAGRAM

LAURIE
- not a "sweet-voiced tot" anymore
- swaggering
- talks to parents a lot

BOTH
- rude
- disrespectful of adults (teachers and parents)
- kind of mean
- likes to slam or bang things
- loud and kind of noisy
- in kindergarten
- kept after school

CHARLES
- likes to hit and kick
- punished by teacher
- gets others in trouble

Fiction

Rereading lets you pick up on details you might have missed the first time. With this one graphic organizer, you can make a powerful comparison and begin to see how much Laurie and Charles have in common. The boy Laurie describes is a lot like Laurie himself.

H Remember

The notes and charts you have made as you read and reread will help you remember Charles and the story about him. Here are two other suggestions to try.

1. Talk about It

One of the best ways to remember a story is to talk about it. Tell a friend who hasn't read it what it's all about. Talk about your favorite parts with someone else who's read it. Share ideas about who would play the main part if it were turned into a movie.

2. Write in a Journal

Try keeping a learning journal. It helps to jot down a paragraph or two about what you read. In fact, you may even want to keep some of the charts or diagrams in the journal as well. Even a few words will come in handy later on when you want to remember what you have read.

Summing Up

When you read a short story, remember to use the reading process and apply the strategy of **using graphic organizers.** Organizers can help you visualize what's happening and understand the **plot organization.** Remember to try one of these useful tools when reading short stories:

- Story Organizer
- Character Map
- Storyboard
- Story String
- Fiction Organizer
- Inference Chart
- Plot Diagram
- Double-entry Journal
- Venn Diagram

Remember that **close reading** can be an effective rereading strategy.

Reading a Novel

Do you like to read novels? If you said no, you should look at *how* you read them. Novels can open up new and fascinating worlds. They can take you to places you've never been, to times long past or far in the future, and inside the hearts and minds of people. They can make you smile or cry. Because of their length, novels can cover broader spans of time than short stories can. They also tell more complicated stories and go more deeply into the lives of characters.

Goals

Here you'll learn how to:

✔ examine the **basic elements of a novel**

✔ use the reading strategy of **synthesizing**

✔ recognize the **plot organization of a novel**

In this lesson, you'll follow the story of the Newbery Medal–winning novel *Roll of Thunder, Hear My Cry* by Mildred D. Taylor. You'll share in the experiences of an African-American farm family in Mississippi during the Great Depression of the 1930s.

Fiction

Before Reading

Most people read novels for personal enjoyment. They get pleasure from following a suspenseful plot, getting to know interesting characters, or learning about a different culture or historical period. But you'll probably also have to read novels for school assignments. When you do, the reading process can help.

A Set a Purpose

Novels are long and often complex. There's a lot going on and a lot to sort out. How can you tell what you need to pay attention to and what's really important? Knowing the basic elements of any story can help you keep focused.

When you read a novel, think of your purpose as answering these questions about *six* elements of the novel:

Setting a Purpose

- **Who is telling the story? (*point of view*)**
- **Who are the main characters, and what are they like? (*characters*)**
- **Where and when does the story take place? What is this place, culture, or historical period like? (*setting*)**
- **What happens? (*plot*)**
- **What is the author's central idea or message? (*theme*)**
- **How does the author express his or her ideas? (*style*)**

As you can see, reading a novel means you have a number of questions to answer and elements to look at. That sounds like a lot, doesn't it? But the good news is that some of those questions you can answer fairly easily and quickly.

B Preview

Before you start to read, take the time to get a general idea of what you can expect. If you have an idea of what a novel is about, you can draw on any prior knowledge you might have—perhaps about the location, the time period, or any other works by the same author. Preview these parts of a novel:

Preview Checklist

✔ the title and author
✔ the front and back covers
✔ any summaries or excerpts from book reviews
✔ any information about the author
✔ any introductory material, such as a preface
✔ any chapter titles or illustrations

Most novels will have several of these parts, but not all of them. From previewing, you often can get a general idea of the plot, characters, setting, and themes. For example, notice how much you can learn from previewing the front and back covers of *Roll of Thunder, Hear My Cry.*

Fiction

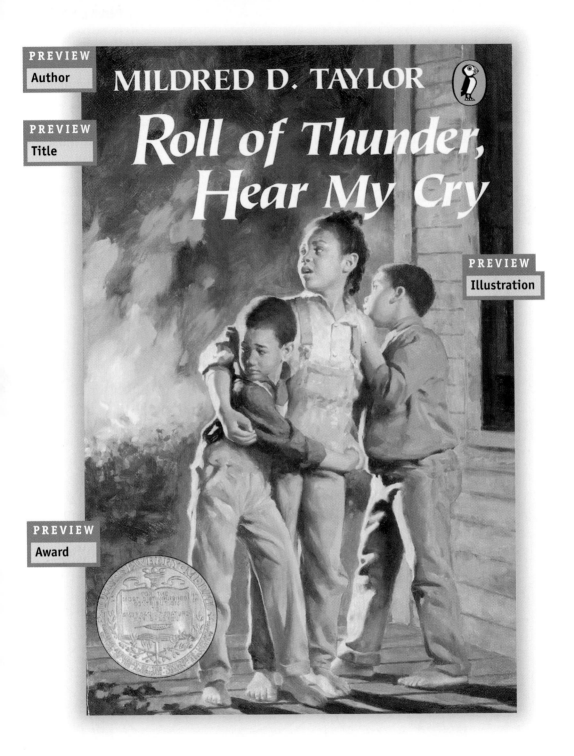

PREVIEW
Author

PREVIEW
Title

PREVIEW
Illustration

PREVIEW
Award

MILDRED D. TAYLOR

*Roll of Thunder,
Hear My Cry*

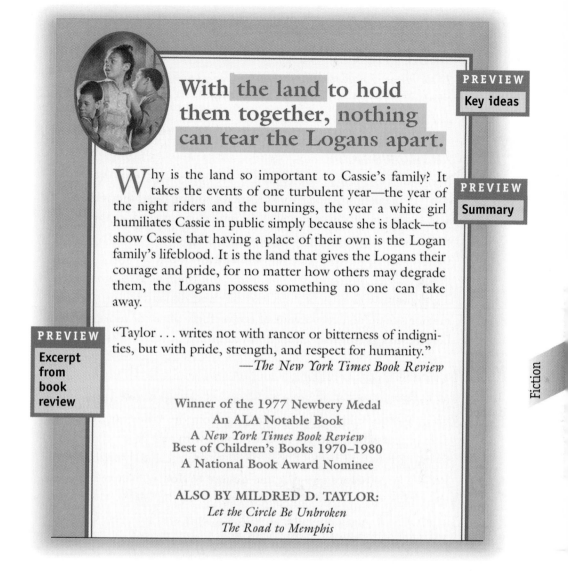

With the land to hold them together, nothing can tear the Logans apart.

Why is the land so important to Cassie's family? It takes the events of one turbulent year—the year of the night riders and the burnings, the year a white girl humiliates Cassie in public simply because she is black—to show Cassie that having a place of their own is the Logan family's lifeblood. It is the land that gives the Logans their courage and pride, for no matter how others may degrade them, the Logans possess something no one can take away.

PREVIEW
Summary

PREVIEW
Excerpt from book review

"Taylor . . . writes not with rancor or bitterness of indignities, but with pride, strength, and respect for humanity."
    —*The New York Times Book Review*

Winner of the 1977 Newbery Medal
An ALA Notable Book
A *New York Times Book Review*
Best of Children's Books 1970–1980
A National Book Award Nominee

ALSO BY MILDRED D. TAYLOR:
Let the Circle Be Unbroken
The Road to Memphis

Fiction

From previewing the front and back covers, you learn that the novel focuses on the Logans, a proud African-American family living in a rural area. You also learn that the novel is about land, family ties, and racism. Now preview the dedication, part of the author's note, and the author's biography that also appear in the book.

DEDICATION

To the memory of my beloved father
who lived many adventures of the boy Stacey
and who was in essence the man David.

PREVIEW

Father's influence on author

AUTHOR'S NOTE

My father was a master storyteller. He could tell a fine old story that made me hold my sides with rolling laughter and sent happy tears down my cheeks, or a story of stark reality that made me shiver and be grateful for my own warm, secure surroundings. He could tell stories of beauty and grace, stories of gentle dreams, and paint them as vividly as any picture with splashes of character and dialogue. His memory detailed every event of ten or forty years or more before, just as if it had happened yesterday. . . .

PREVIEW

Author born in Mississippi

ABOUT THE AUTHOR

Mildred Taylor was born in Jackson, Mississippi, and grew up in Toledo, Ohio. After graduating from the University of Toledo, she spent two years in Ethiopia with the Peace Corps. Returning to the United States, she recruited for the Peace Corps before entering the School of Journalism at the University of Colorado. As a member of the Black Student Alliance, she worked with students and university officials in structuring a Black Studies program at the university.

PREVIEW

Information about author

PREVIEW

Previous book about the Logan family

Mildred Taylor's first book about the Logan family, *Song of the Trees* (Dial), won the Council on Interracial Books Award in the African American category. It was also a *New York Times* Outstanding Book of the Year in 1975. The *Times* called it "Triumphant . . . a true story and truly told"; *Horn Book* said, "The simple story has been written with great conviction and strength"; other reviews called it "absorbing," "powerful," "a moving story."

C Plan

Now you're prepared to read the novel. Even if you've never heard of the book or the author before, you've already built up some background knowledge. The author was born in the South, and the story of the Logan family you're about to read is based partly on the life of her father. Even if you happen to know more about the author or her other books, you still need a plan to help you answer questions about characters, plot, and so on.

Reading Strategy: Synthesizing

One good strategy for reading a novel is **synthesizing.** When you synthesize, you look at a number of parts or elements and pull them together. The idea is to see how those individual parts will fit together.

Before you begin reading, decide on a way to keep track of your ideas and questions about the six elements of a novel: point of view, characters, setting, plot, theme, and style. You might divide your notebook into sections, one for each of these elements.

Filling in a Fiction Organizer is a great way to see how each part affects the work as a whole. This and other ways of taking notes on elements of a novel can help you learn more and enjoy more from the novels you read.

Fiction

FICTION ORGANIZER

POINT OF VIEW   CHARACTERS   SETTING

TITLE

PLOT   THEME   STYLE

During Reading

Usually you'll read a novel at different times over a period of days or weeks. If you find a novel you love, you may feel as though you can't wait to get back to it. You may be tempted to speed through a book to find out what happens at the end. But if you're reading a novel for a class assignment, you'll need to take the time to read it closely rather than just quickly.

D Read with a Purpose

Think back to the questions you want to answer:

- Who is telling the story? (*point of view*)
- Who are the main characters, and what are they like? (*characters*)
- Where and when does the story take place? What is this place, culture, or historical period like? (*setting*)
- What happens? (*plot*)
- What is the author's central idea or message? (*theme*)
- How does the author express his or her ideas? (*style*)

We've listed the questions separately, but as you read, things will be much more jumbled up. For instance, you'll be reading the description of the setting *as* you learn about the characters. We'll look at the elements one by one in this lesson. But as you read or discuss the book in class, you'll no doubt be jumping back and forth from one element to another.

1. Point of View

Have you ever noticed that no two people tell a story in exactly the same way? Each person picks different things to emphasize. That's why **point of view**—the perspective from which an author presents a story—is so important. The person who tells the story in a novel is called the narrator. Look at the beginning of *Roll of Thunder, Hear My Cry*. What can you tell about the narrator?

> from *Roll of Thunder, Hear My Cry*
>
> "Little Man, would you come on? You keep it up and you're gonna make us late."
>
> My youngest brother paid no attention to me. Grasping more firmly his newspaper-wrapped notebook and his tin-can lunch of cornbread and oil sausages, he continued to concentrate on the dusty road. He lagged several feet behind my other brothers, Stacey and Christopher-John, and me, attempting to keep the rusty Mississippi dust from swelling with each step. . . .
>
> "You keep it up and make us late for school, Mama's gonna wear you out," I threatened, pulling with exasperation at the high collar of the Sunday dress Mama had made me wear for the first day of school—as if that event were something special.

NOTE
Narrator has three brothers.

NOTE
First-person pronouns

NOTE
Narrator is a girl.

Fiction

You've learned a lot about the story's point of view. A girl (named Cassie) is telling the story. The pronouns (*I, me, us, my*) are clues that the point of view is first person. Cassie has three brothers (Little Man, Stacey, and Christopher-John). As a reader, you'll experience the story from Cassie's viewpoint.

2. Characters

To understand a novel, you need to keep track of the **characters**. A novelist gives clues about characters by describing how they look, act, speak, think, and feel and how other characters react to them.

Look again at part of the first chapter of *Roll of Thunder, Hear My Cry*. What is Cassie like?

NOTE
Cassie bosses her brother.

NOTE
She likes to be outdoors.

NOTE
She listens to her mother.

NOTE
Cassie is younger than twelve.

NOTE
Cassie can't keep from speaking her mind.

"You keep it up and make us late for school, Mama's gonna wear you out," I threatened, pulling with exasperation at the high collar of the Sunday dress Mama had made me wear for the first day of school—as if that event were something special. It seemed to me that showing up at school at all on a bright August-like October morning made for running the cool forest trails and wading barefoot in the forest pond was concession enough; Sunday clothing was asking too much. Christopher-John and Stacey were not too pleased about the clothing or school either. Only Little Man, just beginning his school career, found the prospects of both intriguing.

"Y'all go ahead and get dirty if y'all wanna," he replied without even looking up from his studied steps. "Me, I'm gonna stay clean."

"I betcha Mama's gonna 'clean' you, you keep it up," I grumbled.

"Ah, Cassie, leave him be," Stacey admonished, frowning and kicking testily at the road.

"I ain't said nothing but—"

Stacey cut me a wicked look and I grew silent. His disposition had been irritatingly sour lately. If I hadn't known the cause of it, I could have forgotten very easily that he was, at twelve, bigger than I, and that I had promised Mama to arrive at school looking clean and ladylike. "Shoot," I mumbled finally, unable to restrain myself from further comment, "it ain't my fault you gotta be in Mama's class this year."

The highlighting and the notes point out just how much you can learn about Cassie in just a few paragraphs. Try using some of these other tools to organize your ideas about characters.

324

FAMILY TREE WEB

Keeping track of the characters in a long novel can be tough. To sort out who's who and how they're related, you might draw a family tree. You can add to the family tree as you learn about the rest of the family members. You can also add other important characters, noting their relationship to one or more members of the family. In the Family Tree Web below, the names of characters you've read about so far appear in black, and the names of some others you'll meet later in the novel are in blue.

Fiction

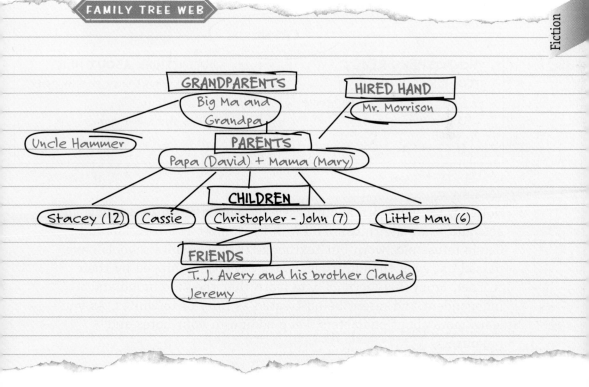

FAMILY TREE WEB

GRANDPARENTS
Big Ma and Grandpa

HIRED HAND
Mr. Morrison

Uncle Hammer

PARENTS
Papa (David) + Mama (Mary)

CHILDREN
Stacey (12) Cassie Christopher - John (7) Little Man (6)

FRIENDS
T. J. Avery and his brother Claude
Jeremy

CHARACTER MAP

Part of the fun of reading is getting to know what
the characters are like. For each main character,
you might start a chart to take notes on
how he or she looks, acts, speaks, feels,
or thinks and how other characters
react to him or her. For example,
you might start a Character Map
like this one for Cassie.

CHARACTER MAP

WHAT SHE SAYS AND DOES	WHAT SHE THINKS AND FEELS
• bosses Little Man • talks back to Stacey	• hates dresses and shoes • prefers woods and pond to school

CASSIE

HOW OTHERS REACT TO HER	WHAT I THINK ABOUT HER
• Stacey tells her to leave Little Man alone.	• understand why she likes to be outdoors • glad she's outspoken

Notice what you learn about Cassie by paying attention to how she
acts and what she thinks. Later on in Chapter 1, Little Man and
Cassie refuse old, worn-out textbooks that the white schools have
passed on, even though it means they will get whipped by their
teacher. From their actions, you learn that they are proud and
independent and resent being treated as inferior to whites. As you
learn more about characters, keep adding to your notes and
organizers.

3. Setting

The place and time in which a story happens is called its **setting**. A novel typically has one *general setting* and a number of *immediate settings*. The general setting is the overall location and time period of the entire story. An immediate setting is the exact place and time in which an individual event happens.

GENERAL SETTING: LOCATION

Chapter 1 describes the general setting of *Roll of Thunder, Hear My Cry*. From the opening passage, you learned that the Logans live in Mississippi. The highlighting and the notes in the following passage point out other important details about the general setting of the novel.

from *Roll of Thunder, Hear My Cry*

Fiction

> NOTE
> **Logan land and surrounding area**

> NOTE
> **Amount of land**

> NOTE
> **Good quality land**

Before us the narrow, sun-splotched road wound like a lazy red serpent dividing the high forest bank of quiet, old trees on the left from the cotton field, forested by giant green and purple stalks, on the right. A barbed-wire fence ran the length of the deep field, stretching eastward for over a quarter of a mile until it met the sloping green pasture that signaled the end of our family's four hundred acres. An ancient oak tree on the slope, visible even now, was the official dividing mark between Logan land and the beginning of a dense forest. Beyond the protective fencing of the forest, vast farming fields, worked by a multitude of sharecropping families, covered two-thirds of a ten-square-mile plantation. That was Harlan Granger land.

Once our land had been Granger land too, but the Grangers had sold it during Reconstruction to a Yankee for tax money. In 1887, when the land was up for sale again, Grandpa had bought two hundred acres of it, and in 1918, after the first two hundred acres had been paid off, he had bought another two hundred. It was good rich land, much of it still virgin forest, and there was no debt on half of it.

GENERAL SETTING: TIME PERIOD

In *Roll of Thunder, Hear My Cry*, understanding the time period is crucial to understanding what happens in the novel. Early on, readers discover that the story begins in the year 1933, during the Great Depression. That's long after slavery was abolished in 1865. However, by the 1930s African Americans in the South still had not gained equal rights. Whites still dominated life across the South.

For example, most of the black farmers in the novel work as sharecroppers on white-owned land. Sharecroppers give a share of the crops they raise to their landlord in place of paying rent. You can learn all of these details about America in the 1930s from the descriptions in Taylor's novel. Read how one African-American sharecropper in the novel describes his financial situation:

from *Roll of Thunder, Hear My Cry*

NOTE
No money

NOTE
Few clothes

. . ."I got no cash money. Mr. Montier [the white landlord] signs for me up at that Wallace store so's I can get my tools, my mule, my seed, my fertilizer, my food, and what few clothes I needs to keep my children from runnin' plumb naked. When cotton-pickin' time comes, he sells my cotton, takes half of it, pays my debt up at that store and my interest for they credit, then charges me ten to fifteen percent more as 'risk' money for signin' for me in the first place. This year I earned me near two hundred dollars after Mr. Montier took his half of the crop money, but I ain't seen a penny of it. In fact, if I manages to come out even without owin' that man nothin', I figures I've had a good year. . . ."

NOTE
Usually owes money

The living conditions of African Americans during this time period are part of the general setting of the novel. They affect what happens in the story. What follows is an example of the kinds of notes a reader might take on the book's general setting. Having notes like these to look back on will make it easier to see how the setting affects other elements, such as plot or theme.

SETTING CHART

ROLL OF THUNDER, HEAR MY CRY

TIME: 1933	PLACE: rural Mississippi
Few blacks own land. Most blacks are sharecroppers, always in debt to white landlords.	Settings are farms and plantations on which cotton is grown. Logans have 400-acre farm next to Granger plantation.

IMMEDIATE SETTINGS: DETAILS

Individual events in the novel take place in a number of immediate settings. You might think of them as scenes. The descriptions of particular places can tell you a lot. Read the description of one bedroom in the Logan house and note the details that help paint the picture of the scene.

Fiction

from *Roll of Thunder, Hear My Cry*

It was a warm, comfortable room of doors and wood and pictures. From it a person could reach the front or the side porch, the kitchen, and the two other bedrooms. Its walls were made of smooth oak, and on them hung gigantic photographs of Grandpa and Big Ma, Papa and Uncle Hammer when they were boys, Papa's two eldest brothers, who were now dead, and pictures of Mama's family. The furniture, a mixture of Logan-crafted walnut and oak, included a walnut bed whose ornate headboard rose halfway up the wall toward the high ceiling, a grand chiffonier with a floor-length mirror, a large rolltop desk which had once been Grandpa's but now belonged to Mama, and the four oak chairs, two of them rockers, which Grandpa had made for Big Ma as a wedding present.

NOTE
Pleasant room

NOTE
Pictures of family

NOTE
Hand-made furniture

IMMEDIATE SETTINGS: IMPORTANCE

The setting reflects the warmth and closeness of the Logans' family life. Now look at this description of one of the spots on the Logan family farm, an area where white men had cut down many trees. Notice how it reveals the family's attachment to the land.

> **from *Roll of Thunder, Hear My Cry***
>
> **NOTE**
> **Trees cut down**
>
> As we neared the pond, the forest gapped open into a wide, brown glade, man-made by the felling of many trees, some of them still on the ground. . . .
>
> Big Ma surveyed the clearing without a word, then, stepping around the rotting trees, she made her way to the pond and sat down on one of them. I sat close beside her and waited for her to speak. After a while she shook her
>
> **NOTE**
> **Grandfather's love for trees**
>
> head and said: "I'm sho' glad your grandpa never had to see none of this. He dearly loved these here old trees. Him and me, we used to come down here early mornin's or just 'fore the sun was 'bout to set and just sit and talk. He used to call this place his thinkin' spot and he called that old pond there
>
> **NOTE**
> **Special names for places**
>
> Caroline, after me."

These brief descriptions of immediate settings reveal a lot of information. They tell about the characters and about two important topics of the novel: 1) attachment to family and 2) attachment to the land. These two bonds form the strong core of the Logans' lives.

4. Plot

A **plot** is a series of events that makes up a story. In a novel, the plot often centers around a conflict, or struggle, between opposing forces. In *Roll of Thunder, Hear My Cry,* the Logans struggle against the racial attitudes in the South.

Decide on a way to help you keep the plot of a novel clear in your head as you read. One possibility is to write brief Summary Notes of what happens in each chapter.

SUMMARY NOTES

CHAPTER 1
Cassie and Little Man get whipped at school for refusing to accept books that whites hand down to blacks. Mama stands by them.

CHAPTER 2
Papa brings Mr. Morrison home to protect the family after the Berrys are burned by some white men.

Another great way to help you remember the events in a plot is to create a brief Timeline of what's going on when.

TIMELINE

October 1933:	Cassie and Little Man get whipped at school. Papa brings Mr. Morrison home.
November 1933:	Logan children stop school bus. T. J. lets Stacey take punishment for cheating, and Stacey beats up T. J.
December 1933:	Cassie is humiliated by Lillian Jean and Mr. Simms. Logans get people to stop buying at the Wallace store.
January 1934:	Mama gets fired after T. J. tells Wallaces that she persuaded people to stop shopping at their store.
Spring 1934:	T. J. starts hanging out with the Simms brothers. Papa gets shot, and Mr. Morrison beats up the Wallaces.
August 1934:	Bank calls up Logans' loan. T. J. robs store with the Simms brothers. Wallaces come to hang T. J. Papa starts fire and prevents hanging. T. J. goes to jail.

Fiction

How Novels Are Organized

Often, but not always, the events that make up a novel's plot are presented in **chronological order**. That means the same order in which they happened in time. Like many short stories, novels often follow the traditional plot structure or something close to it.

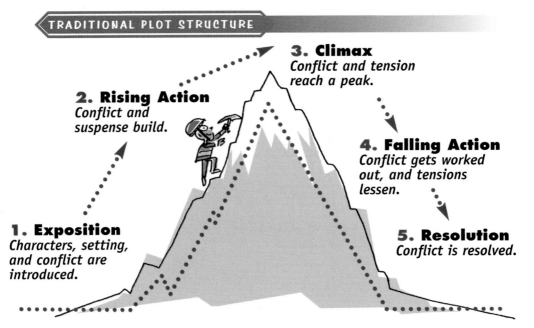

TRADITIONAL PLOT STRUCTURE

3. Climax
Conflict and tension reach a peak.

2. Rising Action
Conflict and suspense build.

4. Falling Action
Conflict gets worked out, and tensions lessen.

1. Exposition
Characters, setting, and conflict are introduced.

5. Resolution
Conflict is resolved.

As you read a novel, be on the lookout for these five parts of the plot. See if you can tell where the suspense starts building or the climax occurs. Make a Plot Diagram like this:

PLOT DIAGRAM

CLIMAX
Papa starts a fire to prevent hanging of T. J.

RISING ACTION
Mama loses job, Papa gets shot, and violence increases.

FALLING ACTION
Men work together to fight fire.

EXPOSITION
Logans are trying to hold on to their land in tough times.

RESOLUTION
T. J. goes to jail, but Logans are unhurt.

5. Theme

A novel's **theme** is a message about life from the author to a reader. It's a statement that makes clear what the book means. The theme (or themes) of a work may be stated directly. Other times you'll need to do some digging around to come up with a theme.

Suppose you've almost finished reading *Roll of Thunder, Hear My Cry* and your teacher has asked you to come to the next class ready to talk about theme. Now's the time to practice your skills in synthesizing. Go back over the notes you've made.

Ask yourself these three questions:

1. What "big idea" is the novel about?

2. What do characters do or say that relates to that topic?

3. What important lessons about life do readers learn?

Let's say in *Roll of Thunder, Hear My Cry* you realize your notes and a lot of class discussion have been about the land. Taylor describes it in detail, and characters talk about it a lot. Here is an organizer that shows how a reader came up with an idea of one possible theme.

Fiction

TOPIC AND THEME ORGANIZER

1. Big idea or topic: **LAND**

2. What characters say or do:
  - Logans risk their lives to hold on to it.
  - Papa always talks about how important land is.

3. What is important to learn: Land is important and worth fighting for.

Of course, there are other "big ideas" in this novel and other possible statements of theme. But using this three-step process will help you come up with a solid theme statement of your own.

6. Style

Style refers to the way an author expresses his or her ideas. An author's style is marked by the kinds of words, sentence structure, and literary devices he or she uses. To analyze an author's style, ask yourself questions like these:

- Does the author use mostly short, simple words and sentences or long, complex ones?

- What sort of feeling do I have about the writing? Is it loose and casual, formal and proper, or something else?

- Do the characters speak in **dialect**? Does their language seem realistic and believable?

- Does the author use sensory language, or words that appeal to the five senses?

- Is there a lot of imagery?

You might copy parts of the novel that stand out for you. Note the kinds of words and language used. Write your reactions to the author's style in a Double-entry Journal. For example, here are some quotes you might write down from *Roll of Thunder, Hear My Cry*.

DOUBLE-ENTRY JOURNAL

QUOTES	MY THOUGHTS AND REACTIONS
• Uncle Hammer speaking to T. J.: "Then if you want something and it's a good thing and you got it in the right way, you better hang on to it and don't let nobody talk you out of it. You care what a lot of useless people say 'bout you you'll never get anywhere, 'cause there's a lotta folks don't want you to make it. . . . "	• I love all the dialect and slang the characters use. • I can hear how Uncle Hammer speaks. • The long sentences make me take time reading it. • It's a very informal feeling.
• Little Man at school: "Then his eyes grew wide, and suddenly he sucked in his breath and sprang from his chair like a wounded animal, flinging the book onto the floor and stomping madly upon it."	• Taylor uses a lot of description—the sights and sounds. • Simile of Little Man being like an animal is a strong image.

E Connect

Besides looking at each of the main elements in a novel, active readers also make connections between characters and events in the novel and their own lives. Get in the habit of asking yourself questions such as these:

> *What was your reaction to major events in the novel?*

> *How did you feel about each character? Which did you like and which did you dislike? Why?*

> *How can you relate what happened in the novel to your own feelings and experiences?*

> *What else have you read that's like this novel?*

Fiction

For example, here's what a reader wrote after reading Papa's advice to Cassie.

---

from *Roll of Thunder, Hear My Cry*

[Papa speaking to Cassie:] ". . . There are things you can't back down on, things you gotta take a stand on. But it's up to you to decide what them things are. You have to demand respect in this world, ain't nobody just gonna hand it to you. How you carry yourself, what you stand for — that's how you gain respect. But, little one, ain't nobody's respect worth more than your own . . ."

Papa seems really wise. I admire him.

My grandma tells me the same thing about earning respect all the time.

Why wait for someone else to tell you what to think about a book? Listen to your own thoughts and feelings as you read.

After Reading

By the time you finish reading a novel, you have invested a lot of time. To get the most from your effort, take the time afterward to think about, digest, and sum up what you've learned.

F Pause and Reflect

First, think back on your purpose in reading a novel. How well do you understand the basic elements of the novel: point of view, characters, setting, plot, theme, and style? Ask yourself questions like these:

Looking Back

- Can I describe the main characters and the setting?
- What is the theme?
- What's the central conflict of the novel?
- Are there parts of the novel that I don't understand?

Now's the time to think about each of the elements and review your notes. Maybe even though you can describe each of the elements separately, you're not sure how they all fit together. Don't give up. That happens all the time. Go back and open up the novel again.

G Reread

Rereading parts of a novel will help you pull together—synthesize—many of your separate ideas.

Rereading Strategy: Using Graphic Organizers

Focus on what you need to look at again. **Using graphic organizers** can help you get a better sense of the whole book or of just a small part. Think about how plot, character, and theme go together, for instance. Or just look at character or theme alone.

Looking at the Whole Novel

When you're reading something short—say a poem or newspaper article—it's fairly easy to keep it all in your mind at once. But when you're reading something long, you'll have to work a little harder at remembering what's there. Review any separate notes you took and use an organizer to collect your ideas. If you tried to fill out a Fiction Organizer, for instance, see where your gaps are. Below is an example of what a completed one might look like.

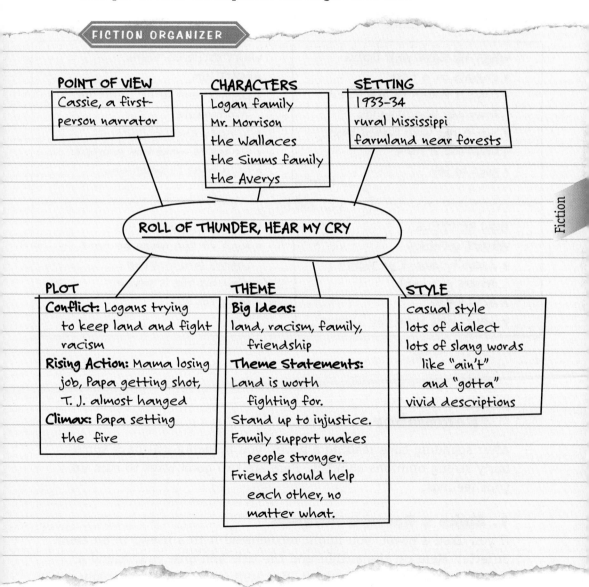

FICTION ORGANIZER

POINT OF VIEW
Cassie, a first-person narrator

CHARACTERS
Logan family
Mr. Morrison
the Wallaces
the Simms family
the Averys

SETTING
1933-34
rural Mississippi
farmland near forests

ROLL OF THUNDER, HEAR MY CRY

PLOT
Conflict: Logans trying to keep land and fight racism
Rising Action: Mama losing job, Papa getting shot, T. J. almost hanged
Climax: Papa setting the fire

THEME
Big Ideas:
land, racism, family, friendship
Theme Statements:
Land is worth fighting for.
Stand up to injustice.
Family support makes people stronger.
Friends should help each other, no matter what.

STYLE
casual style
lots of dialect
lots of slang words like "ain't" and "gotta"
vivid descriptions

Fiction

Looking at One Part

You might also reread to get information about one scene or character. Say, for instance, that as you get toward the end of the novel, you notice that a lot of the plot focuses on T. J. Avery. You can't remember much about him, and your character notes are all about the Logans. It would make sense to reread the parts where T. J. appears. Gather up the details in an organizer such as the one below.

CHARACTER MAP

WHAT HE SAYS AND DOES	WHAT OTHERS THINK ABOUT HIM
• cheats on a test	• Logans realize he's getting
• causes Mama to get fired from her teaching job	into trouble.
• hangs out with Simms boys	• Stacey ends friendship.
• helps rob a store	• Wallaces want him hanged.
• goes to jail	• Papa tries to save him.

T. J. AVERY

HOW HE FEELS ABOUT OTHERS	HOW I FEEL ABOUT HIM
• doesn't care if he gets others in trouble	• mad at him when he gets Logans into trouble
• acts mean	• glad his life is saved
• wants help from the Logans	• sorry for him

H Remember

After spending time reading a novel, you probably will have some fairly strong opinions about it. Here are two good ways to sum up your feelings.

1. Make a Recommendation

If you liked a novel, you might recommend it to a friend in an email or letter. Mention the author and the title and give your friend a general sense of what it's about. Be careful not to give away any surprise endings!

2. Do a Book Review

In a book review, you give your opinions on one or more of the main elements of a novel. To identify your opinions, you might fill out a rating chart similar to the one shown here. Put the chart in your reading journal. Support your ratings with details from the novel.

RATING CHART FOR A NOVEL

PLOT

1	2	3	4	5	6	7	8	9	10
Dull				Interesting				Very interesting	

CHARACTERS

1	2	3	4	5	6	7	8	9	10
Not believable				Somewhat believable				Very believable	

SETTING

1	2	3	4	5	6	7	8	9	10
Not developed				Somewhat developed				Well developed	

THEMES

1	2	3	4	5	6	7	8	9	10
Unclear				Somewhat clear				Clearly stated	

Fiction

Summing Up

As you read a novel, use the reading strategy of **synthesizing** to keep track of the separate elements: point of view, setting, characters, plot, theme, and style. You can increase your understanding and enjoyment of a novel by paying attention to **plot structure** and using tools such as these:

- Fiction Organizer
- Web
- Character Map
- Setting Chart
- Summary Notes
- Timeline
- Plot Diagram
- Topic and Theme Organizer
- Double-entry Journal

Also, **using graphic organizers** can help you as you reread.

Focus on Characters

If the **plot** of a story is *what* happens, then the **characters** are *who* the events happen to. Your understanding of characters in a piece of writing affects your view of other story elements:

- your reaction to the plot
- your opinions of the other characters
- your understanding of the theme

This lesson examines the characters in Theodore Taylor's novel *The Cay*.

Goals

Here you'll learn how to:

✔ **identify and understand a variety of character types**

✔ **recognize how characters influence plot, other characters, and theme**

✔ **use reading tools to analyze characters and track changes in them**

Before Reading

Begin your focus on characters by recognizing how writers reveal what different kinds of characters are like.

Major and Minor Characters

In literature, the main character is the most important character. The action of the plot and the main conflict revolve around him or her. Minor characters are less important characters who interact with the main character and with one another.

Usually it is fairly easy to identify the main character. Often, the title, chapter titles, or picture captions will name the most important character. You can also do a quick skim, looking for the character name that pops up more often than any other. In *The Cay*, for instance, Phillip Enright is the main character. He is the narrator of the story. A quick skim of the first ten pages of *The Cay* tells you that Phillip is from a small family and is adventurous and curious.

Clues about Characters

The way an author develops a character is called *characterization*. Authors scatter character clues throughout a story. You need to pay attention to these sorts of details:

- physical appearance and personality
- speech, thoughts, feelings, and actions
- interactions with other characters
- direct comments by the author

That's a lot to sort out, isn't it? When your focus is character, it's usually smart to plan on using a tool called a Character Map. It will help you keep track of facts and details and draw conclusions about characters. This, in turn, will help you more thoroughly enjoy the story. As you get ready to read, make a Character Map with headings like the ones below.

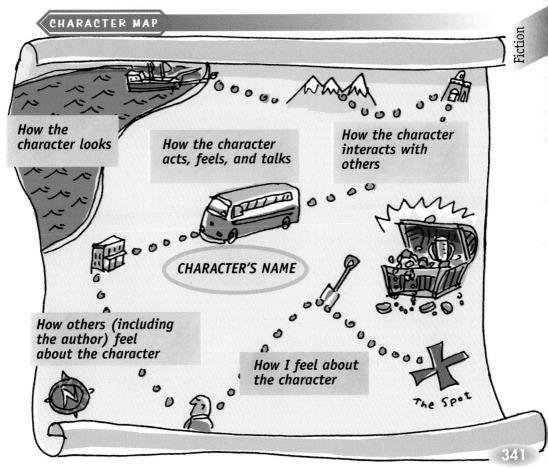

CHARACTER MAP

Fiction

How the character looks

How the character acts, feels, and talks

How the character interacts with others

CHARACTER'S NAME

How others (including the author) feel about the character

How I feel about the character

The Spot

During Reading

It's not like you can totally forget the plot or ignore the theme or setting when your focus is on character. But you do need to pay special attention to the details of what characters say and do, how they are described, and how they interact with others.

Read the following two excerpts from *The Cay*. Note the details given about Timothy, an elderly man who rescues Phillip after an accident.

from *The Cay* by Theodore Taylor

NOTE
How he looks

He was extremely old yet seemed powerful. Muscles rippled over the ebony of his arms and around his shoulders. His chest was thick and his neck was the size of a small tree trunk. I looked at his hands and feet. The skin was alligatored and cracked, tough from age and walking barefoot on the hot decks of schooners and freighters.

He saw me examining him and said gently, "Put your 'ead back downg, young bahss, an' rest awhile longer. Do not look direct at d'sun. 'Tis too powerful."

NOTE
How he interacts with others

NOTE
How others feel about him

I said, "I must have water, Timothy. I'm very hot."

Without answering, he opened the trap in the raft and secured the keg again. It was then that I began to learn what a stubborn old man he could be. I began to dislike Timothy.

"Young bahss," he said, coming back under the shelter, "mebbe before d'night, a schooner will pass dis way, an' if dat 'appens, you may drink d' whole kag. Mebbe d'schooner will not pass dis way, so we mus' make our wattah last."

NOTE
What he thinks

Analyzing Characters

Even a short passage can tell you a lot about a character. Specifics from the story are what you base your conclusions about character on.

Suppose, for instance, that someone wondered how a reader could say that Timothy has good survival skills. Go back to the second excerpt. The description of Timothy preserving the water is the evidence.

Here is a Character Map of Timothy one reader made. How do the reader's ideas compare with yours?

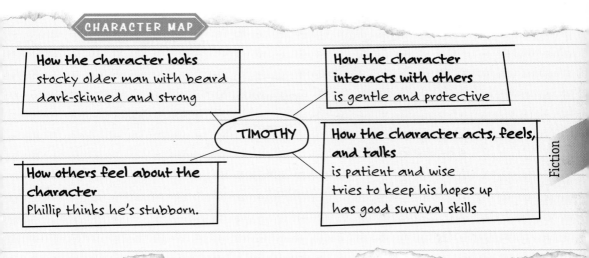

CHARACTER MAP

How the character looks
stocky older man with beard
dark-skinned and strong

How the character interacts with others
is gentle and protective

TIMOTHY

How the character acts, feels, and talks
is patient and wise
tries to keep his hopes up
has good survival skills

How others feel about the character
Phillip thinks he's stubborn.

Fiction

Creating a Portrait

As you read, you'll make additions and changes to your Character Map. Your view of a character is a work in progress. New pages mean new discoveries. Someone will do something unexpected, or you'll realize you missed an earlier clue. When your focus is a character, constantly ask yourself how new information fits with the information you learned earlier.

Get in the habit of talking about the characters with others who have read—or are reading—the story or novel. Two heads can definitely be better than one.

Using graphic organizers, such as a Character Map, is a great way of focusing on characters. If you find yourself pressed for time, try making a Character Web for a character you're thinking about. At the tip of each spoke, write a word that describes the character. When possible, use words that come directly from the story. Below is a Character Web based on *The Cay*.

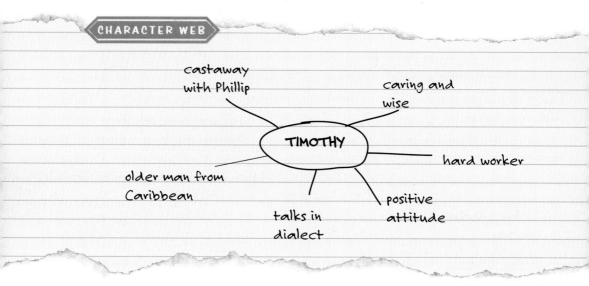

CHARACTER WEB

castaway with Phillip

caring and wise

older man from Caribbean

TIMOTHY

hard worker

talks in dialect

positive attitude

Sometimes you may want to make a Character Web for more than one character. Look at the organizer below for Phillip, the narrator. The phrases describe Phillip during the first half of the novel.

CHARACTER WEB

thick hair and dark tan

adventurous

mean to Timothy

PHILLIP

scared of staying stranded on the island

immature

likes to ask questions

Character and Plot

Understanding characters can be a big help in following the plot of a story or novel. A character's response to plot developments can tell you a lot about the character's personality. And, of course, the events in a plot greatly influence what a character says, does, or feels. When the narrator is a character in the story, it's really important to get a clear picture of him or her. It's through that person that readers get information about what's going on. For instance, if a character is dishonest or sneaky, how much of what he or she says should you believe?

As you read, ask yourself these questions:

What is this character's role in the plot?

How would the plot be different without this particular character?

How do the events in the plot affect this character?

Fiction

Remember that a plot is usually built around a conflict or problem that the main character faces. Focusing on a character's problems can help you understand what's driving the actions of the plot. In *The Cay*, for example, Phillip is the protagonist. The antagonist is the set of obstacles he and Timothy face at sea and on a remote island. Figuring out if Phillip and Timothy are rescued from the island builds the suspense and keeps readers turning pages.

Character and Other Characters

Many times one character's feelings about and conversations with another character are revealing.

As you read, pay attention to what one character says to or about another. Watch how they treat each other. Even a seemingly minor character can color your views in important ways. When one or two characters are patient in a particular situation, for instance, their actions call attention to the impatience of another character. How the main character treats somebody else tells you a lot about the kind of person he or she is.

Read another excerpt from *The Cay*. It describes a seemingly unimportant moment when the main characters introduce themselves to each other.

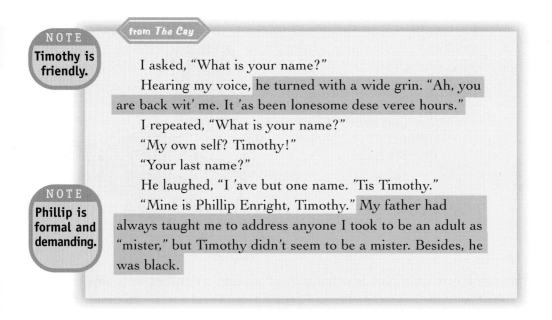

NOTE
Timothy is friendly.

from *The Cay*

I asked, "What is your name?"

Hearing my voice, he turned with a wide grin. "Ah, you are back wit' me. It 'as been lonesome dese veree hours."

I repeated, "What is your name?"

"My own self? Timothy!"

"Your last name?"

He laughed, "I 'ave but one name. 'Tis Timothy."

"Mine is Phillip Enright, Timothy." My father had

NOTE
Phillip is formal and demanding.

always taught me to address anyone I took to be an adult as "mister," but Timothy didn't seem to be a mister. Besides, he was black.

Use an organizer like the Inference Chart on the next page to keep track of what characters can reveal about one another.

INFERENCE CHART

WHAT CHARACTERS SAID OR DID	WHAT I CAN CONCLUDE ABOUT THEM
Phillip and Timothy exchange names.	Timothy is nice to Phillip, but Phillip shows little patience with or respect for Timothy.

Character and Theme

By what they say and do, characters provide readers with clues about the theme. But you need to be on the lookout for them. As you read, pay special attention to *two* sorts of clues.

1. A Character's Statements or Thoughts about Life

It's obvious that some things people say are more important than others, right? When a character at a dinner party says, "Pass the salt," it's probably not too meaningful. But when a character sits back at the table and begins to offer his or her thoughts on life, love, friendship—or some other "big idea"—take note. That's likely to be a clue about theme. Sometimes it's the protagonist whose words lead you to a theme, but sometimes it's not. In *The Cay*, for instance, Timothy offers his general philosophy on people in a conversation one day with Phillip.

from *The Cay*

   Wanting to hear it from Timothy, I asked him why there were different colors of skin, white and black, brown and red, and he laughed back, "Why b'feesh different color, or flower b'different color? I true don' know, Phill-eep, but I true tink beneath d'skin is all d'same."

NOTE
General statement about equality

As you read the rest of *The Cay*, Timothy's words take on added meaning. At first, Phillip doesn't like Timothy because he is different from him. Slowly, Phillip begins to grow up and understand that they are alike in many ways and that he can learn a lot from Timothy.

Fiction

2. A Change in a Character

Looking at how a main character changes can also lead you to a story's theme.

A *static character* is one who remains the same, one who doesn't change. Things happen *to* a static character. A *dynamic character*, in contrast, does change or grow. As you read, ask yourself these questions:

> **Does the character learn anything?**

> **Does the character feel different about himself or herself?**

> **Does the character's physical appearance change?**

> **Do other characters notice differences in him or her?**

If you notice any changes, ask yourself what the author wants you to think about them. Does this excerpt from the middle of *The Cay* give you any clues about the book's theme?

---

from *The Cay*

The rope, I thought. It wasn't for him. It was for me. After a while, I said, "Timothy . . ."

He did not answer, but walked over to me, pressing more palm fronds into my hands. He murmured, "'Tis veree easy, ovah an' under . . ." Then he went back to singing about fungee and feesh.

Something happened to me that day on the cay. I'm not quite sure what it was even now, but I had begun to change.

I said to Timothy, "I want to be your friend."

He said softly, "Young bahss, you 'ave always been my friend."

I said, "Can you call me Phillip instead of young boss?"

"Phill-eep," he said warmly.

NOTE

Big changes in Phillip

Phillip has made it very clear that he has changed. He wants to be Timothy's friend. When you notice a change in a character, ask yourself what caused it and how it might reveal a story's theme.

After Reading

When you finish reading a story or novel, it's time to figure out what you've learned. Specifically, what do you know about the characters? Ask yourself questions like these:

Can I identify the main and minor characters?

Do I know what they are like?

Why do they act the way they do?

Do any of the characters change from the beginning to the end?

How does my view of characters affect my understanding of plot, other characters, and theme?

Fiction

Sometimes when you finish a reading, you'll still have unanswered questions. You may want to return to a particular passage just because you enjoyed it. Or maybe you need to jog your memory about a specific character in order to write a character sketch.

When you reflect on a character, go back to the first description of him or her and the last. Reread these scenes and other important ones in which the character is involved. Make notes about what you find on an organizer or jot down your thoughts about the character in a paragraph or list.

Completing a chart like the one on the next page can help you collect your thoughts about a particular character.

PHILLIP ENRIGHT

BEGINNING	MIDDLE	END
Phillip is adventurous and immature. He doesn't like Timothy because he's different from him.	Phillip begins to grow up. He grows physically stronger and mentally tougher. He becomes friendly with Timothy.	Phillip has learned many new things. He gets to go back home, and he understands life better.

POSSIBLE THEMES: Accept people for who they are, not what they look like.
Don't take life for granted.

Summing Up

- ■ Characters can be major or minor, static or dynamic.
- ■ Understanding characters can help you understand plot, other characters, and theme.
- ■ Use graphic organizers to help you keep track of your ideas about characters.
- ■ Change or growth in a main character often points to the theme.

Focus on Setting

Setting is where and when the story takes place. It's the time, place, and general environment in which the action happens. Settings can be in the past, present, or future or in real or imaginary lands. Sometimes a setting is described in a lot of detail. Other times it's not. In some stories and novels, the setting is extremely important; in others it's not.

Setting is the lens through which a story is seen. This means that you look through the setting to see these important elements of the story:

- mood
- characters
- plot

Goals

Here you'll learn how to:

✔ **spot clues about setting**

✔ **relate the setting to the mood, characters, and plot**

✔ **analyze the setting**

Before Reading

In most stories and novels, the writer gives information about the general setting in the opening paragraphs, usually in the first three to six paragraphs. When your focus is setting, begin by looking for these clues about time and place as you preview:

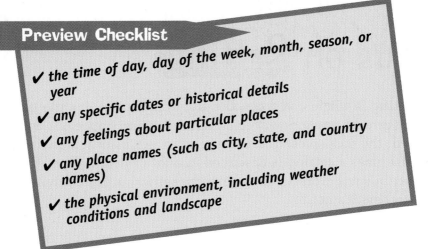

Preview Checklist

✔ the time of day, day of the week, month, season, or year

✔ any specific dates or historical details

✔ any feelings about particular places

✔ any place names (such as city, state, and country names)

✔ the physical environment, including weather conditions and landscape

Below are two paragraphs from the first chapter of Phyllis Reynolds Naylor's novel *Shiloh*. As the novel begins, an eleven-year-old boy named Marty Preston is out for a walk in the West Virginia woods by his home. This passage contains many clues about time and place.

from *Shiloh* by Phyllis Reynolds Naylor

PREVIEW

Physical environment and place names

PREVIEW

Feeling about the setting

PREVIEW

Time of day and season

We live high up in the hills above Friendly, but hardly anybody knows where that is. Friendly's near Sistersville, which is halfway between Wheeling and Parkersburg. Use to be, my daddy told me, Sistersville was one of the best places you could live in the whole state. You ask *me* the best place to live, I'd say right where we are, a little four-room house with hills on three sides.

Afternoon is my second-best time to go up in the hills, though; morning's the best, especially in summer. Early, *early* morning. On one morning I saw three kinds of animals, not counting cats, dogs, frogs, cows, and horses. Saw a groundhog, saw a doe with two fawns, and saw a gray fox with a reddish head. Bet his daddy was a gray fox and his ma was a red one.

Reading Strategy: Close Reading

If your focus is setting, you'll need to pay attention to details. Now's not the time for speed reading or skimming. Do a **close reading**. Take the time to look at and think about particular words and sentences. Ask yourself why the author might have chosen a specific setting or described it in a certain way. You will find that the settings in stories often give you clues about the mood, characters, and plot.

It's a good idea to have a plan for keeping track of your thoughts about setting. Many stories—not to mention long novels—have more than one setting. It would be almost impossible to keep them all straight without writing anything down. Make life easier for yourself by creating a Setting Chart, like the one below. A chart like this one helps you organize the elements of a setting.

SETTING CHART

NOVEL NAME: Shiloh

CLUES ABOUT TIME	CLUES ABOUT PLACE
time of day afternoon	**place names** Friendly, Sistersville, Wheeling, and Parkersburg
season summer	**physical environment** high in the hills

Fiction

During Reading

Why should you keep a close eye on time and place as you read? The answer is because the setting often creates the mood, reveals a lot about the characters, and affects the plot.

Setting and Mood

Mood is the feeling a piece of literature arouses in a reader: happiness, sadness, peacefulness, and so on. Usually, a story's setting will help establish the mood.

Read these next two paragraphs of Naylor's *Shiloh*. As you do, try to feel the mood of the story.

from *Shiloh*

NOTE
Good feelings, a pleasant scene

NOTE
Surprising to see the dog

NOTE
What's wrong with the dog?

My favorite place to walk is just across this rattly bridge where the road curves by the old Shiloh schoolhouse and follows the river. River to one side, trees the other — sometimes a house or two.

And this particular afternoon, I'm about halfway up the road along the river when I see something out of the corner of my eye. Something moves. I look, and about fifteen yards off, there's this shorthaired dog — white with brown and black spots — not making any kind of noise, just slinking along with his head down, watching me, tail between his legs like he's hardly got the right to breathe. A beagle, maybe a year or two old.

How does this description make you feel? What do you think of the mood that's being created? Here is what one reader wrote about it in a Double-entry Journal:

DOUBLE-ENTRY JOURNAL

QUOTE	MY THOUGHTS
"River to one side, trees the other—sometimes a house or two."	Sounds like a pretty place. I can see why Marty would like it.
". . . slinking along with his head down, watching me, tail between his legs like he's hardly got the right to breathe."	Poor dog. Sounds like he's scared. Maybe he's been beaten. Marty's probably worried.

The pleasant scene Naylor starts out describing is interrupted by the appearance of the dog "slinking along." With the description of the "slinking" dog, the whole mood changes. Marty, on seeing the dog, now feels concerned, worried, or even frightened.

Writers often use sensory language (words that appeal to the five senses) to create a certain mood. For example, notice the much happier, carefree atmosphere in the following paragraph. Marty has rescued the dog, which he names Shiloh, from a mean owner; Marty and Shiloh are playing together.

from *Shiloh*

Just out of the woods on the other side of the hill, there's a meadow and I slump down in the grass to rest. Shiloh's all over me, licking my face sloppy wet. I giggle and roll over on my stomach, covering my head and neck with my arms. Shiloh whines and nudges his nose under my shoulder, working to roll me over. I laugh and turn on my back, pulling Shiloh down onto my chest, and for a while we both lay there, panting, enjoying the sunshine, belonging to each other.

NOTE
Physical environment

NOTE
Lots of sensory details

The beautiful natural setting—together with the sights, sounds, and touching of the two friends—creates a mood of fun and happiness.

Fiction

Setting and Characters

Setting can also give you clues about characters. Many times, the character's response to the setting can reveal a lot about the character's personality. For example, think about what Marty's response to walking in the West Virginia hills can tell you. A chart like this one can help you organize your thoughts.

WHAT CHARACTER SAYS OR DOES	MY INFERENCES ABOUT THE CHARACTER
enjoys walking in hills	finds beauty in nature
notices different animals too	knows a lot about nature and animals
likes living where he does	enjoys the country life, not a city boy

Not only does the setting reveal clues about Marty, but it also reveals a lot about Shiloh. For instance, take a close look at the following passage. The time is several hours after Marty has discovered Shiloh. The family is driving through the countryside to return the dog to the man they think owns him.

from Shiloh

NOTE
Shiloh's reaction to where he is

We're in Shiloh now. Dad's crossing the bridge by the old abandoned gristmill, turning at the boarded-up school, and for the first time I can feel Shiloh's body begin to shake. He's trembling all over. . . .

Clearly something about the setting scares Shiloh. His trembling reaction to the depressing landmarks shows he's aware of his surroundings. At this point in the book, neither Marty nor his father is 100 percent sure Shiloh's owner has mistreated him. But Shiloh's reaction to his old home increases their suspicions—and ours.

Setting and Plot

Often a change in setting signals a change in the action or plot. Watching for these setting changes can help you better understand the events that make up the plot of a story.

In the beginning of *Shiloh*, the setting changes as Marty walks home from the woods. The beagle follows him. Notice what happens as they move on and Marty approaches his house.

from *Shiloh*

Once he follows me across the bridge, though, and on past the gristmill, I start to worry. Looks like he's fixing to follow me all the way to our house. I'm in trouble enough coming home with my clothes wet. My ma's mama died of pneumonia, and we don't ever get the chance to forget it. And now I got a dog with me, and we were never allowed to have pets.

If you can't afford to feed 'em and take 'em to the vet when they're sick, you've no right taking 'em in, Ma says, which is true enough. . . .

> **NOTE**
> Moving to a new setting

> **NOTE**
> Possible conflict

Fiction

The change in scenery signals a change in the plot. As a reader, you begin to see things in a new light. Walking by himself in the hills, Marty sees the dog as sad, alone, and not bothering anyone. As he gets near home, though, Marty begins looking at the dog as his parents will look at him. He starts to worry. An important conflict comes out: what if "you can't afford to feed 'em"? The conflict between Marty's wish to have the dog and his parents' concerns causes some of the tension in the plot.

After Reading

Each time you finish reading a
story or novel, you need to pause
for a moment and figure out what
you've learned. When your focus is
setting, you'll want to be sure you
know the general setting—the
time and place the story takes place. Also,
ask yourself if you see how particular scenes
create mood, reveal something about the
characters, and affect
the plot.

If you can't remember details of the setting
or don't understand why it's important, try
one of these tips. Both involve going back
to the book and doing a little rereading.

Tip#1: List Key Settings

You might be able to name several important characters or plot
events in each story fairly easily. But how well can you rattle off
descriptions of the key setting? Make a brief list to refresh your
memory about what happened where. Go through the book quickly
and make some Summary Notes.

SUMMARY NOTES

SETTING	WHAT HAPPENED
woods near Marty's house	Marty finds Shiloh.
Judd Travers's yard	Shiloh's scared when he's taken back.
hills nearby	Marty hides Shiloh to protect him.

Tip #2: Make Sketches

To remember the different settings, try making a Storyboard of each of the main settings. Use a new frame each time the setting changes. Or, keep things simpler and choose only two or three settings to draw. After you've made a sketch of the setting, make some notes about what you have learned from it. Here's how one reader visualized the settings at the beginning and ending of *Shiloh*.

STORYBOARD

SHILOH

Beginning:
Marty—happy out walking in nature

Ending:
Marty—happy to have saved Shiloh

Fiction

Summing Up

■ Writers usually give clues about time and place at the beginning of the story—usually in the first few paragraphs.

■ Setting can help you understand the mood, characters, and plot of a story.

■ A change in the setting often signals a change in action and atmosphere.

Focus on Dialogue

Can you imagine a story in which none of the characters ever spoke to one another? It would be pretty boring, wouldn't it?

Dialogue is the conversations carried on between characters in a piece of writing. Dialogue is more important in some stories than others. But even when there's not a lot of dialogue, it can still help to:

- provide clues about the characters
- explain and advance the plot
- affect the mood

Goals

Here you'll learn how to:

✔ **recognize the form of dialogue**

✔ **appreciate how dialogue affects the plot, characters, and mood**

✔ **use close reading to understand dialogue**

Before Reading

When your focus is dialogue, it's important to recognize what it looks like and how it is used.

Quotation Marks and Speech Tags

In stories and novels, dialogue is almost always set off with quotation marks. You can tell who is speaking in a story by paying attention to the speech tags. A *speech tag* identifies the speaker and gives clues about the speaker's tone of voice.

For example, look at the following dialogue from Mildred D. Taylor's *Roll of Thunder, Hear My Cry*, a novel about an African-American family in the South during the Depression.

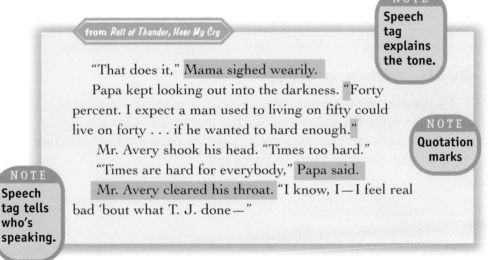

from *Roll of Thunder, Hear My Cry*

NOTE Speech tag explains the tone.

    "That does it," Mama sighed wearily.
    Papa kept looking out into the darkness. "Forty percent. I expect a man used to living on fifty could live on forty . . . if he wanted to hard enough."
    Mr. Avery shook his head. "Times too hard."
    "Times are hard for everybody," Papa said.
    Mr. Avery cleared his throat. "I know, I—I feel real bad 'bout what T. J. done—"

NOTE Quotation marks

NOTE Speech tag tells who's speaking.

Fiction

New Paragraph for New Speaker

Did you notice that Taylor started a new paragraph for each new speaker? This is an important rule for dialogue. Every time someone new begins speaking, the writer begins a new paragraph. Sometimes, following who's speaking in dialogue can be complicated. Keeping track of who says what is an important part of understanding a novel.

Continued Dialogue

Sometimes the same person will continue speaking for more than one paragraph. When the quote continues into the next paragraph, there will be no closing quote until the speaker actually stops speaking. Look at this example when Mr. Logan teaches his daughter Cassie about standing up for what you believe.

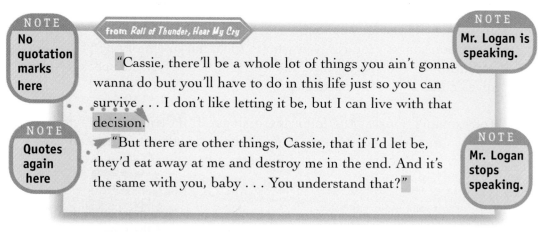

NOTE
No quotation marks here

NOTE
Quotes again here

from *Roll of Thunder, Hear My Cry*

NOTE
Mr. Logan is speaking.

NOTE
Mr. Logan stops speaking.

"Cassie, there'll be a whole lot of things you ain't gonna wanna do but you'll have to do in this life just so you can survive . . . I don't like letting it be, but I can live with that decision.

"But there are other things, Cassie, that if I'd let be, they'd eat away at me and destroy me in the end. And it's the same with you, baby . . . You understand that?"

Quote within a Quote

If the speaker quotes someone else, that second person's quote begins and ends with single quotation marks. Look for the single quotation marks in this paragraph. Here an older woman describes a conversation her husband had years ago.

from *Roll of Thunder, Hear My Cry*

NOTE
Single quotation marks for a quote within a quote

Big Ma chuckled. "That man went right on over to see Mr. Hollenbeck and said, 'Mr. Hollenbeck, I understand you got land to sell and I'd be interested in buyin' me 'bout two hundred acres if yo' price is right.' Ole Mr. Hollenbeck questioned him good 'bout where he was gonna get the money to pay him. . . ."

Keep these rules in mind when you're reading a long conversation between two or more characters. It will help you figure out who's saying what.

During Reading

When your focus is dialogue, you need to keep a close eye on who's talking, what is being said, and how it is being said.

Reading Strategy: Close Reading

It makes sense to use the strategy of **close reading** with dialogue. You may be surprised by all you can learn from the conversations characters have.

"Listen" carefully. Read slowly and "hear" the words. Dialogue often reveals a character's personality, explains and advances the plot, and creates a mood.

Clues about Character

You can tell a lot about people—in real life and in stories—not only by what they do but also by what they say. You can see whether they're well educated, if they have a sense of humor, and what kind of mood they're in.

Look at another excerpt from Mildred D. Taylor's *Roll of Thunder, Hear My Cry*. In this short section, Taylor offers many clues about the character of Cassie, the young narrator, and that of her mother. What character clues can you find?

Fiction

"Yes'm," I murmured, then flared, "But, Mama, that Lillian Jean ain't got the brains of a flea! How come I gotta go 'round calling her 'Miz' like she grown or something?"

Mama's voice grew hard. "Because that's the way of things, Cassie."

"The way of what things?" I asked warily.

"Baby, you had to grow up a little today. I wish . . . well, no matter what I wish. It happened and you have to accept the fact that in the world outside this house, things are not always as we would have them to be."

The kind of words and the tone of voice these two characters use can show just how different they are. Cassie's slang and exaggerated name-calling show her anger. Mama's words are more carefully chosen and serious.

Sometimes you might want to use a Double-entry Journal to record your reactions to especially interesting dialogue and to note inferences about a character. Here's how one reader reacted to a short exchange between Cassie and her grandmother.

DOUBLE-ENTRY JOURNAL

QUOTE	MY THOUGHTS
"Big Ma," I said, "what Mr. Granger need more land for?" "Don't need it," Big Ma said flatly. "Got more land now than he know what to do with."	Cassie's grandmother knows that Mr. Granger is just greedy. She's trying not to lose her temper.

When you read dialogue, you first try to understand what the characters are saying. But, as a reader, you must take the next step and *infer* what words mean.

Clues about Plot

In addition to providing clues about characters, dialogue also can advance a plot. Characters joke around, make plans, and share information. When characters talk, readers can get clues about what's going to happen next and explanations of what has happened before. "Listen" to this conversation as Mrs. Logan tells her family she was fired from her teaching job.

Fiction

from *Roll of Thunder, Hear My Cry*

Papa reached out and touched Mama. She said, "Harlan Granger came to the school with Kaleb Wallace and one of the school-board members. Somebody had told them about those books I'd pasted over . . . but that was only an excuse. They're just getting at us any way they can because of shopping in Vicksburg." Her voice cracked. "What'll we do, David? We needed that job."

Papa gently pushed the stray hair back over her ear. "We'll get by. . . . Plant more cotton maybe. But we'll get by." There was quiet reassurance in his voice.

NOTE
What happened before

NOTE
What might happen

This short conversation fills in some background about past events and suggests what the future might bring.

Clues about Mood

Dialogue can also contribute to the mood of a piece of writing. What the characters say and how they say it can add humor, frustration, sadness, or something else entirely. As you read the passage below from *Roll of Thunder, Hear My Cry*, think about the mood that's created. The Logans have just discovered that their son Stacey is in danger.

NOTE
Tense moment

from *Roll of Thunder, Hear My Cry* by Mildred D. Taylor

"David, not with the shotgun. You can't stop them like that."

"Got no other way," he said, stuffing a box of shells into his shirt pocket.

"You fire on them and they'll hang you for sure. They'd like nothing better."

"If I don't, they'll hang T. J. This thing's been coming a long time, baby, and T. J. just happened to be the one foolish enough to trigger it. But, fool or not, I can't just sit by and let them kill the boy. And if they find Stacey —"

NOTE
Dangerous situation

"I know, David, I know. But there's got to be another way. Some way they won't kill you too!"

"Seems like they might be planning to do that anyway," Papa said, turning from her. . . .

Here's what one reader wrote about that scene in a reading log.

READING LOG

The author does a great job of building up the tension. I can feel how scared the characters are. Mr. Logan wants to protect his son and T. J., but Mrs. Logan is worried about her husband getting killed.

After Reading

Can focusing on dialogue make you a better reader? The answer is *yes*. It can. Dialogue gives you clues about what's happening. Also, dialogue can make a story interesting. Reading dialogue is like listening in on a private conversation. A graphic organizer such as a Thinking Tree allows you to pull together all the clues you found in a story's dialogue.

THINKING TREE: DIALOGUE

PLOT		CHARACTER CLUES		MOOD	
what will happen next	what has come before	what the character says	how the character says it	adds humor	adds tension
Example: "I'll show y'all how we're gonna stop that bus from splashing us."	**Example:** Finally T. J. said, "Okay. See, them Berry's burnin' wasn't no accident. . . ."	**Example:** "You were born blessed, boy, with land of your own."	**Example:** "Ah, man, don't look so down," T. J. said cheerfully.	**Example:** "You wanna be bald, girl?"	**Example:** "Stacey, they've coming after *us*!" "What!" squeaked Christopher-John.

Fiction

You can make your Thinking Tree as big or little—as detailed or simple—as you want. Shrink it if you only need to make a one-minute oral report on dialogue. Add examples if you're writing a paper about it. It will help you see what dialogue adds to the story.

Summing Up

- **Dialogue usually has quotation marks and speech tags.**
- **When someone new begins speaking, a new paragraph is used.**
- **Dialogue can help you understand the plot, characters, and mood.**

Focus on Plot

Plot is the "meat" of a story. It is the series of events that connects the beginning of the story to the end. In a well-written plot, one event leads to another, like stairs on a staircase.

What's important to remember about plot is that it usually moves in chronological order. One stair follows another in a regular pattern from the first event to the last. Another important point is that the individual parts of a plot all work together to add meaning to the story. The events of the plot help build the story's theme.

Goals

Here you'll learn how to:

✔ track the events of a plot

✔ identify the story's subplots and think about a subplot's relationship to the main plot

✔ consider how the plot contributes to a story's theme

Before Reading

When your focus is plot, your first job is to be sure you can follow the action. Knowing that most plots are divided into *five* parts can make that easier.

PARTS OF A PLOT

1. The **exposition** *(or opening) is the first part of a plot. Here the author describes the setting, introduces the characters, and gives background information.*

2. The **rising action** *is the part in which the author describes the conflict or problem that the characters must face. In most stories, the characters don't solve the problem on their first try. As they struggle, tensions rise.*

3. The **climax** *is the turning point of a story. At this point, the problem is at its worst, and the characters may have begun to think of a way to solve it.*

4. The **falling action** *is the part where the author describes how the problem is solved.*

5. The **resolution** *(or ending) comes after the falling action and brings the story to a satisfactory end.*

Use a Plot Diagram such as the one below to keep track of the five parts. As you read, be alert for words such as *next, later,* or *then* that can help you follow the chronological order of events. See if you can tell when one part ends and another begins.

PLOT DIAGRAM

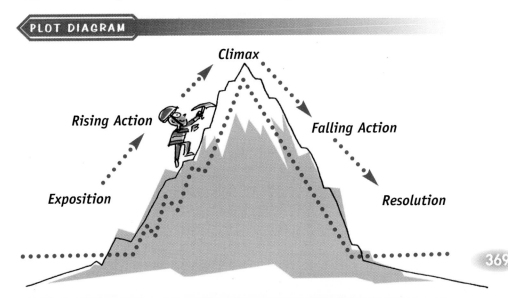

Climax

Rising Action

Falling Action

Exposition

Resolution

Fiction

Getting Background Information

Skimming the beginning paragraphs of a story or novel is a quick way to find information about the first part of the plot. Knowing the setting and characters will give you a head start on what to expect as you read. During your skim, watch for these:

- setting clues (time and place)
- character clues (names and descriptions)
- information about problem or conflict

Each time you find a clue, highlight it or make a note of it on a separate piece of paper. For example, look at the skimming notes this reader made on the opening of Paul Annixter's short story "Last Cover."

Characters are the narrator, brother, fox, and mother.

from "Last Cover" by Paul Annixter

Setting is a house on a winter afternoon.

    I'm not sure I can tell you what you want to know about my brother; but everything about the pet fox is important, so I'll tell all that from the beginning.

    It goes back to a winter afternoon after I'd hunted the woods all day for a sign of our lost pet. I remember the way my mother looked up as I came into the kitchen. Without my speaking, she knew what had happened. For six hours I had walked, reading signs, looking for a delicate print in the damp soil or even a hair that might have told of a red fox passing that way—but I had found nothing.

Problem is a lost fox.

During Reading

When you read for plot, keeping track of the sequence of events is the first step. The second is understanding how the events fit together and why the author might have chosen to describe them in the way he or she did.

Reading Strategy: Using Graphic Organizers

Using graphic organizers can be an excellent strategy for tracking a plot. Instead of driving yourself crazy by trying to remember the details of a plot in your head, write things down. For instance, Storyboards help you pick out and remember individual events. They allow you to see how the events work together to build the conflict to a climax. As an example, look at the Storyboard made to track the action in "Last Cover."

Fiction

STORYBOARD

1. One February, the narrator, Stan, hunts in the woods for a lost pet fox.

2. He, his parents, and brother Colin discuss what might have happened to the pet fox, Bandit.

3. Colin builds a frame for a new picture he's drawn.

4. In March, Colin and Stan find Bandit in the woods. Bandit has a mate.

5. During the summer, Bandit steals chickens from area farms. In September, farmers decide to hunt Bandit down.

6. Bandit outsmarts the hunters several times.

7. Colin and the narrator find Bandit hiding in a pond in the woods.

8. After he learns Bandit is dead, Colin draws a picture of the fox in his hiding spot and gives it to Father.

Understanding Flashbacks

Even in a story as short as "Last Cover," there's more to the plot than you might think at first.

For instance, from the events in the Storyboard, you might think that the story is told completely in chronological order, from beginning to end. The fox runs off in the winter and is killed the next September. But that's not true. The author of "Last Cover" has started somewhere in the middle, switched back in time to fill in some details, and then picked up the story again.

This jump back in time is called a *flashback*. In the middle of one scene, you're taken back to an earlier time. Notice the flashback in this passage from "Last Cover." It starts out describing how upset Colin was that the fox was lost but ends in a description of how Colin had first found the fox.

from "Last Cover" by Paul Annixter

NOTE

Flashback to one and a half years earlier

At supper that night Colin could scarcely eat. Ever since he'd been able to walk, my brother had had a growing love of wild things, but Bandit had been like his very own, a gift of the woods. One afternoon a year and a half before, Father and Laban Small had been running a vixen through the hills with their dogs. With the last of her strength the she-fox had made for her den, not far from our house. The dogs had overtaken her and killed her just before she reached it. When Father and Laban came up, they'd found Colin crouched nearby holding her cub in his arms.

Using certain graphic organizers, like a Story String or a Timeline, can help you spot where the action of the plot has been interrupted. Then, after you've finished reading, you can think about why an author might have used a flashback or how the story would be different if it had been left out.

Understanding Subplots

Many stories and novels often have a main plot plus one or more *subplots*. A subplot always has some elements in common with the main plot, such as characters or setting. But it is less important than—or subordinate to—the main plot.

Think of the subplots as satellites that orbit the main plot. In "Last Cover" the conflict of the main plot centers on Bandit: will he be found, and what will happen to him? But there's also another plot—a subplot. It centers on Colin's love of art and his father's lack of appreciation for it.

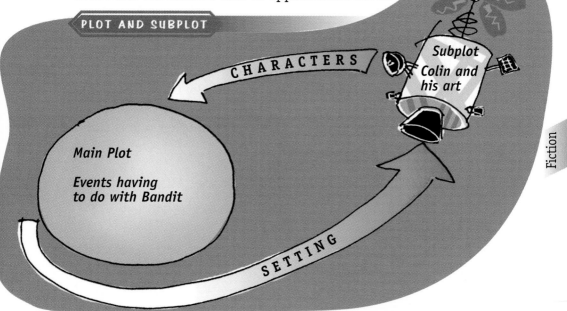

PLOT AND SUBPLOT

CHARACTERS

Subplot
Colin and his art

Main Plot

Events having to do with Bandit

SETTING

Fiction

If what you're reading is a long plot with numerous events or an important subplot, you may decide to make a Storyboard, a Story String, or a Story Organizer for the subplot.

STORY ORGANIZER

"LAST COVER" SUBPLOT

BEGINNING	MIDDLE	END
Father criticizes Colin for making picture frame.	Colin doesn't draw anything.	Father appreciates picture of Bandit hiding.

After Reading

When you finish a story, can you summarize the events to a friend? If the answer is *no,* it's time to do some rereading. Making a list of what the five parts of "Last Cover" are (*exposition, rising action, climax, falling action,* and *resolution*) is a good way to build a plot summary.

But go beyond the facts of what happened. Think about what the events of the plot mean and how the plot contributes to the theme. Try one of these methods to help yourself understand the plot.

1. Ask Questions

Ask questions that get you thinking about why the author arranged the plot in that way. For instance, consider why the author began the story where he or she did. See if you can figure out why one event is described in a lot of detail and another one is skipped over quickly.

In the case of "Last Cover," you might ask yourself:

■ Why did Paul Annixter use the flashback of when Colin first found Bandit?

■ Why did he spend so long on the last scene with Colin's father holding a picture of Bandit?

Look at one reader's ideas about those questions.

> **JOURNAL RESPONSE**
>
> At first I couldn't figure out why the author would want to describe the time when Colin first found Bandit. It just seemed to interrupt the search. But when I went back and read it again, I think I get it. At first the father didn't understand how the fox could mean so much to Colin. That's like at the end, when the father finally realizes how important art is to Colin. I guess one of the "big ideas" of the story is that parents need to understand and support their children.

2. Consider the Climax

The climax is the turning point of the story. If you're having trouble seeing what the events of a story mean, go back to the story's climax and reread this section carefully. Then ask yourself, "What does the action tell me about the theme?"

This Plot Diagram shows the turning point in the action of "Last Cover." Notice how the events of the rising action are far different from the events of the falling action. This is a clue about the theme of the story.

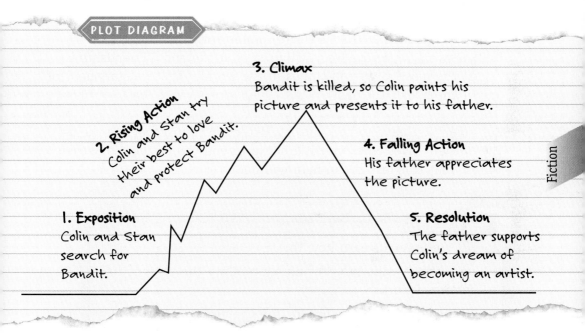

PLOT DIAGRAM

3. Climax
Bandit is killed, so Colin paints his picture and presents it to his father.

2. Rising Action
Colin and Stan try their best to love and protect Bandit.

1. Exposition
Colin and Stan search for Bandit.

4. Falling Action
His father appreciates the picture.

5. Resolution
The father supports Colin's dream of becoming an artist.

Fiction

Summing Up

- ■ **Plots are often divided into five parts: exposition, rising action, climax, falling action, and resolution.**
- ■ **Many stories and novels have a main plot and one or more subplots.**
- ■ **Understanding the action of the plot can help you understand the theme.**

Focus on Theme

A writer's message, or main idea, is the **theme** of the work. The theme is what the writer wants you to remember most. When you understand a story's theme, you understand the underlying idea or message of the work. Most stories, novels, plays, and sometimes poems have more than one theme. Some works, like many mysteries, might have no theme. They're just entertainment.

Some themes are easier to spot than others. A character may say something about life that is clearly important. For instance, in E. B. White's *Charlotte's Web*, Wilbur says at the end, "Friendship is one of the most satisfying things in the world." That's a statement of one of the book's themes.

But often you have to be a bit of a detective to discover the theme. The author leaves clues, but it'll be up to you to put them together. That's what this lesson can help you do.

Goals

Here you'll learn how to:

✔ use a three-step plan for understanding the themes in fictional works
✔ find the writer's support for the themes
✔ understand the difference between a topic and a theme

Before Reading

Here is a three-step plan you can follow when focusing on the themes of a story, novel, poem, or even a play:

Plan for Understanding Theme

Step 1 Find the "big ideas" or general topics in the work.

Step 2 Find out what the characters do and say that relates to the general topics.

Step 3 Come up with a statement of the author's point or message about the topic.

Step 1: Find the "big ideas" or general topics in the work.

When your focus is theme, you'll want to start by figuring out what general topics or "big ideas" the work is about. The author's themes always relate to this subject.

Try to learn about the "big ideas" before you actually begin reading. Maybe you can find a clue in the title, the first paragraph, or any illustrations. Maybe there's a hint in background information. For instance, go back to page 319 and look at information on the back cover of Mildred D. Taylor's novel *Roll of Thunder, Hear My Cry*. Right away you might find out that this book is going to be about an African-American family that deals with racism. Racism is probably going to be mentioned again. It's one of the novel's "big ideas."

Sometimes, though, you're not able to tell much from a quick preview. Did you realize that writers often share general topics? Here is a list of topics that appear over and over in middle school stories.

COMMON TOPICS FOR THEMES

childhood	*growing up*	*loyalty*	*self-reliance*
courage	*hate*	*nature*	*success*
death	*hope*	*patience*	*trust*
faith	*identity*	*patriotism*	*truth*
family	*independence*	*prejudice*	*unhappiness*
freedom	*justice*	*race relations*	*violence*
friendship	*love*	*self-improvement*	*war*

Fiction

During Reading

You should be on the lookout for these "big ideas" as you read. Jot them down, make a list, and keep adding to it as you go. Knowing what the general topics are gives you direction as you move from page to page.

Step 2: Find out what the characters do and say that relates to the general topics.

As you read, watch for details that relate to the general topics you've identified. They are the clues to understanding the themes. They are the evidence or "proof" that a certain topic is, in fact, important to the book or story. These clues often appear in several forms:

- repeated words or ideas
- symbols
- important plot events or dialogue
- changes in characters

What follows are two ways of keeping track of details related to the theme. Try using one of these reading tools the next time you're reading a novel. Notice how actions and quotes from throughout the book are pulled together around the topic of racism.

Summary Notes

Jot down details from each chapter or page of a short work that relate to your topic. Summary Notes work well to help you remember what's important and keep track of details in chronological order.

> SUMMARY NOTES

Racism in Roll of Thunder, Hear My Cry

Chapter 1	African-American students get worst books.
Chapter 4	Wallaces make Logans go in back door of store.
Chapter 6	Mama explains that some white people think they're better.

Double-entry Journal

Using a Double-entry Journal is an excellent way of keeping important passages and your thoughts about them in one place. In the example below, several of Mama's statements to Cassie in Chapter 6 are examined.

> DOUBLE-ENTRY JOURNAL

Quotes	What I Think About It
about Mr. Simms: ". . . he's one of those people who has to believe that white people are better than black people to make himself feel big."	Mama feels bad that Cassie has to learn about prejudice. What she says about slavery and how people don't believe blacks and whites are equal really upsets Cassie. I would feel bad, too.
"White people may demand our respect, but what we give them is not respect but fear. What we give to our own people is far more important because it's given freely."	Mama is very realistic. She wants Cassie to understand that racism can lead to danger. Maybe something bad will happen.

Fiction

If you read all of Taylor's novel, you'll find that she explores several different big subjects in addition to racism. They include these topics:

- family
- pride
- fighting for what you believe in
- the land

family *pride*
fighting for what you believe in *the land*

MILDRED D. TAYLOR
Roll of Thunder,
Hear My Cry

Who says you have to focus on just one thing? Many fictional works—especially long novels—have more than one theme. You may decide to take separate notes or create a separate organizer for each theme topic you're exploring: one for racism, one for family, one for pride, and so on.

After Reading

When you finish reading, it's time to gather up the theme clues you've found and decide what they mean.

Step 3: Come up with a statement of the author's point or message about the topic.

Remember not to confuse topic with theme. Theme is a point made about the topic. For instance, Taylor's theme isn't "racism." That's just a topic. The theme could be that racism is caused by ignorance and insecurity. It could be that learning about racism and prejudice is a painful part of growing up. Very different stories could have very different points to make about the same topic.

Somebody else who's read the same story may come up with a theme statement that's different from yours. That's not a problem. What is a problem is if you can't come up with specific details from the story to offer as evidence for your statement. Stating a theme is not like some mysterious magic trick where a rabbit appears out of thin air. A theme needs to be based on certain things characters say and do.

To pull together your thoughts and notes about theme, try creating a Topic and Theme Organizer. It makes it easy to check that you have plenty of examples and details to support your theme statement. On the next page is one organizer made for *Roll of Thunder, Hear My Cry*.

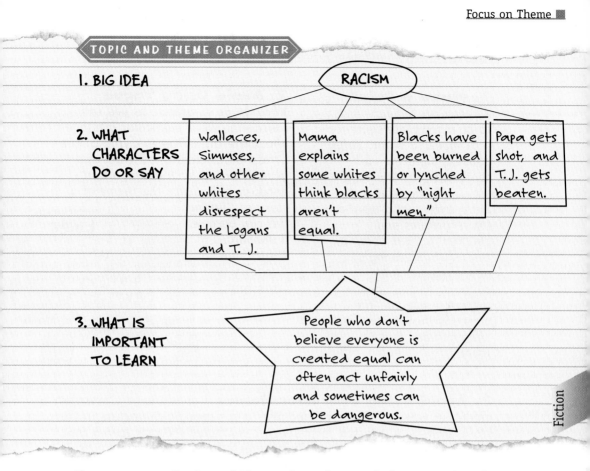

TOPIC AND THEME ORGANIZER

1. BIG IDEA — RACISM

2. WHAT CHARACTERS DO OR SAY

Wallaces, Simmses, and other whites disrespect the Logans and T. J.	Mama explains some whites think blacks aren't equal.	Blacks have been burned or lynched by "night men."	Papa gets shot, and T. J. gets beaten.

3. WHAT IS IMPORTANT TO LEARN — People who don't believe everyone is created equal can often act unfairly and sometimes can be dangerous.

Fiction

You can use a Topic and Theme Organizer to help you write about a theme. You could write a paragraph or whole paper by following your organizer.

WRITING ABOUT THEME

1. Topic Sentence
Sentence that names the topic or big idea

2. Body
Examples that show what the characters do or say that relates to the topic

3. Conclusion
Theme statement of what is important to learn

Make your organizer as simple or as detailed as you want. If you'd read the book, you might have found other examples or stated the theme differently. That's OK. Use the tips on the next page to help you write strong theme statements.

1. Make a Point

A theme statement needs to be a complete sentence that makes a point. Think about completing this sentence: "The theme is _____." Don't fill in the blank with just a word or two ("parents and children"). That doesn't tell us what's being said about parents and children. A much better version would be "The theme is that parents and children need to talk more."

2. Avoid Using Vague Words

Be as precise as you can concerning what particular message about life the writer is trying to get across. Steer clear of abstract and general words, such as important, good, or bad. State the theme of a story as "Telling lies can become a dangerous habit," not "Honesty is important."

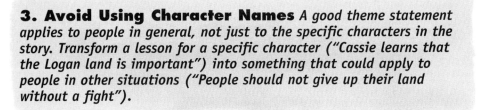

3. Avoid Using Character Names

A good theme statement applies to people in general, not just to the specific characters in the story. Transform a lesson for a specific character ("Cassie learns that the Logan land is important") into something that could apply to people in other situations ("People should not give up their land without a fight").

Summing Up

- A story's theme is different from its topic or subject. The topic is simply what it's about. Theme is the author's point about the topic.

- Follow a three-step plan for understanding theme: find the "big ideas" or topics in the work, pay attention to what the characters do and say that relates to the topics, and write a theme statement.

- Not all interpretations of a work will be exactly the same. You may come up with a theme statement that's different from that of another reader. That's fine, so long as you both can support your ideas with evidence from the text.

Focus on Comparing and Contrasting

At some point, you will be asked to compare and contrast one work of literature to another. Or, you may want to compare two works on your own simply because you're interested in finding out how they are alike and different. You probably do that now when you compare two movies with the same actor or actress or a movie and its sequel. So, when you do compare and contrast, where should you begin? You'll need to decide which type of comparisons to do:

general comparison

specific comparison

When you make a *general comparison*, you compare two entire works: one novel to another novel, one poem to another poem, one story to another story. When you make a *specific comparison*, you compare one literary element of two works—the plots, for example.

Fiction

Goals

Here you'll learn how to:

✔ **use the reading process to make strong comparisons**

✔ **find and organize details from the literary works to back up the points made in your comparisons**

Before Reading

You may know before you read a story or novel that you want to compare it to another, or you may not. But, that's part of what you should think about before you read.

 Am I reading this novel or story just for fun?

Will I write about this work later for school?

Is this an assignment with a specific purpose?

When your goal is comparing and contrasting, you want to find a number of ways in which things are alike and in which they are different. That purpose also helps you to preview.

If you are reading two literary works, preview each one before you read it. Look for the same things you normally would when you read a story or novel:

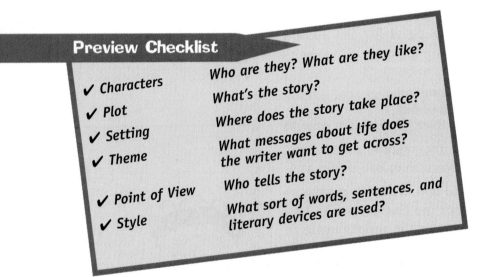

Preview Checklist

✔ Characters — Who are they? What are they like?

✔ Plot — What's the story?

✔ Setting — Where does the story take place?

✔ Theme — What messages about life does the writer want to get across?

✔ Point of View — Who tells the story?

✔ Style — What sort of words, sentences, and literary devices are used?

The rest of this section concentrates on two works you may already know something about: the Greek myth of King Midas and Charles Dickens's *A Christmas Carol*. You can adapt this process to other works.

During Reading

As you read, keep your purpose in mind. Deciding on the best kind of notes to take depends on whether your comparison is general or specific.

Reading Strategy: Using Graphic Organizers

There's a lot to remember when you're reading two stories or novels, especially if they're long. **Use graphic organizers** to help you keep track of the details you'll need in order to make *two* kinds of comparisons.

1. General Comparisons

When you read for general comparisons, you look for what's similar in the two works. Good comparisons don't just happen. To create a good one, you have to read with a purpose and look for parts of each work that will help you make a comparison. Here are the notes one reader made while reading *A Christmas Carol*.

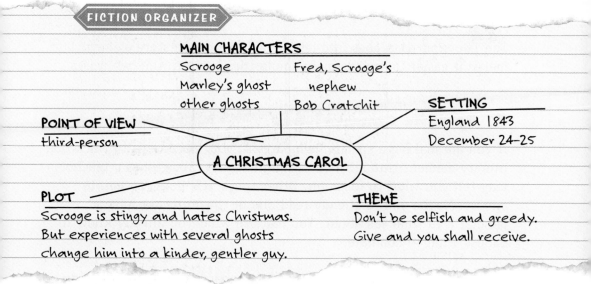

FICTION ORGANIZER

MAIN CHARACTERS
Scrooge   Fred, Scrooge's
Marley's ghost   nephew
other ghosts   Bob Cratchit

POINT OF VIEW
third-person

SETTING
England 1843
December 24–25

A CHRISTMAS CAROL

PLOT
Scrooge is stingy and hates Christmas.
But experiences with several ghosts
change him into a kinder, gentler guy.

THEME
Don't be selfish and greedy.
Give and you shall receive.

It's often helpful to gather details about the two works on a single sheet of paper. Look at the following Two-story Map one reader created.

Fiction

	A CHRISTMAS CAROL	KING MIDAS
MAIN CHARACTER	Scrooge: older businessman rich and powerful	Midas: King rich and powerful
MAIN SETTING	19th-century England Scrooge's home and business	ancient Greece Midas's kingdom
PLOT EVENTS	supernatural— visits from ghosts goes places	supernatural— gets magic powers stays at home
THEME	Being greedy and caring about being rich can lead to unhappiness.	Being greedy and caring about being rich can lead to unhappiness
ENDING	Scrooge learns lesson and changes. Ghosts leave.	Midas sees his wish was foolish. Spell is undone.

The Two-story Map goes into less detail about each story element but makes it easier to see the main similarities between the two works.

2. Specific Comparisons

If you are making a specific comparison, your purpose is to track one literary element through two different stories. Sometimes a teacher may tell you what to focus on. Other times, it'll be up to you to choose. Maybe you've already read one of the stories or have a general idea what it's about. You can use what you already know to choose what to compare.

Let's say you compare the stories of Scrooge and Midas. You decide you're going to focus on the two main characters—what they're like and how they both change. A Venn Diagram is a good tool to help you make a comparison.

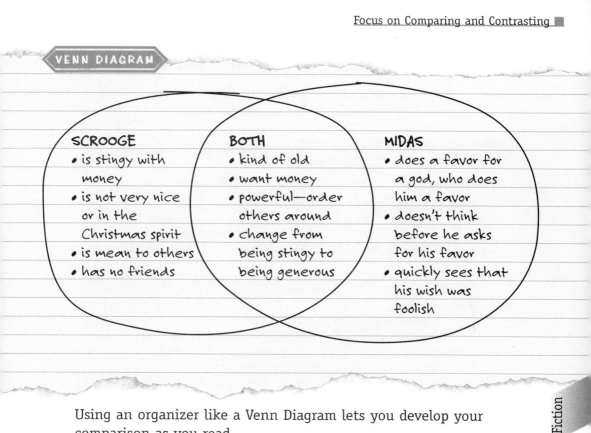

SCROOGE
- is stingy with money
- is not very nice or in the Christmas spirit
- is mean to others
- has no friends

BOTH
- kind of old
- want money
- powerful—order others around
- change from being stingy to being generous

MIDAS
- does a favor for a god, who does him a favor
- doesn't think before he asks for his favor
- quickly sees that his wish was foolish

Fiction

Using an organizer like a Venn Diagram lets you develop your comparison as you read.

After Reading

Once you have finished reading and taking notes, you should have most of the raw material needed for making comparisons between two works. But be patient.

Drawing Conclusions

You will probably want to reread parts of one or both works, if only to fill in places in your organizers. As you reflect, you need to draw a conclusion about how the works are similar and different.

The best conclusions are specific, and they're based on a lot of details from each work. They relate the two works in ways that are not obvious. Good comparisons and contrasts highlight a connection between things that seem to be different or a difference in things that seem to be the same.

Organizing a Comparison or Contrast

Once you have decided on a specific conclusion, organize your comparison or contrast on a clear, sound model.

MODEL OF COMPARISON OR CONTRAST

Opening

• *Topic Sentence*
  Sentence that names what's being compared or contrasted and whether the works are similar or different for at least two reasons

Body

• *Reason One*
  supporting detail or quote from work #1
  supporting detail or quote from work #2

• *Reason Two*
  supporting detail or quote from work #1
  supporting detail or quote from work #2

Conclusion

• *Concluding Sentence*
  Sentence that restates how the works are alike or different or explanation of why the similarities or differences are important

 **Summing Up**

■ Make comparing or contrasting part of your purpose for reading.

■ Decide what kind of comparison you are going to make: general or specific.

■ Use graphic organizers to help you collect and remember the information you need to make good comparisons.

Elements of Fiction

When it comes time to discuss a novel or short story, you need to be familiar with literary words that people use when describing fiction. Twelve of the most important literary terms are included here.

Use this section as you would a glossary. Turn to it as needed. Look up the term, read the example, and study the definition. Then apply what you've learned as you read.

Elements of Fiction

Antagonist and Protagonist   390
Author's Purpose   391
Character   392
Dialogue and Dialect   394
Genre   396
Mood   397
Point of View   398
Plot   400
Setting   402
Style   403
Symbol   404
Theme   405

Fiction

Antagonist and Protagonist

The conflict between a main character and someone or something else forms the plot of many novels and short stories. In S. E. Hinton's novel *Rumble Fish*, Rusty-James is the main character, or protagonist.

EXAMPLE

> from *Rumble Fish* by S. E. Hinton

I was hanging out in Benny's, playing pool, when I heard Biff Wilcox was looking to kill me.

Antagonist Benny's was the hangout for the junior high kids. The high schoolers used to go there, but when the younger kids moved in, they moved out . . . .

Steve was there, and B. J. Jackson, and Smokey Bennet, and some other guys. I was playing pool with Smokey. I was probably winning, since I was a pretty good pool player. Smokey was hacked off because he already owed me some money. He was glad when Midget came in and said, "Biff is lookin' for you, Rusty-James."

Protagonist I missed my shot.

DESCRIPTION

The **protagonist** of a story is the main character, or the one most central to the action of the story. The **antagonist** is the person, thing, or force that works against the protagonist. An antagonist can be another character, a family, a society, a force of nature (such as the freezing cold or a tornado), or a force within the main character.

DEFINITION

The **antagonist** is the person or thing working against the protagonist, or hero, of a work. The **protagonist** is the main character of the story.

Author's Purpose

In the title and first sentence of her myth "How Shiva Got His Blue Throat," author Anita Ganeri makes clear why she is writing.

EXAMPLE

> from "How Shiva Got His Blue Throat" by Anita Ganeri

This is the story of how Lord Shiva, the destroyer, came to have a blue throat.

DESCRIPTION

In this myth, Ganeri does she what she promises in the title. She explains how Lord Shiva got his blue throat.

An author's reason for creating a particular work is called the **author's purpose**. Sometimes the author will state his or her purpose up front, as Ganeri does. Other times you'll need to make inferences (reasonable guesses) about the author's purpose.

There are *four* basic reasons an author might choose to write:

1. to explain or inform

2. to entertain

3. to persuade

4. to enlighten or reveal an important truth

Often, an author may have in mind more than one purpose. But most of the time, one purpose is more important than the others. Recognizing an author's purpose can help you get more out of your reading.

DEFINITION

An **author's purpose** is his or her reason for creating a work. The purpose may be to explain or inform, entertain, persuade, or reveal an important truth.

Fiction

Character

In this passage from Harper Lee's novel *To Kill a Mockingbird*, the narrator, a girl named Scout, describes the family's cook. She is a woman named Calpurnia.

EXAMPLE

from *To Kill a Mockingbird* by Harper Lee

What she was like

What she says, thinks, and does

How she gets along with others

Calpurnia was something else again. She was all angles and bones; she was nearsighted; she squinted; her hand was wide as a bed slat and twice as hard. She was always ordering me out of the kitchen, asking me why I couldn't behave as well as Jem when she knew he was older, and calling me home when I wasn't ready to come. Our battles were epic and one-sided. Calpurnia always won, mainly because Atticus always took her side. She had been with us ever since Jem was born, and I had felt her tyrannical presence as long as I could remember.

DESCRIPTION

A **character** is a person, an animal, or an imaginary creature that takes part in the action of a story. Some stories have many characters, and others have just one or two. Sometimes the author will directly describe a character's appearance, personality, or feelings. Other times the author will leave clues and expect you to draw conclusions about what the person or animal is like. Your job as reader is to watch for and make notes of these clues as you read.

Characterization

The techniques an author uses to develop the personality of a character in a literary work are called **characterization**. An author can give information about a character by describing several aspects of the character:

- physical appearance and personality
- speech, behavior, and actions
- thoughts and feelings
- interactions with other characters

Character, continued

Character Types

Most stories have both main and minor characters. The **main character**, or **protagonist**, is the most important character. The action of the plot revolves around him or her. Often the **antagonist**, the person or thing working against the protagonist, is also a main character. **Minor characters** are less important. They interact with the main characters and one another. Often, readers don't know much about them.

As you read you'll also want to be aware of the differences between static and dynamic characters. **Static characters** stay the same throughout the story. They hardly change at all. In contrast, **dynamic characters** change from beginning to end. They often learn something. That change is something the author expects you as a reader to recognize and interpret. Ask yourself what the author is suggesting by those changes.

Often, understanding how a character develops will help you understand the theme.

DEFINITION

A **character** is a person, animal, or imaginary creature that takes part in the action of a story. An author can develop a character by showing you the character's appearance and personality, speech and behavior, thoughts and feelings, and interactions with other characters.

Fiction

Dialogue and Dialect

At one point in Mark Twain's *Tom Sawyer,* Tom and Becky Thatcher realize they are lost in a cave. Pay careful attention to what Becky and Tom *say.*

EXAMPLE

from *Tom Sawyer* by Mark Twain

Now, for the first time, the deep stillness of the place laid a clammy hand upon the spirits of the children. Becky said— **[Speech tag]**

"Why, I didn't notice, but it seems ever so long since I heard any of the others."

[New paragraph for new speaker] "Come to think, Becky, we are away down below them— and I don't know how far away north, or south, or east, or whichever it is. We couldn't hear them here."

Becky grew apprehensive.

"I wonder how long we've been down here, Tom. We better start back."

"Yes, I reckon we better. P'raps we better." **[Misspellings and unusual expressions]**

"Can you find the way, Tom? It's all a mixed-up crookedness to me."

"I reckon I could find it—but then the bats. If they put both our candles out it will be an awful fix. Let's try some other way, so as not to go through there." **[Suggestion of what might happen next]**

"Well. But I hope we won't get lost. It would be so awful!" and the girl shuddered at the thought of the dreadful possibilities.

DESCRIPTION

The words that characters speak are called **dialogue**. Dialogue can move the plot along and reveal a lot about the characters.

Dialogue and Dialect, continued

Understanding Dialogue

In stories, dialogue is usually set off with quotation marks. Each time a new character speaks, the writer must start a new paragraph. You can tell who is speaking in a story by paying attention to the speech tag. A *speech tag* identifies the speaker and often gives information about the speaker's tone of voice. For example, if you see a quotation followed by the speech tag "Vonya exclaimed," you immediately know that Vonya is the speaker and that she is speaking in an excited tone of voice.

Dialect

Did you notice in the example that Tom uses some unusual words and spellings when he talks? Tom speaks in a **dialect** that is characteristic of certain parts of the South. Tom also speaks in the dialect of children—a shorter, less grammatical version of standard English.

Dialect is a form of language that is spoken in a particular place or by a particular group of people. If you look carefully at Tom's dialect, you can see a pattern of misspellings and mispronunciations ("P'raps"), unique vocabulary ("an awful fix"), and ungrammatical expressions ("a mixed-up crookedness"). These elements are often present in dialect.

Dialect can add freshness, reality, and humor to a piece of writing. It also allows a writer to let characters speak in a way that is faithful to the way they might actually sound if they were real people.

Fiction

DEFINITION

Dialogue is the words spoken by characters in a literary work. Dialogue advances the plot and gives readers clues about the characters' personalities. **Dialect** is a form of language that is spoken in a particular place or by a particular group of people.

Genre

Genre is the name used to identify the category or type of literature. The most well-known literary genres include realistic fiction, science fiction, fantasy, folktales and fairy tales, poetry, drama, and nonfiction.

DESCRIPTION

Although there are always some exceptions, most genres have their own unique characteristics. This chart will help you recognize characteristics associated with particular genres of fiction as well as compare one genre to another.

Genre	EXAMPLE	CHARACTERS	PLOT	SETTING	THEME
REALISTIC FICTION	Roll of Thunder, Hear My Cry	can be people or animals; must be believable to you or me	highly believable conflict: could happen	present-day or recent past	a variety
FANTASY	Harry Potter and the Sorcerer's Stone	combination of realistic characters and characters with magical powers	realistic conflict or completely imaginary	usually realistic world with fantastic qualities	Usually good wins in the end.
FOLKTALE/ FAIRY TALE	"Cinderella"	simple characters; often all good or all evil	conflict usually person vs. person; problems often occur in "threes"	"Once upon a time"; always long ago; castles and forests	Justice is usually important.

DEFINITION

Genre is the category or type of literature. The most well-known fictional literary genres include realistic fiction, science fiction, fantasy, and folktales and fairy tales.

Mood

What feeling do you get from reading this paragraph from Lois Lowry's novel *The Giver*?

EXAMPLE

from *The Giver* by Lois Lowry

He was in a room filled with people, and it was warm, with firelight glowing on a hearth. He could see through a window that outside it was night, and snowing. There were colored lights: red and green and yellow, twinkling from a tree which was, oddly, inside the room. On a table, lighted candles stood in a polished golden holder and cast a soft, flickering glow. He could smell things cooking, and he heard soft laughter. A golden-haired dog lay sleeping on the floor.

Feeling

Sights

Smell and sound

DESCRIPTION

The **mood** of a literary work is the feelings that a writer wants readers to have while reading. It's the atmosphere that's created. Writers can choose words, phrases, and images to create a whole range of moods—from anger and sadness to excitement and fear.

By describing the warm fire, the twinkling lights, the good smells, and the peaceful dog, Lowry creates a mood of happiness or contentment.

In some short works, one mood colors the whole piece. In other longer works, different scenes or plot events have different moods. As you read, keep track of the mood the author creates. Understanding the mood the author is creating will help your understanding of the work as a whole.

DEFINITION

Mood is the feeling that a literary work gives to readers. Writers use words, phrases, and images to create mood.

Fiction

Point of View

In this selection from *The Kid Comes Back* by John R. Tunis, a group of men works to ready a plane for a mission during World War II. Roy is the plane's tail gunner, which means he will ride in the rear of the plane—a dangerous assignment.

EXAMPLE

from *The Kid Comes Back* by John R. Tunis

Third-person pronouns

Roy watched the mechanics readying the plane, as he had done dozens of times before. There were half a dozen of them, on top, underneath, inside, around the gas truck, all chattering in the quiet night air; all oblivious to the task awaiting the ship and the crew who flew her. Snatches of their conversation came to him.

"My wife writes, now she says eggs are sixty cents a dozen...."

Roy's thoughts and feelings

Roy turned away. He had heard them like that, listened to the grease monkeys, watched them do the same thing dozens of times before. Somehow that night they bothered him. All at once he wanted to yell at them as loud as he could. Hey, look, you guys; you up there in the turret, and you, Bud, out on the wing, and you, fella, you gassing her up, and you two in the truck. Look, we're taking this ship up tonight, and maybe we won't come back. Maybe we'll ditch or crash somewhere in France or something. And we've got people at home, same as you have.

DESCRIPTION

The perspective, or vantage point from which an author presents a story, is called **point of view**. *The Kid Comes Back* is told from Roy's point of view. He's angry with the mechanics because they don't seem to be aware of the danger of war. Imagine how different the story would be if it were told from the point of view of one of the mechanics. The literature you read will usually be told either in the first-person or third-person point of view.

Point of View, continued

First-person Point of View

In the *first-person point of view*, the story is told by one of the characters. The character uses pronouns such as *I* or *we* and usually participates in much of the action. Because the story is told from just one character's point of view, however, the reader is limited to knowing only what that character knows, thinks, and feels.

Roll of Thunder, Hear My Cry by Mildred D. Taylor is a good example of a story told from the first-person point of view. Readers experience the story through the eyes of Cassie, a character who is one of the Logan children.

Third-person Point of View

In the *third-person point of view*, the story is told by a *narrator* who is not a character in the story. The narrator, such as the one in *The Kid Comes Back,* will use pronouns such as *she, he,* and *they.* Sometimes this narrator will relate the thoughts and feelings of all the characters. This is called an all-knowing or *omniscient narrator.* More often, however, the narrator will relate the thoughts and feelings of just one character, usually the protagonist. This is called *limited omniscient narration.*

DEFINITION

Point of view is the vantage point from which a story is told. In the first-person point of view, the story is told by one of the characters. In the third-person point of view, the story is told by a narrator who stands outside the story and observes the events as they unfold.

Fiction

Plot

Read this brief summary of Betsy Byars's novel, *The Summer of the Swans.*

EXAMPLE

In the beginning, Sara Godfrey hates everything about herself. One summer day, however, her brother Charlie disappears, and Sara is terrified. Soon, she forgets all about her miseries. When she finally finds him, she cries with joy. At the end, Sara brings Charlie home and realizes that this terrible day has changed her feelings about herself and her family forever.

Events told in chronological order

DESCRIPTION

The person who wrote this summary focused on the **plot** of Byars's novel. Plot is the action of a story. It is the series of related events that the author describes from the beginning of the story to the end. Most plots follow a **chronological order**. In other words, they proceed in the order in which the events happen.

Parts of a Plot

When you are asked to consider a story's plot, you can make your job easier by dividing the plot into five parts: *exposition,* or *opening; rising action; climax; falling action;* and *resolution,* or *ending.*

The **exposition** is the first part of a plot. In the exposition, the author establishes the setting, introduces the main characters, and gives additional background information.

The **rising action** is the series of conflicts or struggles that build a story or a play toward its climax. Tensions rise.

The **climax** is the high point, or turning point, of a story. It is usually the most intense point.

The **falling action** is the action that works out the decision arrived at during the climax. The conflict is—or begins to be—settled.

The **resolution** is the ending. It comes after the falling action and is intended to bring the story to a satisfactory close.

Plot, continued

Plot Diagram

You can keep track of these five parts on a Plot Diagram. A Plot Diagram for *The Summer of the Swans* might look like this:

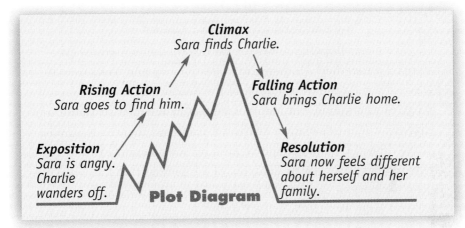

There is no absolute formula for handling each of these five parts of a story. For instance, some stories have many paragraphs of exposition or falling action, and others have only one paragraph. Others have no exposition or falling action at all.

Understanding Conflict

Keep in mind that every plot has a *conflict*. A plot's conflict is the problem that triggers the action. There are *five* main types:

1. **person vs. person** (problem with another character)
2. **person vs. society** (problem with the laws or beliefs of a group of people)
3. **person vs. nature** (problem with the environment)
4. **person vs. self** (problem deciding what to do or think)
5. **person vs. fate** (problem that seems to be uncontrollable)

DEFINITION

Plot is the action or sequence of events in a story. It is based on a key conflict. There are five basic parts of a plot: *exposition, rising action, climax, falling action,* and *resolution.*

Setting

In the paragraph below from *Journey to Topaz*, Yuki and her family arrive at a new place. What clues does the author, Yoshiko Uchida, give you about where and when this is happening?

EXAMPLE

> from *Journey to Topaz* by Yoshiko Uchida
>
> The eager hopeful voices on the bus died down and soon stopped altogether. Mother said nothing more and Yuki herself grew silent. At the western rim of the desert they could see a tall range of mountains, but long before they reached their sheltering shadows the buses made a sharp left turn, and there in the midst of the desert, they came upon rows and rows of squat tar-papered barracks sitting in a pool of white dust that had once been the bottom of a lake. They had arrived at Topaz, the Central Utah War Relocation Center, which would be their new home.

Where they are

What it's like there

Name of place

DESCRIPTION

Could you tell that *Journey to Topaz* takes place somewhere in the Utah desert? You might also have noticed a clue about the time period of the story. The War Relocation centers were built during World War II, so this story must be set in the early to mid-1940s.

If you talk about the where and when of a story, what you're really talking about is the story's **setting**. Understanding a story's setting can give you a context for the events of the plot. It can also give you clues about the mood, or atmosphere, of a story.

DEFINITION

Setting is the time and place in which the action of a literary work occurs. Look for clues about setting in the opening paragraphs of the story or novel.

Style

Read this selection from Louis Sachar's novel *Holes*. Pay attention to the author's choice of words and sentence structure.

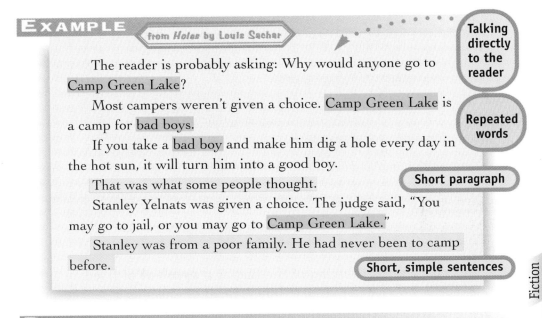

EXAMPLE

from *Holes* by Louis Sachar

The reader is probably asking: Why would anyone go to Camp Green Lake?

Most campers weren't given a choice. Camp Green Lake is a camp for bad boys.

If you take a bad boy and make him dig a hole every day in the hot sun, it will turn him into a good boy.

That was what some people thought.

Stanley Yelnats was given a choice. The judge said, "You may go to jail, or you may go to Camp Green Lake."

Stanley was from a poor family. He had never been to camp before.

Talking directly to the reader

Repeated words

Short paragraph

Short, simple sentences

Fiction

DESCRIPTION

The highlights above mark elements having to do with Louis Sachar's **style**. Style is the way writers express their ideas. It's *how* they say something, not *what* they say. Just as you have a certain style of clothes or of handwriting, so an author has an individual writing style. Thinking about style can help you appreciate the different ways writers can get their ideas across. Style involves these *three* elements:

- word choice
- sentence structure and length
- literary devices, such as figurative language, symbols, dialogue, and imagery

DEFINITION

Style is the way the author uses words, phrases, and sentences to express his or her ideas. Style includes the author's word choice, sentence structure, and use of literary devices.

Symbol

In this excerpt from *The Fragile Flag,* a character thinks about what the American flag represents to him.

EXAMPLE

from *The Fragile Flag* by Jane Langton

Instantly pictures rushed into his head.

The *young faces of the Marines,* firm and controlled, as they marched like clockwork in parade formation. . . .

His *devoted generals,* their service medals flashing. . . .

The *Statue of Liberty* holding up her torch as if she were guarding the American shore against enemies at every hand. . . .

What the flag represents

DESCRIPTION

This character is thinking of the flag as a **symbol** of freedom and democracy. A symbol is something concrete—such as a person, place, or object—that signifies something more than just itself, something abstract, such as a concept or an idea. Writers use symbols as a way to bring meaning and emphasis to their writing.

Some symbols you will probably be familiar with already. A heart stands for love, a dove for peace, and white for innocence. Other symbols will be new to you. Of course, the same object can symbolize different things to different people. To some, a rose might be a symbol of beauty. To others, it may symbolize hidden dangers because of its thorns. You find clues about what the symbol means in the rest of the story.

DEFINITION

A symbol is a person, place, thing, or event used to represent something else. Look for context clues to help you figure out what a symbol means.

Theme

In the last paragraph of Sandra Cisneros's story "Eleven," the main character, Rachel, thinks about her birthday and growing up.

EXAMPLE   from "Eleven" by Sandra Cisneros

I'm eleven today. I'm eleven, ten, nine, eight, seven, six, five, four, three, two, and one, but I wish I was one hundred and two. I wish I was anything but eleven, because I want today to be far away already, far away like a runaway balloon, like a tiny *o* in the sky, so tiny-tiny you have to close your eyes to see it.

Clues about theme

DESCRIPTION

A writer's message, or main point, is the **theme** of his or her literary work. Theme is an answer to the question, "But what does this work *mean?*" Looking for a theme helps you look more deeply into the literature and makes for more enjoyable reading.

Some themes are easy to spot. The writer or a character will either say it directly or give strong clues about it. In the end of "Eleven," for example, Rachel sums up her frustrations with growing up: "I wish I was anything but eleven. . . ." Her statement suggests one of the story's themes: that it's hard to grow up and kids can feel frustrated with themselves and their lives.

Other times, a story's theme is not so easy to find. You will need to infer what the theme is from the work's title, key scenes, characters, symbols, and plot events.

DEFINITION

Theme is the statement about life that the author wants to convey to the reader. Sometimes the writer will make a clear statement about theme. Other times, readers will have to make inferences, or reasonable guesses about it.

Fiction

Reading
Poetry

Reading a Poem

Ways of Reading Poetry

Focus on Language
Focus on Meaning
Focus on Sound and Structure

Elements of Poetry

Poetry

407

Reading a Poem

Poets love words and choose their words very carefully—not just for meaning, but for look and sound. That's one reason why reading poetry is different from any other kind of reading that you will do.

You may sometimes wonder what a certain poem means, why people like poetry so much, or why you should bother with poetry at all. If so, you need to read this chapter. Reading poetry is different from reading prose. Good readers of poetry are always looking for meaning, listening for sounds, and picturing images from poems in their heads.

Goals

Here you'll learn how to:

✔ get more from the **poems you read**

✔ use the strategy of **close reading** on a poem

✔ understand **how poems are organized**

"The fog comes on little cat feet."

" Once upon a midnight dreary..."

" O my luve is like a red, red rose..."

Before Reading

You can read poems for pleasure, but many students read poetry only because their teacher assigned it. Either way, at some point you will probably ask yourself, "What does this poem mean?"

A Set a Purpose

When you get a poetry assignment in school, usually your goal is *to read and understand the poem*. Your purpose in reading the poem most of the time is to answer these two questions:

Setting a Purpose

- **What is the poem saying?**
- **What meaning do I find in the poem?**

Usually there is not one right answer to what a poem means. Poems talk to our senses and feelings and can mean many things to many people. Poems may say more than one thing. But don't start believing that a poem can mean anything you want. What you think a poem means needs to be supported by words or lines in the poem itself.

Poetry

B Preview

Just because a poem may be shorter than a story, textbook chapter, or essay doesn't mean you won't benefit by previewing it. Previewing gets you ready to read.

To preview a poem, look at several items:

poem about
snow
5 miles ahead

Now preview "Winter Poem" by Nikki Giovanni.

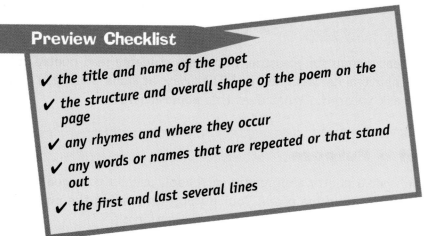

PREVIEW

Title and name of poet

"Winter Poem" by Nikki Giovanni

PREVIEW

Repeated word

once a snowflake fell
on my brow and i loved
it so much and i kissed
it and it was happy and called its cousins
and brothers and a web
of snow engulfed me then
i reached to love them all
and i squeezed them and they became
a spring rain and i stood perfectly
still and was a flower

PREVIEW

No rhymes or punctuation

PREVIEW

Key words in first and last lines

Even from a quick glance at "Winter Poem," you probably learned a lot:

> The poem is about winter and a snowflake in the beginning and ends up being about a flower.

> The poem is short and has no punctuation or rhymes.

> The word *i* is repeated.

Plan

You may have learned much more from your previewing. But at least you can come up with several other specific questions you'll want to answer as you read the poem more carefully. For instance, you might ask yourself:

- What does the snowflake have to do with the flower?
- Why didn't the poet use regular punctuation?
- Is the poet making a point about winter?

Your preview has given you a lot to think about. If you come to poetry with a plan for how to read poems, they will not seem so mysterious or scary or impossible to understand. If you can, plan to read a poem more than once.

Knowing that you're going to read a poem a number of times will help you relax. You won't feel like you have to think about everything at the same time.

PLAN FOR READING A POEM

1. *On a* **first reading,** *read for enjoyment. Get a feeling for the poem's words.*

2. *On a* **second reading,** *read for meaning. Look for clues that help you understand what the poem is saying.*

3. *On a* **third reading,** *study the structure and language of the poem. What kind of poem is it? Does it have a rhyme scheme? How many stanzas are in it? Examine the images, organization, and sounds. Think about how they add to the poem's message.*

4. *On a* **fourth reading,** *read for feeling. What are the mood and tone of the poem? How does this poem make you feel as you read it?*

By reading a poem a number of times and looking at a specific part of it each time, you can break the task of understanding a poem into smaller, easier readings.

Poetry

Even if you read through a poem several times, you will still need a reading strategy. Probably the best strategy for reading poems is called **close reading**. That means going word by word and line by line through a poem. It works especially well with short poems. The plan for reading and rereading a poem four times is, in a way, a kind of close reading.

A reading tool called a Double-entry Journal is a good way of doing close reading and responding to a text. Write lines from the poem on the left side. Choose lines or phrases that catch your attention or seem unusual or important. On the right, react to the words, telling what you think the words mean, how you feel about them, or what conclusions they lead you to make.

QUOTE	MY THOUGHTS ABOUT IT

DOUBLE-ENTRY JOURNAL

During Reading

Now it's time to put your reading plan into effect. Here you will see how going through a poem a number of times can help you unlock a poem's meaning.

D Read with a Purpose

Read slowly. Reading a poem is not the time to rush. Think of what the words mean. Hear how they sound. See how one reader responded to the beginning of "Winter Poem." Note how this reader first tells what he or she enjoyed about Giovanni's poem.

First Reading

DOUBLE-ENTRY JOURNAL—ENJOYMENT

QUOTE	MY THOUGHTS ABOUT IT
"once a snowflake fell on my brow and i loved it so much and i kissed it and it was happy . . ."	The first lines set the tone of a fairy tale. Everything seems so happy. It makes me feel good. The words are simple—like a child telling a story.

Poetry

Active readers respond to a text as they read. They know that their own feelings are an important part of the reading experience. Listen to what you are thinking as you read.

Second Reading

One way to help you sort out a poem's meaning is by using your imagination. Get a picture in your head of what is happening. Can you see someone standing outside in the snow? If you want, make a sketch to capture what's going on in the poem.

Another way to get more deeply into the poem's meaning is to use a reading tool called a Two Per Line. That is, circle the two most important words in each line. So, how do you know what words are the most important? That's a good question. Look for specific words—words that describe what's happening or that give you a strong feeling or image. Look at how one reader tried both making sketches and circling important words in a Double-entry Journal.

DOUBLE-ENTRY JOURNAL—MEANING

QUOTE	MY THOUGHTS ABOUT IT
"i reached to love them all and i squeezed them and they became a spring rain and i stood perfectly still and was a flower"	The speaker loves the snow. When she squeezes the snowflakes, they melt. She feels like she's a flower coming up in the spring. The poem is saying how beautiful nature is.

Don't worry if you're not totally sure about what the poem means. Just jot down a note or two that you can come back to later. Doing the Two Per Line made this reader notice the idea of snow turning into spring rain. What words did you focus on?

Third Reading

At some point in your reading of a poem, you should analyze its
structure and language. Look to see if it rhymes, how it's shaped, and
what images it uses. Think about why the poet might have decided
to write it in this way. Look at the notes this reader made on the
structure and language of Giovanni's poem.

DOUBLE-ENTRY JOURNAL—STRUCTURE AND LANGUAGE

QUOTE	MY THOUGHTS ABOUT IT
"once a snowflake fell on my brow and i loved it so much and i kissed it and it was happy and called its cousins and brothers and a web of snow engulfed me then	There are no capital letters or punctuation or fancy rhymes. It's all one stanza, and there's no regular rhythm.
i reached to love them all and i squeezed them and they became a spring rain and i stood perfectly still and was a flower"	I like the image of a "web" of snowflakes. The snow has human qualities. It's a family.

Poetry

When you focus on the structure of something—a house or a poem—
you pay attention to how it's built. How is it laid out? What parts or
sections are there, how do the parts fit together, and how does the
whole thing look? The reader
who made the notes above
noticed that "Winter Poem"
had no stanza breaks,
punctuation, or regular
rhythm. What else about
the poem's structure and
language caught your eye?

How Poems Are Organized

Knowing a little something about the way different types of poems are organized can help you know what to look at when you're reading. When you think of poetry, what features come to mind? Does a poem have to be broken up into groups of lines called **stanzas**? Does a poem need lots of imagery, a strong rhythm, or rhyming words?

Variety of Poetry

The answer is no. There are no simple formulas for what a poem needs to have or should look like. There are all kinds of poems, so, as a reader, you need to read with an open mind.

In some poems, the sound and rhyme are important; in others, the imagery or figurative language is striking. The key is to ask yourself why the poet put the poem together a certain way.

Understanding a Poet's Choices

So, what do you notice about the organization of "Winter Poem"? It is an example of a poem written in **free verse**. It has no set order or pattern of line length or rhyme. Why would Nikki Giovanni choose to write this poem in free verse? Think about the poem's subject. The title says the poem is about winter, and the first line mentions a snowflake. Falling snow has no real order or regular pattern, does it? It piles up—just as the lines pile up.

Giovanni here uses only one stanza, emphasizing the unity of her idea and feeling. That's also like snow—one clear, simple thing. Individual snowflakes blend together into a "web of snow," and in the poem, individual sentences run into one another without punctuation.

Nikki Giovanni may have had a number of ideas in mind when she created this poem. The point is that you, as a reader, need to stop and think about what the poet was attempting by organizing the poem in a certain way.

Fourth Reading

After reading for enjoyment, meaning, and structure and language, go back to the poem and read for feeling. How does the poem make you feel? What mood is created, and how does it affect you? With almost any literature, you need to listen to your own thoughts as you read. As you read the words, you are thinking something. But, all too often, we never stop to record what we feel about what we're reading.

Note the way this reader recorded feelings about the end of "Winter Poem."

DOUBLE-ENTRY JOURNAL—FEELING

QUOTE	MY THOUGHTS ABOUT IT
"i reached to love them all and i squeezed them and they became a spring rain and i stood perfectly still and was a flower"	This gives me a sense of peace. It's a quiet, beautiful scene. The speaker's love of being out in nature comes through. It makes me feel happy.

Poetry

You probably have somewhat different thoughts about the poem. Perhaps you didn't even like it. That's natural. People have different tastes in clothes or food, so why not poetry? It's OK not to like a poem. Just be ready to explain and support your opinion with some specific parts of the poem.

E Connect

Whether you like to read poetry or you don't, whether you chose a particular poem or your teacher assigned it, make an effort to connect the poem to your own life and experience. Don't just stare at the words on the page. React and relate to them. Read actively.

Only by connecting yourself to the poem will it truly come alive and be memorable for you. Think about how it relates to you and how it's like other poems you've read. Note here a few of the reactions some readers had to Giovanni's poem.

"Winter Poem"

I like the idea of a snowflake having feelings and a family.

once a snowflake fell
on my brow and i loved
it so much and i kissed
it and it was happy and called its cousins
and brothers and a web
of snow engulfed me then
i reached to love them all
and i squeezed them and they became
a spring rain and i stood perfectly
still and was a flower

This poem tells me that I should stop and take notice of beautiful things.

The image of letting raindrops fall on you is nice. I do that in the spring.

After Reading

After reading a poem, many readers want to talk about it. Discussing poems with others after you read is a good idea. But first be sure you've collected your own thoughts about the poem.

F Pause and Reflect

Take a minute after you've read the poem—whether it's only once quickly or four times slowly and carefully—and think. Do you understand the poem? Ask yourself questions like these:

Looking Back

- **Do I feel comfortable explaining what the poem is about?**
- **Do I have a clear picture of the poem in my head?**
- **What particular words or images come to mind?**
- **What is the "big idea" of the poem?**

G Reread

Remember the plan for reading poetry that we suggested on page 411? It included reading the poem four times, each time concentrating on something different. It would be great if readers had the time—and interest—to do this. But let's be honest. You may not always have the chance to read a poem three or four times, especially a long one.

Or, if it's not a question of time, it may be one of motivation. You'll like some poems more than others; some poems will spark your interest or curiosity more than others. But sometimes it's with the ones that puzzle you that rereading pays off the most.

Poetry

Use the strategy of **paraphrasing** to examine particular lines of a poem—maybe ones you especially liked, found surprising, or just didn't get the first time through. When you paraphrase, you translate what the author says into your own words. You can do that in a number of ways:

■ in a conversation with a reading partner or class discussion

■ in a journal entry or summary

■ in a poem modeled on the poem you've read

The point is to capture what's being said but to put it into your own style. Make it sound like you. Below is a Paraphrase Chart one reader made for the last part of "Winter Poem."

PARAPHRASE CHART

LINES	MY PARAPHRASE
"…i stood perfectly still and was a flower"	I didn't move and felt like something alive and beautiful.

MY THOUGHTS
It's not like the speaker is somehow becoming a flower in a magic spell. The speaker is just comparing herself to a flower. She liked feeling the raindrops like a flower might.

H Remember

Sometimes you may want—or need—to remember a poem. How are you going to do that? How can you find a way to make the poem "your own"?

Here are some suggestions.

1. Write in a Journal

Write in your journal about the poem. Describe what it meant to you and how it made you feel. Explore what you did or didn't like about it.

2. Make a Sketch

Draw a picture to go along with the poem. Write about your picture and show how it connects to the poem. Share your sketch with a friend or someone in your family.

Here is the response one reader made to "Winter Poem" in her learning journal.

JOURNAL SKETCH

The description of the snow makes me think of how beautiful everything looks in a snowstorm.

Poetry

Summing Up

Follow a plan for reading a poem several times: once for enjoyment, once for meaning, once for structure and language, and once for the feeling it gives you. **Close reading** is a strategy that helps you take apart a poem word by word and line by line. Note how the poem is organized into **lines and stanzas.** Remember to try one of these helpful tools:

■ **Double-entry Journal**

■ **Two Per Line**

■ **Paraphrase Chart**

Use the rereading strategy of **paraphrasing** to put the poem in your own words.

Focus on Language

You do not usually read poetry just for its language. You're often concerned about its meaning, its sound, its organization, and how it makes you feel. But one part of the richness of poetry *is* its language.

Poets use only a few words, but they make each word count. You can be sure that each word in a poem has been chosen carefully. Poets try to get as much meaning and sound out of each word as they can.

Goals

Here you'll learn how to:

✔ **recognize word connotations, figurative language, and imagery**

✔ **use the strategy of close reading**

✔ **understand how a poem's language affects your reading**

Before Reading

Focusing on a poem's language doesn't mean paying equal attention to every word. But how do you know which words to focus on? When you focus on language, watch for these elements:

- difficult words or unusual phrases
- words that trigger a strong emotional response
- figurative language, such as metaphors and similes
- striking imagery

Notice the notes one reader made about the language in "Words" by Pauli Murray.

"Words" by Pauli Murray

We are spendthrifts with words,
We squander them,
Toss them like pennies in the air—
Arrogant words,
Angry words,
Cruel words,
Comradely words,
Shy words tiptoeing from mouth to ear.

But the slowly wrought words of love
And the thunderous words of heartbreak—
These we hoard.

The idea of spending words is unusual.

I like this comparison to pennies.

Is this personification?

What does this word mean?

Even from one quick look at the poem, the reader has learned a lot. The value of words and how we use them are worth exploring further. What else about the poem's language did you notice?

Poetry

Reading Strategy: Close Reading

When your focus is the language of a poem, you'll want to look closely at the words the poet has chosen. Use the strategy of **close reading** to examine a work word by word and line by line. It's especially useful for shorter selections, where you can really focus on a line or two. Close reading helps you consider the meaning of specific words—by themselves and together with others.

Words in poems can trip you up if you don't know what they mean. They can also trip you up if you don't know how the words are being used. So, you may need to look up key words. But first you need to find out which words are important.

Finding Key Words

As you read, go through the poem line by line to make sure you don't skim over important words. You may want to try doing a Two Per Line to find key words. That means you'll circle or highlight two important words in each line. Focus your attention on one line at a time. Choose words that describe an action, create a mood, or name a person, place, or thing. Notice what's been highlighted in this part of "Words."

TWO PER LINE

Comradely words,
Shy words tiptoeing from mouth to ear.

But the slowly wrought words of love
And the thunderous words of heartbreak —
These we hoard.

Note how some words jump out of the poem when you focus your attention on just two words in each line. But it's not enough to pick out key words. The point is to think about them. Ask yourself how the words affect what you think the poem means and how they make you feel.

Using a Dictionary

Sometimes it's fine to read quickly and skim over words you don't know. But with poems, particularly when your focus is language, it's important to understand what each word means, especially the key words. Trying to understand the language of a poem without knowing the definitions of certain words is like trying to paint a picture without knowing what colors you can use. Keep a dictionary handy. Write definitions in your own words, if necessary.

JOURNAL ENTRY

spendthrifts—people who spend money recklessly or wastefully
wrought—delicately made or carefully put together
hoard—to save or store away; accumulate

Knowing the definitions of these three words helps you see that the poem talks about different things in each stanza. At first, the speaker of the poem describes how people are "spendthrifts," suggesting that we use some words carelessly and wastefully. In the second stanza, the speaker focuses on words people use more carefully. Words having to do with love are carefully and deliberately spoken. These words we store away and collect, as if they have special value.

Poetry

Thinking about Connotations

As a reader of poetry, you also need to look at the denotations and connotations of words. A **denotation** is the meaning of the word you will find in the dictionary. The **connotation** is the emotional response or suggestions that a word triggers within you.

Of course, not all words in a poem will have interesting or important connotations. But some will. For instance, go back to the second line of "Words." What are the denotations and connotations of the word *squander*?

DENOTATION

to spend wastefully or extravagantly

squander

CONNOTATION

to be careless with what you have
to not appreciate something's value

The word *squander* has some negative
connotations. It suggests extreme waste
and carelessness.

We squander them,
Toss them like pennies in the air—
(meaning we use more words than we need)

or

We squander them,
Toss them like pennies in the air—
(meaning we use words carelessly and
don't appreciate their value)

Knowing the connotations of a word or phrase can often help you
understand and enjoy a part of a poem that at first struck you as
strange or confusing. Once you're aware of the connotations of
squander, you can better understand the speaker's point about how
easily we use many words. We toss them out "like pennies in the air."

Examining Figurative Language

Like connotations, **figurative language** goes beyond the literal
meanings of words. Poets often use figurative language to create
pictures and ideas in the reader's mind. Figures of speech—such as
similes, metaphors, and personification—are common examples of
figurative language. As you read the following line from "Words,"
think about the meaning of the words and what pictures you "see"
in your mind.

> ### EXAMPLE OF FIGURATIVE LANGUAGE
>
> "Shy words tiptoeing from mouth to ear."

"Shy words tiptoeing" is an example of personification. The words here seemingly take on human qualities. They have a particular personality and move in a special way.

Not all poems, of course, have personification, similes, or other examples of figurative language. But get in the habit of looking for them. Be alert for descriptions or comparisons that go beyond the literal meaning of the words. With practice, you'll find that examining figurative language will help you enjoy a poem more.

Noticing a Poem's Images

Poets often use **imagery** to help readers create pictures of words. Details that appeal to your senses—sight, hearing, smell, touch, and taste—make descriptions come alive. Use your imagination to picture what you're reading about. What images come to mind as you read these lines?

> ### EXAMPLE OF IMAGERY
>
> But the slowly wrought words of love
> And the thunderous words of heartbreak —
> These we hoard.

By using *wrought*, which means "made delicately or carefully," the poet helps you view love in a certain way. It often takes a period of dating and courtship to find love. When love falls apart, the resulting "heartbreak" strikes with "thunderous" effect. The poet uses the words *wrought* and *thunderous* to create images in your mind as a reader. The poet wants you to imagine hearing the soft, deliberate words of love exchanged between two people and then the booming thunder that arrives with heartbreak.

Sketching the images you "see" can be helpful when you focus on language. What follows is one reader's sketch of the imagery in the first stanza of "Words."

Poetry

We are spendthrift with words,
We squander them,
Toss them like pennies in the air—
Arrogant words,
Angry words,
Cruel words,
Comradely words,
Shy words tiptoeing from mouth to ear.

After Reading

Focusing on a poem's language means picking out key words, looking up unfamiliar words, and considering connotations, figurative language, and imagery. When you've finished reading a poem, ask yourself these questions:

How does the language affect the poem's meaning?

Are particular words or lines still hard to understand?

If there are parts of the poem that puzzle you, it's a good idea to reread the poem again. Use the dictionary to look up other words you may not know and try to picture in your mind how all the separate ideas and images fit together. Try these suggestions.

1. Work with a Partner

Talking about a poem with another person (or with a group) can help you see sides of a poem that you may have missed. Often, someone else will notice something about a poem's language that you didn't see or think about.

- **Read the poem aloud to each other.**
- **Share details you already noticed about the language of a poem.**
- **Discuss what you think the poem means and use particular words to back up your ideas.**
- **Talk with your partner about what certain words mean, their connotations, and what pictures they create in your mind.**
- **Ask yourselves why the poet chose the exact phrase or words he or she did. Try replacing some words with synonyms. Consider how the overall meaning, sound, or mood of the poem would change.**

2. Respond and React

After you've finished examining a poem's language, react to it. At times you can get so caught up in *describing* what's there that you forget to *respond* to it. What words or phrases did you like? What images stuck in your mind? You might want to write down your reactions or thoughts in a journal or try writing a poem modeled on what you read. For example, you could create a poem with similar organization, some of the same language, but with different content. The poem below shows how one reader used "Words"as a model for writing about friendships.

Poetry

POEM MODELED ON "WORDS"

We are careless of our friends,
We ignore them,
Brush them aside as if a lock of hair—
School friends,
Neighborhood friends,
Old friends.

Summing Up

- A poet often chooses a word for its connotations, not just its meaning in the dictionary.

- During a close reading, look for striking imagery, figurative language, or words used in an unusual way.

Focus on Meaning

When you read something, it's natural to want to understand what it means. You want to find the viewpoint of an argument, the main idea of an article, or the theme of a novel. And readers of poetry look for meaning. Of course, there's a lot more to poetry than meaning. People read poems for their interesting use of words, lovely sounds, striking images, and the powerful feelings they stir up. But frequently, a reader's focus is meaning. All too often, however, poems are puzzling. The meaning seems hidden or mysterious. Poets often use words in such unusual and strange ways that the meaning is hard to figure out.

You may get frustrated. Because you don't know what you should be looking for, you give up—on a particular poem or even poetry in general. If you've ever been puzzled by a poem or unsure about how to figure out what a poem means, then read on.

Goals

Here you'll learn how to:

✔ use the strategy of close reading
✔ recognize clues to a poem's meaning
✔ see the difference between a poem's subject and its meaning

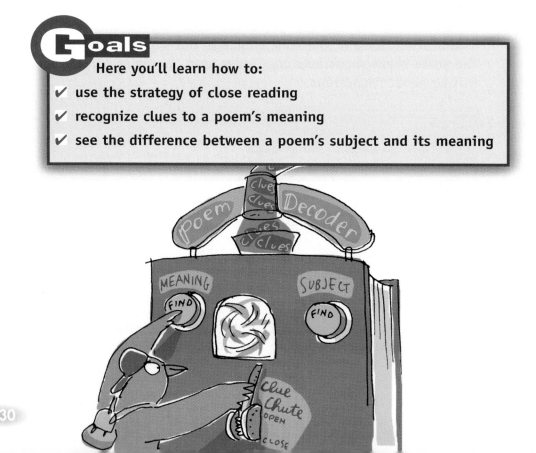

Before Reading

Remember, when you are given a new poem, to follow the reading plan explained on page 411. It's a good idea to read the poem one time just for fun before you focus on its meaning.

Clues to Meaning

On a second reading, look for clues about the poem's meaning.

Pay special attention to these parts:

▪ the title

▪ any words that are repeated or stand out

▪ the first and last several lines

Read through this poem. Note how one reader began to focus on meaning.

Poetry

 "Those Winter Sundays" by Robert Hayden

Sundays too my father got up early
and put his clothes on in the blueblack cold,
then with cracked hands that ached
from labor in the weekday weather made
banked fires blaze. No one ever thanked him.

about the speaker's father and his Sunday routine

I'd wake and hear the cold splintering, breaking.
When the rooms were warm, he'd call,
and slowly I would rise and dress,
fearing the chronic angers of that house,

keeps repeating that it's cold

Speaking indifferently to him,
who had driven out the cold
and polished my good shoes as well.
What did I know, what did I know
of love's austere and lonely offices?

a sad mood— words like "ached," "angers," and "lonely"

a hard question

431

First Thoughts about Meaning

What impression do you get of this poem? You probably see that the speaker is remembering his father. The title, the first line, and the repetition of the word *cold* make sense together. The speaker is describing his memories of what his father used to do on Sundays in winter.

Did you notice anything else? The reader noted several words that create a serious, sad atmosphere. That's something you'll probably want to think more about.

Reading Strategy: Close Reading

Now form a plan to focus on meaning. Here are *five* ways to focus on a poem's meaning:

1. *Look closely at the denotations and connotations of the words.*

2. *Think about what's unusual and important.*

3. *Explore your feelings about the poem.*

4. *Ask yourself what the poet is saying.*

5. *Paraphrase that idea. Put it in your own words.*

One way to focus on meaning is to use the strategy of **close reading**. No skimming is allowed. As you read, keep asking yourself what each word and sentence of the poem means. What the poem makes you think about and how the poem makes you feel will give you the answer.

During Reading

When you focus on a poem's meaning, you think about particular words—what they mean themselves and how they relate to other words.

1. Look at Denotations and Connotations

Begin by looking up unfamiliar words. Knowing the definition, or **denotation**, of the words is the first step in unlocking a poem's meaning. For instance, read the last stanza again. Note the meaning of the highlighted words.

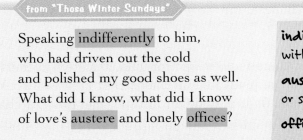

from "Those Winter Sundays"

Speaking indifferently to him,
who had driven out the cold
and polished my good shoes as well.
What did I know, what did I know
of love's austere and lonely offices?

indifferently =
without care or interest

austere = serious
or strict

offices = duties
or responsibilities

Poetry

You can often figure out what a word means from its context. But if you're not sure, use a dictionary or ask a friend. A reader who only thought of *offices* as places of business could find the poem's last line confusing.

The **connotations** of words—the emotional responses you have to them—also provide clues to a poem's meaning. Take, for instance, the word *blueblack* in the second line of the poem. Why is the cold described this way? What other things are *blueblack*? Use a Double-entry Journal to concentrate on the meanings of particular words. Copy a phrase or a line on the left and then write your thoughts and questions about it. Look at how one reader tried to make sense of the word *blueblack*.

QUOTE	MY THOUGHTS
"in the blueblack cold"	It's just a color, a dark blue. But it makes me think of a bruise— like when your skin turns black and blue. It reminds me of being hurt.

2. Think about What's Unusual and Important

Clues to a poem's meaning can be found in important or unusual words, sounds, or images. But how do you know what's important and what's not?

The answer is that there is no magic formula. Different readers will notice different things. It may be an image that creates a striking picture in your mind. Or it may be an unusual metaphor, a change in the rhyme or rhythm, or an unusual grouping of lines. One good way to find the most important words or ideas in a poem is to do a Two Per Line.

After reading a poem once, mark or note on a piece of paper the two words or ideas in each line that seem important to you. Don't worry if your classmates mark other things. Your reading of the poem will be as individual as your fingerprints.

Read the poem again, paying special attention to what you marked in each line. Think about how these words create—and add to—the poem's meaning.

Note the comments one reader made after looking at the key words in the first half of the poem.

from "Those Winter Sundays"

Sundays too my father got up early
and put his clothes on in the blueblack cold,
then with cracked hands that ached
from labor in the weekday weather made
banked fires blaze. No one ever thanked him.

I'd wake and hear the cold splintering, breaking.
When the rooms were warm, he'd call,

TWO PER LINE

WORDS	MY IDEAS
Sundays, father	about his father & Sundays
blueblack, cold	sounds cold and hard
hands, ached	pain in hands—why?
labor, weather	labor = work, weather = cold outside?
No one, thanked	not noticed or thanked
cold, splintering	sounds harsh, like firewood
rooms, warm	sounds cozy—a big change from the cold

Poetry

Below is another way one reader tried to make sense of important parts of "Those Winter Sundays."

DOUBLE-ENTRY JOURNAL

QUOTE	MY THOUGHTS
"Speaking indifferently to him, who had driven out the cold and polished my good shoes as well. What did I know, what did I know of love's austere and lonely offices?"	The father has worked hard. This sounds sad. Is the speaker saying he didn't realize all the father did for him—like building a fire? He wished he hadn't spoken "indifferently."

3. Explore Your Feelings about the Poem

Even though your focus is to understand the poem's meaning, you still should take a moment to note your personal response to what you're reading. How does the poem make you feel? What mood has been created? Your own questions, comments, and reactions will help you find meaning in the poem. Look at one reader's reactions to "Those Winter Sundays."

"Those Winter Sundays"

Sundays too my father got up early
and put his clothes on in the blueblack cold,
then with cracked hands that ached
from labor in the weekday weather made
banked fires blaze. No one ever thanked him.

I'd wake and hear the cold splintering, breaking.
When the rooms were warm, he'd call,
and slowly I would rise and dress,
fearing the chronic angers of that house,

Speaking indifferently to him,
who had driven out the cold
and polished my good shoes as well.
What did I know, what did I know
of love's austere and lonely offices?

Sometimes, I take my father for granted too and forget how hard he works.

This is so sad. He wishes he could go back in time.

As you read, jot down questions, comments, and reactions. Does the poem relate to anything in your life? Does it remind you of any other poems you've read? Use your personal response as another clue for finding meaning in a poem.

After Reading

After you have read the poem a number of times and after you have marked and responded to the text, ask yourself, "Am I getting closer to understanding what the poem means?"

4. Decide What the Poet Is Saying

Deciding what the poet's purpose was can help you discover meaning in a poem. In some poems—not all—the poet tries to send a message or make a point. Look for that message as you would the theme of a story or the main point of an essay. Keep in mind that the *subject* of the poem is not the same thing as the *meaning* of the poem. In "Those Winter Sundays," the subject is the speaker's memories of Sunday mornings in the winter. But that's not the meaning of the poem.

What is the speaker saying about those Sundays? How does he feel about what his father used to do? How does he want the reader to feel about what he's described? Look back over the notes you made, the words you highlighted, and the questions you asked. The meaning of "Those Winter Sundays" is something closer to the idea that often a young child doesn't appreciate or understand how a parent is showing him or her love. The speaker paints a sad picture of a man and a son who were not close.

5. Try Paraphrasing

Paraphrasing part of a poem can be a good way to get at meaning when you read. To paraphrase simply means to put in your own words. So, beside a line or stanza, write down what you think is meant by that line. Translate the text into your own words and your own style. Here's how one reader paraphrased the last two lines:

Poetry

QUOTE	MY PARAPHRASE
"What did I know, what did I know of love's austere and lonely offices?"	When I was younger, I didn't realize that loving and taking care of someone can be so hard.

Don't worry if someone else finds other meaning in the same poem. Different readers can see different things in a poem. That's not the same as saying a poem can mean anything to anybody. What's important is to be able to explain what meaning you do find by drawing on different parts of the poem.

Summing Up

- Look for clues to meaning in the poet's word choices, unusual and important features of the poem, and your personal response.

- The subject of the poem is not the same as its meaning. The meaning is an idea or feeling about the subject.

- Close reading and paraphrasing can help you find meaning in a poem.

Focus on Sound and Structure

When you read a poem, do you pay attention to its sound and structure? Do you listen to the rhymes and rhythms and notice how the words are arranged on the page? Focusing on sound and structure can increase your enjoyment and understanding of poetry.

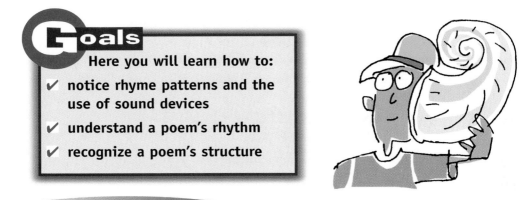

Goals

Here you will learn how to:

✔ **notice rhyme patterns and the use of sound devices**

✔ **understand a poem's rhythm**

✔ **recognize a poem's structure**

Before Reading

Sound and structure are more important in some poems than others. Some poets use a lot of rhyming words or a certain line length; others don't use any rhyme or steady pattern. As a reader, you need to ask yourself why the poet made the poem look and sound the way it does.

When your focus is on sound and structure, look for the following as you preview:

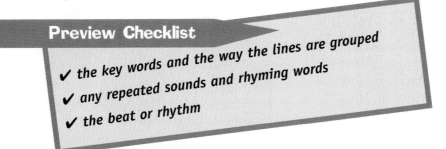

Preview Checklist

✔ the key words and the way the lines are grouped

✔ any repeated sounds and rhyming words

✔ the beat or rhythm

Now preview "The Sloth" by Theodore Roethke, a playful poem about the lazy, tree-dwelling animal.

Poetry

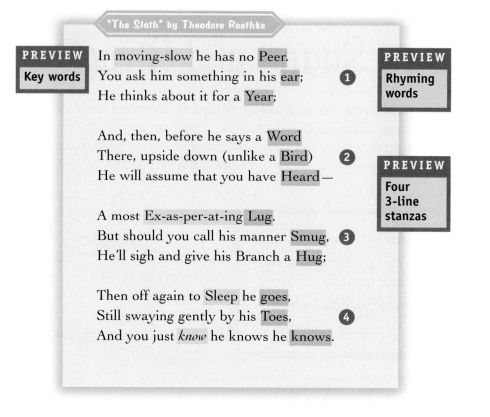

"The Sloth" by Theodore Roethke

PREVIEW

Key words

In moving-slow he has no Peer.
You ask him something in his ear;
He thinks about it for a Year;

And, then, before he says a Word
There, upside down (unlike a Bird)
He will assume that you have Heard—

A most Ex-as-per-at-ing Lug.
But should you call his manner Smug,
He'll sigh and give his Branch a Hug;

Then off again to Sleep he goes,
Still swaying gently by his Toes,
And you just *know* he knows he knows.

PREVIEW

Rhyming words

PREVIEW

Four 3-line stanzas

① ② ③ ④

What did you notice about this poem's sound and structure? Why did Theodore Roethke choose to make his poem look and sound the way it does? That's an important question.

Reading Strategy: **Close Reading**

To understand the sounds and structure of a poem, you need to take the poem apart word for word and line by line. That's why **close reading** is such a good strategy for poems. It will help you go through a poem slowly and see what makes it work.

The Sloth

During Reading

Some poets write in free verse, with no stanza breaks and lines of different lengths. Other poets use a definite rhyme scheme and play a lot with the sounds of words. Still other poets write lines that look and sound like ordinary, everyday conversation. The fact is that poetry follows no absolute rules. It is individual, free, and sometimes even a little wild.

Despite the huge variety in poems, look for these *four* things when you focus on sound and structure:

1. Organization of lines
2. Repeated sounds
3. Rhyme
4. Rhythm or meter

1. Organization of Lines

Structure is another word for organization—the length and arrangement of a poem's lines. So, what can you say about the organization of "The Sloth"? It has four 3-line stanzas. Most of the lines are about the same length.

The **stanzas** can help you understand the poem's meaning. A stanza, like a paragraph, often signals the beginning of a new subject. The punctuation marks in the poem help you separate ideas, and the stanzas help you sort out the images the poet gives you. Roethke introduces a new image in each stanza:

- The sloth is very slow (stanza 1).
- The sloth is difficult to talk to (stanza 2).
- The sloth can be annoying (stanza 3).
- The sloth sleeps upside down (stanza 4).

Did you notice anything else? What about the use of capital letters, for instance, or the way the word *Ex-as-per-at-ing* is spread out?

Poetry

2. Repeated Sounds

A poem's effect on you may come not just from its meaning but also from its sound. Remember that poetry is meant to be seen *and* heard. Try to hear the music that is going on inside poems. Say the words slowly and listen to their sounds.

Think about how the repetition of certain sounds affects your mood as you're reading. You may have noticed the repetition of *know* in the last line. Do you like it? Does it strike you as funny or surprising? A number of other passages contain a sound device called **alliteration**, the repetition of a consonant sound at the beginnings of words.

EXAMPLE OF ALLITERATION

"s" sound	*"Then off again to Sleep he goes, Still swaying gently by his Toes,"*

Do you hear these repeated sounds? How would the poem be different if they weren't there? Put in different words and think about how the effect of the poem would change.

3. Rhyme

You probably noticed the repetition of some other sounds in the poem too. This repetition, called **rhyme**, comes at the ends of the lines. Note how the rhymes in the first two stanzas can be marked.

Poetry

> **RHYME SCHEME**
>
> | | |
> |---|---|
> | In moving-slow he has no Peer. | *a* |
> | You ask him something in his ear; | *a* |
> | He thinks about it for a Year; | *a* |
> | | |
> | And, then, before he says a Word | *b* |
> | There, upside down (unlike a Bird) | *b* |
> | He will assume that you have Heard— | *b* |

Each line is given a letter as a symbol for the end word's sound. Marking the **rhyme scheme** is a quick way to see how much, if any, rhyme was used and whether it is used in any regular pattern.

Ask yourself what effect the rhyme scheme has. Does the rhyme make the poem's meaning clearer or the mood more lighthearted? How would the poem be different if there were no rhyme?

4. Rhythm or Meter

Language has a beat just as music does. In some poems, readers can also notice a clear rhythm. Meter creates a poem's **rhythm.** *Meter* is the pattern of stressed (strong) and unstressed (weak) syllables in a poem. When poets create a rhythm in their poem, they count out the number of stressed and unstressed syllables in each line. Read aloud the following lines and notice how one reader marked the rhythm.

> **LISTENING FOR METER**
>
> ∪ ╱ ∪ ╱ ∪ ╱ ∪ ╱
> In moving-slow he has no Peer.
> da *dum* da *dum* da *dum* da *dum*
>
> ∪ ╱ ∪ ╱ ∪ ╱ ∪ ╱
> You ask him something in his ear;
> da *dum* da *dum* da *dum* da *dum*

each line—
4 stressed beats
4 unstressed beats
8 syllables

As you read, you emphasized (or pronounced louder) some syllables more than others. Can you hear the beats? Both lines have four stressed beats. Be alert for sudden changes in a poem's rhythm. They can be clues to a poem's meaning.

After Reading

Chances are you'll like some poems a lot more than others. Do you have a favorite kind of poetry? Maybe it's poems with strong images and lots of figurative language. Or maybe you prefer poems that tell a story and create a definite mood. For many people, the sound and structure of poems are important parts of the reading experience. Here are two ways to focus on a poem's sound and structure.

1. Connect to the Poem

With poems probably more than any other genre, readers need to make a personal connection to the reading. How does this poem strike you? Most people react first to the poem's subject and what they see as the poem's meaning. But don't forget to respond to the poem's sound and structure.

Note the reaction of one reader to this stanza:

> **from "The Sloth"**
>
> A most Ex-as-per-at-ing Lug.
> But should you call his manner Smug,
> He'll sigh and give his Branch a Hug;

I like the way Ex-as-per-at-ing is spread out. It makes me read it slowly, just like the sloth moves. It's very clever.

2. Reread the Poem

If you find a poem you like, you'll probably enjoy rereading it. You can see in your mind the pictures the words create or listen again to the rhymes and rhythms you liked best. But even if you don't think you "get" a poem, go back and reread. And make a special effort to concentrate on the poem's sounds and structure. It can open your eyes to new ideas and change what you think of a poem. Poems will not always "read" the same way to you each time you return to them.

That's why it will help you to take notes on your reactions to a poem after you reread it. Here, for example, is the journal entry one reader made on the sound and structure of "The Sloth":

JOURNAL ENTRY

I like "The Sloth" because it's different from other poems. I've never read anything like it. The capital letters look strange. A lot of poems are serious, but this one is really funny! The rhymes at the end of the lines are so obvious! The author describes the sloth well, and I can picture him hanging upside down from his tree and being too lazy to talk.

Poetry

Summing Up

- **A poem's sound and structure can give insight into its meaning.**
- **Some poems have regular patterns of rhythm and rhyme, while others don't.**
- **Read a poem aloud to hear its sounds and discover its beat.**

Elements of Poetry

Poems convey an idea or a feeling through carefully selected words and phrases. To unlock the meaning of a poem, you have to consider every word that the poet has chosen. You also need to be familiar with different techniques and styles that a poet may use. This will help you know what to expect from the poetry you read.

Use this part of the handbook like a glossary. Look up a term, read its example, and study its definition. Then apply what you've learned to the reading.

Elements of Poetry

Alliteration	447
Allusion	448
Exaggeration	449
Figurative Language	450
Free Verse	451
Idiom	452
Imagery	453
Lyric Poem	454
Metaphor	455
Mood	456
Narrative Poem	457
Onomatopoeia	458
Personification	459
Repetition	460
Rhyme	461
Rhyme Scheme	462
Rhythm	463
Simile	464
Stanza	465
Symbol	467
Tone and Voice	468

Alliteration

Read the beginning lines of Sara Teasdale's poem "There Will Come Soft Rains." Pay special attention to the repeated sounds that you hear.

EXAMPLE

from "There Will Come Soft Rains" by Sara Teasdale

There will come soft rains and the smell of the ground,
And swallows calling with their shimmering sound;

Repeated sounds

DESCRIPTION

Alliteration is a tool that poets use to create music in poetry. Can you hear the repeated consonant sound? Sara Teasdale repeats the consonant *s*. You can see it and hear it in the words *soft, smell, swallows, shimmering,* and *sound*. Why would a poet use so many words with the same sound? By repeating the sound *s,* Teasdale creates a soft sound, just like falling rain.

DEFINITION

Alliteration is the repetition of the same consonant sound at the beginnings of several words of a line of poetry or a sentence.

Poetry

447

Allusion

Who is this poem talking about? Does it remind you of anything or anybody?

"Alice" by Shel Silverstein

She drank from a bottle called DRINK ME
And up she grew so tall,
She ate from a plate called TASTE ME
And down she shrank so small.
And so she changed, while other folks
Never tried nothin' at all.

References
to a character
in another book

DESCRIPTION

Do you recognize the person the poet is describing? The poet refers to Alice, the little girl in *Alice's Adventures in Wonderland*. You probably wouldn't know that unless you had read the book or seen a movie about her.

Poets often refer to other things outside of their poems. These references are called **allusions**. Allusions can be to real people and historical events as well as to fictional characters and stories. Allusions add extra layers of meaning to poems and make poems richer.

"Talking" to other works of literature is another way poets have fun with writing. They rewrite, comment on, or continue stories when making allusions to them. As a reader, you will appreciate poetry more if you look for allusions to other works as you read.

DEFINITION

An allusion is a reference to something with which the reader is likely to be familiar, such as a person, place, or event from history or literature.

Exaggeration

Notice the way people are described in this poem.

EXAMPLE

"No Difference" by Shel Silverstein

Small as a peanut,
Big as a giant,
We're all the same size
When we turn off the light.

Stretching the truth

Rich as a sultan,
Poor as a mite,
We're all worth the same
When we turn off the light.

Red, black or orange,
Yellow or white,
We all look the same
When we turn off the light.

So maybe the way
To make everything right
Is for God to just reach out
And turn off the light!

Poetry

DESCRIPTION

Sometimes you have to stretch the truth to get your point across or just to make people laugh. Exaggeration like that is a part of everyday speech. Poets also use **exaggeration**, or hyperbole. Here Shel Silverstein stretches the truth about people's size and wealth to make the reader laugh and to make a point about how much alike people are.

DEFINITION

Exaggeration is the obvious stretching of the truth.

Figurative Language

Writing teachers give students the advice to "show, don't tell."
Poetry is about creating images so that a reader can see something.
Notice how Emily Dickinson shows readers what hope is like in the
lines below.

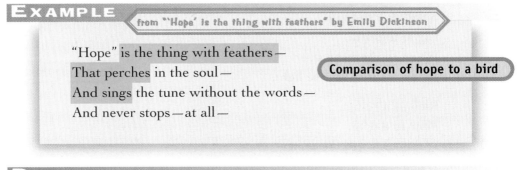

EXAMPLE

from "'Hope' is the thing with feathers" by Emily Dickinson

"Hope" is the thing with feathers—
That perches in the soul—
And sings the tune without the words—
And never stops—at all—

Comparison of hope to a bird

DESCRIPTION

In the lines above, Dickinson describes "hope" as "the thing with
feathers." That's a metaphor. She compares hope to a bird. She
makes hope come alive and gives it the ability to move and to sing.
This is an example of language that goes beyond the words' literal
meanings, or **figurative language**.

Poets want their readers to make connections between things. Poets
use figurative language to make your imagination work and help you
see the world in new ways. After reading this poem, you can now
look at hope differently—something that sings a "tune without
the words."

DEFINITION

Figurative language is made up of all the tools that a poet
uses to create a special effect or feeling. It includes metaphor,
simile, alliteration, personification, and onomatopoeia.

Free Verse

What makes the following piece of writing a poem? Doesn't it sound like everyday speech?

"April Rain Song" by Langston Hughes

Let the rain kiss you.
Let the rain beat upon your head with silver liquid drops.
Let the rain sing you a lullaby.

No rhymes

The rain makes still pools on the sidewalk.
The rain makes running pools in the gutter.
The rain plays a little sleep-song on our roof at night—

No regular rhythm

And I love the rain.

DESCRIPTION

"April Rain Song" is a kind of poetry called **free verse**. The lines in Langston Hughes's poem have no set pattern of rhythms or stressed syllables. It is "free" of formal rhyme patterns and traditional stanzas. Poets use free verse to create lines as short as a breath, to make the reader stop and pause, to emphasize white space around the words of a poem, and to create musical sounds and phrases.

Writing in free verse may look easy, but it isn't. Poets often try to make the words in their poems seem like ordinary conversation. By using the natural rhythms of free verse, poets emphasize the simple beauty and everyday rhythms of language.

DEFINITION

Free verse is poetry written without a regular rhyme scheme, meter, or form.

Poetry

Idiom

Think of the phrase "pull your leg." Its meaning has nothing to do with yanking on someone's leg. The phrase means "joking" or "kidding." What do the highlighted phrases below mean?

EXAMPLE

from "Lean on Me" by Bill Withers

Please swallow your pride if I have things you need to borrow,
For no one can fill those of your needs that you won't let show.

. . .

Just call on me, brother, when you need a hand.
We all need somebody to lean on.

DESCRIPTION

Ordinary expressions made up of words that have meanings other than their literal definitions are called **idioms**. "Swallow your pride" is an idiom, as is "when you need a hand." Bill Withers doesn't expect anyone actually to drink pride or physically to give someone else a hand. He is using idioms because they reflect the way people talk in everyday conversation.

Here is a list of some other idioms you might have heard:

- **raining cats and dogs**—"raining very hard"
- **get a leg up**—"get a start on"
- **lay it on thick**—"exaggerate in praising someone"
- **pass the buck**—"give someone else the blame"
- **teach an old dog new tricks**—"get someone to change old habits"

DEFINITION

An **idiom** is a common phrase made up of words that can't be understood by their literal, or ordinary, meanings.

Imagery

As you read poetry, think about the pictures you see in your mind. Note the images the poet creates in the lines below.

EXAMPLE

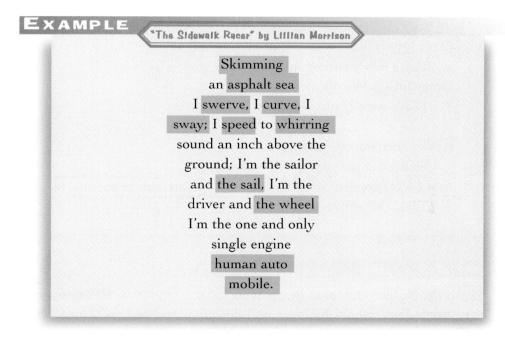

"The Sidewalk Racer" by Lillian Morrison

Skimming
an asphalt sea
I swerve, I curve, I
sway; I speed to whirring
sound an inch above the
ground; I'm the sailor
and the sail, I'm the
driver and the wheel
I'm the one and only
single engine
human auto
mobile.

DESCRIPTION

Poets use **imagery** to present objects, express ideas, or describe feelings and scenes. Usually the words and phrases appeal to your five senses—touch, taste, smell, hearing, and sight. Imagery creates pictures in your mind that stir your emotions and show you things in ways you've never thought of before.

As you read poetry, try to visualize the images or pictures described on the page. Make sketches of them if you can. Images help you "see" what the poem means.

DEFINITION

Imagery is language that appeals to the five senses—touch, taste, smell, hearing, and sight.

Poetry

Lyric Poem

What emotions do the lines from this excerpt express?

EXAMPLE

from "A Red, Red Rose" by Robert Burns

> O my luve is like a red, red rose,
>   That's newly sprung in June.
> O, my luve is like the melodie,
>   That's sweetly play'd in tune.
>
> As fair art thou, my bonie lass,
>   So deep in luve am I,
> And I will luve thee still, my dear,
>   Till a' the seas gang dry.

Expression of personal feelings

DESCRIPTION

You probably get the idea. Burns is expressing his love. He addresses the "bonie lass" whom he loves and describes to her how strong his feelings are. The emotion is very clear, even though it is written in a Scottish dialect.

A **lyric poem** is a lot like a song. A lyric poem is usually short and expresses the emotions of the poet. It tells how the poet sees the world. Most lyric poems use the personal pronouns *I, me, my, we, our,* or *us.*

DEFINITION

A lyric poem is a short poem that directly expresses the poet's thoughts and emotions in a musical way.

Metaphor

At its simplest, a metaphor is a comparison of two unlike things. What is being compared in the poem below?

EXAMPLE

"Fog" by Carl Sandburg

The fog comes
on little cat feet.

It sits looking
over harbor and city
on silent haunches
and then moves on.

Comparison of fog to a cat

DESCRIPTION

Metaphor is a type of figurative language. It's a comparison in which one thing is described as being something else. In "Fog," Sandburg describes the fog as if it were a cat. It's an unusual comparison of two things that don't seem in any way alike. But that's what makes it a good metaphor. It's fresh and new.

A metaphor doesn't just say one thing is something else. A good metaphor inspires you to see the original subject in a new way. Sometimes metaphors are more difficult to spot than similes because they do not use the connective words *like* or *as*. A metaphor gives you a very clear and memorable picture in your head.

DEFINITION

A metaphor is a direct comparison between two unlike things. It does not use the words *like* or *as*.

Poetry

Mood

Writing—and especially poetry—works on your emotions. It creates feelings inside you as you read. What feeling do you get from this part of Edgar Allan Poe's poem?

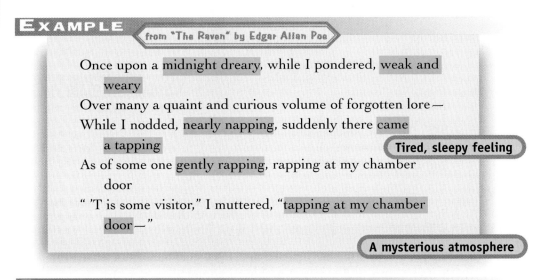

from "The Raven" by Edgar Allan Poe

Once upon a midnight dreary, while I pondered, weak and
   weary
Over many a quaint and curious volume of forgotten lore—
While I nodded, nearly napping, suddenly there came
   a tapping

Tired, sleepy feeling

As of some one gently rapping, rapping at my chamber
   door
" 'T is some visitor," I muttered, "tapping at my chamber
   door—"

A mysterious atmosphere

DESCRIPTION

Poets try to create an overall feeling by introducing a **mood** to their poems. It may be dark and mysterious for a scary poem or cheerful and peaceful for a poem about a spring day. Whatever the mood, it colors the whole poem and creates a feeling in the reader.

Certain words create or set the mood, such as *dreary*, *weak*, and *weary*. Words carry emotional feeling with them. How do you feel when you think about the scene Poe describes—someone almost asleep being startled at midnight by rapping at the bedroom door? The scary, mysterious feeling you get reading these words is part of the mood.

DEFINITION

Mood is the feeling created in the reader by a poem or story. Words, phrases, repetition, rhyme, and exaggeration all work together to create mood.

Narrative Poem

As you read this poem, look for the story it tells.

EXAMPLE

from "Lucinda Matlock" by Edgar Lee Masters

I went to the dances at Chandlerville,
And played snap-out at Winchester.
One time we changed partners,
Driving home in the moonlight of middle June,
And then I found Davis.
We were married and lived together for seventy years,
Enjoying, working, raising the twelve children,
Eight of whom we lost
Ere I had reached the age of sixty.
I spun, I wove, I kept the house, I nursed the sick,
I made the garden, and for holiday
Rambled over the fields where sang the larks,
And by Spoon River gathering many a shell,
And many a flower and medicinal weed—
Shouting to the wooded hills, singing to the green valleys.
At ninety-six I had lived enough, that is all. . . .

Story of a woman's life, from childhood to death

DESCRIPTION

Poems that tell stories are called **narrative poems**. Usually narrative poems have all the parts of a short story, such as character, setting, conflict, and plot. This narrative poem tells the story of Lucinda (the character), who lived by Spoon River (the setting). She raised twelve children, eight of whom died, and she died at age 96 (conflict and plot).

DEFINITION

A narrative poem is a poem that tells a story. Narrative poems usually have all of the elements you would find in a short story: character, setting, conflict, and plot.

Poetry

Onomatopoeia

Look at the different-sounding words in the first stanza of this poem.

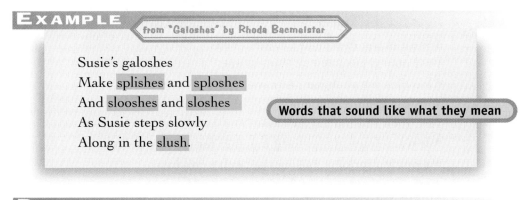

EXAMPLE

from "Galoshes" by Rhoda Bacmeister

Susie's galoshes
Make splishes and sploshes
And slooshes and sloshes
As Susie steps slowly
Along in the slush.

Words that sound like what they mean

DESCRIPTION

Galoshes make *splishes* and *sploshes* and *slooshes* and *sloshes,* which are exactly the sounds made when someone splashes through slush with boots. These words sound like the things they name, and that's what **onomatopoeia** is. Writers use onomatopoeia to add a little fun and power to the words they use. Words like *hiss, bang*, and *buzz* are strong and powerful.

Here are some other examples of onomatopoeia:

zing	*whack*	*plop*
ping	*pow*	*zip*
poof	*wham*	*screech*
clank	*rattle*	*eek*
thud	*smack*	*click*

DEFINITION

Onomatopoeia is the use of words that sound like the noises they describe.

Personification

As you read the following lines, think about how the poet describes grass and rain.

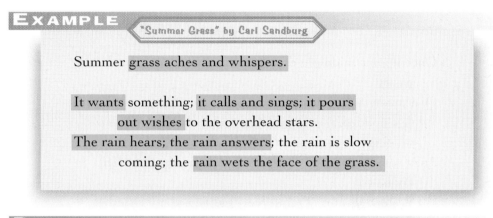

EXAMPLE

"Summer Grass" by Carl Sandburg

Summer grass aches and whispers.

It wants something; it calls and sings; it pours
out wishes to the overhead stars.
The rain hears; the rain answers; the rain is slow
coming; the rain wets the face of the grass.

DESCRIPTION

In the lines above, Sandburg speaks of the grass and rain as if they were human. That's part of what makes the poem interesting. Giving nonhuman objects human qualities adds life to writing, so you can see everyday things in a new way. That is a kind of figurative language called **personification**. Poets use personification to emphasize something in a new way or to make it stand out.

You can find personification in almost any kind of writing. Writers use it to add interest to their writing. Personification gives you a new way of looking at or understanding something.

DEFINITION

Personification is a type of figurative language in which poets give an animal, object, or idea human qualities, such as the ability to hear, feel, talk, and make decisions.

Poetry

Repetition

Poets sometimes repeat things, but they do so for a reason. Note the repetition in these lines.

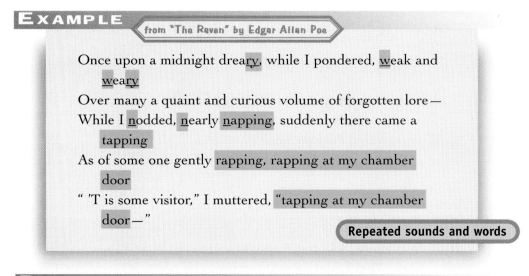

EXAMPLE

from "The Raven" by Edgar Allan Poe

Once upon a midnight dreary, while I pondered, weak and
   weary
Over many a quaint and curious volume of forgotten lore—
While I nodded, nearly napping, suddenly there came a
   tapping
As of some one gently rapping, rapping at my chamber
   door
" 'T is some visitor," I muttered, "tapping at my chamber
   door—"

Repeated sounds and words

DESCRIPTION

Poets repeat sounds and words for effect. **Repetition** helps add a sense of rhythm in a poem, emphasizes important ideas, and sets a mood.

- Repetition holds a poem together with a pattern readers come to expect.
- Repetition creates suspense or adds humor or music.
- Repetition emphasizes meaning.

DEFINITION

Repetition means "to repeat" something. It is the use of any element of language—a sound, word, phrase, or sentence—more than once.

Rhyme

Read this poem about owls and listen for sounds that are the same.

EXAMPLE

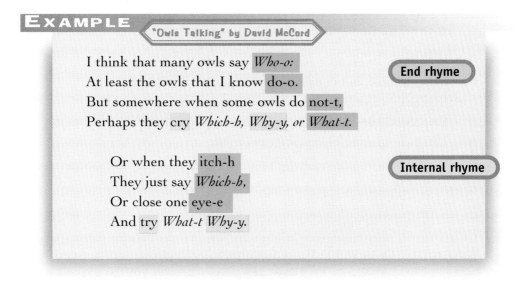

"Owls Talking" by David McCord

I think that many owls say *Who-o:*
At least the owls that I know do-o.
But somewhere when some owls do not-t,
Perhaps they cry *Which-h, Why-y, or What-t.*

Or when they itch-h
They just say *Which-h,*
Or close one eye-e
And try *What-t Why-y.*

End rhyme

Internal rhyme

DESCRIPTION

In the lines above, the words *Who-o* and *do-o* **rhyme**. They are an example of what is called *end rhyme*, because the rhyme is at the end of a line. Do you see (or hear) any other words that rhyme? The word *cry* rhymes with *Why-y*. This is a rhyme, too. It is called *internal rhyme*. Rhyme puts emphasis on certain important words. It helps connect the words with the ideas they express.

You can think of rhyme as a poet's way of emphasizing a particular word or sound. Rhymes add a musical quality to poetry. Often one of the most pleasing aspects of poems is how they sound.

DEFINITION

Rhyme is the repetition of similar sounds. *End rhyme* is the repetition of similar sounds that come at the ends of lines of poetry. *Internal rhyme* occurs within a line when two words have similar sounds.

Poetry

Rhyme Scheme

Read these lines and listen for the end rhymes.

EXAMPLE

from "Adventures of Isabel" by Ogdan Nash

Isabel met an enormous bear,	*a*
Isabel, Isabel, didn't care;	*a*
The bear was hungry, the bear was ravenous,	*b*
The bear's big mouth was cruel and cavernous.	*b*
The bear said, Isabel, glad to meet you,	*c*
How do, Isabel, now I'll eat you!	*c*

DESCRIPTION

Poets use rhyming words to help express feelings and ideas. A pattern of repeated rhymes, or **rhyme scheme**, causes you to expect a sound and look forward to hearing it.

"Adventures of Isabel" has a set pattern to the words that rhyme at the end of each line. Can you hear that the word *bear* sounds like *care?* They rhyme because they have the same ending sound. Can you hear that the word *ravenous* sounds like *cavernous?* They rhyme because they have the same ending sound, but they have a different sound from lines one and two. *You* and *you* is an exact rhyme because the words are exactly the same. So, you can see that the rhyme scheme of this poem is *aa bb cc*.

Poets use rhyme schemes because they add both beauty and a sense of order to a poem. They also provide an added challenge. Poets can't choose any old word. They must choose one that fits the rhyme scheme. Along with this extra layer of difficulty comes the musical quality created by a pattern of rhyming words.

DEFINITION

Rhyme scheme is a repeated regular pattern of rhymes usually found at the ends of lines in a poem.

Rhythm

Read the lines below aloud. As you do, listen for their musical quality. Can you hear how some words are emphasized more than others?

EXAMPLE

"First Fig" by Edna St. Vincent Millay

My candle burns at both ends;
   It will not last the night;
But ah, my foes, and oh, my friends—
   It gives a lovely light!

Stressed syllables

DESCRIPTION

Rhythm is present in both written and spoken language. It gives poetry a musical sound and makes a poem come alive.

What makes rhythm? In a line of poetry, certain syllables get more stress, or emphasis, than other unstressed syllables. In poetry, you can find a rhythm by counting or clapping out the beats in a line. Read the lines above once more. Can you hear the musical beats?

My cán-dle búrns at bóth ends;

It wíll not lást the níght;

But áh, my fóes, and óh, my fríends—

It gíves a lóvely líght!

DEFINITION

Rhythm is the musical quality created by a pattern of beats or a series of stressed and unstressed syllables.

Poetry

Simile

Read these two stanzas from a poem by Eve Merriam and look for things she compares using the words *like* or *as*.

EXAMPLE

from "Simile: Willow and Ginkgo" by Eve Merriam

The willow is like an etching,
Fine-lined against the sky.
The ginkgo is like a crude sketch,
Hardly worthy to be signed.

Comparison of trees to works of art

The willow's music is like a soprano
Delicate and thin.
The ginkgo's tune is like a chorus
With everyone joining in.

Comparison of trees to musical sounds

DESCRIPTION

The poem continues on by comparing the two kinds of trees—willow and ginkgo—to different things and to each other. A **simile** is a comparison using *like* or *as*. Similes are a kind of figure of speech that help you see and understand things in a fresh way. By comparing two unlike things, the poet can create a strong, memorable image. Poets use similes to uncover similarities between things that may otherwise go unnoticed.

DEFINITION

A **simile** is a comparison between two unlike things using the words *like* or *as*.

Stanza

Note how this poem appears on the page and how the lines are organized.

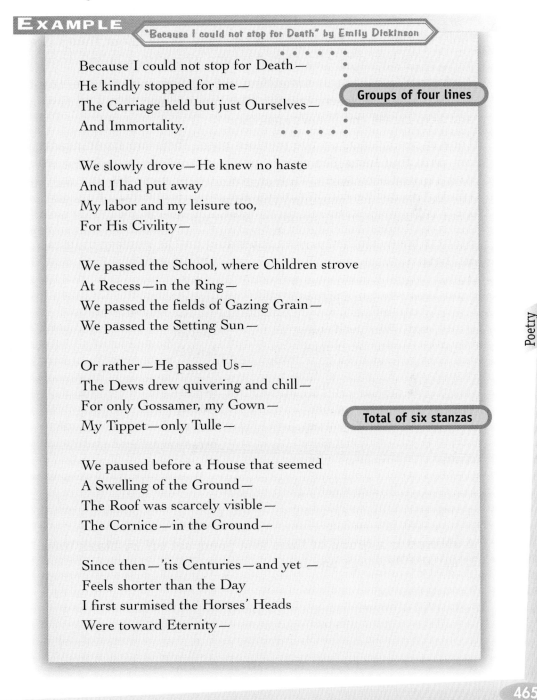

EXAMPLE "Because I could not stop for Death" by Emily Dickinson

Because I could not stop for Death—
He kindly stopped for me—
The Carriage held but just Ourselves—
And Immortality.

Groups of four lines

We slowly drove—He knew no haste
And I had put away
My labor and my leisure too,
For His Civility—

We passed the School, where Children strove
At Recess—in the Ring—
We passed the fields of Gazing Grain—
We passed the Setting Sun—

Or rather—He passed Us—
The Dews drew quivering and chill—
For only Gossamer, my Gown—
My Tippet—only Tulle—

Total of six stanzas

We paused before a House that seemed
A Swelling of the Ground—
The Roof was scarcely visible—
The Cornice—in the Ground—

Since then—'tis Centuries—and yet —
Feels shorter than the Day
I first surmised the Horses' Heads
Were toward Eternity—

Poetry

Stanza, continued

DESCRIPTION

Stanza is an Italian word that means "stopping place" or "place to rest." Like artists, poets concern themselves with the way a poem looks on the page, its shape or form. Poets think about things like how long a line of poetry should be and which lines belong together.

A **stanza** in a poem is something like a paragraph in prose. Stanzas are important in poetry because they give a poem shape on the page and help create the poem's meaning.

Look at the stanzas on the previous page. There are six stanzas, each one with four lines. The speaker in Dickinson's poem tells the story of a journey with Death. Each stanza focuses on a different part of the trip (meeting, beginning the drive, passing different scenes, what she was wearing, stopping, reflecting on what happened).

Stanzas have different names depending on the number of lines in them.

NUMBER OF LINES	NAME
2 lines	couplet
3 lines	tercet
4 lines	quatrain
5 lines	quintet
6 lines	sestet
7 lines	septet
8 lines	octet

DEFINITION

A **stanza** is a group of lines in a poem set off by blank lines. It usually develops one idea.

Symbol

Read the poem "This Is My Rock" and ask yourself what the rock means in the poem.

"This Is My Rock" by David McCord

This is my rock,
And here I run
To steal the secret of the sun;

> **Why the rock is important**

This is my rock,
And here come I
Before the night has swept the sky;

This is my rock,
This is the place
I meet the evening face to face.

Poetry

DESCRIPTION

Symbols are common in everyday life. A blue ribbon or gold medal is a symbol for first place. The Statue of Liberty is a symbol of freedom. A crown is a symbol of a king's power.

A symbol is always itself, but it also suggests another meaning. In the poem above, the rock suggests something solid, safe, and strong. By contrast, the evening suggests darkness, even our fears. In the poem, "evening" and "rock" are used as symbols to stand for something more than what they actually are.

DEFINITION

A **symbol** is something that stands for something else.

Tone and Voice

Read this poem and think about how the speaker feels about the subject he describes.

EXAMPLE   "There's This That I Like About Hockey, My Lad" by John Kieran

There's this that I like about hockey, my lad;
   It's a clattering, battering sport.
As a popular pastime it isn't half bad
   For chaps of the sturdier sort.   **Speaker's attitude toward hockey**
You step on the gas and you let in the clutch;
You start on a skate and come back on a crutch;
Your chance of surviving is really not much;
   It's something like storming a fort.

There's this that I like about hockey, my boy;
   There's nothing about it that's tame.
The whistle is blown and the players deploy;
   They start in to maul and to maim.
There's a dash at the goal and a crash on the ice;
The left wing goes down when you've swatted him twice;
And your teeth by a stick are removed in a trice;
   It's really a rollicking game.   **Person speaker is addressing**

There's this that I like about hockey, old chap;
   I think you'll agree that I'm right;
Although you may get an occasional rap,
   There's always good fun in the fight.
So toss in the puck, for the players are set;
Sing ho! for the dash on the enemy net;
And ho! for the smash as the challenge is met;
   And hey! for a glorious night!

Tone and Voice, continued

The attitude that the writer takes toward the reader or the subject gives a poem its **tone**. Note the highlighted lines. They suggest the poet's tone, or attitude, toward hockey. He points out its rough, brutal side ("storming a fort," "to maul and to maim," "enemy net") yet celebrates its challenge ("rollicking game").

Voice is important in poetry because it lets the reader know who the speaker is in a poem. It may or may not be the poet. A poet usually tries to make sure that the voice in a poem is clear and consistent. Who is the voice in this poem? Look for clues the writer gives.

- Note that the speaker in the title addresses "my lad" and "my boy" and, later in the poem, "old chap."

- The speaker knows a lot about hockey (he uses jargon such as the "left wing") and has watched—or played—many games.

- The speaker has a good vocabulary ("deploy," "maim," "rollicking").

From these few clues, you might infer the speaker in the poem is an adult. He speaks as a fan who knows how rough hockey is yet loves the fun and excitement of the game.

Poetry

DEFINITION

Tone is the attitude the writer takes toward the audience, the subject, or a character. The **voice**, or speaker, is the character or perspective that is taken on by a writer or poet. Often the voice is not identified by name.

Reading
Drama

Reading a Play

Ways of Reading Drama

Focus on Theme
Focus on Language

Elements of Drama

Drama

Reading a Play

Reading a play is very different from reading a short story or novel. In a play, there are no long descriptions of setting or characters. Instead, the entire action of the play is told through dialogue and stage directions. The dialogue reveals what the characters are like and what the plot is. The stage directions help you, as a reader, see the setting in your mind, as well as what the characters look like and how they act.

In this part of the handbook, you'll use the reading process with the Pulitzer Prize–winning play *The Diary of Anne Frank*, written by Frances Goodrich and Albert Hackett.

Goals

Here you'll learn how to:

✔ understand and appreciate the genre of **drama**

✔ use the reading strategy of **outlining**

✔ understand how plays are **organized into scenes and acts**

Before Reading

When you read a play, you use the same reading process as you do for a novel or a short story. In the prereading stage, you establish a purpose for reading, preview parts of the play, and create a plan for reading.

A Set a Purpose

Usually you see a play performed. But in school, you'll probably read and study plays to learn about them as a literary genre. When you read a play for an assignment, you normally have three questions to answer:

Setting a Purpose

■ **What are the main characters like, and what's the relationship among them?**

■ **What is the central conflict, and how is it resolved?**

■ **What is the theme of the play?**

These three broad questions form your purpose in reading.

B Preview

To prepare yourself to read a play, first preview it. You'll gather a lot of clues about the play's subject as you look for these items:

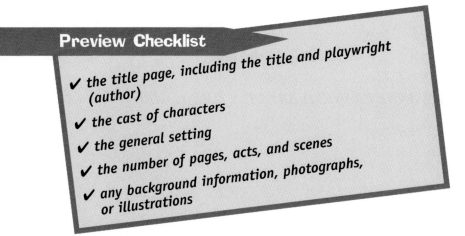

Preview Checklist

✔ the title page, including the title and playwright (author)

✔ the cast of characters

✔ the general setting

✔ the number of pages, acts, and scenes

✔ any background information, photographs, or illustrations

Drama

The Diary of Anne Frank

PREVIEW
Title

Dramatized by
Frances Goodrich
and
Albert Hackett

PREVIEW
Playwrights

Based upon the book

ANNE FRANK: DIARY OF A YOUNG GIRL

PREVIEW
Background
information
about the
source

CHARACTERS

Mr. Frank

Miep

Mrs. Van Daan

Mr. Van Daan

Peter Van Daan

Mrs. Frank

Margot Frank

Anne Frank

Mr. Kraler

Mr. Dussel

The Time:
During the years of World War II and immediately thereafter.

The Place:
Amsterdam

PREVIEW
Cast of characters

PREVIEW
General setting

Drama

Plan

Previewing gives you some general background of the play. You know where and when the action takes place, and you can tell from the cast of characters that two families are involved—the Van Daans and the Franks. The play's title suggests that a girl's diary will be involved somehow. What do you know about World War II? Have you heard of Anne Frank before? (She was a real person.) Draw on what you already know to help you get ready to read. The best strategies for reading a play tend to be ones that allow you to take notes and visualize the stage directions and action.

Reading Strategy: Summarizing

One of the main reading challenges in plays is keeping track of what happens. Plays often have more than one setting, and the action shifts from scene to scene. Because plays are told through dialogue, it may be tough to remember exactly what happened or who said what. **Summarizing** as you read will help you keep track of the main action and ideas.

One good reading tool to help you summarize a play is a Magnet Summary. To create a Magnet Summary, start by selecting a "magnet word." It can be a key word that's repeated in what you read or an idea or feeling. Then connect details to that word. You can use a Magnet Summary to sum up a moment, a scene, or an entire play.

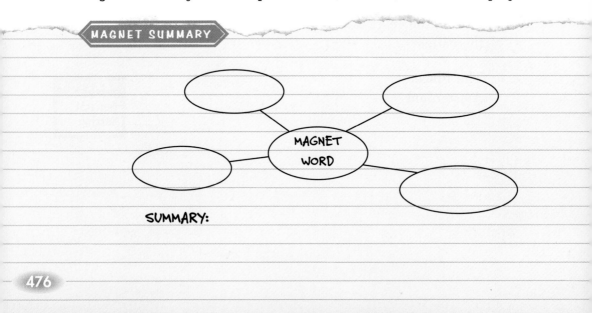

MAGNET SUMMARY

MAGNET WORD

SUMMARY:

During Reading

Now you are ready to start using your plan for reading a play. As you read, think about the one magnet word that best describes the characters, setting, and action.

D Read with a Purpose

Think back to your reading purpose. Remember that after you have finished reading, you want to be able to answer three questions:

▮ What are the main characters like, and what's the relationship among them?

▮ What is the central conflict, and how is it resolved?

▮ What is the theme of the play?

Be an active reader. Have your reading notebook or some index cards handy. Use them to jot down ideas that come to you, quotes you want to remember, or pictures you sketch to help you remember parts of the play. Use as much—or as little—detail as you want: one card or page in your notebook for each scene or act or to pull together the whole play.

What follows is part of the first scene of *The Diary of Anne Frank*. As you read, notice key details about the characters, setting, and action.

Drama

Act One
Scene I

The scene remains the same throughout the play. It is the top floor of a warehouse and office building in Amsterdam, Holland. The sharply peaked roof of the building is outlined against a sea of other rooftops, stretching away into the distance. . . .

The three rooms of the top floor and a small attic space above are exposed to our view. The largest of the rooms is in the center, with two small rooms, slightly raised, on either side. . . .

The room on the left is hardly more than a closet. There is a skylight in the sloping ceiling. Directly under this room is a small steep stairwell, with steps leading down to a door. This is the only entrance from the building below. When the door is opened we see that it has been concealed on the outer side by a bookcase attached to it.

(The curtain rises on an empty stage. It is late afternoon November, 1945.

The rooms are dusty, the curtains in rags. Chairs and tables are overturned.

The door at the foot of the small stairwell swings open. Mr. Frank comes up the steps into view. He is a gentle, cultured European in his middle years. There is still a trace of a German accent in his speech.

He stands looking slowly around, making a supreme effort at self-control. He is weak, ill. His clothes are threadbare.

After a second he drops his rucksack on the couch and moves slowly about. He opens the door to one of the smaller rooms, and then abruptly closes it again, turning away. . . .

from *The Diary of Anne Frank,* continued

As he starts back for his rucksack, his eye is caught by something lying on the floor. It is a woman's white glove. He holds it in his hand and suddenly all of his self-control is gone. He breaks down, crying.

We hear footsteps on the stairs. Miep Gies *comes up, looking for* Mr. Frank. Miep *is a Dutch girl of about twenty-two. She wears a coat and hat, ready to go home. She is pregnant. Her attitude toward* Mr. Frank *is protective, compassionate.)* . . .

NOTE

Miep = young, full of life

Mr. Frank. I've come to say good-bye . . . I'm leaving here, Miep.

Miep. What do you mean? Where are you going? . . . Mr. Frank, you can't leave here! This is your home! Amsterdam is your home. . . . Now that the war is over, there are things that . . .

NOTE

Time = after the war

Mr. Frank. I can't stay in Amsterdam, Miep. It has too many memories for me. Everywhere there's something . . . I'm not the person you used to know, Miep. I'm a bitter old man. . . .

NOTE

Mr Frank = sad and bitter

Miep *(Hurrying up to a cupboard).* Mr. Frank, did you see? There are some of your papers here. *(She brings a bundle of papers to him.)* We found them in a heap of rubbish on the floor after . . . after you left.

Mr. Frank. Burn them.

(He opens his rucksack to put the glove in it.)

Miep. But, Mr. Frank, there are letters, notes . . .

Mr. Frank. Burn them. All of them.

Miep. Burn this?

NOTE

Stage directions introduce Anne's diary.

(She hands him a paperbound notebook.)

Drama

NOTE
The time jumps to Anne's writing three years before.

Mr. Frank (*Quietly*). Anne's diary. (*He opens the diary and begins to read.*) "Monday, the sixth of July, nineteen forty-two." (*To* Miep) Nineteen forty-two. Is it possible, Miep? . . . Only three years ago. (*As he continues his reading, he sits down on the couch.*) "Dear Diary, since you and I are going to be great friends, I will start by telling you about myself. My name is Anne Frank. I am thirteen years old. I was born in Germany the twelfth of June, nineteen twenty-nine. As my family is Jewish, we emigrated to Holland when Hitler came to power."

NOTE
Anne = 13 years old, Jewish

(*As* Mr. Frank *reads on, another voice joins his, as if coming from the air. It is* Anne's *voice.*)

Mr. Frank *and* **Anne.** "My father started a business, importing spice and herbs. Things went well for us until nineteen forty. Then the war came, and the Dutch capitulation, followed by the arrival of the Germans. Then things got very bad for the Jews."

(Mr. Frank's *voice dies out.* Anne's *voice continues alone. The lights dim slowly to darkness. The curtain falls on the scene.*)

Anne's Voice. You could not do this and you could not do that. They forced Father out of his business. We had to wear yellow stars. I had to turn in my bike. I couldn't go to a Dutch school any more. I couldn't go to the movies, or ride in an automobile, or even on a streetcar, and a million other things. But somehow we children still managed to have fun. Yesterday Father told me we were going into hiding. Where, he wouldn't say. At five o'clock this morning Mother woke me and told me to hurry and get dressed. I was to put on as many clothes as I could. It would look too suspicious if we walked along carrying suitcases. It wasn't until we were on our way that I learned where we were going. Our hiding place was to be upstairs in the building where Father used to have his business. . . .

NOTE
Frank family went into hiding.

NOTE
Hiding place = same building where Miep and Mr. Frank are

Remember Important Details

How can you keep track of the plot, the characters, and your ideas about theme all at the same time? Try one of these tools to help you remember important details.

1. Magnet Summary
2. Summary Notes
3. Character Map

1. Magnet Summary

A Magnet Summary organizes information around key concepts called "magnet words." Think of a magnet word as a main idea that attracts details the way a magnet attracts iron or steel objects. These words can help you find the "big ideas" and main themes of the play.

For example, one magnet word you might use for the first scene of *The Diary of Anne Frank* is "memories."

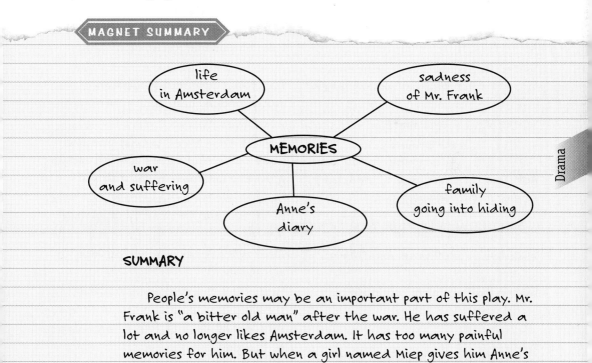

MAGNET SUMMARY

- life in Amsterdam
- sadness of Mr. Frank
- MEMORIES
- war and suffering
- Anne's diary
- family going into hiding

Drama

SUMMARY

People's memories may be an important part of this play. Mr. Frank is "a bitter old man" after the war. He has suffered a lot and no longer likes Amsterdam. It has too many painful memories for him. But when a girl named Miep gives him Anne's diary, he seems interested in it. Anne wrote about the war and when the family went into hiding. Reading it must really stir up her father's memories.

2. Summary Notes

You can also create a scene-by-scene summary, which will help you keep track of the plot and the conflict. Jotting a few Summary Notes on each scene makes it easy to remember what happened.

SUMMARY NOTES

PART OF PLAY	SETTING	KEY EVENTS
Act One Scene I	Place is Franks' hideout in the play. Time is November 1945, after the end of World War II.	Mr. Frank tells Miep he is leaving Amsterdam, and she gives him Anne's diary.
Scene II	back in time to early morning, July 1942	Mr. Kraler helps the Franks and Van Daans get settled in their hideout. Mr. Frank gives Anne a diary.
Scene III	after 6:00 P.M., two months later	The Van Daans argue with Anne. Mr. Kraler brings Mr. Dussel to live in the hideout because the Nazis are rounding up more and more Jews.
Scene IV	middle of the night, several months later	Anne has a nightmare about the Nazis and rejects her mother's offer to stay with her.
Scene V	first night of Hanukkah, December 1942.	Anne gives everyone gifts for Hanukkah. A thief breaks into the warehouse and hears a noise upstairs.
Act Two Scene I	January 1, 1944, late afternoon	A worker who may be the thief blackmails Mr. Kraler. Anne and Peter have become friends. Food rations are cut.
Scene II	evening, April 1944	Anne visits Peter in his room, and he kisses her.
Scene III	night, June 1944	Mrs. Frank catches Mr. Van Daan stealing food and wants him to leave. Miep brings news of the Allied invasion of Europe.
Scene IV	August afternoon, a few weeks later	The Nazis come to take everyone away.
Scene V	again November 1945, in the afternoon	Mr. Frank finishes reading Anne's diary. Mr. Frank, Miep, and Mr. Kraler talk about what happened after the Nazis discovered the hideout.

3. Character Map

A Character Map is another helpful tool, especially as a way to focus on one or two main characters. Create a Character Map for each character you want to understand better. Use it to summarize a character's personality and your feelings about him or her. Here's one for Anne.

CHARACTER MAP

WHAT THE CHARACTER SAYS
- feels that no one understands her
- loves her father but can't stand her mother
- wants to have fun
- fears the Germans
- believes that people are really good at heart

HOW SHE ACTS
- playful, talks a lot
- speaks her mind
- does what she wants despite what others say
- makes gifts for everyone for Hanukkah

ANNE

HOW OTHERS FEEL ABOUT HER
- Van Daans and Dussel scold her for being too loud.
- Mrs. Frank tells her to be quieter and feels hurt by the way Anne acts.
- Peter hates her at first, but then comes to like her.
- Margot and Mr. Frank love her.

MY REACTION TO HER
- likable, good person who deals well with a horrible situation
- always looks on the good side of things
- good at showing or telling how she feels

Drama

How Plays Are Organized

Like most plays, *The Diary of Anne Frank* is divided into **acts** and **scenes**. This play has two acts, each with five scenes. In most plays, a new scene reflects a change in setting—either the place or the time or both. Here the entire story is told as a flashback. It begins at the end of the story in November 1945, after the war, and leaps immediately to July 6, 1942.

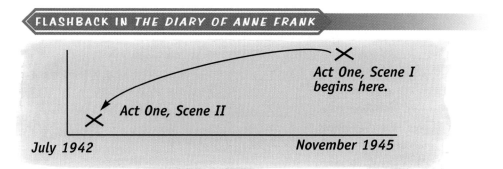

FLASHBACK IN *THE DIARY OF ANNE FRANK*

Act One, Scene I begins here.

Act One, Scene II

July 1942   November 1945

The plots of plays—like novel and story plots—usually have five parts. Even a simple Plot Diagram like the one below will help you see the organization of the play.

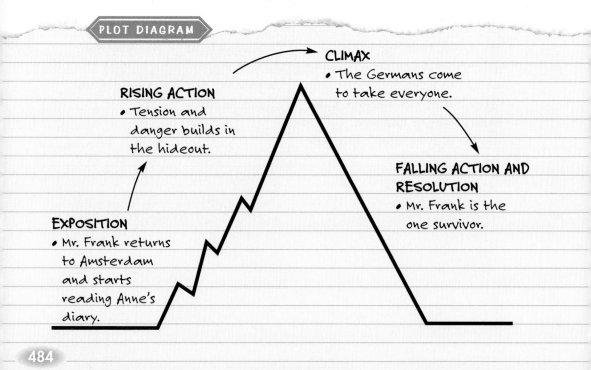

PLOT DIAGRAM

CLIMAX
• The Germans come to take everyone.

RISING ACTION
• Tension and danger builds in the hideout.

FALLING ACTION AND RESOLUTION
• Mr. Frank is the one survivor.

EXPOSITION
• Mr. Frank returns to Amsterdam and starts reading Anne's diary.

E Connect

Some plays, such as *The Diary of Anne Frank*, create strong emotions in readers. As a reader, you need to respect your own feelings about what you read. Record your thoughts. Take the time to jot down notes about how you feel toward certain characters and about the play as a whole.

Remember, you do not have to "love" everything you read. Be honest. All you need to be able to do is to back up your opinion. Here are one reader's reactions to the end of act 2, scene 4. The Nazis have just discovered the hiding place, and Anne is taking one last look around.

---

from *The Diary of Anne Frank*

(The lights dim out. The curtain falls on the scene. We hear a mighty crash as the door is shattered. After a second Anne's voice is heard.)

Anne's Voice. And so it seems our stay here is over. They are waiting for us now. They've allowed us five minutes to get our things. We can each take a bag and whatever it will hold of clothing. Nothing else. So, dear Diary, that means I must leave you behind. Good-bye for a while. P.S. Please, please, Miep, or Mr. Kraler, or anyone else. If you should find this diary, will you please keep it safe for me, because some day I hope . . .

Just hearing her voice—not seeing her—makes this part powerful.

I wonder what Anne thought would happen next.

Interesting last words —I admire her optimism.

Drama

485

After Reading

After you finish reading a play, return to your original purpose in reading and think about what you have learned.

F Pause and Reflect

Take stock of how well you understood the play. Ask yourself questions like these:

Looking Back

- **Can I describe the main characters?**
- **Can I explain the central conflict in the play and summarize the plot?**
- **What is the main message, or theme, of the play?**
- **Do parts of the play confuse or puzzle me?**

Think about each of these questions. If you're unsure about something—what the theme is or why a character acts a certain way—you may need to reread some parts.

G Reread

Sometimes you will want to focus on one specific part of the play. Maybe it's a scene and conversation that you had trouble following. Other times you'll have more general questions: "Do any of the characters change? Does the play teach a lesson about life?"

Rereading Strategy: Visualizing and Thinking Aloud

Visualizing and thinking aloud is a great rereading strategy to use with plays. After all, a play is meant to be seen and heard by an audience, not read alone. Talk with others about what it would be like to see the play performed. What kind of music would be used? How do you imagine the characters would look and sound? Turn back to especially powerful or puzzling moments and share your ideas and questions.

If you like to draw, you might want to create a Storyboard. It can be as detailed as you wish—from one event to a scene-by-scene summary of the whole play. Making some quick notes and sketches can be a simple, fun way to get a clear record of what happens. Below is a Storyboard one reader made for the events of the first act.

STORYBOARD

Act One

Scene I: November 1945 Mr. Frank is back at the hideaway after the war, and Miep gives him Anne's diary.

Scene II: July 1942 The action shifts back in time. The Franks and Van Daans settle into their cramped hiding space.

Scene III: Two Months Later The Franks and Van Daans are getting on one another's nerves, and Mr. Kraler brings Mr. Dussel to hide out with them, too.

Scene IV: Several Months Later Anne has a nightmare and rejects Mrs. Frank's offer of comfort. Anne doesn't get along with Mr. Dussel either.

Scene V: Hanukkah A thief breaks into the warehouse and hears a noise upstairs when Peter knocks over a lamp. The thief may realize Jews are hiding there.

Drama

H Remember

Sometimes you may read a play just for fun. But often, you're reading a play in class, and you'll be asked to do a report or paper on it. If so, you may be looking for a way to help you remember what you read or an interesting topic to explore further. Here are a few possibilities.

1. Do an Oral Reading

If possible, read some of the play aloud or with a group. Ask your partner to take the part of one of the characters.

2. Watch a Movie Version

You can often find film versions of plays. After watching the film version, think about how it compares with the play script.

3. Focus on a Key Passage

Spend time memorizing a line or two that stood out. For example, you might memorize this line from *The Diary of Anne Frank*:

"In spite of everything, I still believe that people are really good at heart."

React to the passage. Explain why it's important to the play as a whole.

Summing Up

When you read a play, remember to use the reading process and the strategy of **summarizing**. Try one of these useful reading tools:

■ Magnet Summary
■ Summary Notes
■ Character Map
■ Plot Diagram
■ Storyboard

Look for the **organization of plays** when you read. Try the rereading strategy of **visualizing and thinking aloud** to focus on key events or dialogue.

Focus on Theme

The **theme** of a play is a message or idea that the playwright wants you to remember. Some plays have one central theme; others have several minor themes. As you think about a play, you'll sometimes want to focus on its theme.

Goals

Here you'll learn how to:

✔ **look for clues about a play's theme**

✔ **use a three-step plan for understanding the theme in a play**

✔ **understand how plot and characters offer clues about theme**

Before Reading

You usually watch—or read—a play for some other purpose than to discover its theme. But, when you come to the end of a play, you naturally want to understand its message. An important reading purpose, then, is to uncover the theme of a play.

Only rarely will the playwright have a character directly state the theme. Most of the time you'll need to be on the alert for bits of dialogue that suggest the broad ideas of the play.

How do you read a play to uncover its theme? Here is a three-step plan for understanding theme:

PLAN FOR UNDERSTANDING THEME

Step 1 *Find the "big ideas" or general topics.*

Step 2 *Find out what the characters do and say that relates to the general topics.*

Step 3 *Come up with a statement of the author's point or message about the topic.*

Drama

Step 1: Find the "big ideas" or general topics.

Start by figuring out what general topics or "big ideas" the play is about. The themes relate to these subjects. Before you even start reading the play closely, you can find some clues about possible topics. When your focus is theme, look for these parts:

- the title page, including the title and playwright

- the beginning of the play and first scene

- the general setting

- any background information, summaries, or illustrations

You may have noticed that some common topics appear over and over in literature. If you have trouble coming up with general topics, check the list below:

COMMON TOPICS FOR THEMES

childhood	*growing up*	*loyalty*	*self-reliance*
courage	*hate*	*nature*	*success*
death	*hope*	*patience*	*trust*
faith	*identity*	*patriotism*	*truth*
family	*independence*	*prejudice*	*unhappiness*
freedom	*justice*	*race relations*	*violence*
friendship	*love*	*self-improvement*	*war*

Go back to pages 474–475 and 478–480, and look at the cover, cast of characters, and beginning of *The Diary of Anne Frank*. What clues can you find about the play's general topics? Right away you can predict that a young girl's diary will be important. For example, in the opening of *The Diary of Anne Frank,* Mr. Frank finds Anne's diary and begins reading. This opening scene suggests a number of other general topics—memories, freedom, prejudice, war, and violence.

During Reading

As you read, keep asking yourself what the author wants you to think about. Looking for these "big ideas" will keep you focused on theme.

Step 2: Find out what the characters do and say that relates to the general topics.

As a reader, watch for the clues about the theme. These clues can appear in many places:

 repeated words or ideas

■ changes in characters

■ plot events or dialogue

■ symbols

Here are two ways of keeping track of your ideas about theme.

Double-entry Journal

A Double-entry Journal works well to pick out key passages and organize your thoughts about them. When your focus is theme, pay special attention to speeches that offer a general lesson or view about life. Read this short passage from act 1, scene 2:

Drama

> **from The Diary of Anne Frank**
>
> **Mr. Frank.** It doesn't matter. I don't want you ever to go beyond that door.
>
> **Anne** *(Sobered)*. Never . . . ? Not even at nighttime, when everyone is gone? Or on Sundays? Can't I go down to listen to the radio?
>
> **Mr. Frank.** Never. I am sorry, Anneke. It isn't safe. No, you must never go beyond that door.
>
> *(For the first time Anne realizes what "going into hiding" means.)*
>
> **Anne.** I see.
>
> **Mr. Frank.** It'll be hard, I know. But always remember this, Anneke. There are no walls, there are no bolts, no locks that anyone can put on your mind. Miep will bring us books. We will read history, poetry, mythology. . . .

NOTE
Important view of life

QUOTE	MY THOUGHTS
"There are no walls, there are no bolts, no locks that anyone can put on your mind."	Mr. Frank's talking about freedom. Even though they're hiding from the Nazis, their minds can be free. He seems like a wise man.

The reader noticed that Mr. Frank seemed to be trying to teach his daughter a general lesson about freedom and not putting limits on yourself. If you think it might be important, you'll want to look for other places in the play where this idea of freedom comes up.

Topic and Theme Organizer

During reading, you act like a collector, picking up information and adjusting your ideas as you go. Use a Topic and Theme Organizer to keep track of the "big ideas" in a play. List the general topics at the top and then fill in details of what the characters do and say below. For example, here are the notes about two general topics one reader jotted down while reading *The Diary of Anne Frank*.

TOPIC AND THEME ORGANIZER

HELPING OTHERS

Miep and Mr. Kraler run errands and bring supplies.

Mr. Dussel is invited.

Van Daans and Franks have to learn to get along and share.

HOPE

Song keeps spirits up at Hanukkah.

They are encouraged by reports of war.

Anne says people are "good at heart."

Your notes can be very informal. Instead of an organizer, just jot down your ideas in your reading notebook as you read. The point is to find out what the characters do and say that relates to the topics you have identified. If you can't come up with several key details, then maybe what you thought was a "big idea" isn't really so important.

After Reading

When you finish a play, you have a pretty good idea about what the main action is and what the major characters are like. Look at your notes. Think about possible themes. Ask yourself what lesson about life a reader could learn from the play and why the playwright may have wanted to write it. Besides looking at your notes and rereading key passages, it's a good idea also to talk about the play with classmates. See if you all found the same key ideas or if you missed anything important.

Step 3: Come up with a statement of the author's point or message about the topic.

After you've finished reading, it's time to review the theme clues you've found and decide what they mean. Be sure not to confuse a play's topic with its theme. For instance, one of the most important topics of *The Diary of Anne Frank* is hope. But that's not a theme. Ask yourself what point *about* hope the play makes. That would be the theme. Here is what one reader wrote about a theme of *The Diary of Anne Frank*:

Drama

JOURNAL ENTRY

Hope

A lesson I learned from <u>The Diary of Anne Frank</u> is that you can't control the bad things that happen to you in life. But you can control how you deal with what happens. Anne Frank kept a positive attitude and kept trying to love people even in a horrible situation. You have to believe in the human spirit after you read this play. The last words Anne says are "I hope . . ."

Theme Statement

People can deal with anything that happens in life if they stay hopeful and look for the good in everything and everybody.

If you read the play, you might have noticed other details and come up with a very different theme statement. That's OK. Just be sure that you can base your statement on plenty of specific examples.

- The theme is a general statement or point about life.
- Use a three-step plan for finding the theme:
  1. Find the big idea.
  2. Notice what the characters do and say that relates to it.
  3. Write a theme statement.
- Look for clues to the theme of a play in key scenes, when characters learn something about themselves or when they offer a general view about life.

Focus on Language

Part of what's fun about seeing a play performed is hearing how the characters sound. You don't usually read a play *just* for its language. But paying attention to the language a playwright uses is an important element of reading and enjoying a play. Sometimes, you'll want to focus on just that one element of drama—its language.

Goals

Here you'll learn how to:

✔ **study the key lines and speeches in a play**

✔ **consider how the stage directions contribute to a play**

✔ **examine the dialogue to see the way it affects characters, plot, and theme**

Before Reading

When you first read a play, you read to find out what happens and to get to know the characters. To examine the language, you'll probably have to look back at the play a second time, focusing just on its language. If possible, you'll have a chance to read at least some of the play aloud—by yourself or with a group. That's the best way to feel the emotions and catch the meanings of particular words. The reason for looking at a play's language is that it can reveal much more than you may have gotten the first time through the play.

Concentrating on a play's language doesn't mean spending a lot of time on each and every word. That would take too much time. When your focus is on language, you look carefully at these three elements:

■ key lines and speeches

■ stage directions

■ dialogue that reveals characters, plot, or theme

Drama

During Reading

As you read, be an active reader. Jot down comments, ideas, or questions about the language of the play on separate sheets of paper. Look for examples of these three aspects of language in *The Diary of Anne Frank*.

1. Key Lines and Speeches

One of the major language elements of a play is its key lines and speeches. Every major drama has a few lines or speeches that stand out. Sometimes a line will grab your attention because of where and when it is spoken. Other times, the words themselves—how they sound, what they mean, or how they make you feel—make you notice them. Your job as a reader is to find those passages and figure out what they add to the overall play.

For example, you might decide to focus on this line from act 2, scene 4, of *The Diary of Anne Frank*:

> **from *The Diary of Anne Frank***
>
> **Anne** *(Going to him)*. I know it's terrible, trying to have any faith . . . when people are doing such horrible . . . I still believe, in spite of everything, that people are really good at heart.

Here one of the central themes of the play is expressed in one telling line: people are basically good. The playwrights say, in effect, if you learn anything from this play, take away the idea that people *are* good.

Another dramatic moment occurs later in the scene when the Germans discover the Franks' hiding place. Mr. Frank tries to set the tone for the others with this simple but eloquent statement:

> **from *The Diary of Anne Frank***
>
> **Mr. Frank** *(Quietly)*. For the past two years we have lived in fear. Now we can live in hope.

2. Stage Directions

As a reader, you need to pay attention to **stage directions**. Don't skip over them. They guide actors and actresses. They describe emotions and facial expressions. Stage directions play an important role in helping you "see" what's going on in a play.

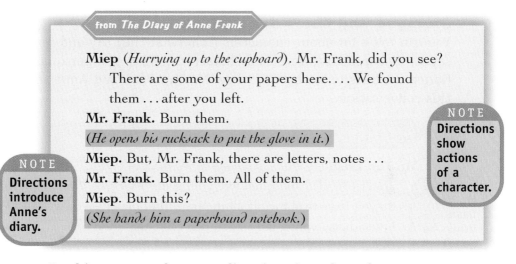

from *The Diary of Anne Frank*

Miep (*Hurrying up to the cupboard*). Mr. Frank, did you see? There are some of your papers here.... We found them ... after you left.

Mr. Frank. Burn them.

(*He opens his rucksack to put the glove in it.*)

Miep. But, Mr. Frank, there are letters, notes ...

Mr. Frank. Burn them. All of them.

Miep. Burn this?

(*She hands him a paperbound notebook.*)

NOTE
Directions introduce Anne's diary.

NOTE
Directions show actions of a character.

In this passage, the stage directions introduce the most important item of all—Anne's diary. Often the stage directions alert the reader to something more subtle. What a character's face looks like or how someone gestures can make the scene come alive in your imagination. Consider this description of Anne just before the Nazis come to take everyone away:

Drama

from *The Diary of Anne Frank*

(*Anne stands, holding her school satchel, looking over at her father and mother with a soft, reassuring smile. She is no longer a child, but a woman with courage to meet whatever lies ahead.*)

NOTE
Directions show important character traits.

The stage directions provide our last "view" of Anne. After this, the lights go out, and only her voice is heard. Without the description of her smile and her courage, readers might imagine that Anne was panicked or crying at this frightening moment. The language in the stage directions helps us see how grown up she has become.

3. Dialogue

One thing that separates plays from other genres is their lack of descriptive details. Except for stage directions, plays are almost all **dialogue**. Because plays are written to be performed and seen, much of what you learn in a play comes through the dialogue.

Dialogue and Character

You can tell a lot about characters from what they say and how they say it. Dialogue often reveals a character's values and personality. Notice the differences between how Mr. Van Daan and Anne talk in this conversation:

---

from *The Diary of Anne Frank*

NOTE
Mr. Van Daan thinks he knows what's right.

Mr. Van Daan (*Restraining himself with difficulty*). Why aren't you nice and quiet like your sister Margot? Why do you have to show off all the time? Let me give you a little advice, young lady. Men don't like that kind of thing in a girl. You know that? A man likes a girl who'll listen to him once in a while . . . a domestic girl, who'll keep her house shining for her husband . . . who loves to cook and sew and . . .

Anne. I'd cut my throat first! I'd open my veins! I'm going to be remarkable! I'm going to Paris . . .

Mr. Van Daan (*Scoffingly*). Paris!

Anne. . . . to study music and art.

NOTE
Anne has strong feelings and determination.

What does this dialogue tell you about Mr. Van Daan? What does it tell you about Anne? You learn about Mr. Van Daan's old-fashioned views about women. But you also learn about how Anne sees herself—studying music and art in Paris. Anne's emotional side comes through in her short sentences with exclamation points, her exaggerations, and her self-confidence.

Sometimes you might want to use a Double-entry Journal to record your reactions to interesting dialogue. Here's what one reader wrote about a disagreement between Anne and her mother:

QUOTE	MY THOUGHTS
"Mrs. Frank. . . . Think how lucky we are! Think of the thousands dying in the war, every day . . . **Anne** (Interrupting). What's the good of that? . . . That's stupid!"	Anne always says what she thinks. She's got a quick temper. She seems like a typical teenager.

Dialogue and Plot

Dialogue in a play also advances the plot. As characters talk, readers get an idea of what might happen in the future and an explanation of what has occurred in the past. Dialogue builds tension. "Listen" to this conversation as Mr. Kraler explains that a man has discovered the hiding place and wants money to keep quiet:

from *The Diary of Anne Frank*

NOTE
Growing tension

Mr. Frank *(To* Mr. Kraler*).* How was it left? What did you tell him?

Mr. Kraler. I said I had to think about it. What shall I do? Pay him the money? . . . or what? I don't know.

Dussel *(Frantic).* For God's sake don't fire him! Pay him what he asks. . . .

This short conversation ties together several parts of the plot. Anne and the others had worried that they'd been discovered before, and they had. In the last scene we learn that it was, in fact, this man that turned them in to the German police.

Drama

Dialogue and Theme

Careful reading of the dialogue is also a way to discover the theme of a play. As a reader, look for passages in which the characters make strong statements about society or people in general. One such moment happens in act 2, scene 3, when Mr. Van Daan is caught stealing food. Notice how Mr. Frank captures the tense mood in these simple words:

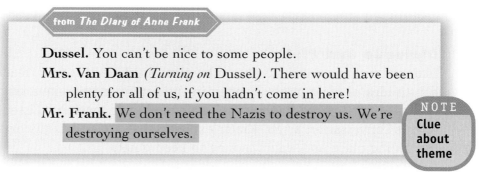

from *The Diary of Anne Frank*

Dussel. You can't be nice to some people.

Mrs. Van Daan (*Turning on* Dussel). There would have been plenty for all of us, if you hadn't come in here!

Mr. Frank. We don't need the Nazis to destroy us. We're destroying ourselves.

> NOTE
> Clue about theme

Note especially the statements made by the "good" characters. Writers, including playwrights, often have one character who serves as the moral voice. Through these "good," moral characters the message of the work is told. In *The Diary of Anne Frank,* Mr. Frank is that character.

After Reading

After you finish rereading a play and studying its language, take the time to think about what you've learned. Think about the most memorable characters and parts of the play. What lines, stage directions, or dialogue do you remember?

You may then want to reread some passages. Go back and find a few of the parts that you like the most. Write out—or make a copy of each passage—to help you remember the character or theme suggested by the words. Jot down your reactions to the language. The example below shows one reader's response to Anne's description of a typical dinner scene.

> **from _The Diary of Anne Frank_**
>
> **Anne's voice.** . . . Our stomachs are so empty that they rumble and make strange noises, all in different keys. Mr. Van Daan's is deep and low, like a bass fiddle. Mine is high, whistling like a flute. As we all sit around waiting for supper, it's like an orchestra tuning up.

JOURNAL ENTRY

I can just imagine the different sounds. The comparison to an orchestra is clever. Anne was a good writer. That must have been a funny scene.

Drama

Summing Up

- **The quotes and speeches are often what makes plays memorable.**
- **The stage directions "show" you what's happening on the stage.**
- **You can learn about the characters, plot, and theme by studying the language of the play.**

Elements of Drama

Like a novel or short story, a drama tells a story and includes such elements as character, setting, plot, and theme. However, unlike other works of fiction, a drama is written to be performed. The written form of a play is called a *script*, and the author is called a *playwright*. A script contains a number of important elements.

Use this section as you would a glossary. Look up the term, read the example, and review the definition.

Elements of Drama

Acts and Scenes	503
Cast of Characters	504
Dialogue	505
Monologue	506
Plot	507
Setting	509
Stage Directions	510
Theme	511

Acts and Scenes

Just as a novel is divided into chapters, a play is broken up into acts and scenes. The acts are the bigger divisions; scenes are the parts within an act.

EXAMPLE

from *Let Me Hear You Whisper* by Paul Zindel

ACT I / Scene 2

(It is the next evening. HELEN *pushes her equipment into the lab. She opens the curtain so she can watch the dolphin as she works. She and the dolphin stare at each other.)*

HELEN: Youuuuuuuuuuuu. *(She pauses, watches for a response.)* Youuuuuuuuuuuu. *(Still no response. She turns her attention to her scrubbing for a moment.)* Polly want a cracker? Polly want a cracker? *(She wrings out a rag and resumes work.)* Yeah, it's four o'clock. Yeah, it's four o'clock. Polly want a cracker at four o'clock?

DESCRIPTION

The passage from *Let Me Hear You Whisper* makes clear the two major divisions of a play: **acts** and **scenes**. Plays have any number of acts, and each act can have any number of scenes. A new scene usually begins whenever the setting—either the time or the place or both—changes. The words *next evening* in the example above alert the reader to the change in scene.

DEFINITION

An act is a group of two or more scenes that form a major division of a play. A scene is one part of the action, usually happening in a particular time and place.

Drama

Cast of Characters

At the beginning of most plays, the playwright gives a list of the characters.

EXAMPLE

from *The Million-Pound Bank Note* by Mark Twain, dramatized

Cast of Characters

Henry Adams	Second Cockney
Lloyd Hastings	First Man
First Cockney	Second Man
Gordon Featherstone	Woman
Abel Featherstone	Third Man
Albert Hawkins	Butler
Servant	Portia Langham
Tod	Sir Alfred
Mr. Smedley	
Hotel Manager	

DESCRIPTION

This **cast of characters** lists everyone in the play. In some scripts, the characters are listed in order of importance. In others, they are listed in the order they appear in the play. Sometimes the playwright includes a short description of each character after his or her name. The cast of characters can help you keep track of who's who in the play, so don't skip over it. The cast list can be a helpful resource to refer to as you read.

DEFINITION

A **cast of characters** is a list that describes who's in the play and often how they are related to one another.

Dialogue

In a play, the characters spend a lot of time talking to one another. Don't skip over this conversation. It's an important part of a play.

EXAMPLE

from *Let Me Hear You Whisper* by Paul Zindel

Speech tags tell who's talking.

DOLPHIN: Help.

(HELEN *opens the curtain. The dolphin and she look at each other.*)

DOLPHIN: Help me.

HELEN: You don't need me. Just say something to them. Anything. They just need to hear you say something. . . . You want me to tell 'em? I'll tell them. I'll just say I heard you say "Help." *(pauses, then speaks with feigned cheerfulness)* I'll go tell them.

DESCRIPTION

A script consists mostly of **dialogue**, or conversation. Through dialogue, a playwright reveals the characters, plot, and themes of a play. In the example above, the dialogue tells the plot: the dolphin needs help and asks Helen for it. The dialogue also reveals what Helen's character is like. Note the *speech tag*—the character's name—to help you keep track of who's speaking. You will need to know which character said what, so use the speech tags as the dialogue goes back and forth between the characters. Notice how the tags are set off in the example by being printed all in capital letters. Note, too, that quotation marks are not used to set off dialogue in plays.

DEFINITION

Dialogue is the conversation between characters in a play.

Drama

Monologue

Sometimes a character speaks when he or she is alone on stage.

from *The Diary of Anne Frank* by Goodrich and Hackett

Anne's Voice. And so it seems our stay here is over. They are waiting for us now. They've allowed us five minutes to get our things. We can each take a bag and whatever it will hold of clothing. Nothing else. So, dear Diary, that means I must leave you behind. Good-bye for a while. P.S. Please, please, Miep, or Mr. Kraler, or anyone else. If you should find this diary, will you please keep it safe for me, because some day I hope . . .

DESCRIPTION

In **monologues**, or soliloquies, a character stands alone on the stage and speaks. These speeches are often important, dramatic moments in a play, because all focus is on one character's thoughts. In the example above, Anne's voice is heard, but the stage is dark. She is not seen.

Although not exactly a monologue, the voice of Anne Frank at the end of the scene functions like one. It allows the character to say something—alone—to the audience. In an *aside*, a character turns to the audience to say something that other characters on stage are not supposed to hear. But in Anne's speech here at the end of the play, she alone speaks to the audience for one last time.

DEFINITION

A **monologue**, or soliloquy, is a speech by one character who is alone on the stage.

Plot

The diagram below shows the traditional way that the action of a play is organized. Many—but not all—plays can be divided into those five parts. The example is from *Let Me Hear You Whisper*.

EXAMPLE

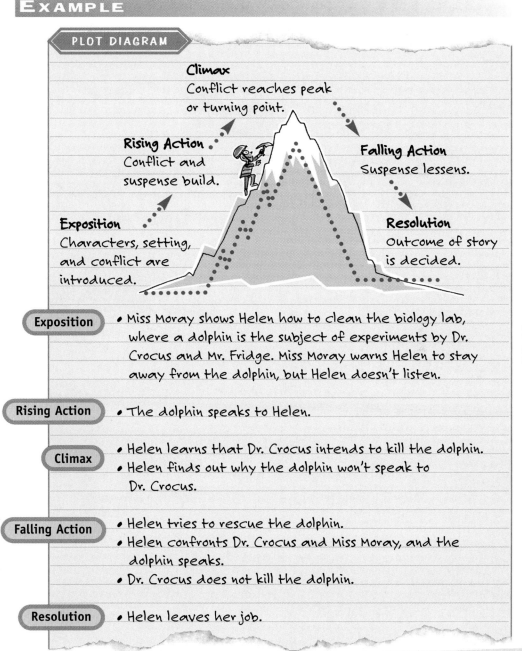

PLOT DIAGRAM

Climax
Conflict reaches peak or turning point.

Rising Action
Conflict and suspense build.

Falling Action
Suspense lessens.

Exposition
Characters, setting, and conflict are introduced.

Resolution
Outcome of story is decided.

Exposition
- Miss Moray shows Helen how to clean the biology lab, where a dolphin is the subject of experiments by Dr. Crocus and Mr. Fridge. Miss Moray warns Helen to stay away from the dolphin, but Helen doesn't listen.

Rising Action
- The dolphin speaks to Helen.

Climax
- Helen learns that Dr. Crocus intends to kill the dolphin.
- Helen finds out why the dolphin won't speak to Dr. Crocus.

Falling Action
- Helen tries to rescue the dolphin.
- Helen confronts Dr. Crocus and Miss Moray, and the dolphin speaks.
- Dr. Crocus does not kill the dolphin.

Resolution
- Helen leaves her job.

Drama

Plot, continued

DESCRIPTION

The **plot** of a play is the action. Like the plot of a novel or a short story, the plot of a play often revolves around a *conflict*.

There are five main types of conflict:

person vs. person
(problem with another character)

person vs. society
(problem with the laws or beliefs of a group)

person vs. nature
(problem with force of nature, such as a blizzard or high winds)

person vs. self
(problem with deciding what to do or think)

person vs. fate
(problem that seems to be uncontrollable)

That struggle between opposing forces builds until it reaches a crisis or a turning point. That moment is the climax.

DEFINITION

Plot is the action or main events in a drama.

Setting

The passage below from the beginning of *Let Me Hear You Whisper* makes clear where and when the action takes place.

EXAMPLE

from *Let Me Hear You Whisper* by Paul Zindel

Setting: *The action takes place in the hallway, laboratory and specimen room of a biology experimentation association located in Manhattan near the Hudson River.*

Overall location of the action

Time: *The action begins with the night shift on a Monday and ends the following Friday.*

Time period

DESCRIPTION

This description of the setting of *Let Me Hear You Whisper* appears in the script immediately after the cast of characters. The **setting** refers to the place and time that a story happens. Like a novel, a play may have one *general setting*—or overall location and time period of the entire story—and several *immediate settings*—or exact places and times at which individual events occur.

When you read a play, note how the setting changes from act to act and scene to scene. In *Let Me Hear You Whisper*, for example, the setting gradually moves from a Monday night to Friday. As you begin each new act or scene, ask yourself how the setting affects the overall mood.

Drama

DEFINITION

Setting is where and when the play takes place. In a play, the setting is usually described in a note or stage directions at the opening of the play and each scene.

Stage Directions

When you go to a play, you can see how the scenery looks and hear how the actors and actresses talk. But when you read a play, you have to depend more on your imagination. Stage directions can help you see the surroundings and imagine just how the characters look and act.

EXAMPLE

from *Let Me Hear You Whisper* by Paul Zindel

MISS MORAY: Now, we'll just move directly into the specimen room. The working conditions will be ideal for you in here.

What the character does or feels

(HELEN *looks ready to gag as she looks around the specimen room. It is packed with specimen jars of all sizes. Various animals and parts of animals are visible in their formaldehyde baths.*)

What the scene looks like

DESCRIPTION

In nearly all plays, **stage directions** are printed in italics and enclosed in parentheses. These directions tell actors and actresses how to speak, how to move, and what to do. Some directions help the director to know how the play should look. Stage directions help a reader picture the setting, characters, and action.

As a reader, note the clues found in stage directions just as you would clues in the dialogue of the play. In the example above, Miss Moray speaks about how "ideal" conditions are, but Helen, in the stage directions, "looks ready to gag." These stage directions give an important clue to Helen's inner emotions and true feelings.

DEFINITION

Stage directions describe details of the setting and sound effects as well as direct characters how to speak their lines, move, act, and look.

Theme

In the speech below, the main character makes a general statement about how people should live their lives. Helen's statement reveals an important message in the play.

EXAMPLE

from *Let Me Hear You Whisper* by Paul Zindel

HELEN: I'm very tired of being a nice person, Miss Moray. I'm going to report you to the ASPCA, or somebody, because . . . and if being a nice person is just not saying anything and letting you pack of butchers run around doing whatever you want, then I don't want to be nice anymore. *(pause)* You gotta be very stupid people to need an animal to talk before you know just from looking at it that it's saying something . . . that it knows what pain feels like. I'd like to see you all with a few electrodes in your heads. Being nice isn't any good. *(looking at dolphin)* They just kill you off if you do that. And that's being a coward. You gotta talk back. You gotta speak up against what's wrong and bad, or you can't ever stop it. At least you've gotta try. *(She bursts into tears.)*

> **Theme statement**

DESCRIPTION

Every now and then a playwright will have a character state the theme of a play directly. The **theme** is the central idea or message. To find the theme, first look for the general topic or "big idea" of the play. Then, look for what the characters say and do that relates to the topic. Last, come up with a statement that explains the author's point or message about the topic.

DEFINITION

Theme is a statement about life around which the playwright builds the play.

Drama

Reading on the Internet

Reading a Website

Elements of the Internet

Reading a Website

Reading email may be simple, but reading a website is not. Reading a website is very different from reading a chapter in a book. When you read a book, you go in one direction, from left to right and from beginning to end. But when you read a website, you can go in any of a number of directions. You jump around. Its links allow you to choose your own path through the material, and it's easy to get lost or just wander around.

Another challenge with websites is evaluating them. Are they accurate? biased or slanted in their point of view? reliable? Be a smart reader. Read critically and don't believe everything you read on a computer screen.

Goals

Here you'll learn how to:

✔ use the reading process for **websites** and a plan for evaluating them

✔ use the strategy of **reading critically** to examine a website

✔ understand the **organization of websites**

Before Reading

There's no doubt about it: surfing the Web can be fun. The animation, the sounds, and the graphics—not to mention the variety of information—can capture your imagination and keep you clicking happily for hours. But it's very easy to get distracted or off track when you're online. That's why the reading process may be even more useful with websites than it is with printed text.

A Set a Purpose

Sometimes you visit websites because you're exploring just for fun. But often you'll use the World Wide Web to find information on a specific subject. Then you need a clear purpose for reading.

When reading a website, ask yourself, "What questions do I have?" Then make a list of those questions. Finding the answers to your questions becomes your purpose for reading.

For example, suppose you are doing a report on dyslexia, a kind of learning disability. Right now, you may not know much about it, so you might have these questions:

Setting a Purpose

■ **What is dyslexia, and how many people have it?**
■ **What causes dyslexia?**
■ **How can dyslexia be treated or cured?**

You may come up with more questions as you go, but answering these will be your general reading purpose. It's fine to expand your purpose for reading as you learn more.

Internet

Keep to Your Purpose

Having a clear purpose is very important when you're using the Internet, especially for research. Start by using a search engine to help you find websites with information you need. You chart your own path through a site, and if you're not careful, you can waste a lot of time with aimless roaming around. You get curious and click. Next thing you know you're off course.

Don't Wander

Wandering around without a purpose is probably the single biggest problem in reading a website. Each link looks tempting. One click and—poof—you're started in a direction that may be completely off your purpose. When you first reach a web page, take a minute to survey it before you click any link.

B Preview

Get a sense of what's there. Think about what, if anything, you already know about the topic and what on the home page can help you get the information you need. When you preview a website, look for these items:

Preview Checklist

✔ the name and overall look of the site
✔ the main menu or table of contents
✔ the first few lines describing the site
✔ any images or graphics that create a feeling for the site
✔ the source or sponsor of the website

Let's say that, after logging onto the Web and searching for "dyslexia," you've just come to the home page of the International Dyslexia Association (IDA). Stop and preview before you click.

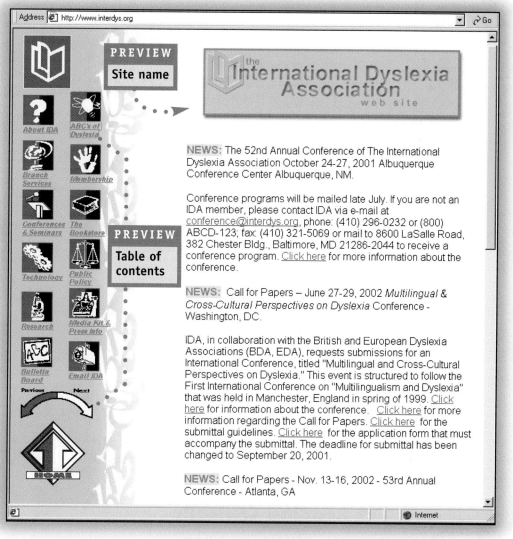

What did you learn from your preview? Does this look like a good site that will have useful information? The organization, the International Dyslexia Association (IDA), seems as if it would be reliable and authoritative. The next step is to see if it has the answers to your questions.

C Plan

Once you decide to give a site a closer look, you'll need a plan to get the information you want. The paragraphs of news don't seem useful; they give information on conferences. Look again at the boxes on the left.

The table of contents gives you an overview of what's available on the site. It's like a menu. For your research, it would probably make the most sense to click on the upper right graphic, *ABC's of Dyslexia,* to get some basic information.

Even if it looks tempting, don't automatically click on the first link you see. That's a common mistake of beginners. Look for the links that are most likely to have the information you want. If a site has no links that look promising, then *don't click*.

Hyperlinks

Reading Strategy: Reading Critically

Once you arrive at a website and know your purpose, you're ready to begin reading. Immediately you face the next biggest obstacle: how do you know you can believe anything you find on the site? That's why you need to use the strategy of **reading critically**.

Here's a simple plan to help you evaluate websites and the information you find on them. Use a Website Profiler to keep track of your ideas.

HOW TO READ A WEBSITE CRITICALLY

1. *First, preview the site. Glance at a few pages. Decide if they have the kind of information that will be helpful to your purpose.*

2. *Take notes on the information you want or print out pages and highlight the key information.*

3. *Then write down the URL, or web address, of the site.*

4. *Last, create a quick profile of the site by looking critically at four elements: its sponsor, its most recent update, its point of view, and its level of expertise.*

WEBSITE PROFILER

NAME	
URL	
SPONSOR	DATE
POINT OF VIEW	EXPERTISE
REACTION	

Internet

During Reading

Now you're ready to put your strategy for reading a website into effect. During your reading, keep your purpose-setting questions in mind. If possible, write out your questions in a notebook or make Study Cards. Keep them beside you at the computer. They will help you stick to your search.

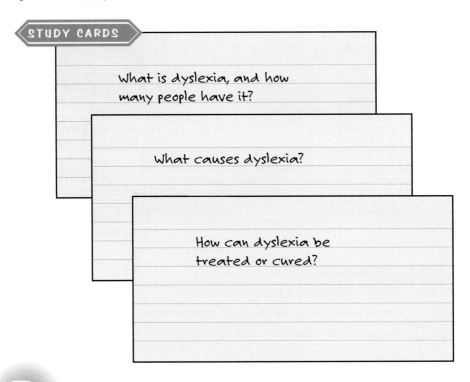

STUDY CARDS

What is dyslexia, and how many people have it?

What causes dyslexia?

How can dyslexia be treated or cured?

D Read with a Purpose

As you skim over the web pages on dyslexia, focus on your questions. After you click on the *ABC's of Dyslexia* graphic, you will see another table of contents. Suppose you choose the link to a page entitled "Adam's Story." Ask yourself, "How useful would this information be?" The answer is "not very." "Adam's Story" tells a personal story and does not contain the answers to your questions.

When a link doesn't look promising, go back to the table of contents. Choose a different link. The best place to find what you need would probably be the "Facts About Dyslexia" link. Do a quick preview of it.

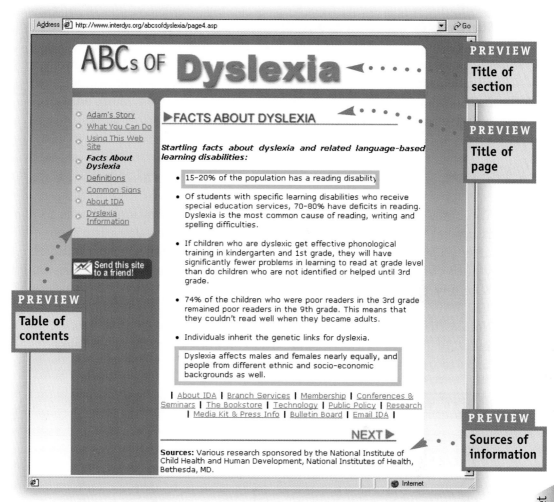

Taking Notes

When you skim this page, you find that it contains the answer to your first question. Write the information you need on a file card or in your notebook or print out the page.

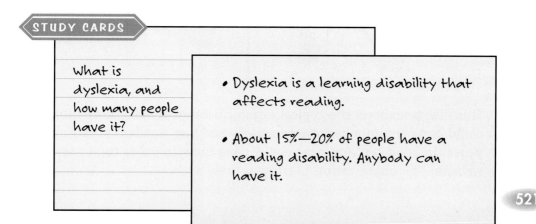

STUDY CARDS

What is dyslexia, and how many people have it?

• Dyslexia is a learning disability that affects reading.

• About 15%—20% of people have a reading disability. Anybody can have it.

Putting It in Your Own Words

One common problem with websites for students is that it's easy to just copy what a website states word for word. That's plagiarism. Put what you learn in your own words. That will help you remember the information better anyway. (If you do decide to use a short phrase or a quote from the source, then be sure to use quotation marks.)

How Websites Are Organized

The home page of the International Dyslexia Association on page 517 is typical of a website. Unlike many books in which you turn page after page and read one page after another in order, a website allows you to choose what you want to read and in what order. You can take any path you want through the links.

Notice that the IDA page contains a table of contents that lists individual pages in the section. You can click on any one of these links to go directly to that page.

ORGANIZATION OF A WEBSITE VS. A BOOK

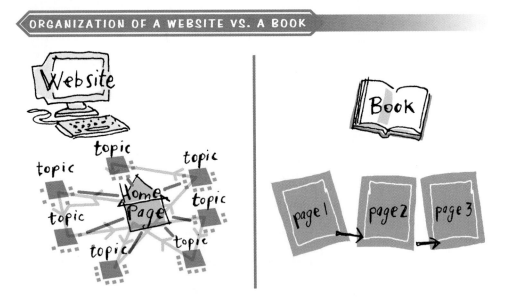

This diagram shows the typical organization of a website. A subject could have any number of topic pages and any number of subtopic pages. In addition, any page could have links to other topics on the website. The organization is truly a "web."

E Connect

When you read a website, you need to take a moment to think about your own feelings. For instance, you may have strong feelings about some topics or information. What you see on websites may anger, surprise, amuse, or worry you. Who you are, what your background is, and what (if anything) you already know about the topic will color your response to a particular website. If you're using information you found, then it's important for you to come to an overall opinion about the site. Here your Website Profiler can come in handy. Especially if you want to use a source later, take a moment to make a few notes.

WEBSITE PROFILER

NAME: International Dyslexia Association
URL: www.interdys.org

SPONSOR: itself	**DATE:** lists events in 2001 and 2002
POINT OF VIEW: The organization helps people with dyslexia.	**EXPERTISE:** It seems to be a good source of information.

REACTION: Site was good but could have been more appealing, such as brighter colors and addition of pictures.

Internet

One thing that makes it fun to use the Internet for research is how fast you can move from page to page, site to site, and topic to topic. But don't be in a rush. Slow down and gather your thoughts about a website.

F Pause and Reflect

First, check that you found information that answers all of your initial questions. Then ask yourself questions like these:

Looking Back

- Can I summarize the most important information?
- Was I confused or puzzled by anything I read?
- What else would I like to know?

A lot of times, the more you research, the more questions you'll have. For example, "What are other types of reading disabilities besides dyslexia?" If you have more questions, write them down. Then go back to search for the answers.

G Reread

Once in a while, you may want to look at a site again to find new information or clear up confusion. But probably most of the time you're looking for information on the Web, you'll want to go back to a site to evaluate the reliability of what you found.

Anyone can post a website—an individual, a government agency, an organization, an educational institution, or a business. Some websites contain biased or even inaccurate information. For this reason, you need to read a website critically and evaluate whether or not the source of the information is reliable.

Rereading Strategy: Skimming

Skimming is a great way not only to review what a website is about and how it's organized but also to evaluate the source fully. This checklist will help you evaluate Internet sources. Go back to pages 517 and 521 and skim the IDA site with this checklist in mind. How would you evaluate its reliability?

HOW TO EVALUATE INTERNET SOURCES

1. Check the source of the site.
The source or sponsor is often named at the top or bottom of the home page.

2. Check the site's credentials.
Credentials are educational degrees, job titles, or other training or experience that makes a person an authority on a subject. To trust the information on a site, you need to know that the people behind it are knowledgeable.

3. Identify its purpose.
Figure out why the site was created. Is its purpose to sell a product and make money, to promote a cause, or to educate people? Its purpose will help you see its point of view.

4. Check the date the site was last updated.
Recent updates suggest the site will probably have up-to-date and accurate information.

5. Question the accuracy if:
- ❑ *the source of the website is not identified*
- ❑ *the source is not well known*
- ❑ *the purpose of the site is to sell a product or promote a cause or political party*
- ❑ *the information is dated*
- ❑ *the text contains obvious errors, grammatical or spelling mistakes, or typos*

Internet

H Remember

To remember what you read on a website, put the information in your own words.

1. Talk about It

Simply tell somebody about it. Describe, for instance, any special features you liked. Talking about a website will help you summarize or put what you learned in your own words.

2. List What You Learned

Write a list of a few of the main things you learned. Jot down the web address in case you want to go back to it later. Your notes can include more information than just the answers to your questions. Anything that impressed you is worth noting. For example, you might write notes like these for the IDA website:

SUMMARY NOTES

(www.interdys.org)

Four things I learned from the IDA website:
1. The cause is not known, but the brain of a person with dyslexia develops and works differently.
2. Dyslexia runs in families.
3. Dyslexia has nothing to do with intelligence. Anyone can have it.
4. Treating dyslexia early can prevent a dyslexic adult from having reading problems.

Summing Up

When you read a website, remember to use the reading process and the strategy of **reading critically**. Because of the **weblike organization**, remember to read with a purpose and not wander. To help you get the information you want and evaluate a site's reliability, try using these tools:

■ Website Profiler
■ Study Cards
■ Summary Notes

When you reread, try the rereading strategy of **skimming.** That will help you find the information you need to evaluate a website.

Elements of the Internet

The Internet is a system of communicating through computers around the world that are connected. It allows people to share information in seconds by having computers send messages back and forth to one another. This part of the handbook describes some basic elements of the Internet.

Elements of the Internet

Bookmark	528
Browser	529
Email	530
Link	532
Search Engine	533
World Wide Web	534

Internet

527

Bookmark

You can save the web addresses of sites you would like to go back to visit. Your web browser may call these "bookmarks" or "favorites," but the idea is the same: places you want to go back and visit.

EXAMPLE

File	Edit	View	Go	Bookmark
				Electronic Library Personal Edition
				Library of Congress
				NBA.com
				Google

DESCRIPTION

A **bookmark** is the address for a website that you would like to visit again. Bookmarks come in handy when you want to find a website quickly. The names and addresses of these sites are stored in a list in the menu at the top of your computer screen.

Bookmarks save you the trouble of typing in each web address perfectly and remembering it each time. On your first visit to a website, you can set a bookmark with your browser software. Then all you need to do is go to that bookmark and click, and you'll be connected directly to that site.

DEFINITION

A **bookmark** is a saved address of a website. It allows users to reach a website with a single click of the mouse.

Browser

A browser is a kind of software tool. Just like a compass helps you find your way, a browser helps you visit and view websites.

EXAMPLE

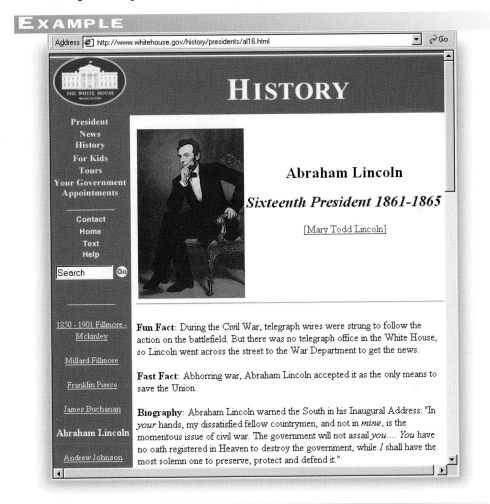

DESCRIPTION

A **browser** is software that helps you explore the Internet. Browsers have features that allow you to store your favorite sites (called "favorites" or "bookmarks"). They also help you look at images or play music. The browser lets you view a site, helps you move from site to site easily, and gives you a home page.

DEFINITION

A **browser** is a software tool that allows you to surf the Web.

Email

An email is a kind of electronic message or letter.

From: "info@wilderness.com" info@wilderness.com
To: davy_crockett@wilderness.net
Date: Thu, Nov. 2, 2000 6:15 AM
Subject: Welcome letter from Wilderness.com

Email address

Header

Thanks for joining Wilderness.com, the Internet's most comprehensive site for nature lovers, outdoor enthusiasts, and environmentalists. You're receiving this email because you have just become a member of the wilderness club.

Body

Your user name is: coyote
Your password is: 456789

To change your information or to unsubscribe to our mailings, click here to access your profile.

http://www.wilderness.com/members/

Thanks for joining Wilderness.com, where wild things just happen.

DESCRIPTION

This message is an example of **email**, which stands for "electronic mail." Email is the most widely used Internet service. Email allows you to send messages to and receive messages from people all over the world.

Most email has a standard form and consists of two basic parts: the *header* and the *body*. Notice that the header identifies who sent the message, to whom it's addressed, the date, and the subject.

To send and receive email, you must have an *email address*. Every email address contains these basic parts:

Email, continued

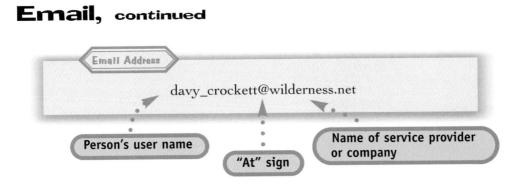

Nowadays you can "talk" to friends using email, sending messages back and forth online. People with common interests exchange a type of email in what are called "chat rooms." No physical room exists. Users simply log on and send messages and wait for a response. Somewhere another user will see the message and respond. The benefit of "chat rooms" is that you can talk to people without their knowing anything about you. For safety reasons, you should *never* give out personal information (phone number, address, school, email address) or agree to meet someone.

Email is a way to reach across states or even countries to exchange messages.

DEFINITION

Email is an electronic message. It has two basic parts: a header and the body of the message. A chat room is a place on the Internet where people send electronic messages back and forth.

Internet

Link

Links allow you to jump directly from one page or site on the World Wide Web to another.

You can spot a link because of the way it looks.

EXAMPLE

Good sites to visit for literature include http://www.bartleby.com/, but you might also try going to www.loc.gov, which is the site for the Library of Congress.

> **Highlighted type and underlining identify links.**

DESCRIPTION

A **link** is the address for another website. A link will jump to another web address because of what is called *hypertext*. That means the text is highlighted like the examples above and gives the address of another web page. Links allow you to make an immediate connection between two things. Where a cross-reference in a book in effect says, "See page 000," a link will go to that place on the World Wide Web with a single click. The home page of most websites is loaded with links, allowing you to click on any of a number of other web addresses.

When you are reading web pages with links in them, try not to click on the first link you see. Preview the entire web page before clicking on a link. That way you can choose the link that looks most promising rather than just the first one you see.

DEFINITION

A link is the address of another website, usually shown in hypertext, that allows you to reach another website with a single click.

Search Engine

How can you find information you want on the World Wide Web? A search engine is the answer. It contains millions of websites covering almost any topic you can imagine.

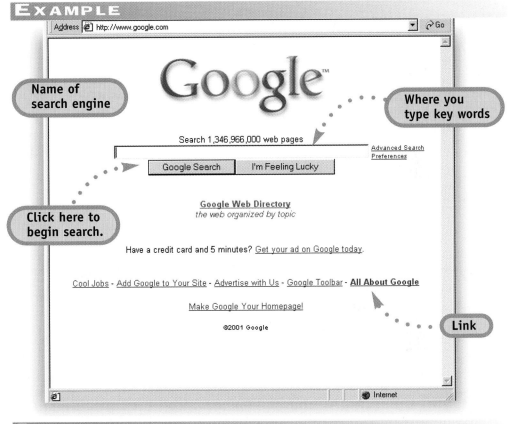

A **search engine** is a tool for helping you find things on the World Wide Web. Search engines work when you type key words into them. Then you usually get a number of "hits" or matches to your search. The key to using search engines is to look closely at the results the search engine found before clicking on any. Choose the ones that look the most promising.

A **search engine** is a tool for helping you find things on the World Wide Web.

Internet

World Wide Web

The page below is an example of what you can find on the World Wide Web. The World Wide Web (www) is a system of computers that are linked together and that have files that can be shared.

EXAMPLE

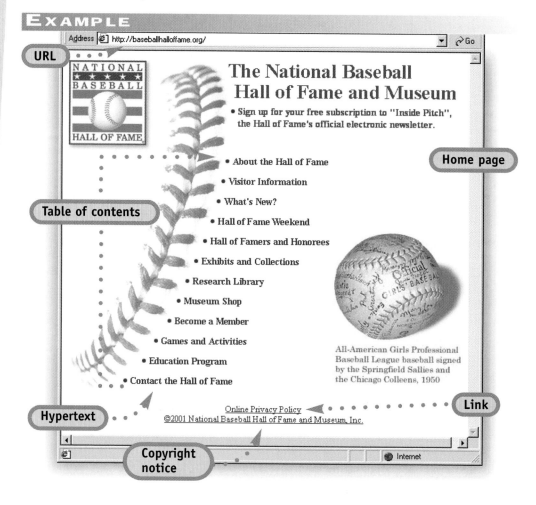

World Wide Web, continued

DESCRIPTION

The example is a home page of a website, which is a group of linked documents on a specific subject. Each document within the site is called a *web page*. Any one document may be longer than one screen or one printed page, and the website itself may be as many as a thousand or more pages. When you go to a website, the first page you see is called the *home page*. The home page introduces the site and serves as a directory (sort of a table of contents) for it.

A click on any of the *links* will take you to another web page. The documents in the website have been linked to one another. This linked information is called *hypertext,* and it can be text, graphics, and small audio and video files. The other links, which often appear in highlighted text and are underlined, may take you to another page in the site or to another website. In the example, a table of contents is shown in the center of the page. By clicking on a topic in the table of contents, you will go to a new page.

Every website and web page has its own address, or URL, which stands for "uniform resource locator." That's how computers know where to look for things on the **World Wide Web**.

Every web address is really a location. When you type www.nasa.gov into your web browser, it sees a location on the World Wide Web. Then, the browser goes to that location. You buy the right to use an address, called a "domain" name. The publishers of this book, for example, paid for the domain name www.greatsource.com. They are the only ones who can use that name. It points only to their website.

DEFINITION

The **World Wide Web** is the system of computers that are joined around the world and that share files. A web address, or URL, is a location of a website or web page. It tells where to look on the World Wide Web to find a website.

Internet

YEAR	TEAM	G	AB	H
1986	OAK	81	205	160
1987	OAK	151	550	143
1988	OAK	149	495	155
1989	BOS	152	520	170
1990	BALT	148	511	152
1991	BALT	152	507	144
1992	BALT	104	390	106

CUTAWAY VIEW WHEEL

81   82   83   84   85   86   87

Reading
Graphics

Reading a Graphic

Elements of Graphics

Reading a Graphic

We live in a "visual age." Look in any textbook, magazine, or newspaper and you'll see lots of graphics. Because so much information appears in visual form, the ability to read charts, graphs, maps, diagrams, and other graphics is more important than ever.

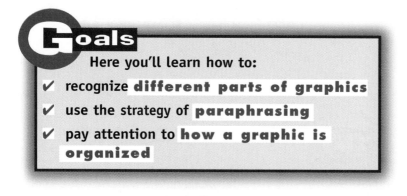

Goals

Here you'll learn how to:

✔ recognize **different parts of graphics**
✔ use the strategy of **paraphrasing**
✔ pay attention to **how a graphic is organized**

Before Reading

The reading process works with graphics just as it does with text. Although many graphics have both visuals and words, the visuals do much or most of the work of communicating the information. Graphics summarize and highlight information, so fewer words are needed.

A Set a Purpose

Your basic purpose in reading a graphic is usually to answer these two general questions:

Setting a Purpose

■ **What is it about?**
■ **What does it say?**

A quick preview will help you answer the first question.

B Preview

When you preview a graphic, pay attention to words and visuals.
Look for these items:

Preview Checklist

✔ the title
✔ any captions or background
✔ any labels
✔ the column and row headings
✔ the key or legend
✔ the scale or unit of measurement
✔ the source

Now preview part of a survey conducted by the Gallup Organization.

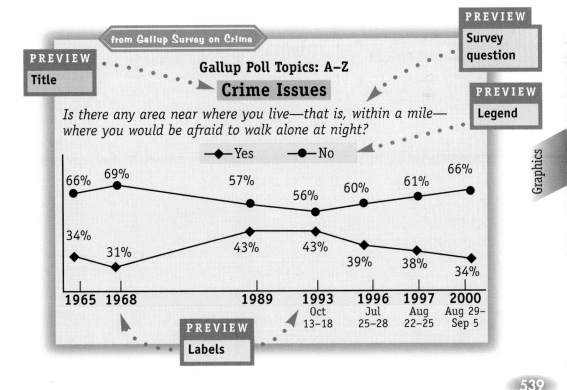

PREVIEW
Survey question

from Gallup Survey on Crime

PREVIEW
Title

Gallup Poll Topics: A–Z

Crime Issues

PREVIEW
Legend

Is there any area near where you live—that is, within a mile—where you would be afraid to walk alone at night?

◆—Yes   ●—No

66%	69%	57%	66%
		56%	60%	61%
34%		43%	43%			
	31%			39%	38%	34%

| 1965 | 1968 | 1989 | 1993 Oct 13–18 | 1996 Jul 25–28 | 1997 Aug 22–25 | 2000 Aug 29– Sep 5 |

PREVIEW
Labels

Graphics

539

Plan

A quick preview tells you a lot. The general topic is crime issues. Specifically, the graphic shows whether people feel safe walking in their neighborhoods. How can you tell what the graphic is saying to you? Here's a five-step plan that will help you attack any graphic:

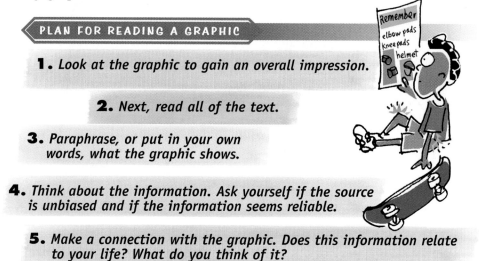

PLAN FOR READING A GRAPHIC

1. Look at the graphic to gain an overall impression.

2. Next, read all of the text.

3. Paraphrase, or put in your own words, what the graphic shows.

4. Think about the information. Ask yourself if the source is unbiased and if the information seems reliable.

5. Make a connection with the graphic. Does this information relate to your life? What do you think of it?

Reading Strategy: Paraphrasing

Putting the information in a graphic into your own words is a good strategy with visuals because it makes you say or write what you are seeing. Explaining information from another source in your own words is called **paraphrasing**. By having to think through information and form sentences, you are more likely to remember it.

You can use a Paraphrase Chart like the one below to walk you through this strategy.

PARAPHRASE CHART

TITLE	
MY PARAPHRASE	
CONNECTION	

During Reading

Now you're ready to read the graphic. The main thing is to put into words the information the graphic gives. Then, after you state that information in your own words, react to it.

D Read with a Purpose

Look back again at the example survey results on page 539. One good way to be sure you read all of a graphic thoroughly is to use your finger. Put your finger on the title. Then put it on the question and legend. Then touch the *yes* and *no* lines and the years along the bottom of the graph.

Next, focus in a little closer. Read the percentages given for *yes* and *no* for each year. Look at the general shapes of the two lines—where they're closer and where they're farther apart. How do these percentages change? How would you put this information in your own words? Here's how one reader paraphrased this information:

PARAPHRASE CHART

MY PARAPHRASE

1. In 1965 and 1968, just under 70% of the people felt safe walking alone at night in their neighborhoods.
2. In 1989 and 1993, a little more than half the people felt this way.
3. Then, in 2000, about 66% of the people thought their neighborhoods were safe at night.

The next step is to think about the information. You might ask yourself, "Is the source a good one? How many people were asked this question?" In this case, the source is the Gallup Organization, which is a well-known survey company. That means you can safely assume that the information is probably reliable and a good number and mix of people were surveyed.

Graphics

How Graphics Are Organized

Understanding the parts of a graphic is the key to unlocking what it has to say. Graphics can be very different from one another, so they can be organized in a number of ways.

Almost every graphic has a title and some other type on it. As a reader, you have to *read* the type. That's the single biggest problem with reading graphics: many people skip the words and numbers. The tendency with graphics is simply to look at them, not read them.

Keep that advice in mind as you read again this graph on crime and think about how the information is organized.

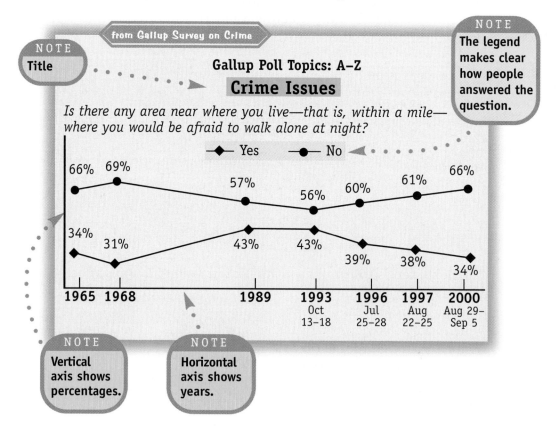

NOTE
Title

from Gallup Survey on Crime

NOTE
The legend makes clear how people answered the question.

Gallup Poll Topics: A–Z

Crime Issues

Is there any area near where you live—that is, within a mile— where you would be afraid to walk alone at night?

— Yes — No

66% 69% 57% 56% 60% 61% 66%

34% 31% 43% 43% 39% 38% 34%

1965 1968 1989 1993 1996 1997 2000
Oct Jul Aug Aug 29–
13–18 25–28 22–25 Sep 5

NOTE
Vertical axis shows percentages.

NOTE
Horizontal axis shows years.

542

Finding the Axes

On the Gallup survey graphic, the years are listed along a bottom rule, or line, called a *horizontal* (or *x*) *axis*. Most graphs have a rule running up the left side as well, called a *vertical* (or *y*) *axis*. In the example, the unit of measurement for the horizontal axis is years. The unit of measurement for the vertical axis is percent of people. These lines and units of measurements are the keys to how the information is organized.

Finding the Legend

Most graphics also have a *legend* that shows how the information is coded. Be sure you understand what symbols are used and what they mean. In this graph, the legend describes that the line with diamond shapes means "yes, people were afraid." The line with the dots means "no, people were not afraid." Understanding the legend is critical for understanding the graphic.

Take time to look closely at the key or legend, because it tells you what information is being shown and how it is coded.

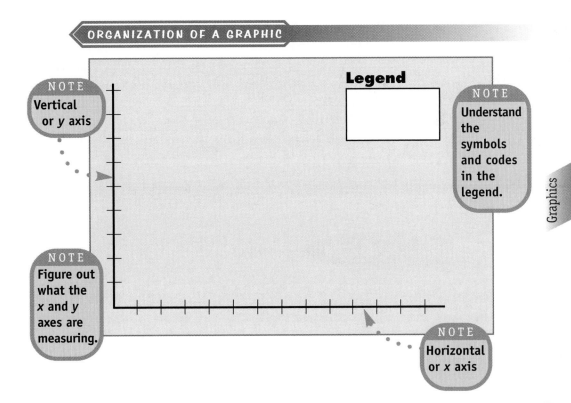

ORGANIZATION OF A GRAPHIC

Legend

NOTE
Vertical
or *y* axis

NOTE
Understand
the
symbols
and codes
in the
legend.

NOTE
Figure out
what the
x and *y*
axes are
measuring.

NOTE
Horizontal
or *x* axis

Graphics

E Connect

Active readers also ask questions, challenge information, and react to what they read. When you read a graphic, ask yourself: "How does this relate to my life? What does this information mean?"

Go back to page 539 and think about the survey results. Do they surprise you? How would you have answered the survey question? What other questions come to mind?

The organizer below summarizes how a reader might use the reading process to organize his or her thoughts about the graphic. How would you have connected to the information?

PARAPHRASE CHART

TITLE	CRIME ISSUES
MY PARAPHRASE	1. In 1965 and 1968, just under 70% of the people felt safe walking alone at night in their neighborhoods. 2. In 1989 and 1993, a little more than half the people felt this way. 3. Then, in 2000, about 66% of the people thought their neighborhoods were safe at night.
MY THOUGHTS	The source is the Gallup Organization, a well-known survey company. The information should be reliable.
CONNECTION	I wonder why people are saying they feel more safe in recent years. Is the crime rate dropping? I feel safe walking where I live.

After Reading

Once you've paraphrased the information in a graphic, you should have a good idea of what it is saying. So why would you need to reread it? Now's the time to give the graphic a closer look with a more critical eye.

F Pause and Reflect

First, think back to your reading purpose. Ask yourself these key questions:

Looking Back

■ **Do I understand what the graphic is about?**
■ **Can I explain in my own words what I learned?**
■ **Does anything about the graphic puzzle me?**
■ **Does the information seem fair and unbiased?**

Some graphics are easier to understand than others. You'll get what they say right away. But others may be more difficult to figure out or evaluate.

G Reread

Look again at the graphic on crime issues and ask yourself, "What conclusions can I draw from this?" Drawing conclusions requires you to analyze the information you're given. The conclusions might be trends, patterns, or other relationships that the data shows.

Rereading Strategy: Reading Critically

Now that you're sure you understand the information, challenge yourself. The facts are clear. You see the changes in how people answered the same question over a period of 35 years. **Reading critically** can help you decide if the facts add up or if the information is slanted in any way.

Occasionally, the text of a graphic directly states the information that it shows. Then the conclusion is already drawn for you. All you have to do is examine the data to see if it supports the conclusion and decide if the information is reliable. As a critical reader, ask yourself questions as you examine a graphic. Take your time drawing conclusions. What follows are one reader's answers to four questions about the Gallup survey on crime.

Graphics

Questions to Ask

CRIME ISSUES GRAPHIC

1. What is being compared or classified?

It compares how safe people feel walking alone at night in their neighborhoods in different years.

2. What similarities and differences in the data do you see?

In 1989 and 1993, fewer people felt safe walking in their neighborhoods than in the other years.

3. Is there anything unusual about the way the data is presented? Is anything left out?

There is a big gap between 1968 and 1989 when no survey was conducted. There's no data at all for the 1970s, so you can't compare by decades. Were different people asked each time—or the same people in the same neighborhoods?

4. What trends or other relationships do you see?

The percentage of Americans who feel safe in their neighborhoods gradually increased between 1993 and 2000.

You can draw a number of conclusions from almost any set of data, and different people may draw different conclusions from the same data. For example, from the survey graphic, one person may conclude that most Americans in 2000 felt pretty safe in their neighborhoods because two-thirds of them were not afraid to walk alone at night. Another person might conclude that Americans felt safest in 1968 and haven't felt as safe since. Still another may be bothered by the fact that we don't know where the people being surveyed were from—big cities or small towns. Questioning the conclusions you draw is part of what it means to read critically.

H Remember

Sometimes it won't be important to recall a particular graphic—say, something in a magazine article you're reading for fun. But when you need to remember what you've learned from a graphic, *do* something with the information. Try one of these suggestions.

1. Talk about It

Tell a friend about what you've read. Summarize what it said or, better yet, show it to him or her. Get another reaction to the information.

2. Make a List

Lists are quick, they are easy, and they help you remember. Here's a list that a reader wrote to remember the Gallup crime graphic:

> **SUMMARY NOTES**
>
> Things I learned about Americans and crime:
> 1. Since 1965, a majority of Americans have felt pretty safe walking at night in their own neighborhoods.
> 2. The fear of walking alone near where you live seems to be decreasing in recent years.

Summing Up

When you read a graphic, use the reading process and the reading strategy of **paraphrasing**. It can help you understand what the information in a visual means. Look also at how the visual is organized, and especially at the **title, legend,** and **labels for the axes** of graphs. These tools can help you understand what the information in a visual means:

- ■ Paraphrase Chart
- ■ Summary Notes

Use the rereading strategy of **reading critically** as you draw conclusions and evaluate whether a graphic is slanted or biased.

Graphics

Elements of Graphics

Graphics need to be read just as much as print. This part of the handbook will describe the most common graphics you're likely to encounter in your reading.

In "Reading a Graphic," you learned how to apply the reading process to one graphic. Now you're ready to take a closer look at the wide variety of other graphics you're likely to come across.

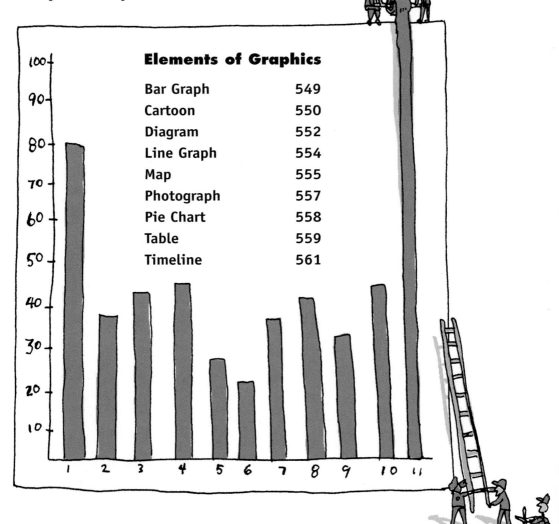

Elements of Graphics

Bar Graph	549
Cartoon	550
Diagram	552
Line Graph	554
Map	555
Photograph	557
Pie Chart	558
Table	559
Timeline	561

Bar Graph

Below is a bar graph about bald eagles. What can you learn from it?

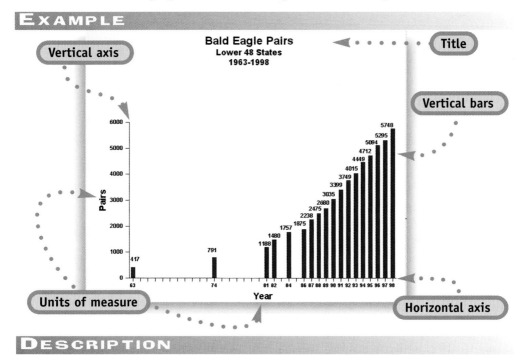

Vertical axis

Title

Bald Eagle Pairs
Lower 48 States
1963-1998

Vertical bars

Units of measure

Horizontal axis

Bar graphs use either vertical or horizontal bars to show quantities or compare amounts of something. A *pictograph* is similar to a bar graph, but it uses symbols or small pictures rather than bars.

Here's how to read a bar graph:

- Read the title to find out what the graph is about.
- Check what's being measured on the vertical axis and on the horizontal axis.
- Check the range of numbers on the graph. Small differences can look a lot bigger if the range is small.
- Try to state in your own words what the graph shows. For example, the graph above shows a big increase in bald eagle pairs from 1963 to 1998.

A **bar graph** uses vertical or horizontal bars to show or compare quantities or amounts.

Graphics

Cartoon

Cartoons are simple drawings that illustrate a point of view. Some cartoons have a caption, and others—like the one below—do not.

EXAMPLE

Two Men In Bottles

DESCRIPTION

A **cartoon** can make a point more quickly and bluntly than persuasive writing, such as an editorial. Besides, the skillful use of humor is one of the most effective ways of persuading people.

Here's how to read a cartoon:

- Identify the subject of the cartoon. If the cartoon has a caption, labels, or any words at all, read these first.

- Look at the way people are dressed, the expressions on their faces, and what they are doing. Did you notice that the man who's laughing doesn't realize he's in a bottle? Sometimes the people may represent people in general, a specific group of people, or a particular person.

Cartoon, continued

- Examine the details, especially objects, pictures, or animals that may be symbols. For example, the donkey is a common symbol of the Democratic Party, and a dove often stands for peace. In the cartoon above, notice symbols for males and females on the elevator buttons.

- Look for irony. *Irony* occurs when the intended meaning is the opposite of what is shown or expected. For example, the cartoon above shows a businesswoman taking the stairs while businessmen take an elevator. The stairs are unexpected.

- Try to state in your own words what is taking place. The cartoon is pointing out that men have an easier path to career success than women and that it's unfair.

DEFINITION

A cartoon is a drawing that uses humor and sometimes words or symbols to express a particular point of view.

Graphics

Diagram

Have you ever heard the expression "A picture is worth a thousand words"? With many subjects, diagrams are the best way to help readers see how something works.

EXAMPLE

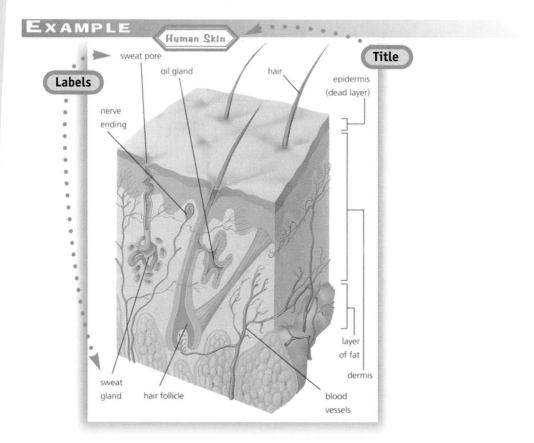

Human Skin

Title

Labels

sweat pore

oil gland

hair

epidermis
(dead layer)

nerve
ending

sweat
gland

hair follicle

layer
of fat

dermis

blood
vessels

DESCRIPTION

It would be difficult to picture in your mind the layers and structures of human skin from words alone. But a **diagram** makes it easier to see and understand.

Here's how to read a diagram:

- Read the title to find out what the diagram shows.
- Read each label and look at the part it identifies.
- Follow any arrows or numbers showing the steps in a process and read any captions.

Diagram, continued

- You don't need to draw conclusions from a diagram. You just need to understand and remember what it shows.

- Diagrams often go along with the text. As you read, you'll need to switch back and forth between the text and the diagrams to understand what is being described.

- Read the text of the diagram more than once. On the first reading, just try to get a general grasp of the subject. When you reread, focus on the details. You may want to make a list of terms and define them in your own words.

  1. **Crown**—visible part of tooth
  2. **Enamel**—hard material that covers the crown
  3. **Dentine**—tough material under the enamel

- To help you remember a diagram, try to redraw it. Just a simple, rough drawing like the one on the right will help you remember.

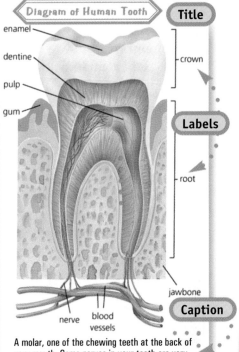

Diagram of Human Tooth — **Title**

enamel
dentine
pulp
gum
crown
Labels
root
jawbone
Caption
nerve
blood vessels

A molar, one of the chewing teeth at the back of your mouth. Some nerves in your teeth are very sensitive to temperature. A hot drink followed by a cold ice cream can make your teeth ache.

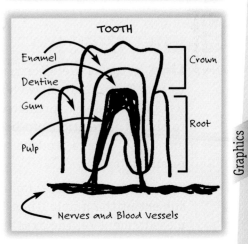

TOOTH

Enamel
Dentine
Gum
Pulp
Crown
Root
Nerves and Blood Vessels

Graphics

DEFINITION

A **diagram** is a drawing with labels that shows or explains something.

Line Graph

Line graphs show a series of data points connected by a line. In the example below, the data points are the number of people at a given time.

EXAMPLE

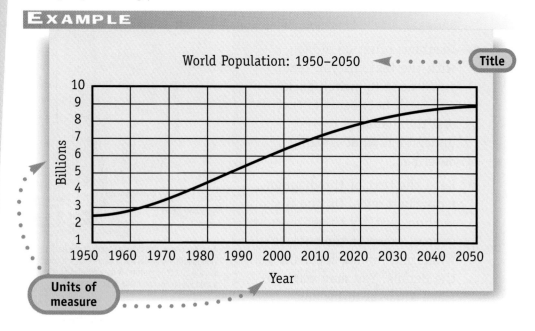

World Population: 1950–2050 ◀ • • • • • • Title

Units of measure • • • • • • • • Year

DESCRIPTION

Line graphs are often used to show changes over time, or trends. This graph shows how quickly the world population has grown—and is predicted to grow. Graphs also can be used to show the relationship between two things, such as the amount of time a student spends studying and the grades he or she gets.

When you read a line graph, read the title to find out the subject of the graph. Then check the labels or units of measurement on the axes to see what the graph compares. Study the slant of the line. The steeper the line, the faster the rate of change.

DEFINITION

A **line graph** shows data plotted at different times or places and usually is used to show a rate of change.

Map

A map shows all or part of the earth's surface or the heavens. Maps provide information about places through lines, colors, shapes, and symbols.

EXAMPLE

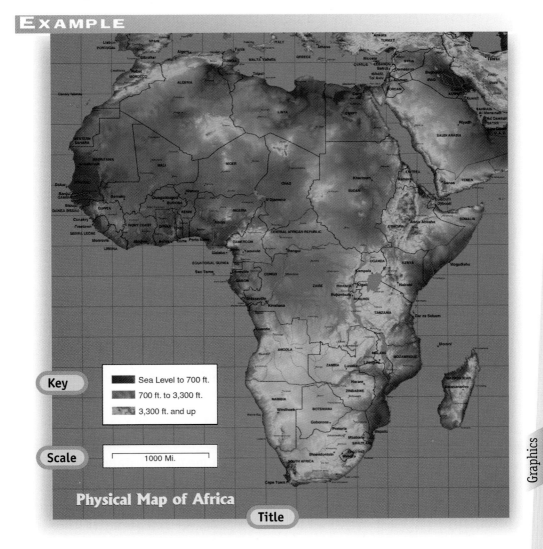

Key

Sea Level to 700 ft.

700 ft. to 3,300 ft.

3,300 ft. and up

Scale

1000 Mi.

Physical Map of Africa

Title

Graphics

555

Map, continued

DESCRIPTION

Maps help to describe the location, distance, and physical features of places. They can help people locate different places. Maps can show almost any kind of information about places—political boundaries, routes, climate, population, natural resources, pollution, economic activity, battles, and land purchases.

Figure out the type of map you're reading.

KINDS OF MAPS

KIND OF MAP	WHAT IT MAINLY SHOWS
Physical	Physical features, such as land elevations, rivers, and lakes
Political	Political units, such as the boundaries between countries, states, and cities
Road	Roads and highways
Historical	Events or political boundaries in the past
Thematic	Information on specific topics, such as climate or population density

Here's how to read a map:

- Read the title to find the subject of the map.
- Look at the map key or legend to find out what the colors or symbols on the map mean.
- Figure out what kind of information the map shows and focus on what you're trying to find out.
- Check the map's scale if you need to measure distances or get an idea of size.

DEFINITION

A **map** is a drawing that shows part or all of the earth's surface and usually includes places such as boundaries between countries, bodies of water, and the like.

Photograph

Photographs show images from real life as they are captured by a camera. You've probably looked at thousands of photographs without examining them very critically. But photographs can carry strong, carefully crafted messages.

EXAMPLE

Photo by Dorothea Lange

DESCRIPTION

When you read a **photograph**, identify the subject and read any caption or text, even text in the photograph. Next, examine some of the choices the photographer made. The chart below highlights some of the elements to look for in a photograph.

ELEMENTS OF PHOTOGRAPHS

ELEMENTS	EFFECTS
Type of shot	Close-up shots encourage the viewer to identify with the subject. Wide-angle shots emphasize the setting.
Positioning of the subject	A photographer can choose how to position the subject by changing the camera angle, by framing, or by cropping. Depending on positioning, the subject can be made to seem important, insignificant, or dominating.
Lighting	Dim light or shadows can create a sad or scary mood. Bright light can produce an optimistic, happy mood.
Color or tone	Bright colors suggest energy and excitement, while dark colors might create a sad or mysterious mood.

DEFINITION

A **photograph** is a picture from real life made with a camera. Usually it is made on a photosensitive surface, such as film or a magnetic disk.

Graphics

Pie Chart

Pie charts, sometimes also called circle graphs, are used to show the parts that make up a whole. They show a circle divided into pieces, or parts.

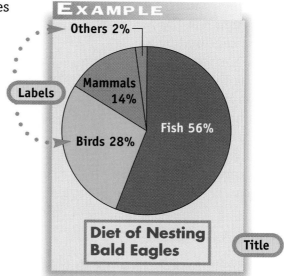

EXAMPLE

Others 2%

Mammals 14%

Labels

Fish 56%

Birds 28%

Diet of Nesting Bald Eagles

Title

DESCRIPTION

Pie charts are used to show the parts that make up a whole. They emphasize the relative size or importance of the different parts. The entire circle equals 100 percent. The pieces of the pie are different parts, or percentages, of the whole.

Here's what to look for in a pie chart:

- Read the title to find the subject.
- Find out what the parts represent by reading the labels or checking the legend.
- Compare the sizes of the pieces of the pie.
- Be aware that pie charts show major factors well but tend to minimize the smaller factors (such as the 2% marked "Other" in the example above).

DEFINITION

A **pie chart** shows parts that make up a whole. It is used to show the relative size or importance of parts.

Table

Tables are among the most common type of graphic. You're probably familiar with tables that present all kinds of data, from statistics on baseball trading cards to population figures in an almanac.

EXAMPLE

Mark McGwire Statistics — **Title**

Row headings

MARK McGWIRE	McGwire, Mark David b: 10/1/63, Pomona, Cal. BR/TR 6'5", 225 lbs Deb: 8/22/86											
YEAR	TM/L	G	AB	R	H	2B	3B	HR	RBI	BB	SO	AVG
1986	Oak-A	18	53	10	10	1	0	3	9	4	18	.189
1987	Oak-A*	151	557	97	161	28	4	49	118	71	131	.289
1988	Oak-A*	155	550	87	143	22	1	32	99	76	117	.260
1989	Oak-A*	143	490	74	113	17	0	33	95	83	94	.231
1990	Oak-A*	156	523	87	123	16	0	39	108	110	116	.235
1991	Oak-A+	154	483	62	97	22	0	22	75	93	116	.201
1992	Oak-A*	139	467	87	125	22	0	42	104	90	105	.268
1993	Oak-A	27	84	16	28	6	0	9	24	21	19	.333
1994	Oak-A	47	135	26	34	3	0	9	25	37	40	.252
1995	Oak-A+	104	317	75	87	13	0	39	90	88	77	.274
1996	Oak-A*	130	423	104	132	21	0	52	113	116	112	.312
	Oak-A*	105	366	48	104	24	0	34	81	58	98	.284
	StL-N	51	174	38	44	3	0	24	42	43	61	.253
	StL-N*	155	509	130	152	21	0	70	147	162	155	.299
Total:	13	1535	5131	941	1353	219	5	457	1130	1052	1259	.264

Year column

DESCRIPTION

A **table** presents data in columns and rows. Tables are used to organize, simplify, and summarize information for easy reference. Look at how much information is packed into a small space. With tables, you need to be able to find a specific number or statistic or compare statistics across years.

Here's how to read a table:

- First, look at the title.

- Next, read *down* the outside column and *across* the top. Note the headings. Make sure you understand what data is being shown in the columns and rows. (For instance, did you know the "SO" means strikeouts?)

Graphics

Table, continued

U.S. Population Data — Title				Years	
POPULATION	1990	1995	1997	1998	1999
Resident population (mil.)	248.8	262.8	267.8	270.2	272.7
Male	121.3	128.3	130.8	132.0	133.
Female	127.5	134.5	137.0	138.2	139.4
Percent of population—					
Under 18 yrs. old	25.7	26.1	26.0	25.9	25.7
65 yrs. old and over	12.5	12.8	12.8	12.7	12.7
White	83.9	83.0	82.7	82.5	82.4
Black	12.3	12.6	12.7	12.7	12.8
Asian and Pacific Islander	3.0	3.6	3.8	3.9	4.0
American Indian, Eskimo, Aleut	0.8	0.9	0.9	0.9	0.9
Hispanic	9.0	10.3	10.9	11.2	11.5
Northeast	20.4	19.6	19.3	19.1	19.0
Midwest	24.0	23.6	23.4	23.3	23.2
South	34.4	34.9	35.2	35.3	35.4
West	21.2	21.9	22.2	22.3	22.4
Metropolitan area	79.8	79.9	80.0	80.1	(N/A)
Households (mil.)	93.3	99.0	101.0	102.5	103.9
Percent one person	24.6	25.0	25.1	25.7	25.6
Families (mil.)	66.1	69.3	70.2	70.9	71.5
With children under 18 yrs. (mil.)	32.3	34.3	34.7	34.8	34.6
Percent one-parent	24.0	26.4	27.6	27.3	27.6

Heading categories

Read down the outside column and across.

- If you don't understand abbreviations or terms used in the column or row headings, look them up or ask someone. For instance, in the population table above, what exactly is a "metropolitan area"? Does it mean a big city and its suburbs? Or would it include even small towns?

- Use your finger or a ruler to find specific data. First, go down the outside column on the left to the correct row. Then, move across that row to the column you're interested in.

- Survey and compare the rows and columns. What similarities and differences or patterns do you see?

- Think for a minute about information that's not included.

DEFINITION

A **table** is a list of statistics or information on a subject, usually arranged in columns and rows.

Timeline

A timeline highlights key events and gives the reader a visual picture of the order in which they occurred.

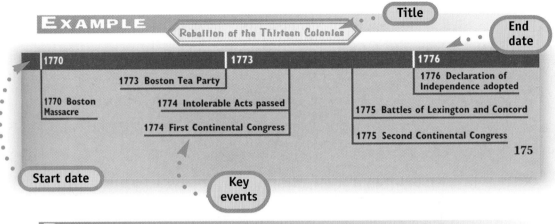

EXAMPLE

Title

End date

Rebellion of the Thirteen Colonies

1770	1773	1776

1773 Boston Tea Party

1770 Boston Massacre

1774 Intolerable Acts passed

1774 First Continental Congress

1776 Declaration of Independence adopted

1775 Battles of Lexington and Concord

1775 Second Continental Congress

175

Start date

Key events

DESCRIPTION

A **timeline** shows when a series of events took place. The events are listed along a horizontal or vertical line. Labels on the timeline usually name a specific year in which an event occurred. Timelines are often used to give either a preview or a summary of the events that are described later or earlier in the book.

Here's how to read a timeline:

- Sometimes there will be a title or caption explaining the general subject. Read it first.

- Look at the start and end dates of the timeline. These dates indicate the span of years that is covered.

- Read each date and event that is highlighted on the timeline. Note what comes before and after each event.

DEFINITION

A **timeline** shows a series of events in time order.

Graphics

Reading
for Tests

Reading a Test and Test Questions

Focus on Kinds of Tests

Focus on Essay Tests
Focus on Vocabulary Tests
Focus on Social Studies Tests
Focus on Math Tests
Focus on Science Tests

Tests

Reading a Test and Test Questions

Tests are a way of life when you're a student. They will be given whether you like it or not. There's no avoiding them. So here's some help when you have to take them.

That's what this part of the handbook will show you—how to prepare better for and perform better on tests by applying the reading process.

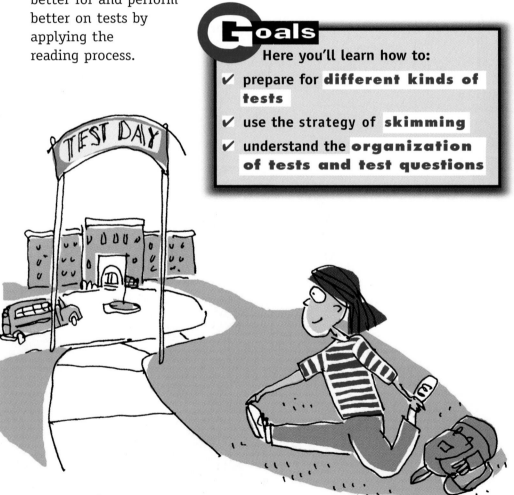

Goals

Here you'll learn how to:

✔ prepare for **different kinds of tests**

✔ use the strategy of **skimming**

✔ understand the **organization of tests and test questions**

Before Reading

Long before you begin reading the first test question, you can start getting ready for the test. Here are a few of the things you can do:

■ Prepare yourself. Get "psyched up" for the test by treating it like a big race or contest.

■ Get plenty of rest and eat well on the days before the exam.

■ Reduce "text anxiety" by getting ready beforehand.

A Set a Purpose

What's your purpose when reading tests? Well, one is certainly to answer the questions correctly.

One way to do that is to remain calm and not get flustered. Some tests can make you panic, so you don't think straight. Take your time, breathe deeply, and be sure you understand each test question and what it is asking. Your reading purpose with tests is simple:

Setting a Purpose

■ **What is the test question asking?**

■ **What information is needed for the answer?**

Learn everything you can about the kind of test you'll take and the kinds of questions that will be on it. Then, study your notes, textbook, and any vocabulary that may help you get ready.

Tests

B Preview

On the day of the test, bring with you all the materials you need. Have several pencils and at least one highlighter. You might also want to bring along your notes, in case you have a few minutes before the test to review them.

When your teacher passes out the test, start with a preview. Page through the test. Read the directions and at least three or four of the questions. Look for the following:

Preview Checklist

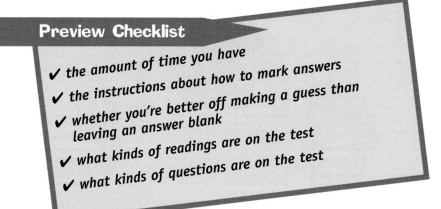

✔ the amount of time you have

✔ the instructions about how to mark answers

✔ whether you're better off making a guess than leaving an answer blank

✔ what kinds of readings are on the test

✔ what kinds of questions are on the test

Now preview the reading test on the next page. Use the Preview Checklist to give you a feeling for what the test will be about and the kinds of questions on it.

PREVIEW

Amount of time and question types

Mid-year Reading Test

60 Minutes—4 Questions, 1 Essay

DIRECTIONS: Answer each question. Choose the correct answer and then fill in the corresponding oval on your answer sheet. Write your essay in the blue test booklet.

Do not linger over problems that seem too difficult. Skip these and return to them later. You will not be penalized for wrong answers.

PREVIEW

Special instructions

Mid-year Reading Test
"Kas-ki-yeh"
from <u>Geronimo: His Own Story</u>

How would you feel if your whole family were under attack? Think about this question as you read this passage from Geronimo's autobiography. Then answer the questions that follow.

PREVIEW

Reading about Geronimo

KAS-KI-YEH

NOTE
Subject of reading

PART 1—THE MASSACRE

In the summer of 1858, being at peace with the Mexican towns as well as with all the neighboring Indian tribes, we went south into Old Mexico to trade. Our whole tribe (Bedonkohe Apaches) went through Sonora toward Casa Grande, our destination, but just before reaching that place we stopped at another Mexican town called by the Indians "Kas-ki-yeh." Here we stayed for several days, camping just outside the city. Every day we would go into town to trade, leaving our camp under the protection of a small guard so that our arms, supplies, and women and children would not be disturbed during our absence.

Late one afternoon when returning from town we were met by a few women and children who told us that Mexican troops from some other town had attacked our camp, killed

NOTE
Important details about who, what, when, and where

Tests

all the warriors of the guard, captured all our ponies, secured our arms, destroyed our supplies, and killed many of our women and children. Quickly we separated, concealing ourselves as best we could until nightfall, when we assembled at our appointed place of rendezvous—a thicket by the river. Silently we stole in one by one: sentinels were placed, and, when all were counted, I found that my aged mother, my young wife, and my three small children were among the slain. There were no lights in camp, so without being noticed I silently turned away and stood by the river. How long I stood there I do not know, but when I saw the warriors arranging for a council I took my place.

NOTE
Important fact

That night I did not give my vote for or against any measure; but it was decided that as there were only eighty warriors left, and as we were without arms or supplies, and were furthermore surrounded by the Mexicans far inside their own territory, we could not hope to fight successfully. So our chief, Mangus-Colorado, gave the order to start at once in perfect silence for our homes in Arizona, leaving the dead upon the field.

NOTE
Key detail

I stood until all had passed, hardly knowing what I would do—I had no weapon, nor did I hardly wish to fight, neither did I contemplate recovering the bodies of my loved ones, for that was forbidden. I did not pray, nor did I resolve to do anything in particular, for I had no purpose left. I finally followed the tribe silently, keeping just within hearing distance of the soft noise of the feet of the retreating Apaches.

NOTE
Subject of paragraph

The next morning some of the Indians killed a small amount of game and we halted long enough for the tribe to cook and eat, when the march was resumed. I had killed no game, and did not eat. During the first march as well as while we were camped at this place I spoke to no one and no one spoke to me—there was nothing to say.

NOTE
Important detail

For two days and three nights we were on forced

marches, stopping only for meals; then we made a camp near the Mexican border, where we rested two days. Here I took some food and talked with the other Indians who had lost in the massacre, but none had lost as I had, for I had lost all.

Within a few days we arrived at our own settlement. There were the decorations that Alope had made—and there were the playthings of our little ones. I burned them all, even our tepee. I also burned my mother's tepee and destroyed all her property.

I was never again contented in our quiet home. True, I could visit my father's grave, but I had vowed vengeance upon the Mexican troopers who had wronged me, and whenever I came near his grave or saw anything to remind me of former happy days my heart would ache for revenge upon Mexico.

> **NOTE**
>
> Key information in first and last sentences of paragraphs

English: Mid-year Reading Test
Multiple-choice Questions

> **PREVIEW**
>
> Several multiple-choice questions

1. Why do Geronimo and his people go into Old Mexico?
   A. for an ambush
   B. to trade
   C. to hunt game
   D. to search for members of their tribe

2. What is the setting for this part of the memoir?
   A. Mexico City and Arizona, 1855
   B. Sonora and Casa Grande, 1958
   C. Kas-ki-yeh and Arizona, 1858
   D. Texas and Arizona, 1858

3. At one point, Geronimo says, ". . . neither did I contemplate recovering the bodies of my loved ones, for that was forbidden." What does *contemplate* mean?
   A. decide to
   B. make preparations for
   C. search for
   D. think about

Tests

4. What do you think Geronimo means when he says, ". . . but none had lost as I had, for I had lost all" (paragraph 6)?

    A. He's upset because his tepee and possessions were all burned.

    B. He's sad because his family is gone forever.

    C. He's worried because he does not know how to get back to Arizona.

    D. He is angry that other tribe members are not grieving.

PREVIEW

One essay question

Essay Question

5. Explain what happens to Geronimo at Kas-ki-yeh. In your short-essay answer, tell how he changes and what caused the changes. Support your answer with evidence from the text.

C Plan

Your preview gave you an idea of the number and kinds of questions you'll be answering. Did you notice that some questions ask for factual recall and others for critical thinking? For question #1, for example, you'll need to find some facts mentioned in the passage. For the essay, you'll make some judgments about what you've read.

Reading Strategy: Skimming

Most tests require you to go back to a passage again and again to look for specific answers to questions. Because of that, a good strategy to use is **skimming**. Skimming—like you did when you previewed—can help you get a general sense of what's there. But skimming can also help you locate specific information.

After you first read a test and begin answering the questions, you probably feel—yikes!—you didn't get *all that* when you read it. Relax. Hardly anyone can answer all of the test questions after one reading.

Most test-takers try to read the passage once and then answer the questions. But good test-takers know how to go back again and again into the passage to find specific information. That's the key strategy for reading tests—knowing what information you need and rereading until you find it.

When you skim, your eyes glance quickly at each page. Use your finger, a note card, or a ruler as a reading tool. By running your finger or ruler down the page, you can gain a sense of the entire passage in as little as 30 seconds.

Tests

During Reading

A careful reading of the test passage is essential. Rushing through it to get to the questions quickly is always a mistake.

D Read with a Purpose

At first, you'll need to read the passage slowly and carefully. Use a highlighter (if you are allowed to) to mark important sentences. Quite often, the first sentence of each paragraph will be important. Also, pay attention to the final sentence of the paragraph, which can give important facts and details.

Look back at the test passage from a school reading test. Notice how one reader highlighted important details in each paragraph. That can help later as you try to find answers to some questions.

Understanding the Question

One big mistake of test-takers is that they are in a hurry and do not read carefully. Read every word in each test question. Be sure you know what it is asking. Some questions can be tricky. Highlight or circle key words. If you hurry, you may not fully understand the question.

Look more closely at the questions about the Geronimo passage. Of the five questions, two ask you to recall a fact. Three of the questions ask you to make an inference or draw a conclusion. These are the two main types of test questions.

TEST QUESTIONS

Fact or Recall

You can find the answer "right there" in the test.

Inference or Conclusion

You must put what the author tells you with what you already know to come up with the answer.

Fact or Recall Questions

With the fact questions, you can find the answer *right there* in the text. Notice how important words in the questions have been highlighted.

---

from Mid-year Reading Test

1. Why do Geronimo and his people go into Old Mexico?
   A. for an ambush
   B. to trade
   C. to hunt game
   D. to search for members of their tribe

2. What is the setting for this part of the memoir?
   A. Mexico City and Arizona, 1855
   B. Sonora and Casa Grande, 1958
   C. Kas-ki-yeh and Arizona, 1858
   D. Texas and Arizona, 1858

You can find the answer to both questions *right there* in the passage. Be sure you pick out the key words in the questions. Every question will have some words that tell you what information to look for. Focus on finding those words.

Test questions also usually go in order through a passage, so with the first question, start at the beginning of the passage. In this case, the very first sentence answers the first question.

---

from Mid-year Reading Test

In the summer of 1858, being at peace with the Mexican towns as well as with all the neighboring Indian tribes, we went south into Old Mexico to trade.

Tests

Inference or Conclusion Questions

Some test questions do not have an answer stated in the passage. You have to think about what you learned in the passage, put that with what you know, and then make an inference or draw a conclusion. Here's an example.

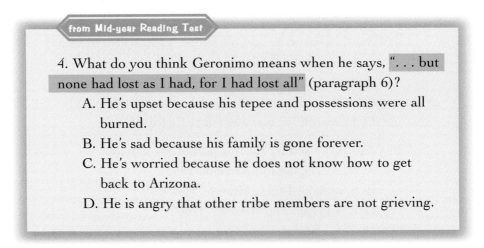

from Mid-year Reading Test

4. What do you think Geronimo means when he says, "... but none had lost as I had, for I had lost all" (paragraph 6)?
  A. He's upset because his tepee and possessions were all burned.
  B. He's sad because his family is gone forever.
  C. He's worried because he does not know how to get back to Arizona.
  D. He is angry that other tribe members are not grieving.

Frequently, test questions point you to a specific part of the passage (for example, paragraph 6) to examine a few words more closely. When that happens, here's what you need to do.

INFERENCE OR CONCLUSION QUESTIONS

First, *go to the part of the passage mentioned.*

Next, *find the words mentioned in the test question.*

Then, *read at least* three *sentences. Read the sentence that has the quote, the* sentence *before* it, *and one or two sentences* after *it.*

Most test-takers only look at the words mentioned in the question. You will score better on tests if you learn to read the sentence before, the sentence with the words mentioned, and the next sentences after the words mentioned in the question.

from Mid-year Reading Test

NOTE
Sentence before

    For two days and three nights we were on forced marches, stopping only for meals; then we made a camp near the Mexican border, where we rested two days. Here I took some food and talked with the other Indians who had lost in the massacre, but none had lost as I had, for I had lost all.

NOTE
Words in question

    Within a few days we arrived at our own settlement. There were the decorations that Alope had made—and there were the playthings of our little ones. I burned them all, even our tepee. I also burned my mother's tepee and destroyed all her property.

NOTE
Sentences after

By reading two sentences after the quote, you see Geronimo mentions his wife and children. That confirms for you the correct answer is "B. He's sad because his family is gone forever." As a reader, you put together what the passage says with the knowledge of how you might feel if you lost your entire family. You make an inference to come up with the answer.

How Tests Are Organized

In most cases, the questions in tests move from easy to hard. The questions about a passage also tend to follow the order of the reading. So, when you are rereading for question #1, look at the beginning of the passage. When you are rereading for question #4, look further along in the passage.

ORDER OF QUESTIONS

paragraph 1	*key information for question 1*
paragraphs 1–3	*key information for question 2*
paragraph 4	*key information for question 3*
paragraph 6	*key information for question 4*

Tests

In other words, if you find yourself unable to answer a question in the *middle* of the test, begin by rereading the *middle* of the passage.

575

E Connect

The idea of making connections to what's on a test may seem crazy. After all, your main focus is just answering the questions, right? Still, as you read a test, think about what you've learned elsewhere. Use these personal connections to help raise your test score.

For example, have you read anything about Geronimo before? Do you know any other story about injustices done to Native Americans? This knowledge can help you answer the questions about the passage.

Some essay questions will ask you to make a personal response to a reading passage. You'll need to form an opinion and back up your opinion with three or more strong supporting details. For example, here is one reader's opinion about the reading.

> **OPINION STATEMENT**
>
> **OPINION STATEMENT**
> I think it's terrible what happened to Geronimo and his people.
> **SUPPORTING DETAILS**
> #1 They came to Mexico as friends, not enemies.
> #2 Their women and children were slaughtered.
> #3 They were surrounded and forced to leave Mexico and the bodies of their loved ones behind.

After Reading

F Pause and Reflect

After you complete the test, take a moment to gather your thoughts. Take stock of what you've done, what you still need to do, and how much time is left. Ask questions like these:

- **Have I answered all of the questions?**
- **Are there answers I should check?**
- **What do I need to spend more time on?**

You meet your reading purpose only if you find all the information you need. So, you'll probably double back and reread. You may want to return to the questions you skipped and give them another try. Sometimes rereading a question a second or third time is all you need to "get it." You'll also want to check the answers to some questions. Make sure you didn't skip anything and look for distracting errors in spelling, punctuation, or grammar that could lower your final score.

G Reread

One excellent strategy to try when you're going over a test is to visualize and think aloud. Suppose you didn't complete one question because it seemed hard. If you couldn't answer the question the first time, what should you do?

Rereading Strategy: Visualizing and Thinking Aloud

With a difficult question, try **visualizing and thinking aloud**. Go through each question again, silently talking yourself through the answer.

> from Mid-year Reading Test
>
> 3. At one point Geronimo says, ". . . neither did I contemplate recovering the bodies of my loved ones, for that was forbidden." What does *contemplate* mean?
>   A. decide to
>   B. make preparations for
>   C. search for
>   D. think about

Find and reread the part of the passage that contains the quote.

NOTE

Passage that contains key word

I stood until all had passed, hardly knowing what I would do—I had no weapon, nor did I hardly wish to fight, neither did I contemplate recovering the bodies of my loved ones, for that was forbidden.

By looking back at the passage, you can narrow down what you think *contemplate* means using context clues. Talk through the possible choices to yourself. Try using the answers instead of *contemplate* in the sentence. Right away, you can cross out two of the answers because they don't make sense.

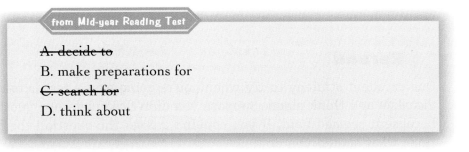

A. decide to

B. make preparations for

C. search for

D. think about

Now you have a better chance of guessing the answer. But, suppose from the context, you can't figure out which of the remaining two answers is correct. Think through the answer in your head. Visualize the scene that's described. Talk to yourself about the question.

THINK ALOUD

I'm not sure if <u>contemplate</u> means "think about" or "make preparations for." Geronimo seems to be standing still, deciding what to do. He says that recovering the bodies is "forbidden." Since he knows he's not permitted to do anything with the bodies, it's unlikely he'd "make preparations for" recovering them. He probably just thought about it. This makes me think that D is correct.

H Remember

Often, when you finish a test, you may just want to forget about it. You're happy it's over and want to go on to something else. But sometimes, you can learn a few things by thinking back on what the test asked.

1. Ask Questions and Find Answers

If you had trouble with a question, ask a classmate how he or she answered it. Write down the question or concept that gave you trouble. Chances are good you will run into it again, if not in that class then later in another one. So, look up the word or idea that puzzled you. Ask your teacher about it.

2. Go Over It

If you get a test back, look it over. Sometimes you'll spend class time going over a test. Pay attention to what the teacher says about the questions, sample answers, or tips on preparation for the next test. Even if you don't go over a test together, or have to turn it back in, read any comments carefully. If you missed a question, be sure you understand why. Looking over a previous test is one way of getting ready for the next one.

Summing Up

Remember when you read a test to use the reading process. Preview the test questions and get a sense of how the test is organized. Apply the reading strategy of **skimming** during the test. Think how test questions can be divided into **two basic types**:

- Factual or Recall
- Inference or Conclusion

That will help you know what you need to do to answer them. Remember, too, that the rereading strategy of **visualizing and thinking aloud** is helpful for answering the last few questions and for checking your work.

Tests

Focus on Essay Tests

On many tests, you will be asked to write a brief essay or respond to a question in several paragraphs. Usually the essay has to be written in a short period of time and, often, after you've had to answer a number of multiple-choice, true-false, or other objective questions.

You're tired, and the essay is still waiting for you. But the job can be a lot easier than you think.

Goals

Here you'll learn how to:

✔ **read an essay question and get ready for an essay test**

✔ **use graphic organizers to help you get ready to write**

Before Reading

Most tests have at least two parts. The first contains factual questions—multiple-choice, true-false, matching, and so on. The second part of the test often will be writing an essay. As you preview the test, look to see if you have to write an essay. You may also have to read a passage before you write. Plan to leave at least 15–20 minutes for the essay part of the test.

Once you see an essay question, be sure to preview it. Read it over. Get an idea of what you'll be writing about later. Giving your brain some advance warning will help you be ready when it's time to write.

During Reading

After you finish the factual or short answer part of the test, relax a minute. Reading is not the difficult part of essay tests. In fact, it can be the easiest part, but you can't hurry through it.

Reading Directions

Read the question and writing prompt (if there is one) carefully. Many students blow the essay question because they don't take time to read it carefully.

SAMPLE ESSAY QUESTION

DIRECTIONS: Write an opinion essay about wearing school uniforms. First, read the prompt below. Then, decide how you feel and offer support for your opinion. Proofread your work when you've finished.

Prompt: Some public schools have made it a rule that students wear uniforms to school. How do you feel about the idea of wearing uniforms at your school? Write an essay stating your opinion. Support it with 3–4 convincing reasons.

What did you learn? What's the assignment? As a reader, you look for key words in the directions and what they tell you about what to write. By doing this, you can spot five things in these directions.

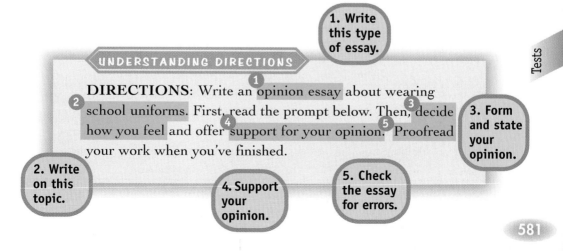

1. Write this type of essay.

UNDERSTANDING DIRECTIONS

DIRECTIONS: Write an opinion essay about wearing school uniforms. First, read the prompt below. Then, decide how you feel and offer support for your opinion. Proofread your work when you've finished.

2. Write on this topic.

3. Form and state your opinion.

4. Support your opinion.

5. Check the essay for errors.

Planning the Essay

You need a plan for timed writings. You may feel rushed and in a hurry, but you don't want to write whatever pops into your mind. Your score depends in part on how well you follow directions. To help you follow the directions, use a Main Idea Organizer like the one below. It can help you sort out what you will say. This is an all-purpose organizer. You can use it for almost any essay test.

MAIN IDEA ORGANIZER

MY IDEA		
DETAIL 1	DETAIL 2	DETAIL 3
CONCLUDING SENTENCE		

You may not always need—or have the time—to complete an organizer in detail. The point is to think through what you want to say and make some notes for yourself—a list of several points or words. Make sure you have all of the elements asked for in the writing prompt. Plan to write an essay of at least five to six sentences.

MAIN IDEA ORGANIZER

MY IDEA I think school uniforms should be a choice, rather than something students have to do.		
DETAIL 1	DETAIL 2	DETAIL 3
Being a kid is all about expressing yourself. The clothes you choose can tell others a lot about you.	School uniforms are expensive. It would be better for us to use the money for books or software.	Uniforms can make our school-to-school rivalries worse. This might lead to more fights in public places.
CONCLUDING SENTENCE School uniforms might make sense for some schools, but they won't work here at Eleanor Roosevelt Middle School.		

After Reading

After you write your essay, go back and read it over. First, look at the "big picture"—what you've said and how you've organized it. Read what you've written and answer these questions to help you revise:

■ Have I answered the question clearly and completely?

■ Is my main idea clear?

■ Have I included enough supporting details?

■ Is my essay easy to follow, with an introduction, body, and conclusion?

■ Have I included the five things asked for in the directions?

After you've got the "big things"—content and organization—set, it's time to look at the "little things." Remember that proofreading for errors can affect your score. On most essay tests, even the simplest spelling, punctuation, or usage mistakes will count against you. So take the time to check your work and make your corrections neatly!

Summing Up

■ **Read the question carefully, looking for key words that tell you what to write.**

■ **Plan your response by making notes or using a graphic organizer.**

■ **Leave enough time to read your essay, make any revisions, and check for errors.**

Tests

Focus on Vocabulary Tests

Vocabulary tests check your knowledge of words and word parts. Some vocabulary tests also look at your ability to understand analogies, which are the relationships between word pairs.

Goals

Here you'll learn how to:

✔ **improve your knowledge of words and vocabulary tests**
✔ **build your vocabulary**
✔ **understand word analogies and use context clues**

Before Reading

Most vocabulary tests have at least two parts. The first part has sentences with blanks that you are to complete, or it asks for synonyms, antonyms, or definitions of words. The second part of many vocabulary tests is a series of word analogies.

The best way to improve your vocabulary is to read more. That's all you have to do. Read. Read at least an hour every day, and your vocabulary will grow (just like the hair on your head) without your knowing it.

Reading exposes you to all different kinds of words, over and over again. That's the secret to building your vocabulary. Read every day, and the number of words in your vocabulary will go up. If you don't read much, you'll have to work a great deal harder to learn new words.

Vocabulary tests can be difficult to prepare for, unless your teacher or school has a good vocabulary program. Here are a few ideas for preparing for vocabulary tests by starting a vocabulary program of your own.

Tip #1: Use Flash Cards or a Vocabulary Notebook

Flash cards can help you memorize key words and their definitions. Find a set of index cards and then cut each card in half, so the pack is small enough to fit in your pocket. Write key words on the front of the cards and definitions on the back. Test yourself on the cards as often as you can. Keep them in your pocket or backpack and pull them out whenever you have some "downtime"—while riding in the car or waiting for a bus. (You can also use a vocabulary notebook, if you prefer that to cards.)

Tip #2: Learn Prefixes, Suffixes, and Roots

Before a test, brush up on your knowledge of prefixes, suffixes, and roots. You will find lists of the most common ones in the Almanac in the back of this handbook (see pages 685–692). Read through the lists. Put the most common prefixes, suffixes, and roots on flash cards and study them. After all, once you know *auto-* means "self," you're on your way to knowing half of a big word family.

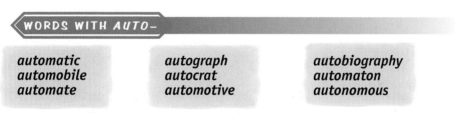

WORDS WITH *AUTO—*

automatic	*autograph*	*autobiography*
automobile	*autocrat*	*automaton*
automate	*automotive*	*autonomous*

Many vocabulary tests are quite long, so do a quick preview. If you see words you know, answer the questions that contain these words right away. That will start you off with confidence.

During Reading

After your preview, begin working through the test. If you come to a word you're unsure of, first eliminate the answers that are obviously wrong. Look for word parts that can give you clues about meaning. If you don't recognize any word parts, use sound-alikes or context clues to help you predict the correct answer.

Tests

Tip #3: Use Context Clues

You can also use context clues to help you find the meaning of an unknown word. The *context* of a word is the words or sentences nearby. Authors will often include synonyms, definitions, descriptions, or other information that will help you figure out a word's meaning.

For example, read the test question below. What context clues can you find about the meaning of the underlined word?

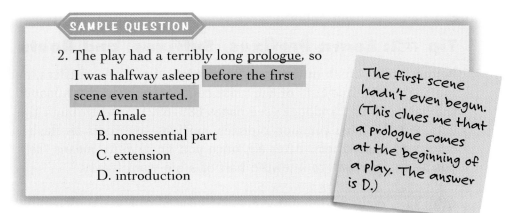

SAMPLE QUESTION

2. The play had a terribly long <u>prologue</u>, so I was halfway asleep before the first scene even started.

 A. finale

 B. nonessential part

 C. extension

 D. introduction

The first scene hadn't even begun. (This clues me that a prologue comes at the beginning of a play. The answer is D.)

Tip #4: Understand Analogies

Word analogies test your ability to figure out relationships between words. You need to look at a pair of words (for example, *cold : frigid*) and decide how they are related.

COMMON KINDS OF WORD ANALOGIES

Set and subset (*color : blue*)
Succession or pattern (*zig : zag*)

Synonyms (*dry : parched*)
Antonyms (*cold : hot*)

Greater than or less than (*skyscraper : house*)
Relationship (or proportion) to each other (*adult : child*)

Your job is to first figure out how the word pair is related and then choose another pair that shows the same relationship.

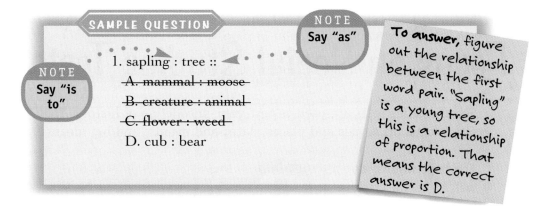

SAMPLE QUESTION

NOTE Say "is to"

NOTE Say "as"

1. sapling : tree ::
   A. mammal : moose
   B. creature : animal
   C. flower : weed
   D. cub : bear

To answer, figure out the relationship between the first word pair. "Sapling" is a young tree, so this is a relationship of proportion. That means the correct answer is D.

After Reading

When you finish the vocabulary test, you'll need to check your answers for mistakes. You are looking for careless errors, perhaps because you read a question too quickly or marked the answer carelessly.

Be sure you've completed each item. If you have time, rework a few of the analogies that gave you the most trouble. But try not to doubt yourself. If you tried your best, stick with your answers. Unless you see something is obviously wrong, the chances are that your first instinct about an answer is as good as or better than your second or third guess at it. After reading, you want to proofread your answers, not outsmart yourself.

Summing Up

- **The best way to improve your knowledge of vocabulary is to read a lot.**
- **Before you take a vocabulary test, study words, prefixes, suffixes, and word roots.**
- **Drawing on your memory, using context clues, and knowing the kinds of analogies will help you do well on vocabulary tests.**

Tests

Focus on Social Studies Tests

Social studies tests are used to test your knowledge of history. They often focus on names and places, dates and events, and big ideas.

The best way to do well in social studies is to do the reading in your textbook over the course of the year and to read outside of class. But you can also do some things to get ready for a test.

Goals

Here you'll learn how to:

✔ get ready for social studies tests

✔ preview common elements on social studies tests, including maps and other graphics

✔ use your time well and think through possible answers

Before Reading

When preparing for a social studies test, begin with your textbook. If the test is a final or mid-term, go back through the chapters you have been studying. Begin studying for a social studies test well before the day of the test. Study these items:

Names, dates, people, and places Try to learn one or two names, dates, and places from each chapter.

Key terms and concepts Look especially at the words in boldface in your textbook. Try to learn these terms.

Class notes What your teacher talks about in class will probably be on the test.

End-of-chapter questions Be sure you know something about the topics mentioned in these questions.

Maps, timelines, graphs, primary sources, and political cartoons Learn how to read these materials.

Tip #1: Create a Top Ten List

How can you study everything? You don't have to study everything; that would be an impossible job. Make it easy on yourself by creating a Top Ten List of topics to study. Include topics discussed in class and key terms from your reading. Learning even a few points on ten major topics could help you a lot. Here's a Top Ten List of topics in American history.

TOP TEN LIST

1. Pilgrims
2. American Revolution
3. Slavery
4. Civil War
5. World War I
6. Great Depression
7. World War II
8. Civil Rights
9. Cold War
10. Vietnam

You can use this idea with almost any subject. You might even list just five things. That's OK. The trick is to simplify things—a textbook chapter, several handouts, or a whole semester course.

Tip #2: Learn How to Read Graphics

Read through the part in this handbook or your history textbook about reading a map or other graphics. Questions about charts, timelines, graphs, and maps are frequently on social studies tests. Learn to read the titles, labels, captions, and map legends.

Tip #3: Use Graphic Organizers

Create Study Cards, Concept Maps, or other organizers to help you keep track of what you know. Making an organizer can help you review the subject yourself.

Tip #4: Preview the Test

Be sure to preview the directions and the questions on the test. You can read the first few questions in each part of the test or one or two on each page, but don't try to read *every* word.

Tests

Once you have previewed the test, begin by answering the easiest questions first. Work carefully through these questions one at a time. You'll want to save as much time as possible for the more challenging parts. If you can, use a highlighter or pencil to mark up the test. If a question seems hard, come back to it later. You may need to read it more carefully. Consider this example:

SAMPLE QUESTION

17. Lincoln's main goal throughout the Civil War was to:
    A. abolish slavery throughout the nation
    B. preserve the Union
    C. break the South's dependence on cotton
    D. end British control of the western territories

Tip #5: Rule Out Wrong Answers

Social studies tests often have multiple-choice questions, and with them it helps to rule out wrong answers. If you don't know the *right* answer immediately, look for answers you know are *wrong*. Cross out those first.

Tip #6: Think Through the Answer

When you finish the easiest questions, return to the more challenging ones and think through the answers. Rule out the wrong answers and work through the best ones.

SAMPLE QUESTION

17. Lincoln's main goal throughout the Civil War was to:
    A. abolish slavery throughout the nation
    B. preserve the Union
    C. break the South's dependence on cotton
    D. end British control of the western territories

A. I know he wanted to do this.

B. The Union was most important to him. B is correct.

C. I haven't ever heard this one.

D. No way this is right.

Tip #7: Read the Question for Clues

Read and reread each hard question. Remember that the question itself can give you a clue about the correct answer. The words *main goal* in the previous question suggest whichever answer seems *most* important.

Tip #8: Read the Graphics

Just as you have to read and reread each difficult question, you also have to read any graphics. Take time to notice all the parts of each visual, or graphic. Ask yourself what is being shown. The questions written for graphics are designed to make you draw conclusions to get information from them. Consider this question:

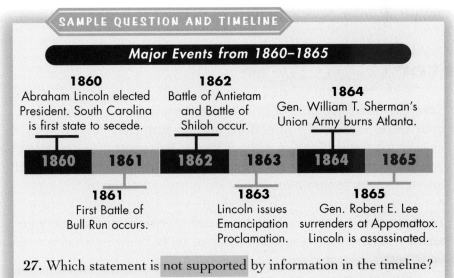

SAMPLE QUESTION AND TIMELINE

Major Events from 1860–1865

1860
Abraham Lincoln elected President. South Carolina is first state to secede.

1862
Battle of Antietam and Battle of Shiloh occur.

1864
Gen. William T. Sherman's Union Army burns Atlanta.

| 1860 | 1861 | 1862 | 1863 | 1864 | 1865 |

1861
First Battle of Bull Run occurs.

1863
Lincoln issues Emancipation Proclamation.

1865
Gen. Robert E. Lee surrenders at Appomattox. Lincoln is assassinated.

27. Which statement is not supported by information in the timeline?
   A. The Battle of Antietam followed the First Battle of Bull Run.
   B. General Robert E. Lee surrendered one year after the burning of Atlanta.
   C. South Carolina seceded two years before the Battle of Antietam.
   D. Lincoln was assassinated one year after the Battle of Shiloh.

What period in history does the timeline cover? Read *from left to right*. Note each date and then read the text with it. Work on understanding the graphic before you tackle the question.

Tests

I need to look at each possible answer and find the one that the timeline doesn't support.

- Answer A is supported. (Antietam was in 1862. Bull Run was in 1861.)
- Answer B is supported. (Lee surrended in 1865, and Atlanta burned in 1864.)
- Answer C is also supported. (South Carolina seceded two years before Antietam.)
- So, that leaves D. (The assassination was in 1865. That's three years after Shiloh, not one.) The timeline doesn't support D. So D is the correct answer.

Questions like this one can be challenging. Check each possible answer in order. Take your time, work through it, and don't give up!

After Reading

Save the last few minutes of the test period for a quick check of your work. Review the directions and be sure that you filled in an answer for every blank or answer space. Return to the questions you found the hardest. Try these one more time. You may find the answer comes to you more easily on a second attempt.

The best thing you can do is to reread questions and check your answers. Then, after the test, you can relax knowing that you did your best.

Summing Up

- **Begin studying for a social studies test by reviewing your textbook.**
- **Take a few minutes to preview the test questions.**
- **Read each question carefully. You may need to reread some questions more than once.**
- **Study the details of graphics before trying to answer questions about them.**

Focus on Math Tests

Much of your success on a math test will depend on you. You need to study carefully and thoroughly for small quizzes, chapter tests, and big mid-term or unit exams. You'll need to review key terms, memorize important formulas, and do practice problems.

Goals

Here you'll learn how to:

✔ **prepare for a math test**

✔ **use your time well during a math test**

✔ **understand word problems, equations, and graphics**

Before Reading

Preparing for a math test can take a few hours or a few days. A lot will depend on how well you already know the material. If possible, plan to study with one or more classmates.

Getting Ready

As you review earlier homework assignments, quizzes, and tests, do some of the problems again to make sure you still know how to solve them. Skim the chapter or chapters in your math book and do the practice problems.

Several days before the test, memorize key rules, terms, and formulas. Also review any diagrams, charts, and graphs that relate to the topics covered on the test. Be sure you know how to "read" these visuals. Questions about them will probably be on the test.

Tests

Previewing

When your teacher passes out the test, begin with a quick preview. Look to see how many questions you'll be asked to answer and how much time you'll be given. Try to get a sense for which questions will be easiest. Mark these with a star.

Think of taking the test in two parts. During the first part, you answer all of the easy questions. During the second part, you work on the hard ones, and in the last five minutes, you check your work.

During Reading

Begin working on the first starred problem. If you're not sure of an answer, make notes in the margin (or on scratch paper) so that you don't forget your first thoughts about the problem. After making your notes, move on to the next problem. For example:

> **SAMPLE QUESTION**
>
> 5. Is 1 a composite, prime, or neither?
>
> *1 is definitely not a prime.*
> *Is it a composite?*

When you've finished the easier starred problems, go back to the beginning to work on the challenging questions. Remember, some problems only look difficult.

Eliminating Wrong Answers

Use number sense to eliminate answers that are clearly wrong. Test questions often look harder than they actually are.

> **SAMPLE QUESTION**
>
> 57. $69.3 + (27.4 \times 3) =$
> A. 151.5
> B. 109.2
> ~~C. 139~~
> ~~D. 225~~
>
> *Because two of the numbers in this equation involve decimals, I can assume that the answer will involve a decimal as well. I can eliminate C+D right off the bat.*
> *(Correct answer is A.)*

Estimating the Answer

Estimate the answer, if you can. Often by doing some rough calculations, you can rule out one or two answers. Your chances of picking the right answer then get a lot better.

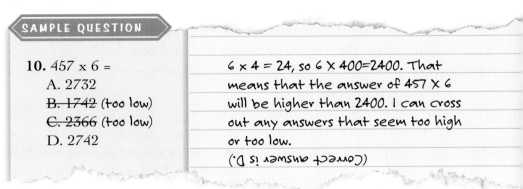

SAMPLE QUESTION

10. 457 x 6 =
   A. 2732
   B. ~~1742~~ (too low)
   C. ~~2366~~ (too low)
   D. 2742

6 x 4 = 24, so 6 x 400=2400. That means that the answer of 457 x 6 will be higher than 2400. I can cross out any answers that seem too high or too low.

(Correct answer is D.)

Visualizing the Answer

Try to visualize what word problems are saying. That will make them easier to understand. The math part of this problem is easy. The difficult part is sorting out what the question describes and what it is asking for.

SAMPLE QUESTION

1. Near Chicago, planes take off from two major airfields. One of the fields is capable of sending up a plane every 3 minutes. The other field is capable of sending up 2 planes every 3 minutes. At these rates, what is the total number of planes the two airfields could send up in 90 minutes?

   A. 20   B. 90   C. 130   D. 82

I need to figure out how many planes take off from each field and then add those totals.

1 plane every 3 minutes = 30 planes every 90 minutes.

2 planes every 3 minutes = 60 planes every 90 minutes.

(Correct answer is B.)

Tests

Trying Easier Choices First

Sometimes the only way to solve a math problem is to try solving it with the given answers. When you do that, first rule out any answers that look wrong. Then try the easier choices first, the ones with fewer digits or no decimals, for example. After all, why solve a bunch of hard problems when you might have gotten the answer by trying the easy one first?

SAMPLE QUESTION

4. Solve for the variable:
57 is x% of 90.

~~A. $x = 33.33$~~
B. $x = 63.33$
C. $x = 59$
~~D. $x = 127$~~

57 is more than half of 90, so A can't be right. 57 is less than 90, and D is more than 100%, so D can't be right. This means that the answer is either B or C. Since C is a simpler number, I'll try it first. 90 × .59 = 53.1 That means C is wrong.

(Correct answer is B.)

After Reading

If you're like many students, you probably left the problems involving figures (triangles, squares, rectangles), graphs, charts, and drawings for the very end. These problems may scare some students, even though they can be among the easiest on the test.

To solve a problem with a graphic, you often need to use formulas you've learned in class. That's what makes these problems hard, and this is why it's so important to study these formulas *before* the day of the test. Knowing just a few formulas can help you a lot on math tests, because important formulas are tested again and again.

Begin by looking at the graphic. Note anything that is special or different about it. Then, read the question with a highlighter in hand, marking the most important parts.

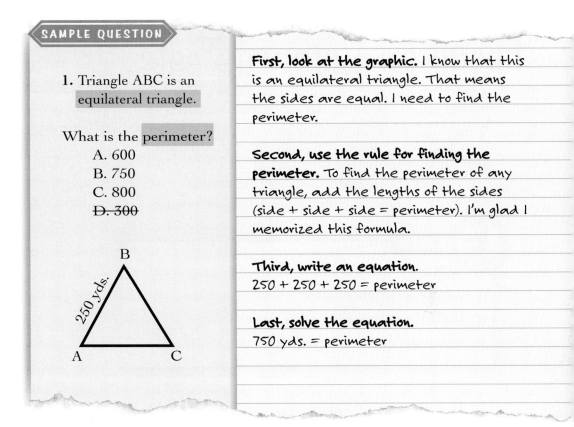

SAMPLE QUESTION

1. Triangle ABC is an equilateral triangle.

What is the perimeter?
  A. 600
  B. 750
  C. 800
  D. 300

B

250 yds.

A   C

First, look at the graphic. I know that this is an equilateral triangle. That means the sides are equal. I need to find the perimeter.

Second, use the rule for finding the perimeter. To find the perimeter of any triangle, add the lengths of the sides (side + side + side = perimeter). I'm glad I memorized this formula.

Third, write an equation.
250 + 250 + 250 = perimeter

Last, solve the equation.
750 yds. = perimeter

After you've finished the most challenging problems on the test, go back and check your work. Be sure you haven't skipped any questions and that your answers are legible.

As a general rule, try to check at least one-third of the problems before you hand in the test. This means leaving a good five or so minutes at the end of the test for checking answers.

Summing Up

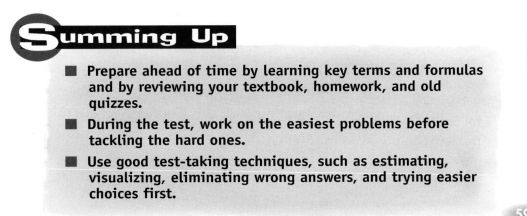

- Prepare ahead of time by learning key terms and formulas and by reviewing your textbook, homework, and old quizzes.

- During the test, work on the easiest problems before tackling the hard ones.

- Use good test-taking techniques, such as estimating, visualizing, eliminating wrong answers, and trying easier choices first.

Tests

Focus on Science Tests

Since much of the vocabulary in science is different from your everyday vocabulary, learning science sometimes seems like learning a whole new language. When you are preparing for science tests, spend time learning the language of science. You'll also need to think like a scientist and learn the scientific method.

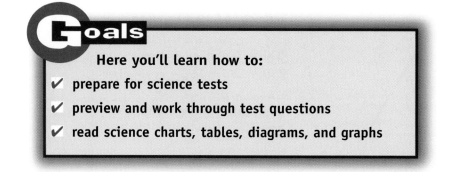

Goals

Here you'll learn how to:

✔ **prepare for science tests**

✔ **preview and work through test questions**

✔ **read science charts, tables, diagrams, and graphs**

Before Reading

The time to start preparing for a science test is not the night before. It's every day. Make it a habit to read carefully the material assigned in your science texts. Next, try to learn basic science terms, such as *molecule, ecology, photosynthesis, virus,* and so on.

Learn to take science notes—on what you do in class and what you read on your own. Predict what some test questions might be, based on what the teacher explained and the class discussed. By learning how to take good notes, you can come back and review and refresh your memory before the test day.

Even if you have already read your textbook and taken good notes, following a few tips can lead you to prepare for science tests in a way that will help you score better.

Tip #1: Make Visuals

Because science often describes the steps in a process, it's a good idea to draw a picture or visual. A picture is easier to remember than written notes. For example, one picture can help you remember the whole principle of the food chain or the steps in the metamorphosis of a caterpillar into a butterfly.

Tip #2: Skim for Science Terms

Look through chapters in your science textbook for key terms. Often they appear in boldface type within the chapter. The glossary in the back of your science book can also be an excellent resource for science terms. Use the glossary to search for definitions of words or concepts you don't know. Read the definition of a key term several times. Read it once to yourself, once out loud, and again to yourself. Repeating the terms and their definitions out loud will help you remember them. Try quizzing yourself on them. Read the term and try to give its definition.

Tip #3: Learn How to Read Graphics

Almost all science tests will have some charts or graphs you will have to read. Be sure you are comfortable with how to read them *before* the test. Review the graphics in your textbook and go over examples you have discussed in class. If necessary, review the pages in this handbook on reading charts and graphs.

Tip #4: Preview the Questions

When the teacher hands out the test, first preview it. Notice the time limit and any special instructions. Read the questions quickly to see what you will be asked to do on the test. Put a star by the questions that you know will be easy to answer. Glance at any charts, tables, or diagrams. You may need to save extra time for these graphics. Note whether or not you have an essay question to answer. Then, go back and start at the beginning, answering the easier questions first.

Tests

During Reading

You'll likely see a number of different kinds of factual questions on tests—from true-false and matching to fill-in-the-blank and multiple-choice. Make sure you read each question carefully. If you don't know what's being asked, how can you answer correctly? Make some notes or highlight important information in the question itself. Talk yourself through the question by eliminating any answers that are obviously wrong. Try to visualize what's being asked.

When you come to questions on graphics, ask yourself, "What is this graphic trying to show me?" Then read the question itself, highlighting key information you need to find. Understanding graphics can take time, but having a plan in mind will help you do well on science tests.

How to Read a Chart or Table

Most charts and tables have rows (going across) and columns (going down).

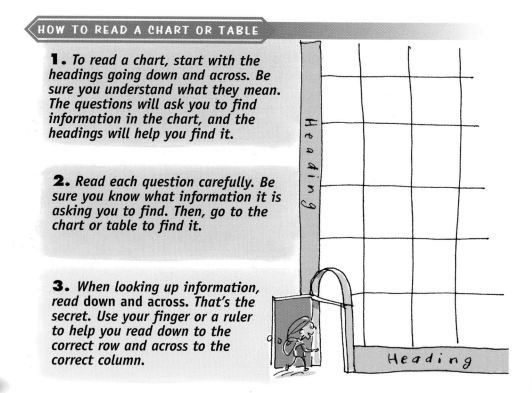

HOW TO READ A CHART OR TABLE

1. To read a chart, start with the headings going down and across. Be sure you understand what they mean. The questions will ask you to find information in the chart, and the headings will help you find it.

2. Read each question carefully. Be sure you know what information it is asking you to find. Then, go to the chart or table to find it.

3. When looking up information, read down and across. That's the secret. Use your finger or a ruler to help you read down to the correct row and across to the correct column.

Charts

SAMPLE QUESTIONS AND CHART

Planet	Made of	Atmosphere	Weight (of object that is 100 pounds on earth)		Gravity (compared to earth)
Jupiter	liquid and gas	helium, hydrogen	234 pounds		greater
Uranus	rock	helium, hydrogen, methane	91 pounds		less
Neptune	frozen gas	helium, methane, hydrogen	118 pounds		greater

1. Which planet has no methane in its atmosphere?
2. If you weighed 200 pounds on earth, how much would you weigh on Neptune?

To answer, find the "Atmosphere" heading of the chart and then sort through the facts. (The answer is Jupiter.)

To answer, find the section for Neptune under the "Weight" column. Double the Neptune weight. (The answer is 236 pounds.)

Tables

SAMPLE QUESTION AND TABLE

Green Tea

Nutrition Facts
Serving Size 1 tea bag (2g)
Servings Per Container 24

Amount Per Serving

Calories 0

	% Daily Value*
Total Fat 0g	0%
Sodium 0mg	0%
Potassium 20mg	1%
Total Carbohydrate 0g	0%
Protein 0g	
Folic Acid	2%

Not a significant source of calories from fat, saturated fat, cholesterol, dietary fiber, sugars, vitamin A, vitamin C, calcium and iron.

*Percent Daily Values are based on a 2,000 calorie diet.

INGREDIENTS: 100% Natural Green Tea

5. This beverage contains 1% daily value of what?
   A. protein
   B. potassium
   C. carbohydrates
   D. total fat

To answer, read down the "% Daily Value" column to find the 1% figure. Then move across to the left for the answer. (The answer is B.)

Tests

How to Read a Diagram

A diagram is a drawing designed to show how something works, how it is constructed, or how its parts relate to one another.

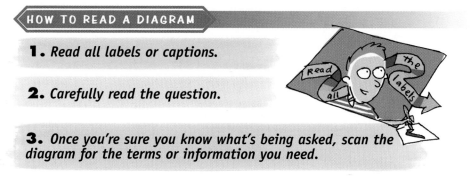

HOW TO READ A DIAGRAM

1. Read all labels or captions.

2. Carefully read the question.

3. Once you're sure you know what's being asked, scan the diagram for the terms or information you need.

Diagrams

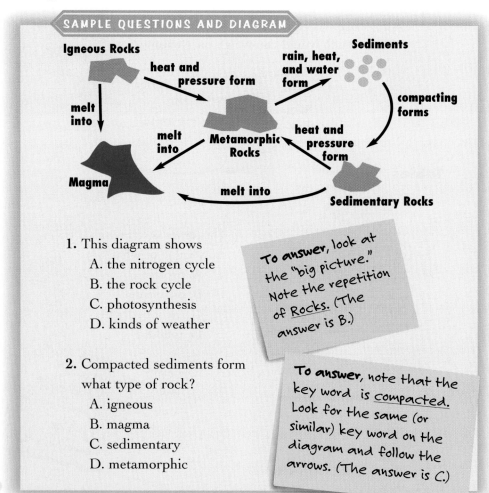

SAMPLE QUESTIONS AND DIAGRAM

Igneous Rocks — heat and pressure form — rain, heat, and water form — Sediments — compacting forms — heat and pressure form — Metamorphic Rocks — melt into — melt into — melt into — Magma — Sedimentary Rocks

1. This diagram shows
   A. the nitrogen cycle
   B. the rock cycle
   C. photosynthesis
   D. kinds of weather

To answer, look at the "big picture." Note the repetition of Rocks. (The answer is B.)

2. Compacted sediments form what type of rock?
   A. igneous
   B. magma
   C. sedimentary
   D. metamorphic

To answer, note that the key word is compacted. Look for the same (or similar) key word on the diagram and follow the arrows. (The answer is C.)

How to Read a Graph

Your job on many science tests will be to read a graph and summarize or interpret the information it contains.

HOW TO READ A GRAPH

1. Read the title to learn what's being shown.

2. Read the labels on the x and y axes (that is, the words on the bottom and the left). The test questions will ask you to find information in the chart, so learn what these labels mean.

3. Read the question. Now use the graph to find the information you need. Remember, when looking up information, read up and across.

Graphs

Line graphs have L-shaped grids. The horizontal line of the grid often stands for passing time. The vertical line shows the subject of the graph.

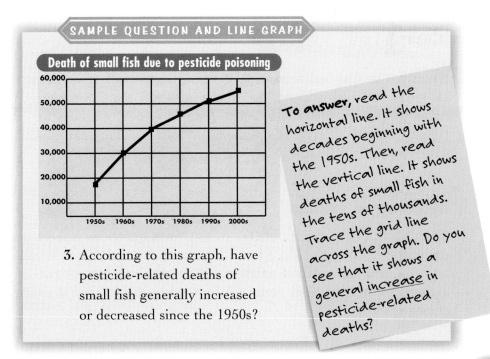

SAMPLE QUESTION AND LINE GRAPH

Death of small fish due to pesticide poisoning

3. According to this graph, have pesticide-related deaths of small fish generally increased or decreased since the 1950s?

To answer, read the horizontal line. It shows decades beginning with the 1950s. Then, read the vertical line. It shows deaths of small fish in the tens of thousands. Trace the grid line across the graph. Do you see that it shows a general _increase_ in pesticide-related deaths?

Tests

Bar Graphs

Some graphs are called bar graphs because they use bars (or columns) to stand for the subjects of the graphs. Unlike line graphs, bar graphs show only one point in time.

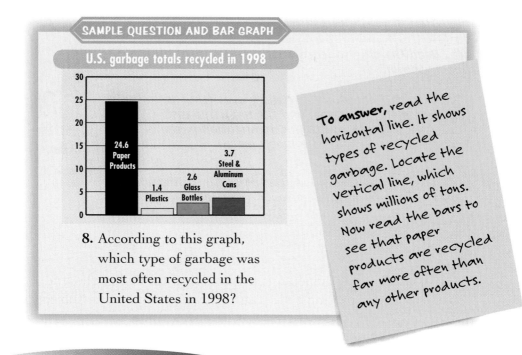

SAMPLE QUESTION AND BAR GRAPH

U.S. garbage totals recycled in 1998

24.6 Paper Products

1.4 Plastics

2.6 Glass Bottles

3.7 Steel & Aluminum Cans

8. According to this graph, which type of garbage was most often recycled in the United States in 1998?

To answer, read the horizontal line. It shows types of recycled garbage. Locate the vertical line, which shows millions of tons. Now read the bars to see that paper products are recycled far more often than any other products.

After Reading

When you've finished answering the questions on the test, return to the ones that you skipped. Read each question again and review any notes you made. Sometimes, when you come back to a question, you simply read the directions again and understand them better. That's worth repeating: *Be sure you read the directions carefully.*

Making a Guess

If you're still not sure about the answer for a question, make a guess. Answer every question on a test unless your teacher has said you'll be penalized for incorrect answers. Try to eliminate one or two answers to increase your chances of guessing correctly on a multiple-choice question.

Checking Your Work

Save the last few minutes of the test period to check your work. Scan your answers to be sure you haven't made any careless mistakes or skipped any questions. Check that you haven't marked more than one answer for a question.

If you have time, spot-check a couple of questions that gave you the most trouble. Reread each question and then reread your answer. Make sure what you've written can be easily read. That's especially important if you've changed your mind. Erase old answers well before rewriting your new answer.

- **Prepare for science tests by reading the text, making visuals of key science processes, learning science terms, and practicing how to read graphics.**
- **Preview the test and start with the easier questions.**
- **Be sure to read all questions and directions carefully.**

Tests

Improving
Vocabulary

- Learning New Words
- Building Vocabulary Skills
- Understanding Specialized Terms and Vocabulary Tests

new words

Improving Vocabulary

Try to imagine a life without words. That's tough to do, because words are so important to the things you do every day. Words help you learn, read, and talk to friends and family. Without them, you can't do much of anything.

Learning New Words

Words are something you want to collect, something individual and distinct, like songs or photos. You don't want just one or two; you want a lot of them. Words enable you to unlock meaning from what you read. They help you understand, connect ideas, create new ideas, write, and talk about your thoughts and feelings to others.

Building Vocabulary Strength

After you think of words as something you'd like to collect, you realize you can't do without them. Building a vocabulary is like pumping iron or training for swimming. By training for and practicing a sport, you improve a little with each workout. You develop your breathing, muscle strength, technique, and concentration—allowing you to compete at a higher level. It's the same with learning vocabulary. The more you learn, the easier it is to read and understand more.

When you see a new or unfamiliar word, you may feel like skipping over it, but don't. Learn what the word means.

Being a Word Collector

It's easy to learn new words. Here's one tried and true way to become a word collector.

1. Ready, Set, Record!

In a journal or notebook, set aside a section of about ten pages for each category of new words you'll jot down.

A. RECORD UNFAMILIAR WORDS

When you hear or read a new word that's important to know, jot it down in your journal or notebook. First, note the title of the book. Then write the word and the page on which the word appears. Be sure to put the word under a general subject, such as Science or English.

VOCABULARY JOURNAL

Sept. 12
    History

    reincarnation, p. 23
    dynasty, p. 26
    abundant, p. 26
    covenant, p. 30

Sept. 21
    English

    To Kill a Mockingbird by
    Harper Lee

    apothecary, p. 2
    piety, p. 3
    imprudent, p. 4

    Science

    cilia, p. 83
    mollusks, p. 85
    mantle, p. 87

Vocabulary

B. LOOK THEM UP

Find the meaning of each word by using your textbook's glossary or a dictionary. Read the definitions, examples of how the word works in sentences, and any history given for the word.

from *American Heritage Student Dictionary*

a•poth•e•car•y (ə-pŏth´-ĭ-kĕr´-ē) *n., pl.* **a•poth•e•car•ies.**
A person trained in the preparation of drugs and medicines; a pharmacist. [First written down about 1387 in Middle English and spelled *apotecarie*, from Late Latin *apothēcārius*, clerk, from Greek *apothēkē*, storehouse.]

C. WRITE THE DEFINITIONS

Next, jot down the definition beside the word in your vocabulary journal. Put the definition that relates to the way the word was used by your teacher or in the book you were reading.

VOCABULARY JOURNAL

apothecary, p. 2—a druggist or pharmacist

Another method is to get a file box and make file cards for your vocabulary words. Here's what you need for that:

- lined 3 x 5 index cards
- index-card box

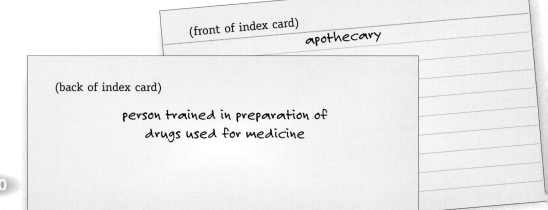

(front of index card)
apothecary

(back of index card)

person trained in preparation of
drugs used for medicine

D. SAY THE WORDS

If you need help saying the word, jot down the word divided into syllables from your dictionary. Place the vowel markings and accent marks, so you know which syllables to emphasize when you say the word.

Students often wonder which definition to record because words in English often have a number of meanings. Here are some tips that can help you make that decision.

TIPS FOR LEARNING DEFINITIONS

1. Recall the situation surrounding the word or refer back to the place you found the word. That's why you record the page number.

2. Reread the word and the sentences around it to get an idea of the way the author used it.

3. Write, in your own words, the definition that relates to the way the word was used. If possible, give an example.

4. Jot down one or two other definitions that might be helpful.

VOCABULARY JOURNAL

ENTRY	MEANING
homogeneous mixture	a material in which you can't see different particles, even under a microscope **Examples:** vinegar, saltwater Another name for a homogeneous mixture is solution.
desultory	to go from one subject to another and show no interest or connections **Example:** a desultory or rambling conversation

Vocabulary

2. Move Words into Long-term Memory

To make a new word part of your vocabulary, you need to see or use a word at least seven or eight times. That sounds like a lot, but it's easier than you'd think. Here's a plan for memorizing the words you write in your vocabulary journal.

MEMORIZING WORDS

1. Set aside short periods of time (eight to ten minutes) several days each week.

2. Select several vocabulary words to review.

3. Read the word. Try to recall the definition and example.

4. Check the meaning of the word to see if your memory was on target. If it was, go to the next entry.

5. Reread the word, its definition, and the example two to three times if you were unable to recall the correct meaning.

6. Highlight words that you need to study so you can cover these again.

7. Put a check beside the words you knew.

8. Try to use the word in a sentence. Write or say the sentence.

You will be surprised how well this plan for memorizing new words works. Try it for a while. You'll soon find that it becomes a habit and an easy way to collect new words.

3. Start Owning Words

You want to "own" the new words you come across. That means you know how to use them in conversation or in writing. The more you include a new word in your thinking, speaking, and writing, the better chance you have of making the word part of the daily vocabulary you use. Try following several tips.

TIPS FOR USING NEW WORDS

1. *Try to use the new word when you answer in class and when you speak to friends and family.*

2. *Include the new word when you write answers to questions at school and when you plan and write paragraphs, letters, and essays.*

3. *Think about the word's meaning when you meet it again in your reading. Ask yourself, "Did I learn something new about this word's meaning?"*

Boosting Your Vocabulary

You can make learning new words easy or hard. It's your choice. The important point is that you can learn new words anytime, and you can learn words in a variety of ways.

1. Read for Fun

The "fun" reading you do on your own offers the best way to learn new words. Like a detective searching for clues, be on the lookout for new words. You'll meet hundreds of new words in the sports pages, the magazine articles, and the novels you read. Instead of skipping over words you don't know, ask yourself, "Do I really know what this means? Can I give the meaning for this word?" If you can't, put the word in your vocabulary journal, even if you think you sort of know it. You may just need to hear the meaning of the word one or two more times before it becomes part of your vocabulary.

2. Listen and Ask

As young children, we first learn language by asking, "What's that mean?" We listen to what our parents say and ask them when we hear words we don't understand. Now you probably hear new words all the time in conversations, especially when you are around people who are older than you are. All you need to do is ask, "What's that word mean?" You will find this one of the easiest ways to learn new words, because you have a place and person to help you remember where and what you heard.

Vocabulary

3. Play Word Games

You can learn a lot of words just by playing games. Try working the crossword puzzles that appear in newspapers and magazines. Some of them may be hard, but you'll learn a lot of words by working them. You can also play word games like Scrabble® or Boggle®. These are easy ways to test yourself and your word knowledge—and have fun while doing it!

4. Go on a Scavenger Hunt

For fun or just to pass time, collect five or six words from your vocabulary journal. Write them on a page in your notebook. Then go looking for places where the words are used. Listen to the radio, watch TV, read the newspaper, and listen to the conversations of your parents and friends until you hear or see one of the words used again. When you hear or see one of the words used, note who used it and what it meant. Keep track of how long it takes you to "find" the five or six words. Next, do it with a second set of words. You will find yourself becoming a better listener, and you will learn lots of words just by keeping your eyes and ears open.

Building Vocabulary Skills

How can you build your vocabulary throughout your lifetime? What do you need to do that? Among other things, you need to master a few tools (a dictionary and a thesaurus) and some knowledge that will help you add words to your vocabulary anytime you read (context clues).

Becoming a Context Clue Expert

All readers bump into words they don't know while reading. But it's not always possible to look up words in the dictionary. Sometimes a dictionary isn't handy. Other times, especially when you're into an exciting mystery or adventure, you just don't want to stop. Get in the habit of searching for the clues that authors leave. These are called context clues.

Spotting Context Clues

Context clues are the words, phrases, and sentences around the word you don't know. Many sentences and paragraphs include enough information for you to put on your detective cap and figure out the meaning of new words as you read. Look at this example. Can you figure out the meaning of the following highlighted words?

> **from *Lyddie* by Katherine Paterson**
>
> She [Lyddie] saw the overseer's impeccable wife with the end of a towel in either hand briskly polishing her husband's head, just above the ears, then carefully combing back the few strands of grayish hair from one ear to the other.

The wife, who is impeccable, takes great pains to clean her husband's head after a day's work at the mill. Use what the wife does to figure out what *impeccable* means. She's cleaning him up and making him look neat, and that's exactly what *impeccable* means.

Vocabulary

615

Was she [the overseer's wife] a meek, <u>obedient</u> little woman, <u>or someone like Mrs. Cutler</u>, who would rule him as he ruled the girls under his watchful eye?

Here the author uses a similar word immediately after the unfamiliar word. *Obedient* offers a clue for the meaning of *meek*. Another clue is that the author describes an opposite character—a wife who rules her husband. By using both context clues, you realize *meek* probably means that the wife doesn't challenge her husband and sees him as the decision maker.

Kinds of Context Clues

Writers are usually thoughtful of their readers. When they use a long, difficult word, they often provide clues that allow you to figure out the word's meaning. Becoming familiar with the different types of context clues will help you get more out of reading and help you do better on standardized tests.

1. DEFINITIONS OR SYNONYMS

Often a writer will give a synonym or a definition of a tough word. This occurs when a writer senses a word is difficult to understand. To help the reader, the explanation is in simpler terms. A definition or synonym follows a comma, a dash, or such words as *or, is called, that is,* and *in other words*.

This type of clue will appear frequently in your science, history, and mathematics textbooks.

Most castles had high walls and were surrounded by <u>a water-filled ditch</u> called a moat.

2. CONCRETE EXAMPLES

Writers sometimes provide examples that illustrate and make clear a difficult concept or idea. The example can often help you figure out the meaning of a new word or concept. Sometimes authors use these signal words that tell you an example is coming: *such as, including, for instance, to illustrate, are examples of,* and *for example.*

from *Physical Science*

Oxygen, carbon, water, sugar, and salt are examples of materials classified as substances. A substance is either an element or a compound.

Note that the examples can be in the sentence before, in the same sentence, or in a sentence after the difficult word.

3. CONTRAST CLUES

To make clear the meaning of a challenging word, authors will sometimes include the opposite meaning or a situation that illustrates the opposite meaning.

from *Growing Up In Coal Country* by Susan Campbell Bartoletti

Nippers, spraggers, and mule drivers envied the miners and laborers, whose strength was measured in coal.

In this example, you learn what nippers and spraggers are not like—the miners and laborers. You also learn they "envied" them, suggesting that their position is lower and less important than that of the laborers and miners. Often it is important to learn what a word does *not* mean, because that will help you learn what it *does* mean. Here, from this one sentence, you can tell nippers and spraggers are low-level workers in coal mines.

Vocabulary

4. DESCRIPTION CLUES

Often you will find a description of a word that you don't know. For example, you might read the word *epidemic* in one paragraph and not realize what it means until you read the next paragraph.

> **from *Ida B. Wells* by Dennis and Judith Fradin**
>
> . . . Ida was at her grandmother's farm when a yellow fever epidemic broke out in Memphis, fifty miles from Holly Springs, and in Grenada, Mississippi, eighty miles from Ida's home. An infectious disease of warm regions, yellow fever is carried by mosquitoes. . . .

At first, from the immediate context, you can tell *epidemic* means "an infectious disease." But *epidemic* refers to a widespread disease. That becomes clearer in the next paragraph, which tells the number of people who got the disease.

> **from *Ida B. Wells***
>
> Most of the town's thirty-five hundred people fled. Of the fifteen hundred people who remained in Holly Springs, all but about sixty contracted the disease. . . .

5. WORDS OR PHRASES THAT MODIFY

Sometimes modifiers—such as adjectives, adverbs, or phrases and clauses—contain clues to a word's meaning.

> **from *Cleopatra* by Diane Stanley and Peter Vennema**
>
> The city buzzed with rumors that Caesar was planning to make himself king, with Cleopatra as his queen, and that the capital would be moved to Alexandria.

The underlined clauses describe events that readers can tell are unlikely and probably aren't true. From them you can infer that the word *rumor* means a false story.

6. CONJUNCTIONS SHOWING RELATIONSHIPS AND CONNECTING IDEAS

Conjunctions show relationships between words and allow readers to link unknown ideas to known ones. *And, but, or, nor, for,* and *yet* are all coordinating conjunctions. Common subordinating conjunctions are *since, because, even though, if, just as, when, whenever, until,* and *although*.

> **from *Experiencing World History***
>
> Isolation would prove to be a bad mistake for China, <u>for</u> <u>they were cut off</u> from the learning and the excitement of new ideas that were developing, especially in Europe.

The clause after the conjunction *for* explains what *isolation* means—being "cut off" or "separated."

7. REPEATING WORDS

Often writers repeat a difficult word in familiar and new situations. This way you can construct an unfamiliar word's meaning by using what you already know. By using the word a number of times, the writer helps ensure that readers will understand what it means. This happens especially with important words that the reader needs to know, as in this example.

> **from *Coming to America: The Story of Immigration* by Betsy Maestro**
>
> America is a nation of immigrants. <u>Immigrants</u> are people who come to a new land to make their home. All Americans are related to <u>immigrants</u> or are <u>immigrants</u> themselves.

Note that the author also gives here a definition of *immigrants*. The second sentence defines the word, and the next one gives examples of it.

Vocabulary

8. UNSTATED OR IMPLIED MEANINGS

Many times the meaning becomes clear when you study the situation the word appears in or draw on your own knowledge and experience of similar situations.

from *Rescue: The Story of How the Gentiles Saved the Jews in the Holocaust* by Milton Meltzer

Most Italian Jews were assimilated and well-educated middle-class people. Their families had lived in Italy for generations. Indeed, before the birth of Christ some 8,000 Jews were settled on the banks of the Tiber River.

It's easy to figure out the meaning of *assimilated* here. The writer tells you that the Jews had been in Italy for thousands of years, so you can infer that they fit in Italian culture and were part of it. That's what *assimilated* means—"to be fully absorbed by or blended in."

Beyond Context Clues

Sometimes you will come across words that have few or no context clues. That can make finding their meanings frustrating. When that happens, you can check in a dictionary or ask your reading partner or a family member. Or jot down the word, the page it appears on, and the book's title. Then, you can look it up in a dictionary or ask someone later.

Think of words you can't figure out with context clues as delicious, special challenges that will be a treat to learn.

Understanding Roots, Prefixes, and Suffixes

Knowledge of word parts can be very important know-how for you to have.

Word parts are prefixes, suffixes, and word roots (sometimes called base words). Knowing word parts can quickly multiply the number of new words you can understand. With them, you act like a detective, using the clues from word parts to help you to figure out meanings of words you've never seen.

If you want to learn 20 to 30 new words, you can spend time memorizing the words and their definitions. However, within a few days you may forget most of the words' meanings. It's more efficient to learn the meaning of word parts: prefixes, suffixes, and roots. They can help you understand—and more easily remember—what dozens of words mean.

Word Roots

A word's *root* is the part of the word that carries the most meaning. Knowing the meanings of common Greek and Latin roots arms you with the tools to unlock the meanings of dozens of related words. Consider, for example, the Latin root *port*, which means "to carry." Knowing it can help you unlock the meaning of many related words.

WORDS WITH *PORT*

porter	*exportable*	*reporter*
portable	*deport*	*importer*
importable	*deportation*	*portage*
import	*important*	*portfolio*
export	*report*	

If you understand that there are two Latin roots that mean "light"— *luc* and *lum*—you can begin to figure out some of the meanings of the words on the next page.

Vocabulary

luminous	lucent	illumine	illuminate	illuminator
lucid	lucidity	translucent	translucence	illuminative
luminescent	luminosity	lumen	luminary	luminaria
luminousness	lucidly	illumination		

For a list of word roots, see the Almanac (page 689).

Prefixes

Knowing the meanings of *prefixes* can help you figure out the meanings of many words. Prefixes can be added onto the beginnings of many English words to change the words' meanings. Look what happens when you add the prefix *anti-*, meaning "against," to *social*, which means "getting along well with others or living and interacting with a group." The new word, *antisocial*, means "keeping to oneself, *not* interacting with others." See the Almanac (page 685) for a list of prefixes.

Suffixes

A *suffix* is a letter or group of letters put at the end of a word or part of a word. When you add a suffix to the end of a word, you often change the word's function as well as its meaning. That is, you change its part of speech. The examples below show how adding different suffixes changes the part of speech and meaning of words. The examples are from the Latin roots *claim* and *clam* (which mean "to shout").

Word	Part of Speech	Meaning
clam*ant*	*adjective*	*noisy*
clamor*er*	*noun*	*one who makes noise*
clam*or*	*verb*	*to make loud sounds*
claim*ant*	*noun*	*a person who makes a claim*
exclaim*ed*	*verb*	*shouted suddenly*
exclam*ation*	*noun*	*noisy talk; outcry*
exclama*tively*	*adverb*	*in a noisy manner*
exclama*tory*	*adjective*	*expressing emotion*

See the Almanac (page 687) for a list of suffixes.

Putting Word Parts Together

Learning the meanings of word parts is a super way of enlarging your vocabulary. A good place to start is with the general tips below.

TIPS ABOUT WORD MEANINGS

1. *Most words in English are built from at least one root:*
narrate, scribe, serve, mariner, lunar, vagrant

2. *Words do not always have both a prefix and a suffix.*
Words with no prefix or suffix:
sleep, light, plead, eat, mold

Words with one prefix:
promote, retract, detract, consent

Words with one suffix:
signal, regretful, creation, mechanize

3. *Words can have more than one root, prefix, or suffix.*
Words with two or more roots:
anthropology, barometer,
photograph, psychology

Words with two prefixes:
unenlighten, intercontinental,
unextraordinary, deconstruct

Words with two suffixes:
anonymously, mindlessly,
brightened, embarrassingly

4. *Often the spelling of a base word changes when it is combined with a prefix or suffix.*
Words in which the spelling of the base word changes:

brief	move	exclaim
brevity	mobile	exclamation

Learning Word Parts

Now that you know about word roots, prefixes, and
suffixes, what do you do with them? Here are
a few ideas to help you learn word parts,
because the more you learn, the more
words you will know. Each week try
some of these tips for learning a few
roots, prefixes, and suffixes.

Tip #1: Collect Roots and Related Words

1. Work on one root a week. (That's also
   a good way to learn new prefixes and
   suffixes.)

2. Keep your roots and related word lists in
   a notebook.

3. Write the root and its meaning.

4. Brainstorm a list of words that come from the
   root. See the example below. If you can,
   identify any prefixes and suffixes in the words.

5. Check your dictionary to make sure the list is correct.

6. Add to the list any new words you find in
   the dictionary.

ROOT LIST

Word Root <u>cert</u>

<u>from Latin meaning "sure"</u>	Prefixes	Suffixes
certain		<u>-ain</u>, adjective
certify		<u>-ify</u>, verb
recertify	<u>re-</u>, again	
certification		<u>-cation</u>, noun
certainly		<u>-ly</u>, adverb
uncertain	<u>un-</u>, no, not	
certifier		<u>-er</u>, noun
certifiable		-able, adjective

Tip #2: Play Word Games

One painless way to learn word roots, prefixes, and suffixes is through word games. For example, here is a way to use them in the card game known as Concentration.

THE CONCENTRATION GAME

1. Choose five to ten roots, prefixes, or suffixes.

2. Make a file card for each one.

3. Then, on another set of file cards, write the meaning for each root, prefix, or suffix.

4. Mix the file cards. Place the cards face down on a table.

5. On each turn, turn over two cards. Try to match the root, prefix, or suffix with its meaning.

6. Each time you make a match, keep the two cards. The object of the game is to remember where the root, prefix, or suffix is and to match it with its meaning.

Tip #3: Use the Words

Another easy way to learn different word roots, prefixes, and suffixes is to practice using them each week. The secret of accomplishing something difficult is to make it easy. Make the job easier by concentrating on one word part each week.

1. Choose one new root, prefix, or suffix each week. Learn its meaning and five or six related words that use it.

2. Read the root, prefix, or suffix and five or six related words at least once.

3. Try using one of the words with the new root, prefix, or suffix in conversation at least once a day.

4. Make a habit of using the word in writing sometime during the week. In no time, you will find you know the meanings of a lot of word roots, prefixes, and suffixes.

Vocabulary

Dictionary Dipping

Just as you wouldn't try to sail the sea without a good ship, neither should you try to understand the English language without a good dictionary. A dictionary is an indispensable tool for readers.

The Right Tool for the Job

In fact, it's helpful to own two dictionaries: a large, hardbound dictionary and a smaller, paperback dictionary. Collegiate dictionaries offer a great deal of information about a great many words. But they are written for college students, so their definitions can sometimes be difficult to understand. Most bookstores will have a "student" or "junior" dictionary that is written for middle school students. Whichever dictionary you choose, keep the hardbound dictionary on or near your desk at home, so it's handy while you do your homework.

You might want to carry a smaller dictionary with you in your backpack at school. It will help you quickly find the meanings of most new words and check spellings. If the paperback dictionary doesn't have the word you need, jot the word down on a page in your vocabulary notebook. Then, look up the word at home, in your larger, more complete hardbound dictionary.

What's in Dictionaries?

Larger dictionaries contain more words and tell more about them than smaller, paperback dictionaries. But almost any dictionary can help you with the most common kinds of questions you'll have.

■ How is a word spelled and pronounced?

■ What does a word mean?

■ How can a word be divided at the end of a line of writing?

■ How is the word spelled when an ending is added?

Note the differences in these three dictionary entries.

from *American Heritage Dictionary* — **Paperback dictionary**

im-mune (ĭ **myoōn´**) *adj.* **1.** Exempt. **2.** Resistant to infection by a specific pathogen. [<Lat. *immūnis*.]

from *American Heritage Student Dictionary* — **Student dictionary**

im-mune (ĭ **myoōn´**) *adj.* **1.** Protected from disease naturally or by vaccination or inoculation: *I'm immune to chicken pox since I had it when I was young.* **2.** Relating to or producing immunity: *the body's immune response to a vaccine.* **3.** Protected; guarded; safe: *The fort made the harbor immune from attack.* [First written down in 1440 in Middle English, from Latin *immūnis*.]

from *American Heritage College Dictionary* — **Collegiate dictionary**

im-mune (ĭ **myoōn´**) *adj.* **1.** Not subject to an obligation imposed on others; exempt: *immune from taxation.* **2.** Not affected by a given influence; unresponsive: *immune to persuasion.* **3.** *Immunol.* Of, relating to, or having immunity to infection by a specific pathogen. — *n.* A person who is immune. [ME < Lat. *immūnis*.]

Vocabulary

Learning to Use a Dictionary

Knowing the parts of a dictionary can help you look up words. Page 629 shows a list of some of the most important parts of a dictionary.

(1) **olive /omission**

(2) ol•ive (ol´ iv) *n.* **1.a.** The small, oval, greenish or blackish fruit of the Mediterranean region, having a single hard seed. Olives are eaten as a relish or pressed to extract olive oil. **b.** The tree **(3)** bearing such fruit. **2.** A dull yellowish green. [First written down before 1200 in Middle English, from Greek *elaia.*]

olive branch *n.* **1.** A branch of an olive tree, regarded as a symbol of peace. **2.** An offer of peace.

olive oil *n.* Oil pressed from olives, used in salad dressings, for cooking, as an ingredient of soaps, and as an emollient.

O•lym•pi•a (ŏ lĭm´ pē ə *or* ə lĭm´ pē ə) *n.* A plain of southern Greece in the northwest Peleponnesus. It was the site of the ancient Olympic games. The statue of the Olympian Zeus was one of the Seven Wonders of the World.

om•e•let (om´ ə lit *or* om´ lit) *n.* A dish of beaten eggs, cooked and often folded around a filling, as of cheese. [First written down in 1611 in **(4)** Modern English, from Old French *amlette.*]

(5) o•men (o´ m ən) *n.* A thing or an event regarded as a sign of future good or bad luck. [First written down in 1582 in Modern English, from Latin *ōmen.*]

om•i•nous (om´ ə nəs) *adj.* **(6)** Being a sign of trouble, danger, or disaster. **—om´i•nous•ly** *adv.* **— (7)** **om´i•nous•ness** *n.*

o•mis•sion (o mish´ ən) *n.* **1.** The act of omitting something or the state of having been omitted: *the omission of several* **(8)** *letters from a word.* **2.** Something that has been omitted: *several omissions from the guest list.*

1 Guide Words

At the top of each dictionary page are two guide words. They tell you the first and last word on that dictionary page. Use the guide words to help you locate the entry you want to find.

2 Entry Word

Entry words are listed in alphabetical order and are shown in bold-face type. Entry words show how a word is spelled and let you know if the word should be capitalized. They also show how the word can be divided into syllables.

3 Definitions

When a word has more than one definition, the dictionary numbers each one. When looking up a word, always read all the meanings, and then choose the one that fits best for your purpose. The first meaning is not always the most important or main one.

4 Word History

Some of the entries will tell you the origin of the word, or etymology. This part tells from what languages a word was derived.

5 Pronunciation

Right after the entry word the pronunciation is shown in parentheses. It looks unusual because the respelling shows how to say the word. It also shows where the stressed, or accented, syllable is.

6 Part of Speech

In italics right after the respelling you'll find the abbreviation for the part or parts of speech of the word. When other forms of the entry word are given after the definition, the parts of speech, syllables, and respellings are also included.

7 Inflected Forms

At the end of a dictionary entry are other forms of the word, especially when their spellings might give you trouble.

8 Illustrative Example

Often a dictionary entry will give an example in a phrase or sentence for one or more definitions. The examples show exactly how a word can be used with *that* particular meaning.

Vocabulary

Reading a Thesaurus

Using a thesaurus can help you be a better reader and writer. Like the dictionary, a thesaurus is a tool that will open your eyes to dozens of new words and help you choose just the right one. By using a thesaurus, you will expand your vocabulary, and that will aid you as a reader.

A thesaurus is a book of synonyms—that is, words that have the same or nearly the same meaning. All of the words that mean "old" are grouped together (*aged, elderly, mature, advanced, senior*), as are all of the words that mean "press" (*push, shove, ram, compress, squeeze, bear, mash*). Many entries in a thesaurus also list antonyms, or words that have opposite meanings. For example, the antonyms listed for "old" are *young, immature, modern, up-to-date,* and *current.*

from *American Heritage Student Thesaurus*

Entry word

Part of speech

Illustrative examples

Antonyms

Synonyms

pretty *adjective* **1. attractive, beautiful, lovely, good-looking, fetching, cute, comely, fair** My little sister looks very pretty in her new holiday dress. **2. clever, adroit, deft, sharp, smart, ingenious, shrewd, imaginative** He pulled off a pretty business deal. **3. bad, terrible, horrible, awful, ghastly, dire, unpleasant, appalling** The situation has come to a pretty pass. **4. large, huge, great, big, fat, generous, immense, sizable** He made a pretty profit on the transaction. ◆ *adverb* **fairly, quite, rather, somewhat, very, reasonably, moderately** It's pretty cold out for a late spring day. •➤ Antonyms: *adjective* **1. plain, ugly, unattractive 2. clumsy, unimaginative 3. good, pleasant 4. small, paltry, little**

Understanding Specialized Terms and Vocabulary Tests

Building a strong vocabulary will help you day in and day out in school. You will understand more about what you're learning in your classes and what you read in your textbooks, and you'll do well on vocabulary test questions.

School Terms

You've probably noticed that different sports have their own vocabularies. Basketball fans talk about free throws, technical fouls, zone defenses, screens, and jams. Like sports, your school subjects have their own special vocabularies. By learning the special language for your classes, you jump-start your ability to understand the material.

1 Record Key Terms

When you start studying a new subject—such as earth science, technology, algebra, or civics—you're bombarded with unfamiliar vocabulary. For example, in algebra, you'll meet such terms as *variable, quadratic equation, absolute value, inverse, integers, exponents, property of zero,* and *prime factorization.*

Each of these unfamiliar terms is essential to understanding the concepts in the text. To do well in your classes, you need to learn these specialized terms.

Become a collector of terms in your classes. Set aside a part of your vocabulary notebook to add terms from each class.

> **VOCABULARY JOURNAL**
>
> **CIVICS TERMS**
> **amnesty**—general pardon given by the government to people who have broken the law
> **boycott**—way of protesting in which people do not buy goods and services or deal in other ways with the people they are protesting against
> **checks and balances**—system in which political power is divided among the branches of government, with each having some control

Vocabulary

2 Get Savvy about Textbooks

Most textbooks begin with introductory material that discusses the subject and introduces the key terms. In a history textbook, you might find 5 or 10 new words in the introduction and as many as 30 or 40 new words in the first few chapters. Learning these new, specialized terms will help you learn the material more easily. Placing the list of the terms at the very beginning of the chapter is a way of saying, "These terms are important. Focus on them and learn them."

As you read a textbook chapter, you'll usually find these key terms highlighted in italics, boldface type, or colored print. Specialized vocabulary exists because it describes something not easily explained in another way. For example, *bicameral* is a specialized government term that means "having two legislative chambers or houses." It's a lot easier to say *bicameral* than to say all that.

At the back of most textbooks is a glossary with a list of all the highlighted terms. Look up the meanings of the new, specialized vocabulary you find in textbooks. You'll understand more when you know the specialized lingo used in your books.

TIPS FOR LEARNING SCHOOL TERMS

1. *Read the list of new words in a chapter.*

2. *Find each word in the chapter as you read and see how it is used.*

3. *Then, at the end of the chapter, reread the list. How many words do you know?*

4. *Write any words you don't know in your vocabulary notebook or create index cards for the words you don't recall.*

5. *Use the glossary of your textbook to find definitions for the words.*

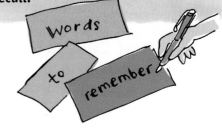

3 Use Webs and Concept Maps

Terms are easier to understand when you can connect them to other words and ideas. That's where a Concept Map can help. A Concept Map is a way of organizing important information using a visual design.

Creating the map helps you pull together a lot of details and can be more useful than plodding through a chapter yet again. For example, look at the Concept Map for *digestion* below. At the center of the map is the key word or concept you want to review.

CONCEPT MAP

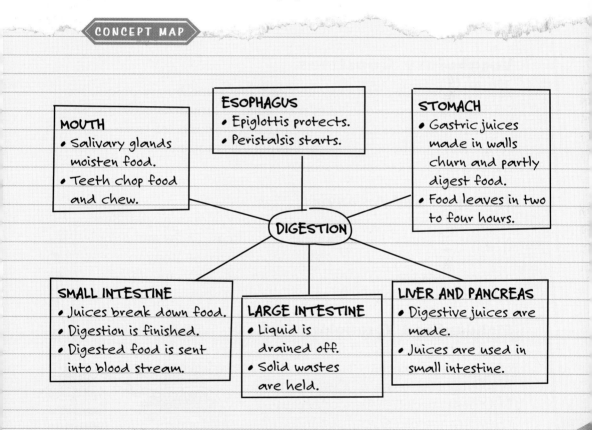

MOUTH
- Salivary glands moisten food.
- Teeth chop food and chew.

ESOPHAGUS
- Epiglottis protects.
- Peristalsis starts.

STOMACH
- Gastric juices made in walls churn and partly digest food.
- Food leaves in two to four hours.

DIGESTION

SMALL INTESTINE
- Juices break down food.
- Digestion is finished.
- Digested food is sent into blood stream.

LARGE INTESTINE
- Liquid is drained off.
- Solid wastes are held.

LIVER AND PANCREAS
- Digestive juices are made.
- Juices are used in small intestine.

Vocabulary

4 Learn Specialized Terms

Many students put off reading or studying key terms until the last day or minute before the test. Cramming information into your brain in a hurry can result in mixing up ideas, forgetting information, and generally doing poorly. Instead of putting off learning new words, make it a part of your everyday study routine. Spend a few minutes on vocabulary before you begin other studying—say, the first five to ten minutes. Learn to budget your time. Study the words slowly and for short periods of time, but do it every day or every other day. Over a period of time, learning new words will become a habit—and one that pays off.

Vocabulary Questions

Your teachers will often put questions about vocabulary on quizzes. Standardized tests probe your knowledge of hundreds of words. So the more you understand about the inner workings of these vocabulary questions—analogies, synonyms, antonyms, definitions— the better you'll be able to score.

Synonyms and Antonyms

Vocabulary tests often ask about synonyms and antonyms. Synonyms are pairs of words that have similar meanings. *Chaos* and *disorder* are synonyms, as are *inattentive* and *distracted*. Antonyms are pairs of words that have opposite meanings. *Light* and *dark* are antonyms, as are *humility* and *pride*.

Standardized Vocabulary Tests

Vocabulary sections of standardized tests usually include questions that ask you to find the synonym or antonym of a word. These tests pose special challenges because the words are often not used in a sentence or paragraph. You need to know the meaning of a word really well to succeed on these tests.

Let's look first at some of the different kinds of questions you're likely to see on standardized vocabulary tests.

SYNONYM QUESTION

Choose the word that is a synonym of each word below.

1. REVELRY
    A. worries
    B. preparations
    C. merrymaking
    D. lighthearted

First, think about the base word *revel*. It has something to do with "fun." If you know what *revel* means, cross out *preparations* and *worries*. That leaves you with *merrymaking* and *lighthearted*. *Revelry* is a noun, not an adjective like *lighthearted*, so the answer must be *merrymaking*. Take a look at a second question.

ANTONYM QUESTION

Choose the word that is an antonym of each word below.

1. ARID
    A. chilly
    B. windy
    C. river
    D. humid

First, you know from geography that deserts are arid because they are so dry. Here you need to find the opposite of *arid*, which would be *wet* or *moist*. You can cross out *chilly* and *windy*, because those answers are not even close to being right. A river is wet, but it's a noun, a body of water. You may not be sure what *humid* means, but that has to be the right answer. *Humid* is like the *humidity* you hear about in a weather report. Humidity is the amount of water in the air, so *humid* must be correct.

Vocabulary

Preparing for Vocabulary Tests

The best preparation for vocabulary tests is to read—and read some more. Your vocabulary will grow daily, a little at a time, without your even knowing it. Another great way to prepare is to keep a vocabulary notebook and collect the words you come across. Here are a few other tips so you can ace vocabulary tests.

VOCABULARY TEST-TAKING TIPS

1. *Read the directions carefully. Know whether you are looking for synonyms or antonyms.*

2. *Read the word and ask yourself if you've seen it in your reading or heard others use it. Perhaps you know the meaning of the word parts.*

3. *Cross out the answer choices you know won't work. You can usually immediately cross out one or two choices.*

4. *Use your knowledge of the word's part of speech and choose the answer that is the same part of speech.*

Analogies

An analogy shows a relationship between two things. An analogy question has two sets of words that share a common relationship. Once you figure out the relationship of the first pair of words, you can complete the analogy.

How to Read Analogy Questions

Here is an analogy: *pencil : pen :: shirt :*_____. You read an analogy this way: *pencil* is to *pen* as *shirt* is to_____. The single colon stands for "is to." The double colon stands for "as." Read each word slowly. Now is not the time to skim.

SAMPLE ANALOGY QUESTIONS

1. *pencil* : *pen* :: *shirt* : _____
    a. striped   b. pants   c. cotton   d. buttons
2. *panic* : *terror* :: *reveal* : _____
    a. mask   b. artistic   c. disclose   d. cover

Types of Analogies

Become familiar with the kinds of relationships that analogies present. Then, when you read analogies, identify exactly what's being compared in the sample pair before selecting your answer.

1. ANALOGIES IN WHICH WORD ORDER IS NOT IMPORTANT

RELATIONSHIPS IN ANALOGIES

1. Synonyms

surge : rise :: renew : _____

a. alive   b. restore   c. dead   d. drain

2. Antonyms

vicious is to *kind* as *reckless* is to _____

a. careful   b. risk   c. unsafe   d. healthy

3. Rhyming Words

thatch : catch :: loud : _____

a. quiet   b. crowd   c. cloudy   d. noise

4. Homophones

gilt : guilt as _____

a. reed : read   b. jump : jumped

c. core : court   d. bruise : bruises

5. Parts of the Same Thing

lens : frame :: _____

a. dominoes : checkers   b. propeller : wing

c. miner : gold   d. count : number

6. Two Examples from the Same Class

meteor is to *comet* as *dolphin* is to _____

a. porpoise   b. net   c. ocean   d. boat

(Answers: 1.b, 2.a, 3.b, 4.a, 5.b, 6.a)

Vocabulary

2. ANALOGIES IN WHICH WORD ORDER IS IMPORTANT

Always select an answer that is in the same order as the example.

RELATIONSHIPS IN ANALOGIES

1. Different Forms of the Same Word

describe : description :: organize : _____

a. organizing   b. organization   c. organizer   d. organ

2. Name and Location

state : Virginia :: city : _____

a. Michigan   b. town   c. Phoenix   d. river

3. Class and Example of That Class

female : ewe :: _____

a. cattle : herd   b. grease : slimy

c. hockey : soccer   d. musician : harpist

4. Item and Who Uses It

car is to *motorist* as *gymnasium* is to _____

a. principal   b. guidance counselor   c. coach   d. driver

5. Item and What It Does

scissors : cut :: _____

a. ruler : straight   b. operator : telephone

c. orbit : spacecraft   d. microscope : magnify

6. Item and a Word That Describes It

knife : sharp :: ravine : _____

a. rock   b. dangerous   c. river   d. crevice

7. Whole and Part

computer : screen :: woodpile : _____

a. leaves   b. houses   c. sand   d. logs

(Answers: 1.b, 2.c, 3.d, 4.c, 5.d, 6.b, 7.d)

RELATIONSHIPS IN ANALOGIES, continued

8. Action and Where It Takes Place

deposit is to *bank* as *flood* is to _____

a. evacuate   b. river   c. boat   d. waves

9. Action and Who Does It

applaud : audience :: _____ _____

a. thief : steal   b. perform : singer

c. happy : sad   d. racehorse : gallop

10. Sequence

spring : summer :: _____ _____

a. morning : early   b. time : hour

c. month : June   d. morning : afternoon

(Answers: 8.b, 9.b, 10.d)

Summing Up

You can take several steps in learning new words. One is to begin keeping a vocabulary journal in which you write down the new words you meet in your reading. You should also learn how to use context clues, a dictionary, and a thesaurus. Focus some attention on specialized school subject terms. They can help you understand more of what you read in your textbooks. Then, before any standardized tests, review the various kinds of analogies so you'll be prepared—not surprised—when you see analogy questions.

vocabulary

ABCDEFGHIJKLMNOPQRSTUVWXYZ

total

Reader's
Almanac

- Strategy Handbook
- Reading Tools
- Word Parts: Prefixes, Suffixes, and Roots

Strategy Handbook

This part of the handbook explains reading strategies that can help you become a better reader. Think of a strategy as a way of finding and unlocking meaning in what you read. Choose different strategies depending on what and why you're reading.

Key Strategies

Close Reading	642
Looking for Cause and Effect	644
Note-taking	646
Outlining	648
Paraphrasing	650
Questioning the Author	652
Reading Critically	654
Skimming	656
Summarizing	658
Synthesizing	660
Using Graphic Organizers	662
Visualizing and Thinking Aloud	664

Close Reading

Close reading means reading word for word, sentence by sentence, or line by line. It is like putting one part of a reading under a microscope and studying how the words look, sound, and work together.

Close reading is a good strategy to use with shorter selections, such as poems or speeches, or with small parts of a longer work. Choose parts that you know are important to the meaning of the selection as a whole.

Using the Strategy

To do a close reading, first you'll need to read the selection slowly and carefully.

1. Select and Read Choose a key passage or a few lines. If you're allowed to write on the page, use a highlighter or pen to mark important words. If you can't write on the page, cut sticky notes into narrow strips and use these strips to mark important parts in the selection.

2. Analyze Then, look at each passage you chose word for word. Ask yourself questions like these:

- Why did the writer use this particular word?
- What does this mean?
- Why is this important?
- What's special or unusual about the words used here?
- What do the words mean, but also what do they suggest?

By answering these questions, you'll figure out what the passage means.

3. React Finally, make connections to what you've read. Your personal reactions to a word or phrase can help you understand the author's message. This can help you figure out the effect the writer wants to create.

Record your thoughts about individual words, phrases, or lines in a Double-entry Journal. For example, here is one reader's reaction to part of a poem by Edgar Allan Poe.

DOUBLE-ENTRY JOURNAL

QUOTE	MY THOUGHTS AND FEELINGS
"In the silence of the night How we shiver with affright At the melancholy meaning of the tone! For every sound that floats From the rust within their throats Is a groan."	The word "shiver" adds to a scary atmosphere. The sound of the bells must be creepy. It's strange to think of a bell as making a groan.

You can use the information you've uncovered from your close reading to support your ideas about the work. You need to have reasons to back up your view of the reading. By telling what individual words and phrases mean, you have all the reasons you need to support your view.

DEFINITION

Close reading means reading word for word, sentence by sentence, or line by line. Use close reading when a work is short or when you come to a paragraph or section that is particularly important. Assume that every word you read carries meaning and contributes to the mood, tone, and message of the selection.

Looking for Cause and Effect

Writers often explain *why* things happen. The events or situations that happen first are the "causes." The event or events that happen as a result are the "effects."

Using the Strategy

You'll find writers explaining cause and effect in much of the nonfiction you read, including textbooks and biographies. As a reader, you make connections as you read and as you see relationships among ideas and events. When you think back on what you read, you can see how causes lead to effects.

1. Read Read the selection all the way through first. Highlight or use sticky notes to record your ideas or questions as you go, including any notes you can make about cause-effect relationships.

2. Create an Organizer Next, create an organizer that shows cause and effect in the reading. Look at the different organizers that follow. Choose the one that you think will work best for you.

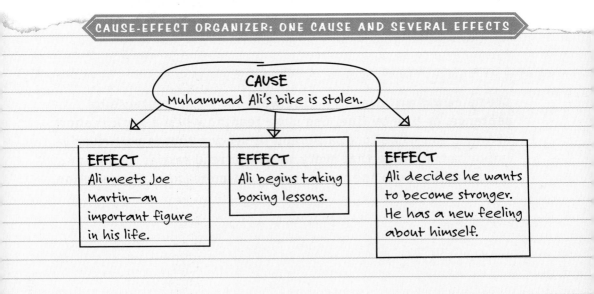

CAUSE-EFFECT ORGANIZER: ONE CAUSE AND SEVERAL EFFECTS

CAUSE
Muhammad Ali's bike is stolen.

EFFECT
Ali meets Joe Martin—an important figure in his life.

EFFECT
Ali begins taking boxing lessons.

EFFECT
Ali decides he wants to become stronger. He has a new feeling about himself.

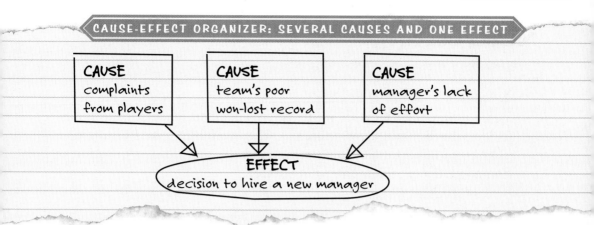

CAUSE-EFFECT ORGANIZER: SEVERAL CAUSES AND ONE EFFECT

CAUSE	CAUSE	CAUSE
complaints from players	team's poor won-lost record	manager's lack of effort

EFFECT
decision to hire a new manager

3. Revise the Organizer As you read—or reread—you may need to add to or revise your organizer. Keep in mind that many writers will describe the effect first and mention the causes later. Also, sometimes you can identify a chain reaction of causes and effects: A will cause B and C, and then B and C will cause D.

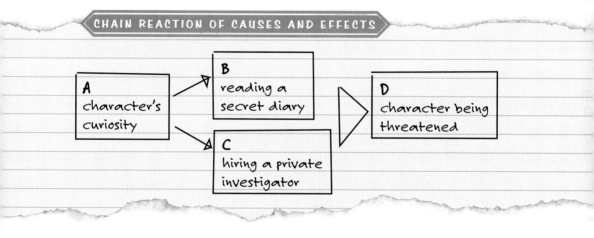

CHAIN REACTION OF CAUSES AND EFFECTS

A	B	D
character's curiosity	reading a secret diary	character being threatened
	C	
	hiring a private investigator	

DEFINITION

Looking for cause and effect means focusing on the process by which one event brings about another. In cause-effect writing, the event or events that happen first are the "causes." The event or events that happen as a result are the "effects."

Note-taking

Writing is a way of remembering. That's why readers who take good notes understand more of what they read. Good readers make notes before, during, and after a reading. They watch for parts of a text that seem important or interesting, and they jot down a question or comment. They review their notes later.

Using the Strategy

After you preview the reading, choose the note-taking tools you will use. Here are four that work well:

1. Summary Notes Jot down the most important details, terms, or events in Summary Notes. Chapter-by-chapter notes make sense with longer works—novels, plays, textbooks, and so on. Assign one blank page in your notebook per chapter. For long works, you may even want to divide each note page into two or three parts, as in the example:

SUMMARY NOTES

Chapter 1: "The Mighty Erie Canal"

Dates and Place
1817–1825
New York state, from Buffalo to Albany
Names
Governor DeWitt Clinton (wants to build the Erie Canal)
Problem
Canal will cost $7 million. Clinton's enemies are angry at the high cost.
Outcome
Clinton refuses to take no for an answer. He decides to charge a canal toll to recover money the state put out for construction.

2. Timeline or Sequence Notes Another kind of notes is Timeline or Sequence Notes. These help you follow the order of events and the time period in which they occurred.

3. Key Word Notes This is a 2-column note-taking technique. Notes from the reading are written on one side of the page, and key words that organize the notes are written on the other.

KEY WORD NOTES

KEY WORDS	NOTES FROM "THE MIGHTY ERIE CANAL"
Erie Canal	historic waterway connecting Great Lakes with New York City via the Hudson River
DeWitt Clinton	governor of New York
1825	beginning of Canal construction, Oct. 25 opening
price	$7 million

4. Class and Text Notes This is another type of 2-column notes. In the left column, write notes from class—what's covered by your teacher. In the right column, write notes from your reading.

CLASS AND TEXT NOTES

CLASS NOTES	TEXT NOTES
Bill of Rights keeps government from limiting personal freedoms.	• first 10 amendments • added to Constitution in 1791 • originally 12 proposed

DEFINITION

Note-taking can help you remember key facts and details from a reading. In addition, it can help you think through important information until you truly understand it.

Almanac

Outlining

Outlines organize information into topics and subtopics. Broad, general ideas are treated as main headings. Each of these is divided into two or more smaller topics, called subtopics. The subtopics can be divided still further into smaller subtopics.

OUTLINE

KINDS OF WAVES

I. Seismic Waves
   A. characteristics
      1. P wave — strongest type of body wave
      2. longitudinal
      3. travel through either liquid or solid matter
   B. effects
      1. result in liquid or solid vibrating uncontrollably
      2. vibrations - compression or expansion of rocks
II. Sound Waves
   A. characteristics
      1. pure tone — the simplest sound wave
      2. characterized by frequency
   B. behavior
      1. light waves and sound waves — same actions
      2. reflect and scatter

NOTE

These heads correspond with major heads in chapter.

NOTE

Important details are listed under subtopics.

Using the Strategy

Concentrate on listing only the most essential facts and details. Try making Topic and Sentence Outlines and using outlining to understand your textbooks.

1. Topic Outlines A Topic Outline lists the major topics covered in a reading. It can contain many or a few specific details. Topics are stated briefly in words or phrases rather than complete sentences.

2. Sentence Outlines A Sentence Outline contains the major points in the reading, along with specific details. Points are written as complete sentences. Use Sentence Outlines to make notes on longer selections, since this type of outline offers a more complete record of what the reading is about.

3. Outlines and Textbooks When outlining material in textbooks, pay attention to the headings and subheadings in the texts. These headings can help you decide what to write. Often the headings in the text can become major topics or subtopics in your outline. As you read, take notes directly in outline form. Paraphrase important facts and details and write them in the appropriate sections. In addition, you'll want to be sure to note key terms and their definitions.

DEFINITION

Outlining can help you keep track of the most important topics and details in a selection, especially nonfiction. Topic Outlines use words or phrases to describe key information. Sentence Outlines use complete sentences to list major points as well as supporting details.

Paraphrasing

When you paraphrase, you use your own words to tell what you've read, heard, or seen. Paraphrasing is a helpful strategy to use with visuals, such as charts, diagrams, maps, math problems, and pictures. It allows you to put pictures into words.

Paraphrasing can help you make sense of the information you read. If you can't understand what the author is saying, try using your own words. State the meanings of difficult terms or a hard-to-understand sentence or passage in words that make sense to you. Besides graphics, paraphrasing works well with parts of textbooks, essays, articles, and poems.

Using the Strategy

Rephrasing what somebody else wrote can give you a new way to unlock meaning.

1. Preview Get ready to paraphrase by getting a sense of the one general topic or subject of the selection. Preview the graphic or skim the reading. Ask yourself questions like these:

- What is this graphic or selection all about?
- What clues hint at the meaning or main idea?
- What other important facts and details stand out?

At this point, you are looking only for the general subject.

2. Take Notes To paraphrase a graphic, start by reading the title and any text. In most long readings, you'll want to focus in on a key passage or important group of lines. Write your general thoughts and questions in the margins or on sticky notes as you read.

from "The Raven" by Edgar Allan Poe

Ah, distinctly I remember it was in the bleak December;
And each separate dying ember wrought its ghost upon the
　　floor.
Eagerly I wished the morrow: —. . .

Speaker is recalling an unpleasant moment. What does "wrought its ghost" mean?

3. Put the Material in Your Own Words The key to paraphrasing is using *your* words, not those of someone else. An easy way to do that is to think about how you would explain something to a friend or a younger brother or sister. Just talk through what you would say. Then, organize your thoughts a little so that they are perfectly clear. You may want to reread a passage several times and look up any unfamiliar words.

Put quotation marks around any key words or phrases that you borrow from the source. Quote as little as possible. Most of the words should be your own.

PARAPHRASE CHART

LINES	MY PARAPHRASE
"And each separate dying ember wrought its ghost upon the floor."	Every piece of hot coal or wood made a faint image on the floor.

MY THOUGHTS
I like how Poe compares ashes of the fire to a ghost. It makes you think something spooky will happen.

DEFINITION

Paraphrasing is using your own words to describe what you've seen, heard, or read.

Almanac

Questioning the Author

DESCRIPTION

As a reader, you often have questions about why an author used a particular word or made a character do or say a particular thing. You cannot easily telephone or email an author to get answers about why he or she wrote a story or essay a certain way. But you can focus on an author's decision by asking yourself questions.

If you figure out why the author is writing, you'll have an easier time understanding what he or she is trying to say and why certain words or details were included.

Using the Strategy

Questioning the author can be an important strategy for understanding the author's ideas or message.

1. Read and Ask Questions Start to ask yourself questions from the moment you begin reading. Write them down. Suppose you had a chance to talk with the author. What sort of questions would you ask him or her?

- What is the author trying to teach me?
- Why did the author begin the way he or she did?
- What is the reason for including that event, that detail, or that character?
- How does this fit with my previous knowledge or experience?
- How does what the author says at the end go with what's said earlier?
- Why did the author use that word or phase?
- What am I supposed to think of this?
- What point is the author trying to make?
- Where did the author get his or her ideas?

2. Infer Answers and Draw Conclusions Of course, the author won't actually answer the questions you ask, but he or she will leave clues that can help you infer the answers. You can make better inferences about what's happening because you have the author's purpose in mind.

You'll probably need to do some rereading to come up with answers to the questions you've written. Don't worry if you can't answer them all. Write the best answers you can think of at the time. If possible, share your ideas with classmates. Be honest about what seemed hard or confusing.

3. Evaluate As a final step, ask yourself what the author's purpose was and how well it was met.

EVALUATING AUTHOR'S PURPOSE

Author's Purpose:	Questions to Ask:
Explain	*Have you learned something helpful as a result of the reading?*
Entertain	*Did you enjoy the selection? Did it make you laugh or cry? Would you recommend it to others?*
Persuade	*Have you changed your mind as a result of the reading?*
Enlighten	*Did the reading help you think about a topic or idea in a new way?*

DEFINITION

Questioning the author is the process of asking questions as you read about why the author made the choices he or she did.

Almanac

Reading Critically

Reading critically means understanding and evaluating the point a writer is trying to make. To do that, you need to move beyond the facts and details on the page and consider what those facts and details mean. Read the lines and read between the lines. Think about what's missing or has been left out.

Critical readers know they can't always trust that they're getting the full story. They know to look a little bit deeper and ask themselves questions:

- Is there something missing here?
- Has the author considered both sides of the question?
- How believable or trustworthy is the evidence?

Reading critically can help you find out if there's another side to the story. It can help you decide whether you can really believe what you read.

Using the Strategy

Follow these steps to use the strategy of critical reading:

1. List First, think of or write out a list of "critical reading" questions to ask yourself as you're reading:

- What is the main idea or viewpoint of the writing?
- How well does the writer support the main idea with evidence?
- How authoritative and reliable are the sources?
- How convincing is the evidence?
- Could there be another side to the story? If so, what is it?
- What has the author *not* mentioned?
- How truthful is the speaker or narrator?

2. Be an Active Reader As you read, keep focused on the main idea and what evidence supports it. Look for answers to your critical reading questions. Pay special attention to this question: "Are the sources used authoritative and reliable?" This question will be particularly important if your source is the Internet.

3. Evaluate Create a Critical Reading Chart to help you evaluate your thoughts about the selection. It can help you decide whether or not you can believe what you've read.

CRITICAL READING CHART

1. Is the main idea or viewpoint clear?	
2. What evidence is presented?	
3. Are the sources authoritative and reliable?	
4. Is the evidence convincing?	
5. Is there another side of the story?	

DEFINITION

Reading critically means finding and evaluating the author's main idea or message in a piece of writing. This involves testing the evidence to see if it is authoritative and reliable.

Skimming

Skimming is a strategy that works well with almost any kind of reading. Skimming is particularly effective with selections that are long or challenging. Skimming can give you an overall sense of what a reading is about. It also works well when you are reading to find one specific bit of information.

You might want to skim a text for many reasons. Good readers know that skimming has a variety of uses:

1. It helps familiarize you with the topic and important ideas.

2. It gives you a "heads up" about challenging words or concepts.

3. It helps you locate essential information in the text.

4. It serves as a quick review of material that you need for a test or presentation.

Using the Strategy

When you skim, you don't read each word or sentence carefully. Let your eyes roam down each page of the selection.

1. Skimming for General Ideas To get a general idea of what a reading is about, pay particular attention to these text elements:

- the title
- the table of contents or "chapter-at-a-glance" features
- the length and difficulty of the selection
- any captions
- any illustrations, photographs, or other visuals
- any headings
- any boldface terms or concepts
- any repeated words
- the first and last paragraphs

2. Skimming for Specific Information Often you need to look for specific information—a fact in an article or test, a time on a train schedule, and so forth. You may be looking for one tiny detail in the middle of a sea of information. Use skimming to help you sift through all of the information. If you see that a paragraph or column of information is *not* what you need, move on. With skimming, you first read for topics to help locate the general subject you need. Later, concentrate on the specific details you need to find.

3. Skimming Paragraphs The secret to skimming paragraphs is to identify the one key subject in a paragraph. Once you identify the subject of a paragraph, you know if it contains the information you need. Try circling or writing in the margin a key word naming the subject of a paragraph. That way you know if you need to skim the facts or details in that paragraph or skip them.

4. Skimming on Tests Many times you will need to skim a selection to answer test questions about it. For instance, if you can write on the test, circle a key word or phrase that suggests the subject of each paragraph. That will help you later. If a test question asks about the feeding habits of whales, skip the paragraphs about other animals. Skim paragraphs in the article until you find ones that talk about what whales eat. Then, start reading there.

DEFINITION

Skimming means glancing quickly through a selection. When you skim, you look through a selection to get a sense of the topics and important ideas. Once you find the general subject you need, then begin reading more closely there, sentence by sentence.

Almanac

Summarizing

Summarizing is a strategy that works well for any type of reading. When you summarize, you retell the main events or ideas in a selection using your own words. Because you're leaving out details, your summary will be much shorter than the original.

Using the Strategy

The key to summarizing is knowing how to find the main points or ideas.

1. Summarizing Literature First, read the selection all the way through, taking some notes as you go. A good summary will tell you:

- title and author
- point of view
- characters
- setting
- plot
- theme
- style

Knowing what you are looking for as you read will help you summarize. You might also want to create a simple organizer to help you take notes.

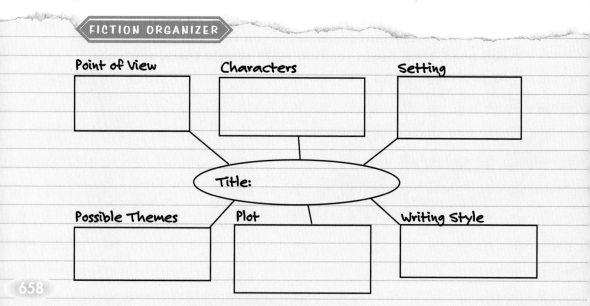

FICTION ORGANIZER

Point of View

Characters

Setting

Title:

Possible Themes

Plot

Writing Style

2. Summarizing Nonfiction When you want to summarize nonfiction, you read looking for key details. Ask yourself what the subject is, what is said about it, and what three to four things stand out. Look for these kinds of things with nonfiction:

- the general subject
- what the author says about the subject
- the supporting details
- any key words and phrases
- any definitions and explanations

Use an organizer like the one below to help you summarize a nonfiction selection.

NONFICTION ORGANIZER

TITLE:

SUBJECT:

INTRODUCTION:

BODY:

CONCLUSION:

DEFINITION

Summarizing is telling the main events or ideas in a selection in your own words. The strategy of summarizing will improve your ability to comprehend and remember what you've read.

Almanac

Synthesizing

When you synthesize, you look at a number of parts or elements and pull them together. You consider various parts and figure out how they make a whole.

Synthesizing is a good strategy for almost any kind of text—fiction and nonfiction. But it's especially useful for long works because it helps you keep track of details from throughout the work.

Using the Strategy

Synthesizing is like gathering up the pieces of a puzzle and turning them this way and that until you figure out how they all fit together.

1. Using Synthesizing with Fiction To evaluate a novel or story, you need to look at many different elements, such as the plot, characters, and setting. As a reader, you want to look at a number of parts of a novel at once. Use synthesizing to look closely at certain details throughout a work or to see how different elements are connected. Take notes on each element as you read.

KEY TOPICS

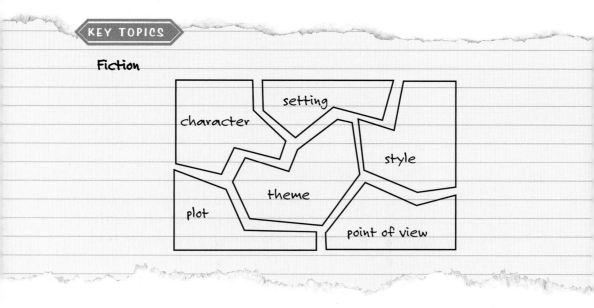

Fiction

character · setting · style · theme · plot · point of view

2. Using Synthesizing with Nonfiction

As a reader of nonfiction, you also need to look at a number of things at once about a subject. You want to see how the beginning fits with the end or how the details in one paragraph connect to those in another. In a biography or autobiography, for example, you want to know how the person grew up, what events shaped his or her life, what character traits the person has, and so on. You have to keep track of a lot. You want to synthesize, or pull together, all of the information into one clear picture of the person. With biographies and autobiographies, focus on key topics, such as childhood, school, character traits, and major achievements.

KEY TOPICS

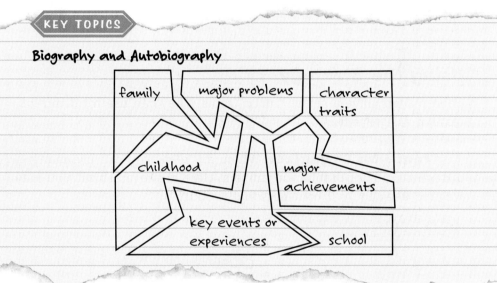

Biography and Autobiography

family | major problems | character traits

childhood

major achievements

key events or experiences | school

3. Evaluating What You Learn

When you've finished reading, look closely at individual parts and pieces. That will help you to create a thorough evaluation of the subject. Pull together the different elements of the story or article. Ask yourself how the details add up and what were the strongest and weakest parts.

DEFINITION

Synthesizing means reflecting on a number of individual elements of a text and deciding how they affect the selection or subject as a whole.

Almanac

Using Graphic Organizers

As a reader, you often need help in seeing ideas. Graphic organizers help you do that.

Graphic organizers are "word pictures." You create them to help you organize and visualize important ideas in a reading. You can use graphic organizers with fiction or nonfiction. With fiction, they can help you keep track of important events in the plot, inferences about characters, and clues about setting and theme. Use them with nonfiction to help you identify and sort important facts and details and to evaluate evidence.

Using the Strategy

Good readers have a set of trusty "tools" they can use for different reading assignments.

1. Create an Organizer When you read, you can use many different kinds of graphic organizers. Here are several that you may want to keep in your own personal toolkit.

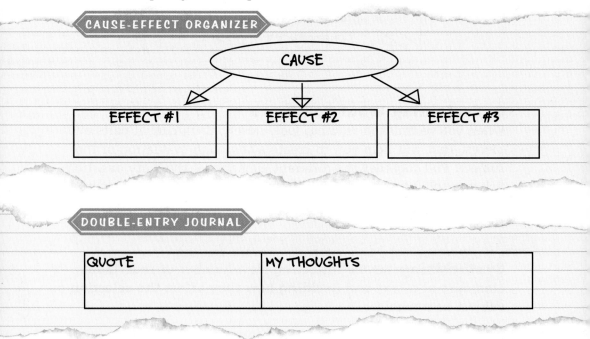

CAUSE-EFFECT ORGANIZER

CAUSE

EFFECT #1 EFFECT #2 EFFECT #3

DOUBLE-ENTRY JOURNAL

QUOTE	MY THOUGHTS

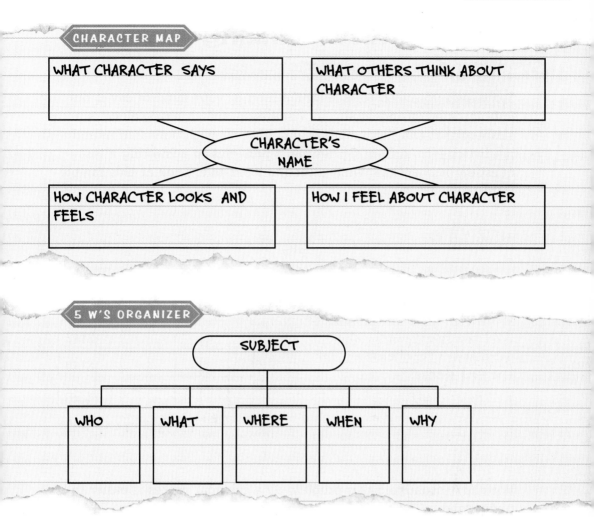

CHARACTER MAP

WHAT CHARACTER SAYS

WHAT OTHERS THINK ABOUT CHARACTER

CHARACTER'S NAME

HOW CHARACTER LOOKS AND FEELS

HOW I FEEL ABOUT CHARACTER

5 W'S ORGANIZER

SUBJECT

WHO | WHAT | WHERE | WHEN | WHY

2. Try Different Organizers Practice makes perfect when using graphic organizers. Try different kinds of organizers as you read. Stick with the ones that work best for you. See "Reading Tools" on pages 666–684 for more graphic organizers.

DEFINITION

Graphic organizers are "word pictures." They are the charts, webs, diagrams, and any other visuals you draw that can help you understand a work of fiction or nonfiction.

Visualizing and Thinking Aloud

DESCRIPTION

Sometimes you need to "see" something in your mind or say it out loud in order to understand it. Visualizing and thinking aloud is a strategy that can help you do that. It works with both fiction and nonfiction—from figuring out math problems to answering a test question or imagining what a setting looks like. Look at this sample word problem.

EXAMPLE

In June, Alma earned $127 the first week, $182 the second week, $159 the third week, and $207 the fourth week. What were Alma's total earnings for the four weeks?

June

S	M	T	W	T	F	Sat
						$127
						$182
						$159
						$207

(The answer is $675.)

Note how visualizing this problem on a calendar makes it easier to understand.

Visualizing Most readers visualize as they read. It's something that you do almost automatically. When you visualize, you make "mental pictures" or "mental movies" of the text as you read. The strategy of visualizing involves focusing on the pictures that form in your mind as you read and drawing what you "see."

Thinking Aloud This strategy involves talking to yourself about what you're reading. Focus on what's important, ask yourself questions, or keep a running record of your ideas and reactions. With this strategy, you help yourself "hear" the ideas in your head by saying them out loud quietly to yourself. Often, thinking aloud and visualizing go together. Doing one helps you do the other.

Using the Strategy

The more you practice visualizing and thinking aloud, the easier it will become. Follow these steps:

1. Read and Sketch You may want to make a very quick sketch next to each math problem, science concept, or process as you read. Even if your drawing is corny, it may help you remember. Make room in your notebook for sketches. Your drawings do not need to be masterpieces. Even simple stick figures can be better than nothing.

You can use visualizing with any kind of reading, even fiction. In that case, you'll be drawing pictures of characters, events, settings, ideas, and so on—anything that helps you make sense of important details and facts. For example, by sketching a scene you may create a useful map or help yourself remember the climax of a story or novel.

2. Listen to Your Thoughts As you sketch, try talking to yourself about what you're doing. Trying to explain a process or passage to yourself can help you make sense of it. The act of putting a story or essay into your own words will help you understand it better.

3. Review and Reflect Use your sketches to remind yourself of important details. They can help refresh your memory about what you've read. Go through why you drew what you did. Talk to yourself about your sketches.

DEFINITION

Visualizing and thinking aloud involves making a mental picture or sketch of the words on the page and talking through your ideas about what you're reading.

Reading Tools

This part of the Almanac lists reading tools that can help you get more out of your reading. Think of this section as your toolkit. When you read, you build meaning. Which tool can best help you get the job done?

Reading Tools

Argument Chart	667	Paraphrase or Retelling Chart	676
Cause-Effect Organizer	667	Plot Diagram	676
Character Development Chart	668	Process Notes	677
Character Map	668	Setting Chart	677
Class and Text Notes	669	Storyboard	678
Classification Notes	669	Story Organizer	678
Concept Map	670	Story String	679
Critical Reading Chart	670	Study Cards	679
Double-entry Journal	671	Summary Notes	680
Fiction Organizer	671	Thinking Tree	680
5 W's Organizer	672	Timeline or Sequence Notes	681
Inference Chart	672	Topic and Theme Organizer	681
Key Word or Topic Notes	673	Two Per Line	682
K-W-L Chart	673	Two-story Map	682
Magnet Summary	674	Venn Diagram	683
Main Idea Organizer	674	Viewpoint and Evidence Organizer	683
Nonfiction Organizer	675	Web	684
Outline	675	Website Profiler	684

ARGUMENT CHART

An Argument Chart is a tool to examine and analyze persuasive writing, such as a speech, magazine article, or editorial.

Viewpoint	Support	Opposing Viewpoint
Put the writer's viewpoint here.	*Write three or four ways the writer supports the position here.*	*Note if the writer considers other viewpoints here.*

See an example on page 253.

CAUSE-EFFECT ORGANIZER

A Cause-Effect Organizer is a tool to help you sort out what are causes and what are the effects coming from them. It shows the relationship between them.

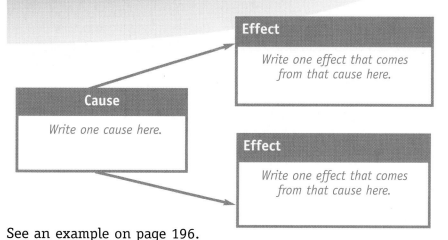

Effect

Write one effect that comes from that cause here.

Cause

Write one cause here.

Effect

Write one effect that comes from that cause here.

See an example on page 196.

CHARACTER DEVELOPMENT CHART

A Character Development Chart helps you follow how characters change in a story, play, or novel. The changes in a character help you understand the theme.

Beginning	Middle	End
Write what the main character is like at the beginning.	*Describe what the character is like in the middle of the story here.*	*Note how the character is at the end of the story here.*

Possible Themes:	
	Write one or two ideas about the theme here.

See an example on page 350.

CHARACTER MAP

A Character Map helps you understand and analyze a character in a story, play, or novel. This tool helps you see how you—and other characters—feel about the character.

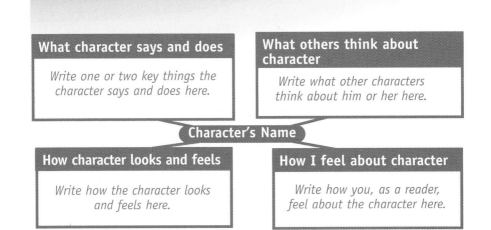

What character says and does

Write one or two key things the character says and does here.

What others think about character

Write what other characters think about him or her here.

Character's Name

How character looks and feels

Write how the character looks and feels here.

How I feel about character

Write how you, as a reader, feel about the character here.

See an example on page 326.

CLASS AND TEXT NOTES

Use Class and Text Notes to connect what your teacher says in class with what you're reading in your textbook. These 2-column notes help you organize your ideas.

Class Notes	Text Notes
Note key ideas from class here.	*Write notes you took from reading the textbook here.*

See an example on page 108.

CLASSIFICATION NOTES

Use Classification Notes to help you organize separate types or groups and sort out characteristics about them.

Make a column for each major type or group.

Label each column here.		
Write important details or characteristics here.	*Write important details or characteristics here.*	*Write important details or characteristics here.*

See an example on page 110.

Almanac

A Concept Map helps you organize everything you know about a concept or idea. It works especially well with big ideas, such as *democracy*, *photosynthesis*, and *population*.

Create an organizer with one box surrounded by five to seven boxes.

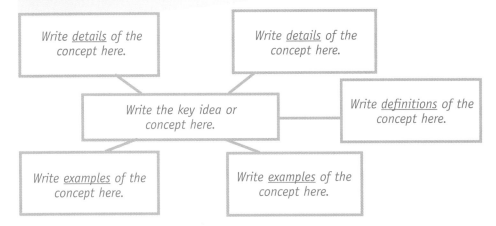

Write <u>details</u> of the concept here.		Write <u>details</u> of the concept here.
	Write the key idea or concept here.	Write <u>definitions</u> of the concept here.
Write <u>examples</u> of the concept here.	Write <u>examples</u> of the concept here.	

See an example on page 138.

CRITICAL READING CHART

Use a Critical Reading Chart to analyze the information an author gives you. The chart will help you identify the facts, opinions, evidence, and main idea or viewpoint.

Create an organizer with these five questions.

1. Is the main idea or viewpoint clear?	*Then record the main point here.*
2. What evidence is presented?	*Note the evidence here.*
3. Are the sources authoritative and reliable?	*List and comment on sources here.*
4. Is the evidence convincing?	*Evaluate the evidence here.*
5. Is there another side of the story?	*Write another possible viewpoint here.*

See an example on page 228.

DOUBLE-ENTRY JOURNAL

A Double-entry Journal helps you interpret a text. With a Double-entry Journal, you can figure out what you think about a character's words, what lines of poetry mean, or how you react to an author's main idea.

Quote	My Thoughts
Write a key quote or several lines here.	*Write what you think or feel about the lines of the text here.*

See an example on page 413.

FICTION ORGANIZER

Use a Fiction Organizer to collect all of the key information about a story, novel, or play.

Fill in the information from the text in the boxes of the organizer below.

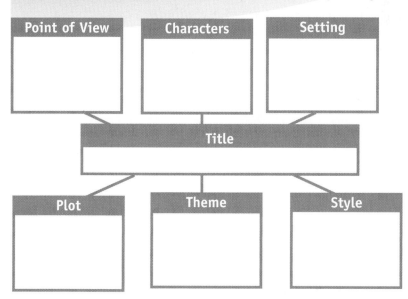

See an example on page 337.

5 W'S ORGANIZER

With nonfiction, use a 5 W's Organizer to gather key information about a subject. By asking yourself a reporter's questions (*who, what, where, when,* and *why*), you can learn most of the important information about a subject.

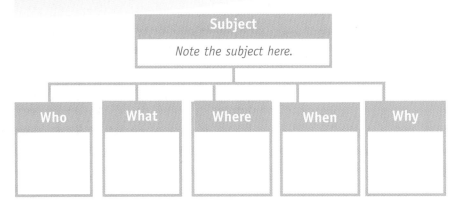

Label each box below the subject with one of the 5 W's. Write notes that answer each question in the boxes.

See an example on page 222.

INFERENCE CHART

Use an Inference Chart when you have to read between the lines and look a little closer at part of a reading—a character, a description, or a particular detail or event. This chart helps you draw conclusions about what you read.

Text	What I Conclude
Write part of the text, a detail, or an event here.	*Write what conclusions you draw about the meaning of it here.*

See an example on page 308.

KEY WORD OR TOPIC NOTES

Use Key Word or Topic Notes to help you stay organized and pull out the main ideas from your reading. Key Word or Topic Notes work well for taking notes on textbooks and other nonfiction.

Divide your notebook into two columns. Make the right side wider than the left side.

Key Words or Topics	Notes
Note the key words or main topics here. These are the main things to study.	*Take notes about each key word or topic here.*

See an example on page 130.

K-W-L CHART

Use a K-W-L Chart with nonfiction. This chart helps you draw on what you already know about a subject, focus what you want to know, and identify what you learned.

What I Know	What I Want to Know	What I Learned
Put down what you already know about the topic here.	*Write two to four questions you have about the topic here.*	*Write important information and answers to your questions after you read here.*

See an example on page 92.

MAGNET SUMMARY

Use a Magnet Summary to help you organize your thoughts after reading. It works with any kind of writing. Choose one word that is important to what you have read. Then, collect all of the other words, ideas, and details you can think of around it and summarize your ideas about the "magnet word."

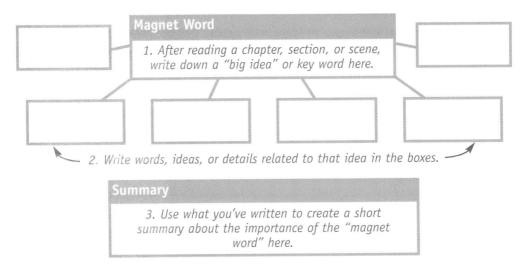

Magnet Word

1. After reading a chapter, section, or scene, write down a "big idea" or key word here.

2. Write words, ideas, or details related to that idea in the boxes.

Summary

3. Use what you've written to create a short summary about the importance of the "magnet word" here.

See an example on page 481.

MAIN IDEA ORGANIZER

A Main Idea Organizer helps you sort out the big ideas and the smaller details. This tool works best with nonfiction, such as biography, magazine articles, persuasive writing, and textbooks.

Main Idea	Write what you think is the biggest, most important idea here.	
Detail	**Detail**	**Detail**
Next write details here.	Next write details here.	Next write details here.
Conclusion	Finally, write the conclusion the author makes here.	

See an example on page 182.

NONFICTION ORGANIZER

A Nonfiction Organizer helps you sort out what you learn in essays, articles, speeches, editorials, and so on. It divides these nonfiction works into three parts: introduction, body, and conclusion.

Subject	Write the general subject here.
Introduction	Describe the ideas in the first one or two paragraphs here.
Body	Write three or four details, points, or topics from the middle here.
Conclusion	Note what happens or what the author says in the last paragraph or two here.

See an example on page 261.

OUTLINE

An Outline helps you understand the organization of what you're reading. Use words or phrases (Topic Outline) or full sentences (Sentence Outline) to sort out main ideas, topics, and subtopics.

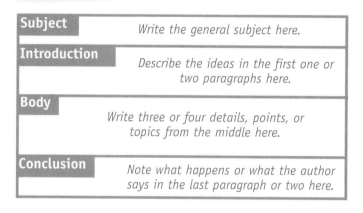

First, find the two, three, or four main topics and write them here.

I. Main Topic 1	
A. subtopic	*Under each main topic,*
B. subtopic	*write two or*
C. subtopic	*more subtopics.*
II. Main Topic 2	
A. subtopic	
B. subtopic	
C. subtopic	

See an example on page 180.

Almanac

PARAPHRASE OR RETELLING CHART

A Paraphrase or Retelling Chart helps you do two things at once. It helps you understand parts of a text or graphic by putting them in your own words and helps you collect your own thoughts about the work.

Lines	My Paraphrase
Write two or three lines from a text or facts from a graphic here.	*Tell in your own words what these lines mean here.*

My Thoughts

Note your own ideas or reaction to what's said here.

See an example on page 420.

PLOT DIAGRAM

A Plot Diagram shows you how a story is organized. It highlights the five main parts of a story.

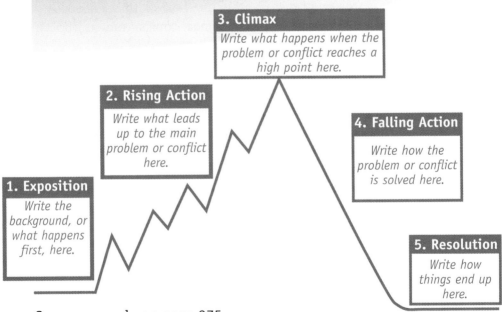

3. Climax
Write what happens when the problem or conflict reaches a high point here.

2. Rising Action
Write what leads up to the main problem or conflict here.

4. Falling Action
Write how the problem or conflict is solved here.

1. Exposition
Write the background, or what happens first, here.

5. Resolution
Write how things end up here.

See an example on page 375.

PROCESS NOTES

To keep track of a series of steps, stages, or events, use Process Notes. They work especially well for science and history, which often tell about how things develop or work.

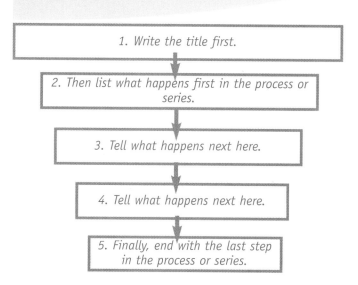

1. Write the title first.

2. Then list what happens first in the process or series.

3. Tell what happens next here.

4. Tell what happens next here.

5. Finally, end with the last step in the process or series.

See an example on page 140.

SETTING CHART

To help you understand fiction and keep track of details about when and where a story took place, create a Setting Chart. You may want to make a chart for each major scene or setting.

Clues about time	Clues about place
Write details about the time here—date, season, year, general time period, and so on.	Write details about where the story is happening here—place names, regions, physical environment, and so on.

See an example on page 353.

Almanac

STORYBOARD

A Storyboard can help you keep track of events in a story, novel, or play. It works best for longer works that have a lot of events. A Storyboard helps you remember what happened and in what order things happened.

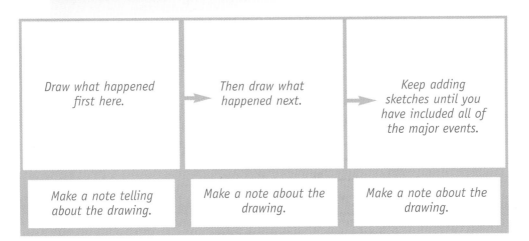

See an example on page 487.

STORY ORGANIZER

A Story Organizer is a chart that helps you sort out what happens in a story. It highlights the three main parts of a story, even if the story is really complex and has lots of characters and events.

Beginning	Middle	End
Write what happens first here.	*Write what happens in the middle of the story here.*	*Write what happens at the end of the story here.*

See an example on page 373.

STORY STRING

To keep track of a series of events in a story, novel, or play, use a Story String. It helps you see a chain of events and keep the time order straight, so you can remember what caused what in the story.

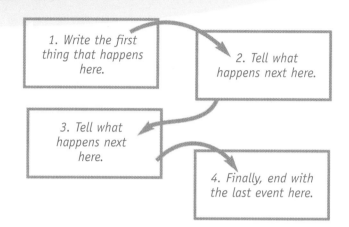

1. Write the first thing that happens here.

2. Tell what happens next here.

3. Tell what happens next here.

4. Finally, end with the last event here.

See an example on page 307.

STUDY CARDS

Use Study Cards to help you learn key terms, facts, and ideas from your reading. Study Cards are also useful for helping you memorize vocabulary words, study for tests, and keep track of research notes.

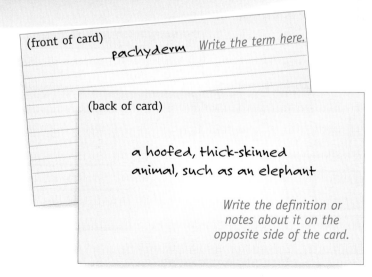

(front of card)

pachyderm   Write the term here.

(back of card)

a hoofed, thick-skinned animal, such as an elephant

Write the definition or notes about it on the opposite side of the card.

See an example on page 109.

Summary Notes help you focus on the most important parts of what you're reading, whether it's fiction or nonfiction. Make your summary as detailed as you want. You can create a summary for each page in your textbook, each scene in a play, each chapter in a book, each graphic in an article, and so on.

Title or Topic	Write the title or topic here.
Main Point	Write what you think is the main point or idea here.
1. 2. 3. 4.	List three or four smaller, related points that support the main idea here.

See an example on page 232.

THINKING TREE

A Thinking Tree works well when you have little or no idea what a reading will be about. It helps you see connections among different ideas or details. Use a Thinking Tree to list an author's ideas and branch related ideas off one another.

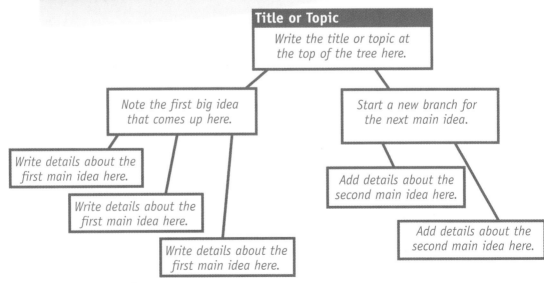

See an example on page 139.

TIMELINE OR SEQUENCE NOTES

Use a Timeline or Sequence Notes to keep track of a series of dates or events. They work best when you need to put events in order. Stories and plays sometimes jump back and forth in time, and a timeline can help you keep track of what happens.

1. List what happens first and the date (if available) here.

2. List what happens next here, along with the date.

3. Continue listing events and dates until the end.

See an example on page 213.

TOPIC AND THEME ORGANIZER

A Topic and Theme Organizer helps you find the theme in a story, novel, or play. First, list the big idea or main topic. Then, tell what the characters say or do related to the topic. Finally, come up with a theme statement that says what's important to learn based on those details.

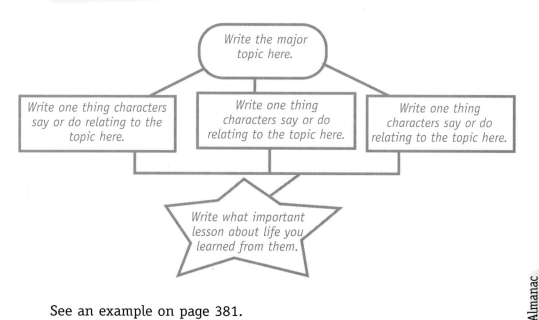

Write the major topic here.

Write one thing characters say or do relating to the topic here.

Write one thing characters say or do relating to the topic here.

Write one thing characters say or do relating to the topic here.

Write what important lesson about life you learned from them.

See an example on page 381.

Almanac

681

TWO PER LINE

To understand poetry or fiction, do a Two Per Line. Pick a key paragraph or passage. Write it out, mark the two most important words in each line, and then write your ideas about the passage.

Text	My Ideas
1. Write a paragraph or several lines here. 2. Circle or highlight the two most important words in each line or sentence.	3. Tell what you think the paragraph or lines mean here.

See an example on page 435.

TWO-STORY MAP

Use a Two-story Map to compare and contrast the major elements of two works. This reading tool will help you organize your ideas about the works.

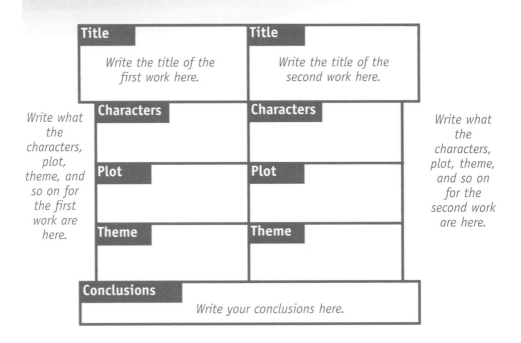

Write what the characters, plot, theme, and so on for the first work are here.

Title	Title
Write the title of the first work here.	Write the title of the second work here.

Characters | **Characters**

Plot | **Plot**

Theme | **Theme**

Write what the characters, plot, theme, and so on for the second work are here.

Conclusions

Write your conclusions here.

See an example on page 386.

VENN DIAGRAM

To compare two characters, stories, poems, settings, essays, and so on, use a Venn Diagram. This tool will help you see what's different and what's the same when you compare two things.

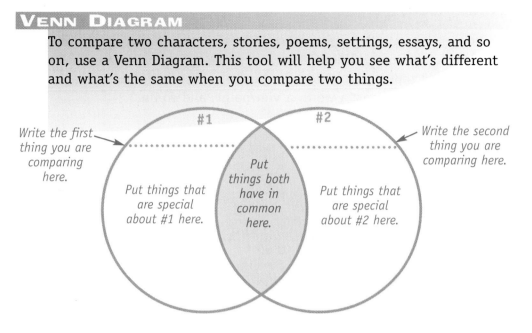

Write the first thing you are comparing here.

Write the second thing you are comparing here.

#1

#2

Put things that are special about #1 here.

Put things both have in common here.

Put things that are special about #2 here.

See an example on page 313.

VIEWPOINT AND EVIDENCE ORGANIZER

For nonfiction such as essays, articles, and speeches, use a Viewpoint and Evidence Organizer to help you figure out what an author's opinion is and how well it is supported.

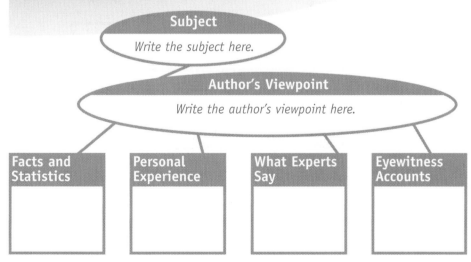

Subject

Write the subject here.

Author's Viewpoint

Write the author's viewpoint here.

Facts and Statistics	Personal Experience	What Experts Say	Eyewitness Accounts

Write notes about how the author used each kind of evidence here.

See an example on page 243.

Almanac

WEB

Webs are great all-purpose organizing tools for taking notes. They work for fiction and nonfiction and link supporting details with main ideas and topics. Use Webs to organize and brainstorm ideas about a character, an event, a word, a viewpoint, and so on.

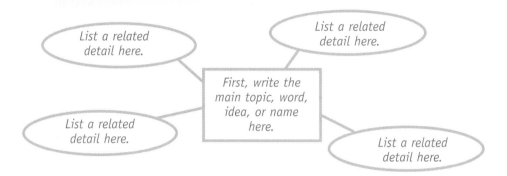

See an example on page 344.

WEBSITE PROFILER

To check out how trustworthy a website is, use a Website Profiler. It looks at who made the site, when it was updated, its point of view, and how good its information is. A Website Profiler helps you judge how reliable a site is.

Name (URL)		Write the name and URL here.	
Sponsor		**Date**	
Tell who created or pays for the site here.		Note when the site was last updated here.	
Point of View		**Expertise**	
Write the site's point of view here.		Tell where the information on the site comes from here.	
Reaction			
	List your thoughts about the site here.		

See an example on page 523.

Word Parts:

Prefixes, Suffixes, and Roots

Prefixes

Prefixes are word parts added to the beginning of a root or base word to create a new meaning.

Prefixes	Meanings	Examples
a-	not, without	amoral, apart
ab-	away from	abstract, absent
ad-	to, toward, against	addition, additive
ante-	before	antebellum, antecedent
anti-	against, opposite	antiwar, antisocial
arch-	original, chief	archbishop, archangel
auto-	self	automobile, automatic
be-	to cause, become	befriend, beneath
bi-	two	biped, bilingual
circum-	around	circumference, circumnavigate
co-	together	coworker, copilot
con-	with, together	construct, contemplate
contra-	against	contradict, contraband
counter-	against, in opposition	counteract, counterspy
de-	down, away from	descend, detract
demi-	half	demiglaze, demigod
dia-	through, across	diagnosis, diagonal
dis-	the reverse of	disagree, disable
dys-	not normal	dysfunction, dystrophy
en-	to cause, provide	enlighten, enable
epi-	to, against, added on	epicenter, epigram
ethno-	race, nation	ethnic, ethnicity
ex-	out of, away from	expel, external
extra-	outside, beyond	extracurricular, extraordinary
fore-	previously, in front of	forefathers, forefront

Prefixes	Meanings	Examples
hydro-	water	hydroelectric, hydrosphere
hyper-	extra, beyond, over	hypercritical, hyperactive
hypo-	under, below	hypodermic, hypocenter
il-	not	illegal, illegitimate
im-	not	immovable, immobile
infra-	below, underneath	infrastructure, infrared
inter-	between	interstate, interview
intra-	inside of	intramuscular, intramural
ir-	not	irregular, irrelevent
iso-	equal	isobar, isosceles
mal-	bad	maladjusted, malevolent
meta-	change, transform	metacognition, metamorphosis
micro-	small	microwave, microscope
mid-	middle	midterm, midtown
mini-	small	minibus, minivan
mis-	wrongly, badly	mistake, mistrust
mono-	one, single	monopoly, monorail
multi-	many	multimillionaire, multitude
neo-	new, recent	neoclassic, neophyte
non-	not, against	nonplus, nonsense
ob-	in the way of	obstruct, obstacle
octa-	eight	octagon, octet
omni-	all, general	omnipotent, omnipresent
pan-	whole	panacea, panorama
para-	alongside, similar	paramedic, paraphrase
per-	through	percussion, perceive
peri-	all around	perimeter, periscope
poly-	many, more than one	polygon, polytheism
post-	after, later	postmortem, postscript
pre-	earlier, before	prejudge, preview
pro-	in favor of	proclaim, project
proto-	earliest, original	prototype, protoplasm
pseudo-	false, pretend	pseudonym
quadri-	four	quadrant, quadrilateral
re-	back, again	reappear, return
retro-	backward	retroactive, retrospect
self-	by oneself	self-control, self-rule

Prefixes	Meanings	Examples
semi-	half	semifinal, semiformal
sub-	under, less than	subhead, subzero
super-	over, more than	superhuman, superstar
tetra-	four	tetralogy, tetrahedron
trans-	across, through	transact, transcend
tri-	three	triangle, tripod
ultra-	beyond	ultrasound, ultraviolet
un-	not, reverse of	unarm, unaware
under-	below, beneath	underground, underwear
uni-	single, one	unicycle, uniform
up-	upper, upward	upheaval, uprising
vice-	in place of	vice president, viceroy

Suffixes

Suffixes are combinations of letters (such as *-ance*) or single letters (such as *-s*) added to the end of base words or word parts. What follows is a sampling of common suffixes. Note the parts of speech they indicate and the examples of words that use them.

Suffixes that form nouns	Examples
-age	garbage, luggage
-al	funeral, portal
-ance	reluctance, allowance
-ant	claimant, attendant
-ee	devotee, employee
-ence	independence, audience
-ent	dependent, student
-er, -or, -ar	peddler, monitor, cellar
-ess	actress, address
-ette, -et	kitchenette, booklet
-hood	neighborhood, statehood
-ian, -ion	musician, information
-ism	Buddhism, communism
-ist	journalist, novelist
-ment	judgment, amusement

Suffixes that form nouns	Examples
-ness	kindness, happiness
-ure	future, creature

Suffixes that form adjectives	Examples
-able	expendable, dependable
-al	personal, optional
-er	messier, better
-est	cutest, smartest
-ful	disdainful, hopeful
-ible	edible, incredible
-ic	bionic, tonic
-ical	historical, tropical
-ish	bluish, skittish
-ive	divisive, pensive
-less	childless, mindless
-ous	joyous, religious
-some	loathsome, worrisome
-y	tasty, worthy

Suffixes that form adverbs	Examples
-erly	easterly, westerly
-fully	beautifully, dutifully
-ly	angrily, merrily
-ward	backward, forward
-ways	sideways, always
-wise	likewise, clockwise

Suffixes that create verb forms	Examples
-ate	congratulate, concentrate
-ed	joked, ripped
-en	brighten, eaten
-fy, -ify	notify, rectify
-ing	frightening, stunning
-ize, -yze	familiarize, analyze
-n	known, grown

Greek and Latin Roots

Knowing the meanings of common Greek and Latin roots can help you figure out the meanings of dozens of related words.

Roots	Origins	Meanings	Examples
aero	Greek	air	aerobics, aerate
agri	Latin	field	agriculture, agrarian
alter	Latin	other	alternate, altercation
ambi	Latin	both	ambiguous, ambidextrous
amo	Latin	love	amorous, enamored
ang	Latin	bend	angle, triangle
anim	Latin	life, spirit	animate, animal
ann, enn	Latin	year	annual, biennial
anthropo	Greek	human	anthropology
apt, ept	Latin	fasten	inept, aptitude
aqua	Latin	water	aquaduct, aquarium
arch	Greek	primitive	archaic, archetype
art	Latin	skill	artisan, artist
aud	Latin	hear	audible, audition
baro	Greek	weight	barometer, isobar
belli	Latin	war	bellicose, rebellion
biblio	Greek	books	bibliography, bible
bio	Greek	life	biology, biosphere
brev	Latin	short	abbreviate, brevity
cam	Latin	field	campus, campaign
cap	Latin	head	captain, decapitate
cardi	Greek	heart	cardiac, cardiogram
cede, ceed	Latin	go, yield	precede, succeed
centr	Latin	center	central, eccentric
cert	Latin	sure	certain, certify
cess	Latin	go, yield	cessation, process
chron	Greek	time	chronic, chronicle
cide, cise	Latin	cut, kill	scissors, suicide
claim, clam	Latin	shout	clamor, exclaim
clar	Latin	clear	clarity, declare
cline	Latin	lean	decline, incline
cogn	Latin	know	incognito, recognize

Roots	Origins	Meanings	Examples
commun	Latin	common	communal, commune
corp	Latin	body	corpse, corporation
cosm	Greek	universe	cosmos, microcosm
crat	Greek	rule	autocrat, bureaucrat
cred	Latin	believe	credit, incredible
cycl	Greek	circle, ring	bicycle, cyclone
dem	Greek	people	democrat, epidemic
dic	Latin	speak	dictate, verdict
div	Latin	separate	divide, division
domin	Latin	rule	dominate, dominion
duc	Latin	lead	conduct, educate
fer	Latin	bear, carry	ferry, transfer
firm	Latin	strong	affirm, confirm
flect	Latin	bend	deflect, reflect
form	Latin	shape	transform, uniform
frag	Latin	break	fragile, fragment
fug	Latin	flee	fugitive, refuge
gen	Greek	birth, race	generate, progeny
geo	Greek	earth	geography, geology
grad	Latin	step, stage	graduate, gradual
gram	Greek	letter	grammar, telegram
graph	Greek	write	autograph, graph
grat	Latin	pleasing	gratify, ungrateful
hab, hib	Latin	hold	habitat, prohibit
hom	Latin	alike	homogeneous, homogenize
hydr	Greek	water	hydrant, hydroelectric
imag	Latin	likeness	image, imagery
init	Latin	beginning	initial, initiate
integ	Latin	whole	integer, integrate
jud, jur, jus	Latin	law	judge, jury, justice
laps	Latin	slip	elapse, relapse
liber	Latin	free	liberate, liberty
log, logy	Greek	word	dialogue, prologue
luc	Latin	light	lucid, translucent
lum	Latin	light	illumine, luminous
luna	Latin	moon	lunar, lunatic
man	Latin	hand	manual, manipulate

Roots	Origins	Meanings	Examples
mar	Latin	sea	mariner, submarine
mater, matr	Latin	mother	maternal, matron
mech	Greek	machine	mechanic, mechanize
mens, ment	Latin	mind	demented, mental
migr	Latin	depart	migrate, migrant
miss, mit	Latin	send	missile, submit
mon	Latin	warn	admonish, monitor
mort	Latin	death	mortal, mortician
mot, mov	Latin	move	promote, remove
narr	Latin	tell	narrate, narrative
nat	Latin	born	nation, native
nav	Latin	ship	naval, navigate
not	Latin	mark	denote, note
nun, noun	Latin	declare	enunciate, announce
nov	Latin	new	innovate, novel
numer	Latin	number	enumerate, numeral
ocu	Latin	eye	binocular, oculist
opt	Greek	visible	optic, optician
opt	Latin	best	optimal, optimist
orig	Latin	beginning	aborigine, origin
pater, patr	Latin	father	paternal, patriarch
path	Greek	feeling	empathy, pathos
pend	Latin	hang	appendix, suspend
phon	Latin	sound	telephone, phonics
photo	Greek	light	telephoto, photograph
phys	Greek	nature	physical, physician
poli	Greek	city	metropolis, police
pop	Latin	people	populace, popular
port	Latin	carry	import, porter
psych	Greek	mind	psyche, psychology
put	Latin	think	deputy, computer
ques	Latin	ask, seek	quest, question
rect	Latin	straight	erect, rectangle
rid	Latin	laugh	deride, ridicule
rupt	Latin	break	erupt, rupture
san	Latin	health	insanity, sanitary
scend	Latin	climb	ascend, transcend

Roots	Origins	Meanings	Examples
sci	Latin	know	conscience, science
scop	Greek	see	microscope, periscope
scribe	Latin	write	inscribe, describe
script	Latin	written	transcript, script
sect	Latin	cut	dissect, intersect
sed	Latin	settle	sedate, sediment
sens	Latin	feel	sensation, senses
sign	Latin	mark	insignia, signal
sim	Latin	like	similar, simile
sol	Latin	alone	desolate, solitary
solv	Latin	loosen	solvent, resolve
son	Latin	sound	sonar, sonnet
spec	Latin	see	inspect, spectator
sta	Latin	stand	static, stagnant
strict	Latin	draw tight	constrict, restrict
struct	Latin	build	construct, instruct
sum	Latin	highest	summary, summit
tact, tang	Latin	touch	contact, tangent
ten	Latin	hold	tenant, tenure
terr	Latin	land	terrace, terrain
the	Greek	god	monotheism, theology
therm	Greek	heat	thermal, thermos
tract	Latin	pull, drag	attract, tractor
trib	Latin	give	contribute, tribute
turb	Latin	confusion	disturb, turbulence
urb	Latin	city	suburb, urban
vac	Latin	empty	evacuate, vacant
vag	Latin	wander	vagrant, vague
var	Latin	different	variety, vary
ver	Latin	truth	verdict, veracity
vic	Latin	conquer	conviction, victor
vid	Latin	see	evidence, video
voc	Latin	voice	advocate, vocal
void	Latin	empty	avoid, devoid
vol	Latin	wish, will	benevolent, volition
volv	Latin	roll	involve, revolve
vor	Latin	eat	herbivorous, voracious

Acknowledgments

44 "Mother" from THE SEVENTH CHILD by Freddie Mae Baxter. Copyright © 1999 by Freddie Mae Baxter. Reprinted by permission of Alfred A. Knopf, a division of Random House, Inc.

48 Copyright © 1982 by Annie Dillard. Reprinted by permission of HarperCollins Publishers, Inc.

52 (60, 61, 156, 157, 158, 159, 160, 162, 163, 166, 167, 168, 591) From *Creating America: A History of the United States* by Jesus Garcia, Donna M. Ogle, C. Frederick Risinger, Joyce Stevos and Winthrop D. Jordan. Copyright © 2001 by McDougal Littell Inc. All rights reserved. Reprinted by permission of McDougal Littell Inc.

58 (**342, 346, 347, 348**) From THE CAY by Theodore Taylor, copyright © 1969 by Theodore Taylor. Used by permission of Doubleday, a division of Random House, Inc.

62 Excerpt from GRAY WOLF, RED WOLF by Dorothy Hinshaw Patent. Text copyright © 1990 by Dorothy Hinshaw Patent. Reprinted by permission of Houghton Mifflin Company. All rights reserved. Fair Use

63 Excerpt from BIG BLUE OCEAN by Bill Nye. © 1999 by Bill Nye. Reprinted by permission of Hyperion Books. Fair Use

69 (70, 71, 72, 77, 78) From *America's Past and Promise* by Lorna Mason, Jesus Garcia, Frances Powell, and C. Frederick Risinger. Copyright © 1995 by Houghton Mifflin Company. All rights reserved. Reprinted by permission of McDougal Littell Inc.

85 (87, 88, 89, 90, 96) From *Geography: The World and Its People* by the National Geographic Society, David G. Armstrong, Richard G. Boehm, and Francis P. Hunkins. Copyright © 2000 by The McGraw-Hill Companies, Inc.

102 (103, 104, 105, 113) From *Prentice Hall Science Explorer Earth Science* by Michael J. Padilla, Ioannis Miaoulis, Martha Cyr, Joseph D. Exline, Jay M. Pasachoff, Barbara Brooks Simons, Carole Garbuny Voge, and Thomas R. Wellnitz. © 2001 by Prentice Hall, Inc. Used by permission of Pearson Education, Inc.

120 (121, 127) From *Passport to Mathematics: An Integrated Approach, Book 2* by Roland E. Larson, Laurie Boswell, and Lee Stiff. Copyright © 1997 by D.C. Heath and Company. All rights reserved. Reprinted by permission of McDougal Littell Inc.

133 (134, 135, 136) From *Prentice Hall Exploring Life Science* by Joan Hopkins, Susan Johnson, David LaHart, Maryanna Quon Warner & Jill Wrig. © 1999 by Prentice Hall, Inc. Used by permission of Pearson Education, Inc.

174 (175, 176) From NOT THAT YOU ASKED by Andrew A. Rooney, copyright © 1989 by Essay Productions, Inc. Used by permission of Random House, Inc.

190 (191, 193, 194, 195, 200) Reprinted by the permission of Russell & Volkening as agents for the author. Copyright © 1955 by Ann Petry, renewed 1983 by Ann Petry.

206 (207, 210, 211, 214) From UP FROM SLAVERY by Booker T. Washington, copyright © 1986 by Viking Penguin Inc, introduction and notes. Used by permission of Viking Penguin, a division of Penguin Putnam Inc.

221 (224, 225, 226, 227) © 2001, *Los Angeles Times*. Reprinted with permission.

236 (237, 238, 239) Copyright 2000 National Wildlife Federation. Reprinted from the August/September issue of *National Wildlife Magazine*

248 (250, 251, 252) © Tribune Media Services, Inc. All rights reserved. Reprinted with permission.

296 (297, 298, 299, 300, 301, 302, 303) "Charles" and excerpt from "Charles" from THE LOTTERY AND OTHER STORIES by Shirley Jackson. Copyright © 1948, 1949 by Shirley Jackson. Copyright renewed 1976, 1977 by Laurence Hyman, Barry Hyman, Mrs. Sarah Webster, and Mrs. Joanne Schnurer. Reprinted by permission of Farrar, Strauss and Giroux, LLC.

318 (319) From ROLL OF THUNDER, HEAR MY CRY by Mildred D. Taylor, Puffin cover illustration by Max Ginsburg, © 1991 by Max Ginsburg, cover illustration. Used by permission of Puffin Books, an imprint of Penguin Putnam Books for Young Readers, a division of Penguin

320 (323, 324, 327, 328, 329, 330, 334, 335, 361, 362, 364, 365, 366, 367, 379) From ROLL OF THUNDER, HEAR MY CRY by Mildred D. Taylor, copyright © 1976 by Mildred D. Taylor. Used by permission of Dial Books for Young Readers, an imprint of Penguin Putnam Books for Young Readers, a division of Penguin Putnam Inc.

352 (354, 355, 356, 357) Reprinted with the permission of Atheneum Books for Young Readers, an imprint of Simon & Schuster Children's Publishing Division. From SHILOH by Phyllis Reynolds Naylor. Copyright © 1991 Phyllis Reynolds Naylor.

370 (372) © 1974 by Paul Annixter.

410 (413, 414, 415, 417) © By Permission of Nikki Giovanni.

423 © The Estate of Pauli Murray, Reprinted by Permission of The Charlotte Sheedy Literary Agency.

431 "Those Winter Sundays." Copyright © 1966 by Robert Hayden, from ANGLE OF ASCENT: New and Selected Poems by Robert Hayden. Used by permission of Liveright Publishing Corporation.

440 (443) "The Sloth" copyright 1950 by Theodore Roethke, from THE COLLECTED POEMS OF THEODORE ROETHKE by Theodore Roethke. Used by permission of Doubleday, a division of Random House, Inc.

447 "There Will Come Soft Rains" by Sara Teasdale. Reprinted with permission of Wellesley College Special Collections.

448 Copyright © 1974 by Evil Eye Music, Inc. Used by permission of HarperCollins Publishers.

449 Copyright © 1974 by Evil Eye Music, Inc. Used by permission of HarperCollins Publishers.

451 From THE COLLECTED POEMS OF LANGSTON HUGHES by Langston Hughes, copyright © 1994 by The Estate of Langston Hughes. Used by permission of Alfred A. Knopf, a division of Random House, Inc.

452 From "Lean on Me" by Bill Withers, copyright © 1972 by INTERIOR MUSIC. International copyright secured. All rights reserved. Used by permission.

453 From WAY TO GO! by Lillian Morrison. Copyright © 2001 by Lillian Morrison. Used by permission of Marian Reiner for the author.

455 "Fog" from CHICAGO POEMS by Carl Sandburg, copyright 1916 by Holt, Rinehart and Winston and renewed in 1944 by Carl Sandburg, reprinted by permission of Harcourt, Inc.

457 "Lucinda Matlock" from SPOON RIVER ANTHOLOGY by Edgar Lee Masters. Originally published by the Macmillan Company. Permission by Hilary Masters.

458 "Galoshes" from STORIES TO BEGIN ON by Rhoda W. Bacmeister, illustrated by Tom Maley, copyright 1940 by E.P. Dutton, renewed © 1968 by Rhoda W. Bacmeister. Used by permission of Dutton Children's Books, an imprint of Penguin Putnam Books for Young Readers, a division of Penguin Putnam Inc.

459 "Summer Grass" from GOOD MORNING, AMERICA, copyright 1928 and renewed 1956 by Carl Sandburg, reprinted by permission of Harcourt, Inc.

461 From ONE AT A TIME by David McCord. Copyright © 1952 by David McCord. By permission of Little, Brown and Company (Inc.)

462 Copyright © 1936 by Ogden Nash, renewed. Reprinted by permission of Curtis Brown, Ltd.

463 "First Fig" by Edna St. Vincent Millay. From COLLECTED POEMS, HarperCollins. All rights reserved. Copyright 1922, 1950 by Edna St. Vincent Millay. Reprinted by permission of Elizabeth Barnett, literary executor.

464 Excerpted from "Simile: Willow and Ginkgo" in A SKY FULL OF POEMS by Eve Merriam. Copyright © 1964, 1970, 1973 by Eve Merriam. Used by permission of Marian Reiner.

465 Harvard University Press and the Trustees of Amherst College.

467 From ONE AT A TIME by David McCord. Copyright © 1929 by David McCord; First appeared in SATURDAY REVIEW. By permission of Little, Brown and Company (Inc.).

468 Reprinted with the permission of Scribner, a Division of Simon & Schuster, Inc., from THE AMERICAN SPORTING SCENE by John Kiernan. Copyright © 1941 by John Kiernan and John W. Golinkin, copyright renewed © 1969 by John Kiernan.

474 (475, 478, 479, 480, 485, 491, 496, 497, 498, 499, 500, 501, 506) From THE DIARY OF ANNE FRANK by Frances Goodrich and Albert Hackett, copyright © 1956 by Albert Hackett, Frances Goodrich Hackett, and Otto Frank. Used by permission of Random House, Inc.

503 (505, 509, 510, 511) Copyright © 1970 by Zindel Productions, Inc. First appeared in LET ME HEAR YOU WHISPER, published by Harper & Row Publishers, Inc. Reprinted by permission of Curtis Brown, Ltd.

504 Used with permission of PLAYS Magazine (www.playsmag.com).

517 (521) © International Dyslexia Association. *At the time of publication of this book, The International Dyslexia Association was creating a new website.*

533 © Google, Inc.

534 © National Baseball Hall of Fame

559 Courtesy of Major League Baseball

597 Copyright © 1998 by Great Source Education Group, Inc. All rights reserved.

601 © Unilever, Inc.

621 (622, 623, 624, 685, 686, 687, 688,

689, 690, 691, 692) Used by permission of the author.

PHOTO CREDITS

69 Courtesy of Southwest Museum, Los Angeles CA (photo# LS.7458)

71 *top*, **78** *top* © Bettmann/Corbis

71 *bottom*, **78** *bottom*, **168** *middle* From A Pictographic History of Oglala Sioux by Amos Bad Heart Bull, Plate# 147, Courtesy of University of Nebraska Press

72, 77 Smithsonian Institution, National Anthropological Archives, Neg# 2906

85 © David Allen Harvey/National Geographic Society

90, 96 © James P. Blair/National Geographic Society

102 *bottom*, **157** *left*, **166** The Granger Collection

102 *top* © Russ Lappa

103 *top* Photograph courtesy of Peabody Essex Museum, Salem, MA

104 *top* © Norbert Wu/Stock Market

105 *top*, **113** Scripps Institute of Oceanography

105 *bottom* © Scott Camazine/Photo Researchers

121 *top*, **127** *top* © Mark Antman/Image Works

134 *top* © Chris Baker/Stone

134 *bottom* © Nina Lampen/Phototake

157 *right* Culver Pictures

159, 163 Courtesy of McDougal Littell

160 *top*, **168** *top* © R. Kord/H. Armstrong Roberts

160 *bottom* © Jim Zintgraff/ Courtesy of Rock Art Foundation, San Antonio TX

165 Western History Collection, University of Oklahoma Libraries

167 James Otis Arguing Against writs of Assistance in the Old Towne House mural by Robert Reid, 1901 (detail), Courtesy of Commonwealth of Massachusetts Art Commission

168 *bottom* © Corbis

221 © Leo Sorel

236 © Stephen M. Kajiura

237, 239 © Norbert Wu

238 © Jeff Rotman/Jeff Rotman Photography

539, 542 "The Gallup Poll" a registered trademark of The Gallup Organization, Princeton, NJ. All rights reserved. Reprinted with authority. www.gallup.com

© 2001 - The Gallup Organization

549 U.S. Fish & Wildlife Service

550 © Jules Stauber/CCC, www.c5net

551 © Clay Bennett

552, 553 Diagrams by Mike Saunders reproduced from *The Young Oxford Book of the Human Being* by David Glover, by permission of Oxford University Press.

554 U.S. Census Bureau, International Data Base 5-10-00

557 Library of Congress/National Archives, Washington D.C.

560 U.S. Census Bureau

The editors have made every effort to trace the ownership of all copyrighted selections found in this book and to make full acknowledgment for their use. Omissions brought to our attention will be corrected in a subsequent edition.

Author and Title
Index

A

"Adventures of Isabel" (Nash), 462

"Alice" (Silverstein), 448

"America the Not-so-Beautiful" (Rooney), 174–176, 179, 183

Annixter, Paul, "Last Cover," 370, 372

"April Rain Song" (Hughes), 451

B

Bacmeister, Rhoda W., "Galoshes," 458

Baxter, Freddie Mae, The Seventh Child, 44

Bald Eagle Pairs (U.S. Fish and Wildlife Service), 549

Ball, Charles, Slavery in the United States, 59

Barry, Dave, online interview with, 282

Bartoletti, Susan Campbell, Growing Up in Coal Country, 617

"Because I could not stop for Death" (Dickinson), 465

Big Blue Ocean (Nye), 63

The Boys' War (Murphy), 281

"British Troops and Taxes" in Creating America: A History of the United States, 156

Burns, Robert, "A Red, Red Rose," 454

Byars, Betsy, The Summer of the Swans, 400

C

Call of the Wild (London), 57

Career Opportunities (cartoon), 551

The Cay (Taylor), 58, 342, 346, 347, 348

"Cell Growth and Division" in Prentice Hall Exploring Life Science, 133–136

"Charles" (Jackson), 296–303, 310

"Cheating," 287

Chicago Tribune, 283

Cisneros, Sandra, "Eleven," 405

Cleopatra (Stanley and Vennema), 618

Colker, David, "Robots get ready to rumble," 221, 224–227, 229, 230

Coming to America: The Story of Immigration (Maestro), 619

"Connections to Algebra: Variable and Equations" in Passport to Mathematics: An Integrated Approach, Book 2, 120–121, 127

Courier from Warsaw (Nowak), 51

Creating America: A History of the United States, 52, 60, 61, 156, 157, 158, 159, 160, 162, 163, 164, 165, 166, 167, 168

"Creating a New Nation" in Creating America: A History of the United States, 168

D

The Diary of Anne Frank (Goodrich and Hackett), 474–475, 478–480, 485, 491, 496–501, 506

Dickinson, Emily,
"Because I could not stop for Death," 465
"Hope is the thing with feathers," 450

Diet of Nesting Bald Eagles(chart), 558

Dillard, Annie, "Living Like Weasels," 48

E

"Effects of the New Deal, 1929–1941" in Creating America: A History of the United States, 159

"Eleven" (Cisneros), 405

Experiencing World History (King and Lewinski), 619

"Exploring the Ocean" in Prentice Hall Science Explorer Earth Science, 102–105, 113

F

"First Fig" (St. Vincent Millay), 463

"The First People in America" in Creating America: A History of the United States, 52

Fisher, Leonard Everett, Galileo, 276

"Fog" (Sandburg), 455

Forbes, Steve, "A Uniformly Good Idea," 274

Fradin, Dennis and Judith, Ida B. Wells, 291, 618

The Fragile Flag (Langton), 404

Freedman, Russell, Lincoln, 286

"The future doesn't belong to the fainthearted" (Reagan), 258–259

G

Galileo (Fisher), 276

Gallup poll, 539, 542

"Galoshes" (Bacmeister), 458

Ganeri, Anita, "How Shiva Got His Blue Throat," 391

Geography: The World and Its People, 85, 87, 90, 95, 96

Geronimo: His Own Story, "Kas-ki-yeh," 567–569, 573, 575, 578

Giovanni, Nikki, "Winter Poem," 410, 418

The Giver (Lowry), 397

Goodrich, Frances, The Diary of Anne Frank, 474–475, 478–480, 485, 491, 496–501, 506

Google (website), 533

Gray Wolf, Red Wolf (Patent), 62

Growing Up in Coal Country (Bartoletti), 617

H

Hackett, Albert, The Diary of Anne Frank, 474–475, 478–480, 485, 491, 496–501, 506

Harriet Tubman: Conductor on the Underground Railroad (Petry), 190–191, 193–195, 200

Hayden, Robert, "Those Winter Sundays," 431, 433, 435, 436

Hinton, S. E., Rumble Fish, 20, 390

Holes (Sachar), 403

"Hope is the thing with feathers" (Dickinson), 450

Houghton Mifflin Social Studies, 289

"How Shiva Got His Blue Throat" (Ganeri), 391

Hughes, Langston, "April Rain Song," 451

Human skin (diagram), 552

Human tooth (diagram), 553

I

Ida B. Wells (Fradin and Fradin), 291, 618

"Indian Wars" in America's Past and Promise, 69–72, 77, 78

The International Dyslexia Association (website), 517, 521

J

Jackson, Shirley, "Charles," 296–303, 310

Journey to Topaz (Uchida), 402

K

"Kas-ki-yeh" from Geronimo: His Own Story, 567–569, 573, 575, 578

The Kid Comes Back (Tunis), 398

Kieran, John, "There's This That I Like About Hockey, My Lad," 468

"A Killer Gets Some Respect" in National Wildlife Magazine, 236–239, 243

*King, Experiencing World History, 619

L

Lange, Dorothea (photo), 557

Langton, Jane, The Fragile Flag, 404

"Last Cover" (Annixter), 370, 372

Lauber, Patricia, Volcano: The Eruption and Healing of Mount St. Helens, 284

"Lean on Me" (Withers), 452

Lee, Harper, To Kill a Mockingbird, 392

Let Me Hear You Whisper (Zindel), 503, 505, 507, 509, 510–511

*Lewinski, Experiencing World History, 619

Lincoln (Freedman), 286

"Living Like Weasels" (Dillard), 48

London, Jack, Call of the Wild, 57

Lopez, Barry, "The Raven," 278

Lowry, Lois, The Giver, 397

"Lucinda Matlock" (Masters), 457

Lyddie (Paterson), 615, 616

M

Maestro, Betsy, Coming to America: The Story of Immigration, 619

Maps in *Creating America: A History of the United States,* 163–164
Map of Africa, 555
Masters, Edgar Lee, "Lucinda Matlock," 457
McCord, David
   "Owls Talking," 461
   "This Is My Rock," 467
Meltzer, Milton, *Rescue: The Story of How the Gentiles Saved the Jews in the Holocaust,* 620
Merriam, Eve, "Simile: Willow and Gingko," 464
"Meteorides, Meteors, and Meteorites," 277
The Million-Pound Bank Note (Twain), 504
Momaday, N. Scott, *The Way to Rainy Mountain,* 275
Morrison, Lillian, "The Sidewalk Racer," 453
Murphy, Jim, *The Boys' War,* 281
Murray, Pauli, "Words," 423, 424, 427, 428

N
Nash, Ogden, "Adventures of Isabel," 462
National Baseball Hall of Fame (website), 534
National Wildlife Magazine, "A Killer Gets Some Respect," 236–239, 243
Naylor, Phyllis Reynolds, *Shiloh,* 352, 354, 355, 356, 357
"No Difference" (Silverstein), 449
Nowak, Jan, *Courier from Warsaw,* 51
Nye, Bill, *Big Blue Ocean,* 63

O
"Owls Talking" (McCord), 461

P
"Parents, Not Cash, Can Enrich a School" (Royko), 248, 250–252, 254
Patent, Dorothy H., *Gray Wolf, Red Wolf,* 62
Paterson, Katherine, *Lyddie,* 615, 616
Petry, Ann, *Harriet Tubman: Conductor on the Underground Railroad,* 190–191, 193–195, 200
Physical Science, 617
Poe, Edgar Allan, "The Raven," 456, 460, 651
"Population" in *Geography: The World and Its People,* 87–90

R
"The Raven" (Lopez), 278
"The Raven" (Poe), 456, 460, 651
Reagan, Ronald, "The future doesn't belong to the fainthearted," 258–259
"A Red, Red Rose" (Burns), 454

Rescue: The Story of How the Gentiles Saved the Jews in the Holocaust (Meltzer), 620
"The Road to Revolution" in *Creating America: A History of the United States,* 166
"Robots get ready to rumble" (Colker), 221, 224–227, 229, 230
Roethke, Theodore, "The Sloth," 440, 444
Roll of Thunder, Hear My Cry (Taylor), 318–320, 323, 324, 327, 328, 329, 330, 335, 361, 362, 364, 365, 366
Rooney, Andy, "America the Not-so-Beautiful," 174–176, 179, 183
Royko, Mike, "Parents, Not Cash, Can Enrich a School," 248, 250–252, 254
Rumble Fish (Hinton), 20, 390

S
Sachar, Louis, *Holes,* 403
St. Vincent Millay, Edna, "First Fig," 463
Sandburg, Carl
   "Fog," 455
   "Summer Grass," 459
The Seventh Child (Baxter), 44
Shiloh (Naylor), 352, 354, 355, 356, 357
"The Sidewalk Racer" (Morrison), 453
Silverstein, Shel
   "Alice," 448
   "No Difference," 449
"Simile: Willow and Gingko" (Merriam), 464
Slavery in the United States (Ball), 59
"The Sloth" (Roethke), 440, 444
Stanley, Diane, *Cleopatra,* 618
"Summer Grass" (Sandburg), 459
The Summer of the Swans (Byars), 400

T
Taylor, Mildred D., *Roll of Thunder, Hear My Cry,* 318–320, 323, 324, 327, 328, 329, 330, 335, 361, 362, 364, 365, 366
Taylor, Theodore, *The Cay,* 58, 342, 346, 347, 348
Teasdale, Sara, "There Will Come Soft Rains," 447
"There's This That I Like About Hockey, My Lad" (Kieran), 468
"There Will Come Soft Rains" (Teasdale), 447
"This Is My Rock" (McCord), 467
"Those Winter Sundays" (Hayden), 431, 433, 435, 436
"Three Worlds Meet" in *Creating America: A History of the United States,* 160

"Tighter British Control" in *Creating America: A History of the United States,* 167
To Kill a Mockingbird (Lee), 392
Tom Sawyer (Twain), 394
Tunis, John R., *The Kid Comes Back,* 398
"Turkeys" (White), 279
Twain, Mark
   The Million-Pound Bank Note, 504
   Tom Sawyer, 394
Two Men in Bottles (cartoon), 550

U
Uchida, Yoshiko, *Journey to Topaz,* 402
"A Uniformly Good Idea" (Forbes), 274
Up from Slavery (Washington), 206–207, 210–211, 214

V
Vennema, Peter, *Cleopatra,* 618
Volcano: The Eruption and Healing of Mount St. Helens (Lauber), 284
"Vote 'YES' For a New School," 280

W
Washington, Booker T., *Up from Slavery,* 206–207, 210–211, 214
The Way to Rainy Mountain (Momaday), 275
White, Bailey, "Turkeys," 279
The White House (website), 529
"Winter Poem" (Giovanni), 410, 418
Withers, Bill, "Lean on Me," 452
"Words" (Murray), 423, 424, 427, 428

Z
Zindel, Paul, *Let Me Hear You Whisper,* 503, 505, 507, 509, 510–511

Skills and Terms Index

A

Active reading, 43–45, 413, 655
  asking questions, 44, 45
  clarifying, 44, 45
  marking or highlighting, 44, 45
  predicting, 44, 45
  reacting and connecting, 44, 45
  visualizing, 44, 45
Acts in drama, 503
Alliteration in poetry, 442, 447
Allusion in poetry, 448
Analogies, 586–587, 636–639
  antonyms in, 586, 637
  description in, 638
  different forms of same word in, 638
  examples in, 637, 638
  greater than or lesser than in, 586
  homophones in, 637
  reading questions in, 636
  relationship to each other in, 586, 638, 639
  rhyming words in, 637
  sequence in, 639
  set and subset in, 586, 637, 638
  succession or pattern in, 586
  synonyms in, 586, 637
Answers
  choosing best, on standardized vocabulary tests, 635
  in math tests
    eliminating wrong, 594
    estimating, 595
    trying easier choices first, 596
    visualizing, 595
  in social studies tests
    ruling out wrong, 590
    thinking through, 590
Antagonist, 390
Antonyms
  in analogies, 586, 637
  in vocabulary questions, 634
Appeal to ignorance, 288
Argument, 274
  persuasive writing in making, 247, 254–255
Argument chart, 249, 253, 255, 667
Author
  purpose of, 391
  evaluating, 653
  questioning of, 185, 240, 652–653
Autobiographer, 204
Autobiographies
  organization of, 213
  reading process for, 204–217
  reading and rereading strategies
    looking for cause and effect, 216
    synthesizing, 208–209
  reading tools for, 209, 212, 213, 214, 216

B

Bandwagon, 263, 288
Bar graphs, 549, 603
Biographer, 188
Biographical subject, 188
Biographies, 188
  key events in, 198
  organization of, 196–199
  place in, 198
  reading process for, 188–203
  reading and rereading strategies
    looking for cause and effect, 192
    outlining, 202
  reading tools for, 192, 196, 198, 199, 202, 203
  subject in, 199
  time in, 197
Boldface terms as textbook element, 156
Bookmarks for the Internet, 528, 529
Book reviews, 217, 339
Broad generalization, 263, 288
Browsers for the Internet, 529
Buried lead, 229

C

Caption in diagram, 552, 553
Cartoons, 550–551
Cast of characters in drama, 504
Cause-effect order, 56, 59, 644–645
Cause-effect organizer, 59, 644–645, 662, 667
  in autobiographies, 216
  in biographies, 192, 196
  in history textbooks, 82
  in nonfiction, 275
  in science textbooks, 111
Characterization, 392
Characters, 340–350, 392–393
  analyzing, 343
  antagonist as, 390
  avoiding names of, in making theme statements, 382
  cast of, in drama, 504
  clues about, 341
  creating a portrait of, 343
  in dialogue, 363–364, 498–499
  dynamic, 348, 393
  main, 393
  major, 340
  minor, 340, 393
  in novels, 323–326
  plot and, 345
  protagonist as, 390
  reading tools for
    character development chart, 350, 668
    character map, 341, 343, 663, 668
      for autobiographies, 212
      for biographies, 199

      for drama, 483
      for novels, 326, 338
      for short stories, 306
    character webs, 212, 326, 344
    inference chart, 347, 356
    Venn diagram, 313
  relations with other characters, 346
  setting and, 356
  static, 348, 393
  theme and, 347–348
  types of, 393
Charts, 63
  reading, for science tests, 600–601
  as textbook element, 157
Chat rooms, 531
Chronological order, 57, 77, 196, 276
Circular thinking in propaganda, 263, 288
Clarification, 44, 45
Classification, 56, 63, 112, 277
Classification notes, 110, 669
Class notes, 108, 647, 669
Climax, 369, 375, 400
  in plays, 484, 507
  in short stories, 309
Close reading, 312–313, 642–643
  in focusing on dialogue, 363
  in focusing on setting, 353
  in novels, 332
  for poetry, 412, 423, 432, 440
Comparison-contrast, 278, 383–388
  drawing conclusions and, 387
  organizing, 388
  previewing, 384
  reading tools for
    fiction organizer, 385
    two-story map, 386
    Venn diagram, 387
Comparison-contrast order, 42, 56, 62
Concept maps, 670
  in building vocabulary, 633
  for geography textbooks, 93
  for science textbooks, 137, 138
Concepts, focusing on, in science textbook, 132–142
Conclusions, drawing, 41, 653
  for comparison-contrast, 387
  in reading graphics, 546
Conflict in plot, 508
Connecting, 35
Connotations, 279
  in poetry, 425–426, 433–434
Context clues, 586
  comparisons and contrasts as, 617
  conjunctions showing relationships and connecting ideas as, 619
  definitions as, 616
  descriptions as, 618
  examples as, 617
  in improving vocabulary, 615–620
  modifying words or phrases as, 618
  repeating words as, 619

synonyms as, 616
unstated or implied meanings as, 620
Continued dialogue, 362
Couplets, 466
Critical reading chart, 655, 670
for newspaper articles, 228
for settings, 245
for speeches, 223

D

Definition, 277
Definitions
as context clues, 616
in dictionaries, 629
Denotations, 279
in poetry, 425–426, 433–434
Details, 51, 53, 54, 60–61
in biography, 196–199
in magazine articles, 242
in newspaper articles, 229
in speeches, 262
supporting, 289–290
Diagrams, 552–553
making sense of, in word
problems, 149
reading, for science tests, 602
in retelling information, 142
Dialect, 394–395
Dialogue, 360–367
clues about character in, 363–364,
498–499
clues about mood in, 366
clues about plot in, 365
continued, 362
defined, 360
dialect and, 394–395
in drama, 498–500, 505
paragraphing for, 361
plot and, 499
quotation marks for, 361
quotes within quotes, 362
reading tools for
double-entry journal, 364
thinking tree, 367
speech tags for, 361
theme and, 500
Dictionaries, 626–629
definitions in, 629
entry word in, 629
guide words in, 629
illustrative examples in, 629
inflected forms in, 629
part of speech in, 629
pronunciation in, 629
using, 425
word history in, 629
Directions, reading, for essay tests, 581
Domain, 535
Double-entry journal, 643, 662, 671.
See also Journals
for dialogue, 364
for drama, 491–492, 499
for essays, 185

for novels, 334
for poetry, 185, 355, 412, 413,
414, 415, 417, 434, 435
for setting, 355
for short stories, 312
for theme, 379
Drama
acts and scenes in, 503
cast of characters in, 504
dialogue in, 498–500, 505
focusing on language in, 495–501
focusing on theme in, 489–494
key lines and speeches in, 496
monologue in, 506
organization of, 484
plot in, 507–508
reading process for, 472–501
reading and rereading strategies
summarizing, 476
visualizing and thinking aloud,
487
reading tools for, 476, 481, 482,
483, 484, 487, 491–492, 499
script for, 502
setting in, 509
stage directions for, 510
theme in, 511
Dynamic characters, 348, 393

E

Editorials, 280
Either/or, 288
Email, 530–531
End rhyme, 461
Essays
expository, 172, 181
finding main idea in, 179
finding supporting details in,
179–180
narrative, 172, 181
opening in, 182
organization of, 181–182
parts of, 172
reading process for, 172–187
reading and rereading strategies
outlining, 177–178, 180
questioning the author, 185
reading tools for, 181, 182, 185
Essay tests, 580–583
Evaluating, 42, 655
Exaggeration in poetry, 449
Exposition, 369, 400
in plays, 484, 507
in short stories, 309
Expository essays, 172, 181
Expository paragraphs, 55

F

Fact and opinion, 281
Falling action, 369, 400
in plays, 484, 507
in short stories, 309
Family tree web for novels, 325
Favorites for the Internet, 529

Fiction
antagonist in, 390
author's purpose in, 391
characters in, 340–350, 392–393
comparing and contrasting in,
383–388
dialect in, 394–395
dialogue in, 360–367, 394–395
genre in, 396
mood in, 397
novels as, 315–339
plot in, 368–375, 400–401
point of view in, 398–399
protagonist in, 390
setting in, 351–359, 402
short stories as, 294–314
style in, 403
symbols in, 404
synthesizing with, 660
theme in, 376–382, 405
Fiction organizer, 658, 671
for comparison-contrast, 385
for novels, 321, 337
for short stories, 308
Figurative language, 426–427
alliteration as, 447
metaphors as, 426, 434, 455
onomatopoeia as, 458
personification as, 426, 459
in poetry, 450
similes as, 426, 464
5 W's organizers, 663, 672
for history, 73, 74
for newspaper articles, 220, 222
5 W's questions, 67, 229, 283
Flashbacks, 372, 481
Free-reading, 265
Free verse, 416, 451
Funnel pattern organizer for essays, 182

G

General comparison, 383, 385–386
General setting in drama, 509
Genre, 396
Geographic order, 77
Geography textbooks, 84–99
organization of, 94–95
reading process for, 84–99
reading and rereading strategies
graphic organizers, 91
note-taking, 98
reading tools for, 91, 92, 93, 95, 98
Glossary as textbook element, 158
Graphic organizers, 54, 662–663. *See
also* Reading tools
in character analysis, 344
in comparing and contrasting, 385
for geography textbooks, 91
in plot analysis, 371
as rereading strategy, 336
for science textbooks, 139–140
for short stories, 305
for social studies tests, 589

Graphics
  bar graphs as, 549
  cartoons as, 550–551
  diagrams as, 552–553
  drawing conclusions in reading,
    546
  in geography textbooks, 95
  line graphs as, 554
  maps as, 555–556
  organization of, 542–543
  photographs as, 557
  pictographs as, 549
  pie charts as, 558
  reading, 537–547
  reading and rereading strategies
    paraphrasing, 540
    reading critically, 545
  reading tools for, 540, 541, 544,
    547
  tables as, 559–560
  timelines as, 561
Graphs, 15
  reading, for science tests, 603–604
  as textbook element, 159
Greek roots, 689–692
Guess, check, and revising, in solving
  word problems, 151
Guide words in dictionaries, 629

H

Headings
  in finding subject of paragraph, 49
  in skimming, 270
  as textbook element, 160–161
Highlighting text, 44, 45, 270
History textbooks
  organization of, 77
  reading process for, 66–83
  reading and rereading strategies
    note taking, 73–76
    outlining, 80–81
  reading tools for, 73, 75, 76, 81, 82
Home page, 529, 535
Homophones in analogies, 637
Horizontal axis, 543
Hypertext, 532, 535

I

Idioms in poetry, 452
Illustrations as textbook element, 165
Imagery in poetry, 427, 453
Immediate settings in drama, 509
Implied main idea, 52
Index as textbook element, 162
Inference chart, 672
  for autobiographies, 214
  for characters, 347
  for nonfiction, 285
  for setting, 356
  for short stories, 308
Inferences, making, 40, 52, 653
Inflected forms in dictionaries, 629

Information
  diagrams in retelling, 142
  getting background, in plot, 370
  redrawing/retelling, for science
    textbooks, 142
  remembering and using, 272
  skimming for specific, 657
Informational reading, 265
Informative speech, 256
Internal rhyme, 461
Internet. See also Websites
  bookmark for, 528, 529
  browser for, 529
  email for, 530–531
  evaluating sources on, 525
  link for, 532
  search engine for, 533
  World Wide Web for, 534–535
Interviews, 282
Inverted pyramid organization, 229
Irony in cartoons, 551

J

Jargon, 270
Journals. See also Double-entry journal
  drama, 493, 501
  learning, 115
  for magazine articles, 246
  math, 130
  poetry, 420–421, 425
  short stories, 314
  vocabulary, 609–611, 631

K

Key lines in drama, 496
Key terms, recording, in building
  vocabulary, 631
Key topic notes, 660, 661
  in reading autobiographies, 209,
    212
Key word notes, 647, 673
  for math textbooks, 130
  for science textbooks, 109
Key words
  in finding subject of paragraph, 49
  in poetry, 424
K-W-L chart, 673
  for geography textbooks, 91, 92

L

Labels in diagram, 552
Language, focusing on
  in reading drama, 495–501
  in reading poetry, 422–429
Latin roots, 689–692
Leads, 220, 229, 283
  buried, 229
Legend, 543
Line graphs, 554, 603
Links for the Internet, 516, 518, 532,
  535
Listening in boosting vocabulary, 613
Loaded words, 263, 264, 288
Location order, 56, 58, 77

Long-term memory, moving words into,
  612
Looking for cause and effect, 192,
  216, 644–45
Lyric poems, 454

M

Magazine articles
  organization of
    time order, 242
    viewpoint-details order, 242
  reading process for, 234–246
  reading and rereading strategies
    questioning the author, 240
    reading critically, 245
  reading tools for, 240, 242, 243,
    245
Magnet summary, 674
  for drama, 476, 481
Main character, 393
Main idea, 179, 284–285
  finding, in paragraphs, 50–54,
    60–61
  implied, 52–53
Main idea organizer, 53, 54, 582, 674
  for essays, 182
  for essay tests, 582
  for geography textbooks, 93
  for nonfiction, 285
  for magazine articles, 240
  for speeches, 262
Maps, 555–556
  historical, 556
  physical, 555, 556
  political, 556
  road, 556
  as textbook element, 163–164
  thematic, 556
Marking text, 44, 45
Math tests, 593–597
Math textbooks
  focusing on word problems in,
    143–154
  organization of, 126–127
  problem-solving plan, 124
  reading process for, 118–146
  reading and rereading strategies
    note-taking, 129–130
    visualizing and thinking aloud,
      123, 125–128, 145–146
  reading tools for, 123, 125, 126,
    128, 130, 145, 146, 148, 149,
    150, 151, 152, 153
  use simpler numbers, 153
  work backward, 152
Meaning, focusing on, in reading
  poetry, 430–438
Metaphors, 426, 434, 450
  in poetry, 455
Meter in poetry, 443–444
Minor characters, 393
Monologue in drama, 506

Mood, 397
  clues about, in dialogue, 366
  in poetry, 417, 456
  setting and, 354–355

N

Narrative essays, 172, 181
Narrative paragraphs, 55
Narrative poems, 457
Natural sciences, 100
Newspaper articles
  lead, 220
  organization of, 229
    inverted pyramid, 229
  reading process for, 218–233
  reading and rereading strategies
    reading critically, 222–223
    summarizing, 232
  reading tools for, 222, 223, 228,
    232, 233
Nonfiction
  autobiographies as, 204–217
  biographies as, 188–203
  elements of
    argument or persuasive
      writing, 274
    cause and effect, 275
    chronological order, 276
    classification, 277
    comparison and contrast, 278
    connotation, 279
    definition, 277
    denotation, 279
    editorial, 280
    fact and opinion, 281
    interview, 282
    lead, 283
    main idea, 284–285
    problem and solution, 286
    propaganda techniques,
      287–288
    topic sentence and supporting
      details, 289–290
    viewpoint, 291
  essays as, 172–187
  magazine articles as, 234–246
  newspaper articles as, 218–233
  persuasive writing as, 247–255
  real-world writing as, 265–272
  speeches as, 256–264
  summarizing, 659
  synthesizing with, 661
Nonfiction organizer, 659, 675
  for speeches, 261
Note-taking, 646–647
  classification notes, 110, 669
  class notes, 108, 647, 669
  key topic notes, 209
  key word notes, 109, 130, 647,
    673
  page-by-page notes, 75
  in paraphrasing, 650–651
  process notes, 51, 110, 140, 677

sequence notes, 76, 116
study cards, 98, 109, 140
summary notes, 75, 232, 233,
  331, 358, 378, 484, 526, 547,
  646, 680
text notes, 108, 647, 669
timeline notes, 76
web notes, 75
for websites, 521
Novels, 315–339
  characters in, 323–326
  organization of
    chronological order, 332
    plot structure, 332
  plot in, 331
  point of view in, 323
  previewing, 317–320
  reading process for, 315–339
  reading and rereading strategies
    synthesizing, 321
    using graphic organizers, 336
  reading tools for, 321, 325, 326,
    329, 331, 332, 333, 334, 337,
    338
  setting in, 327–330
  style, 334
  theme, 333
Numbers
  order of, in word problems, 147
  using simpler in solving word
    problems, 153

O

Octet, 466
Onomatopoeia in poetry, 458
Opinion, 281
Opposing viewpoint in persuasive
  writing, 249, 250, 252, 253
Order of importance, 60–61
Organizational schemes
  cause-effect, 56, 59, 82, 111,
    192, 196, 216, 275, 644–645
  chronological, 77, 196, 213, 232,
    276, 368
  classification, 56, 63, 112
  comparison-contrast, 42, 56, 62
  geographic, 77
  inverted pyramid, 229
  location order, 56, 58, 77
  order of importance, 56, 60–61
  problem-and-solution, 112, 124,
    150–154, 286
  in real world writing, 269
  time order, 56, 57, 77, 196, 213, 242
  topic, 94
  viewpoint-details order, 242
  web, 522
Outlines, 648–649, 675
  as reading strategy , 80–81, 177
  sentence, 178, 180, 649
  topic, 81, 94, 649
Oversimplification, 288

P

Paragraphs. *See also* Organizational
  schemes
  classification, 63
  descriptive, 55
  expository, 55
  finding main idea in, 50–54
  finding subject in, 48–49
  narrative, 55
  persuasive, 55
  for showing dialogue, 361
  steps to understanding, 47–54
Paraphrase chart, 651, 676
  for graphics, 540, 541, 544
  for poetry, 420, 438
Paraphrasing, 650–651
  for graphics, 540
  for poetry, 420
Partner, working with, 122, 154,
  428–429
Part of speech in dictionaries, 629
Pattern in analogies, 586
Pausing and reflecting, 35–36
Personification in poetry, 426, 459
Persuasive paragraphs, 55
Persuasive speech, 256
Persuasive writing, 55, 274
  argument, 249
  critical reading as reading strategy
    for, 249
  propaganda techniques, 263
  reading, 247–255
  reading tools for, 248, 249, 253, 255
  viewpoint, 247
Photographs, 557
  elements of, 557
  as textbook element, 165
Physical maps, 555, 556
Physical sciences, 100
Pictographs, 549
Pie charts, 558
Plain folks appeal, 263
Planning, 33
Plays. *See* Drama
Playwright, 502
Plot, 368–375
  characters and, 345
  climax in, 369, 375, 400, 484
  conflict in, 401
  in dialogue, 365, 499
  in drama, 507–508
  exposition in, 369, 400, 484
  falling action in, 369, 400, 484
  flashbacks and, 372, 484
  getting background information in,
    370
  in novels, 331, 332
  in plays, 484
  reading strategy for, 371
  reading tools for
    plot diagram, 309, 332, 369,
      375, 401, 484, 507, 676
    storyboard, 371
    story organizer, 373

resolution in, 369, 400, 484
rising action in, 369, 400, 484
setting and, 357
subplots in, 373
Plot diagram, 369, 375, 401, 676
  for drama, 484, 507
  for novels, 332
  for short stories, 309
Poetry, 407–469
  alliteration in, 442, 447
  allusion in, 448
  choices of poet in, 416
  connecting to, 444
  connotations in, 425–426,
    433–434
  denotations in, 425–426, 433–434
  enjoyment of, 413
  exaggeration in, 449
  exploring feelings about, 417, 436
  figurative language in, 415,
    426–427, 450
  first reading, 411, 413
  focusing on language in reading,
    422–429
  focusing on meaning in, 414,
    430–438
  focusing on sound and structure
    in, 439–445
  fourth reading, 411, 417
  free verse in, 451
  idioms in, 452
  imagery in, 427, 453
  key words in, 424
  lyric, 454
  metaphors in, 455
  meter in, 443–444, 463
  mood in, 417, 456
  narrative, 457
  onomatopoeia in, 458
  organization of, 416, 441
  personification in, 459
  reading plan for, 411
  reading process for, 407–421
  reading and rereading strategies
    close reading, 412–417, 423,
      432, 440, 642
    paraphrasing, 420, 437–438
  reading tools for, 185, 355, 412,
    413, 414, 415, 417, 420, 434,
    435, 438
  repetition in, 442, 460
  rereading, 445
  rhyme in, 442–443, 461–462
  rhythm in, 443–444, 463
  second reading, 411, 414
  similes in, 464
  stanzas in, 416, 441, 465–466
  structure of, 415
  symbols in, 467
  third reading, 411, 415
  tone in, 468–469
  variety of, 416
  voice in, 468–469

Point of view, 313, 323, 398–399
  first-person, 399
  limited omniscient narration, 399
  omniscient narrator, 399
  third-person, 399
Political maps, 556
Predicting, 44, 45
Prefixes, 585, 622, 685–687
Preview as textbook element, 166–167
Previewing, 33
  autobiographies, 205–207
  bibliographies, 189–191
  comparison-contrast, 384
  drama, 473–475
  essays, 173–176
  geography textbooks, 86–90
  graphics, 539
  history textbooks, 68–72
  magazine articles, 235–239
  math textbooks, 119–121
  newspaper articles, 220–221
  novels, 317–320
  persuasive writing, 248
  poetry, 409–410
  science textbooks, 101–105,
    132–136
  setting, 352
  short stories, 295–303
  speeches, 257–259
  tests, 566–570
  websites, 516–517
Problem and solution
  for nonfiction, 286
  for science textbooks, 112
Process notes, 51, 677
  for science textbooks, 110, 140
Pronunciation in dictionaries, 629
Propaganda techniques, 263, 287–288
Protagonist, 390
Purpose
  identifying, 266
  reading with, 34
  setting, 32
    for autobiographies, 205
    for biographies, 189
    for drama, 473
    for essays, 173
    for geography textbooks, 85
    for graphics, 538
    for history textbooks, 67
    for magazine articles, 235
    for math textbooks, 118
    for newspaper articles, 219
    for novels, 316
    for poetry, 409
    for reading tests, 565
    for science textbooks, 101
    for short stories, 295
    for websites, 515

Q
Quatrain, 466
Questioning, 44, 45
  of the author, 185, 240, 652–653

Questions
  analogy, 636
  asking, about plot, 374
  5 W's, 67, 229, 283
  previewing, for science tests, 599
  for readers, 29
  reading, for clues, for social
    studies tests, 591
  vocabulary, 634–636
  working through, for social studies
    tests, 592
  for writers, 28
Quintet, 466
Quotation marks, 361
  single, 362

R
Reacting and connecting, 44, 45
Reader's Handbook
  goals of, 14–15
  organization of, 17–21
  using, 16
Readers, questions for, 29
Reading
  active, 43–45, 413, 655
  autobiographies, 204–217
  biographies, 188–203
  charts, 600–601
  close, 312–313, 353, 363, 412,
    423, 432
  critical, 518–519, 545–546,
    654–656
  defined, 24
  diagrams, 602
  directions for essay tests, 581
  drama, 472–501
  essays, 172–187
  finding place for, 46
  finding time for, 46
  free, 265
  graphics, 537–547
  graphs, 603–604
  informational, 265
  kinds of, 15
  for magazine articles, 234–246
  modeling good, 14
  for newspaper articles, 218–233
  novels, 315–339
  paragraphs, 47–54
  for persuasive writing, 247–255
  poetry, 407–445, 440
  for real-world writing, 265–272
  reasons for, 25
  short stories, 294–314
  for speeches, 256–264
  tables, 600–601
  tests, 564–579
  textbooks, 65–169
    geography, 84–99
    history, 66–83
    math, 131, 143–154
    science, 100–116, 132–142
  thesaurus, 630
  visualizing, 26–27

websites, 514–526
Reading critically, 222–223, 654–655
  for graphics, 545–546
  for magazine articles, 245
  for persuasive writing, 249
  for speeches, 260
  for websites, 518–519
Reading process, 26–29
  connecting, 35
  pausing and reflecting, 35–36
  planning, 33
  previewing, 33
  reading with a purpose, 34
  remembering, 36
  rereading, 36
  setting a purpose, 32, 34
Reading skills
  comparing and contrasting, 42
  drawing conclusions, 41
  evaluating, 42
  making inferences, 40
Reading strategies. *See also* Rereading
  strategies
  cause and effect, 644–645
    for autobiographies, 216
    for biographies, 192
  close reading, 642–643
    in focusing on dialogue, 363
    in focusing on setting, 353
    in focusing on sound and
      structure, 440
    for poetry, 412, 423, 432
  critical reading, 518–519, 654–655
    for newspaper articles, 222
    for persuasive writing, 249
    for speeches, 260
  graphic organizers, 336, 662–663
    in character analysis, 344
    in comparing and contrasting,
      385
    for geography textbooks, 91
    in plot analysis, 371
    for science textbooks, 139–140
    for short stories, 305
  note-taking, 646–647
    for geography textbooks, 98
    for history textbooks, 73–76
    for science textbooks, 106–107
  outlining, 648–649
    for biographies, 202
    for essays, 177–178, 180
  paraphrasing, 650–651
    for graphics, 540
  questioning the author, 652–653
    for essays, 185
    for magazine articles, 240
    for short stories, 240
  skimming, 656–657
    for real-world writing, 269
    for tests, 571
  summarizing, 476, 658–659

synthesizing, 660–661
  for autobiographies, 208–209
  for novels, 321
visualizing and thinking aloud,
  664–665
  for drama, 484
  for math textbooks, 123,
    125–126, 128, 145, 146
Reading tools. *See also* Graphic
organizers
  argument chart, 249, 253, 255,
    274, 667
  cause-effect organizer, 59, 82,
    111, 192, 196, 216, 275, 644,
    645, 662, 667
  character development chart, 350,
    668
  character maps, 199, 306, 326,
    338, 341, 343, 483, 663, 668
  classification notes, 110, 277, 669
  class notes, 108, 647, 669
  concept map, 93, 137, 138, 633,
    670
  critical reading chart, 223, 228,
    245, 655, 670
  diagrams, 142, 149, 552–553, 602
  double-entry journal, 185, 312,
    334, 355, 364, 379, 412, 413,
    414, 415, 417, 434, 435,
    491–492, 499, 643, 662, 671
  evidence organizer, 243, 683
  fiction organizer, 308, 321, 337,
    385, 658, 671
  5 W's organizer, 73, 74, 220, 222,
    229, 663, 672
  inference chart, 214, 285, 308,
    347, 356, 672
  key topic notes, 209, 212, 660,
    661
  key word notes, 109, 130, 647,
    673
  K-W-L chart, 91, 92, 673
  magnet summary, 476, 481, 674
  main idea organizer, 53, 54, 93,
    182, 240, 262, 285, 582, 674
  nonfiction organizer, 261, 659,
    675
  outlines, 80–81, 94, 178, 180,
    481, 648–649, 675
  paraphrase chart, 420, 438, 541,
    544, 651, 676
  plot diagrams, 309, 332, 369, 375,
    401, 484, 507, 676
  process notes, 51, 110, 140, 677
  retelling chart, 676
  scene-by-scene summary notes,
    482
  sequence notes, 76, 116, 646
  setting chart, 329, 353, 677
  storyboard, 307, 359, 371, 487,
    678
  story organizer, 305, 373, 678
  story string, 242, 307, 679

study cards, 98, 109, 140, 203,
  520, 521, 679
summary notes, 75, 95, 232, 233,
  331, 358, 378, 482, 526, 547,
  646, 680
text notes, 108, 647, 669
thinking tree, 76, 107, 115, 139,
  367, 680
timeline, 198, 213, 276, 331, 561,
  646, 681
topic and theme organizer, 333,
  381, 492, 681
topic notes, 673
two per line, 414, 435, 682
two-story map, 386, 682
Venn diagram, 313, 387, 683
viewpoint organizer, 243, 683
webs, 50, 75, 212, 325, 326, 344,
  633, 684
website profiler, 519, 523, 684
Real-world writing, 265–272
  identifying reading purpose, 269
  organization of, 269
  reading plan for, 266
Redrawing/retelling information for
  science textbooks, 142
Relationship to each other in
  analogies, 586, 637, 638, 639
Remembering, 36
Repetition
  as context clue, 619
  in poetry, 460
Rereading, 36
  autobiographies, 215
  biographies, 201
  in drama, 486
  essays, 184
  geography textbooks, 97
  for graphics, 545–546
  history textbooks, 80
  magazine articles, 244–245
  math textbooks, 129
  newspaper articles, 231
  novels, 336–338
  poetry, 419, 445
  science textbooks, 114
  short stories, 336
  tests, 577–578
  for websites, 524
Rereading strategies. *See also* Reading
  strategies
  close reading, for short stories,
    312–313
  critical reading
    in focusing on settings, 245
    in graphics, 545–546
  graphic organizers, for novels, 336
  looking for cause and effect
    in autobiographies, 216
    in biographies, 192
  note-taking, for geography
    textbooks, 98

note-taking, for math textbooks, 129–130
outlining, for history texts, 80–81
paraphrasing, for poetry, 420
questioning the author, 245
skimming as
  for science textbooks, 114–115
  for websites, 525
summarizing as, for newspaper articles, 232, 233
visualizing and thinking aloud, 487
  for tests, 577–578
Resolution, 369, 400
  in plays, 484, 507
  in short stories, 309
Responding and reacting in reading poetry, 428–429
Retelling chart, 676
Rhyme
  in analogies, 637
  in poetry, 442–443, 461, 462
Rhyme scheme, 443, 462
Rhythm, 443–444
Rising action, 369, 400
  in plays, 484, 507
  in short stories, 309
Road maps, 556
Roots, 585, 621–622, 624
  Greek and Latin, 689–692

S

Scenes, in drama, 503
School terms, learning, 631–634
Science tests, 598–605
Science textbooks, 100–116
  focusing on concepts in, 132–142
  organization of
    cause-effect order, 111
    classification, 112
    problem-solution order, 112
  reading process for, 132–142
  reading and rereading strategies
    note-taking, 106–107
    skimming, 114–115
  reading tools for, 107, 108, 109, 110, 111, 112, 115, 116, 137, 138, 139, 140, 192
Script for drama, 502
Search engine for the Internet, 516, 533
Sentence outlines, 649
  for essays, 178, 180
Sentences
  finding main idea in, 50–51
  making sense of, in word problems, 148
Septet, 466
Sequence notes, 646
  for history textbooks, 76
  for science textbooks, 116
Sestet, 466
Set/subset in analogies, 586
Setting, 351–359, 402

characters and, 356
critical reading as rereading strategy for, 245
double-entry journal for, 355
in drama, 509
listing key, 358
making sketches, 359
mood and, 354–355
in novels, 327–330
plot and, 357
previewing, 352
reading strategy for, 353
reading tools for
  inference chart, 356
  setting chart, 329, 353, 677
  storyboard, 359
  summary notes, 358
Setting chart, 353, 677
  for novels, 329
Short stories, 294–314
  characters in, 313
  organization of, 309
  point of view in, 313
  previewing, 295–303
  reading process for, 294–314
  reading and rereading strategies
    close reading, 312-313
    using graphic organizers, 305
  reading tools for, 305, 306, 307, 308, 309, 312, 313
Similes, 426
  in poetry, 464
Single quotation marks, 362
Skimming, 656–657
  for general ideas, 656
  for science terms, 599
  for science textbooks, 114–115
  for specific information, 657
  on tests, 571, 657
  for websites, 525
Snob appeal, 263
Social studies tests, 588–592
Social studies textbooks. See Geography textbooks; History textbooks
Soliloquy in drama, 506
Sound, focusing on, in poetry, 439–445
Specific comparison, 383, 386–387
Speeches
  in drama, 496
  graphic organizers for, 261, 262
  identifying main idea and support, 262
  informative, 256
  loaded words in, 264
  parts of, 261
  persuasive, 256
  propaganda techniques in, 263–264
  reading critically as reading strategy for, 260
  reading process for, 256–264

Speech tags, 361
Stacking the deck, 263
Stage directions in drama, 497, 510
Standardized vocabulary tests, 634–636
Stanzas in poetry, 441, 461, 465–466
Static characters, 348
Storyboard, 678
  for drama, 487
  for plot, 371
  for setting, 359
  for short stories, 307
Story organizer, 678
  for plot, 373
  for short stories, 305
Story string, 679
  for magazine articles, 242
  for short stories, 307
Straw man exaggerating, 288
Structure, focus on, in poetry, 439–445
Study cards, 679
  for biographies, 203
  for geography textbooks, 98
  for science textbooks, 109, 140
Study guide for science textbooks, 141
Style, 403
  in novels, 334
Subject, finding, in paragraphs, 48–49
Subplots, 373
Suffixes, 585, 622, 687–688
Summarizing, 658–659
  for autobiography, 217
  for drama, 476
  for essay, 186
  for literature, 658
  for nonfiction, 659
Summary notes, 646, 680
  chapter-by-chapter, 331
  in focusing on setting, 358
  in focusing on theme, 378
  for graphics, 547
  for history textbooks, 76
  for newspaper articles, 232, 233
  scene-by-scene, 482
  for websites, 526
Supporting details, 53, 179, 249, 262, 289–290
Support in persuasive writing, 249, 250–252, 253
Symbols, 404
  in poetry, 467
Synonyms, 616
  in analogies, 586, 637
  in vocabulary questions, 634
Synthesizing, 660–661
  with fiction, 660
  with nonfiction, 661

T

Table of contents as textbook element, 168–169
Tables, 559–560
  reading, for science tests, 600–601
Tercet, 466

Tests
 creation of
  for geography textbooks, 99
  for math textbooks, 130–131
 essay, 580–583
 math, 593–597
 organization of, 575
 questions on
  fact or recall, 572, 573
  inference or conclusion, 572, 574
 reading, 564–579
 science, 598–605
 skimming on, 657
 social studies, 588–592
 vocabulary, 584–587
Textbooks, 65–169
 elements of, 155–169
  boldface terms, 156
  charts, 157
  glossary, 158
  graphs, 159
  headings, 160–161
  illustrations, 165
  index, 162
  maps, 163–164
  photos, 165
  preview, 166–167
  table of contents, 168–169
  titles, 160–161
 geography, 84–99
 history, 66–83
 math, 117–131, 143–154
 science, 100–116, 132–142
 vocabulary in, 632
Text notes, 647, 669
 for science textbooks, 108
Thematic maps, 556
Theme, 368, 376–382, 405
 characters and, 347–348, 378
 common topics for, 377, 490
 defined, 376
 in drama, 489–493, 500, 511
 in novels, 333
 reading tools for, 378, 379, 381
 steps in understanding, 377–381, 489
 tips for making statements on, 382, 493
Theme statements, 382, 493
Thesaurus, reading, 630
Thinking aloud, 664–665
 for drama, 487
 for math textbooks, 123, 126, 128, 146
 for tests, 577–578
Thinking tree, 680
 for dialogue, 367
 for science textbooks, 107, 115, 139
Timeline notes, 646
 in reading history textbooks, 76
Timelines, 561, 681
 for autobiographies, 213

for biographies, 198, 203
for nonfiction, 276
for novels, 331
Time order, 56, 57, 77, 242
Titles
 in diagram, 552
 as textbook elements, 160–161
 in finding subject of paragraph, 49
Tone in poetry, 468–469
Topic and theme organizers, 681
 for drama, 492
 for novels, 333
 for theme, 381
Topic notes, 673
Topic organization in geography textbook, 94
Topic outlines, 81, 649
Topic sentence and supporting details, 289–290
Two per line, 682
 for poetry, 414, 435
Two-story map, 682
 for comparison-contrast, 386

U
URL, 519, 535
Using graphic organizers, 662–663

V
Venn diagram, 683
 for comparison-contrast, 387
 for short stories, 313
Vertical axis, 543
Viewpoint organizer and evidence, 243, 683
Viewpoints, 291
 in persuasive writing, 247, 249, 252, 253
Visualizing, 26–27, 44, 45, 664–665
 in reading drama, 487
 in reading math textbook, 123, 125, 145
 for tests, 577–578
Visuals
 making, for science tests, 599
 reading, for social studies tests, 591
Vocabulary
 analogies in, 586–587, 636–639
 antonyms, 634
 boosting, 613–614
 building strength in, 608
 improving, 607–639
 journal for, 609–611, 631
 notebook for, 585
 prefixes, 585, 622, 685–687
 roots, 585, 621–622, 624, 689–693
 school terms in, 632–634
 specialized terms in, 631–634
 suffixes, 585, 622, 687–688
 synonyms, 634
 tests for, 584–587, 634–636
Voice in poetry, 468–469

W
Web notes in reading history textbooks, 75
Web page, 532, 535
Webs, 684
 in building vocabulary, 633
 character, 326, 344
 character trait, 212
 family tree, for novels, 325
 in finding main idea, 50
Website profiler, 519, 523, 684
Websites. *See also* Internet
 evaluation of, 525
 organization of, 522
 reading process for, 514–526
 reading and rereading strategies
  reading critically, 518
  skimming, 525
 reading tools for, 519, 523, 526
 reliability of, 524–525
 sponsor of, 519
 table of contents in, 535
 taking notes, 521
 update of, 519
Word collector, being a, 608–609
Word games in boosting vocabulary, 614, 625
Word history in dictionaries, 629
Word problems, 143–154
 diagrams in, 149
 four-step plan for, 144
 order of numbers in, 147
 problem-solving tips for, 150–154
 sentences in, 148
 use of words in, 147
 visualizing and thinking aloud, 145
Word roots, 585, 621–622, 624
Words
 avoiding vague, in making theme statements, 382
 in improving vocabulary, 625
 loaded, 263, 264, 288
 modifying, as context clues, 618
 moving, into long-term memory, 612
 parts of, 621
  learning, 624–625
  putting together, 623
 repeated, as context clues, 619
 start owning, 612–613
 in word problems, 147
Working backward, in solving word problems, 152
World Wide Web, 534–555
 browser, 529
 home page, 529, 535
 link, 532
 web address, 535
Writers, questions for, 28
Writing
 about theme, 381
 persuasive, 55, 247–255, 274
 process, 28
 real-world, 265–272